CONCEPTS AND THEIR ROLE IN KNOWLEDGE

The Ayn Rand Society (www.aynrandsociety.org), founded in 1987 and affiliated from its inception with the American Philosophical Association, Eastern Division, has as its constitutional purpose "to foster the study by philosophers of the philosophical thought and writings of Ayn Rand." Since 1988, the society has sponsored some twenty programs at Eastern Division meetings, and in 2008 it began sponsoring programs at Pacific Division meetings as well.

In furtherance of its purpose, the society is publishing, with the University of Pittsburgh Press, a series of volumes called Ayn Rand Society Philosophical Studies. Each volume will be unified around a theme of importance both to philosophy generally and to Rand's philosophical system, Objectivism, in particular, and will be intended to be of interest both to philosophers unfamiliar with Rand and to specialists in her thought. The volumes will contain, for the most part, previously unpublished materials that pertain to Rand's philosophical work; the aim is to present professional studies that will advance understanding both of the philosophical issues involved and of the thought of this seminal and still underappreciated philosopher.

The Series
Metaethics, Egoism, and Virtue: Studies in Ayn Rand's Normative Theory, 2011

Ayn Rand Society Philosophical Studies

Allan Gotthelf, Editor
James G. Lennox, Associate Editor

Gregory Salmieri, Consulting Editor

CONCEPTS AND THEIR ROLE IN KNOWLEDGE

Reflections on Objectivist Epistemology

Allan Gotthelf, Editor

James G. Lennox, Associate Editor

AYN RAND SOCIETY PHILOSOPHICAL STUDIES

University of Pittsburgh Press

Published by the University of Pittsburgh Press, Pittsburgh, Pa., 15260
Manufactured in the United States of America
Printed on acid-free paper
10 9 8 7 6 5 4 3 2 1

Library of Congress Cataloging-in-Publication Data

Concepts and their role in knowledge : reflections on objectivist epistemology / Allan
Gotthelf, editor, James G. Lennox, associate editor.
    pages cm. — (Ayn Rand Society philosophical studies)
  Includes bibliographical references and index.
  ISBN 978-0-8229-4424-9 (alk. paper)
  1. Rand, Ayn. 2. Objectivism (Philosophy) 3. Knowledge, Theory of. I. Gotthelf, Allan,
1942– editor of compilation.
  B945.R234C66 2013
  121'.4—dc23   2013003756

CONTENTS

Preface   ix

Part One: Essays

Ayn Rand's Theory of Concepts: Rethinking Abstraction
and Essence   3
ALLAN GOTTHELF

Conceptualization and Justification   41
GREGORY SALMIERI

Perceptual Awareness as Presentational   85
ONKAR GHATE

Concepts, Context, and the Advance of Science   112
JAMES G. LENNOX

Part Two: Discussion

Concepts and Kinds

Rand on Concepts, Definitions, and the Advance of Science:
Comments on Gotthelf and Lennox   139
PAUL E. GRIFFITHS

Natural Kinds and Rand's Theory of Concepts: Reflections
on Griffiths   148
ONKAR GHATE

Definitions

Rand on Definitions—One Size Fits All? Comments on Gotthelf   163
JIM BOGEN

Taking the Measure of a Definition: Response to Bogen   173
ALLAN GOTTHELF

Concepts and Theory Change

On Concepts that Change with the Advance of Science: Comments on
Lennox   185
RICHARD M. BURIAN

Conceptual Development versus Conceptual Change: Response to
Burian   201
JAMES G. LENNOX

Perceptual Awareness

In Defense of the Theory of Appearing: Comments on Ghate and
Salmieri   215
PIERRE LE MORVAN

Forms of Awareness and "Three-Factor" Theories   226
GREGORY SALMIERI

Direct Perception and Salmieri's "Forms of Awareness"   242
BILL BREWER

Keeping Up Appearances: Reflections on the Debate over Perceptual
Infallibilism   247
BENJAMIN BAYER

Uniform Abbreviations of Works by Ayn Rand   269

References   271

List of Contributors   283

Index   287

The first volume in this series, *Metaethics, Egoism, and Virtue: Studies in Ayn Rand's Normative Theory,* focused on aspects of Ayn Rand's ethical theory. The present volume explores a more fundamental area of her philosophic thought: her epistemology or theory of knowledge.

Rand thought of metaphysics and epistemology as the two fundamental areas of philosophy, and she grounded the rest of her philosophic system, Objectivism—including her ethics and politics—in her views on the nature of reality and of knowledge. As we will see in the opening essays in this volume, metaphysics is for her prior to epistemology, but most of the philosophic action is in epistemology. She spoke of having "a new approach to epistemology" and part of the aim of this volume is to bring that approach to the fore and to encourage reflection upon its significance. One aspect of that new approach was to give centrality in the understanding of human knowledge to the nature of *concepts*. Consider, for instance, that the title of a monograph she wrote on her theory of concepts is *Introduction to Objectivist Epistemology.* In some ways the first two essays in this volume make the understanding of that choice of title their theme. Allan Gotthelf provides a general introduction to the Objectivist theory of concepts and its view of their role in human knowledge, focusing on the way the theory arises out of a rethinking of two traditional notions that have, for better or worse, shaped both presentations and criticisms of prior theories: abstraction and essence. Gotthelf explores the relation of commensurability, which Rand identifies as the basis for concepts; the process of "measurement-omission" by which she held that concepts are abstracted; and her (nonrealist but nonsubjectivist) view of essences as epistemological rather than metaphysical. He closes with a discussion of how facts about the ontological basis of concepts and facts about the way a human consciousness must operate if it is to achieve knowledge jointly generate norms for the formation of concepts and their definitions. This serves as a lead-in to the next essay.

The subject of the second essay, by Gregory Salmieri, is how Rand's theory of concepts constitutes an introduction to an epistemology—more specifically, he considers how Rand's theory of concepts bears on the issue of how propositional knowledge is justified. The essay begins by situating Rand's theory of concepts (as presented by Gotthelf) in Rand's wider conception of consciousness as an "active process" of "differentiation and integration." In the second part of the essay, he discusses Rand's view that the process of "conceptualization" itself includes not just the formation of concepts, but the formation of an ever growing body of propositional knowledge. In elaborating this position, Salmieri goes beyond Rand's stated views, incorporating ideas of Leonard Peikoff's and of his own, into a sketch of a view of judgment and inference that is based on (and arguably implicit in) Rand's theory. The final section of the chapter discusses the norms for concepts and judgments implied by Rand's theory, and how adherence to these norms renders concepts and conclusions justified—or, in Rand's terms, *valid*. It also discusses the nature and structure of this justification, including the respects in which it is and is not a necessary condition for knowledge, and the respects in which it need and need not be self-conscious.

Gotthelf and Salmieri both discuss briefly how Rand's theory of concepts and conceptual knowledge rests on her view of sense-perception as a direct, automatic, nonconceptual (and nonpropositional) form of *awareness*. As such, perception constitutes a basic and unquestionable form of knowledge. In the third essay, Onkar Ghate develops the view in detail, comparing and contrasting it with another direct realist presentationalist theory, the Theory of Appearing developed by William Alston.

Rand held that a proper understanding of concepts and their formation—including the process of *conceptualization* Salmieri describes—is crucial to understanding the growth of human knowledge and, in particular, the ongoing development of science. James G. Lennox reflects on her thought in this area, in the fourth essay, "Concepts, Context, and the Advance of Science," showing how essentials of her theory of concepts and definition allow us to understand how concepts are able to preserve their identity across significant changes in scientific theory, thereby facilitating rather than undermining the expansion of scientific knowledge. In the final section of his essay, Lennox illustrates this sort of process by means of a biological case study of conceptual reclassification in response to important advances in the understanding of evolution and development.

All four of these essays were presented at workshops and conferences between 2003 and 2007. Most of these presentations had commentators. Those we invited to publish in this volume kindly agreed to revise their commentaries, at least in a limited way, and they are published here along with responses, either by the original authors or, in special cases, by others who are sympathetic to their views. The discussions, with responses, came to ten in total, which appear in part 2, under the following four headings:

Concepts and Kinds

Paul E. Griffiths commented on the first presentations of Gotthelf's and Lennox's essays, at a meeting the Ayn Rand Society held with the APA Eastern Division in 2003. A lightly revised version prepared by Griffiths in 2004 and reviewed in 2010 appears here.

At a 2004 Concepts Workshop at the University of Pittsburgh, Onkar Ghate provided some reflections on Griffiths's original presentation. His reflections, revised in the light of Griffiths's revised comments, are published here, in lieu of responses from Gotthelf and Lennox. Griffiths subsequently supplied some questions for Ghate to answer, which he has done.

Definitions

Jim Bogen has substantially revised for publication his comments on a later version of Gotthelf's essay, both of which were presented at a Pittsburgh-Texas joint conference on Concepts and Objectivity: Knowledge, Science, and Values, in 2006. Allan Gotthelf responds to Bogen's current comments, drawing to some extent on oral responses he gave at that 2006 meeting.

Concepts and Theory Change

Richard Burian has substantially revised for publication here the comments he presented, on a version of Lennox's essay, at that same 2006 meeting. James Lennox responds to Burian's current comments, drawing to some extent on oral responses he gave at that meeting.

Perceptual Awareness

Because Ghate used William Alston's Theory of Appearing as a "foil," comparing and contrasting it with his own theory, we invited Pierre Le Morvan, a former student of Alston's and a prominent defender of the Theory of Appearing, to comment on the discussions of perception in Ghate and Salmieri.

At a workshop on Perception, Consciousness, and Reference held at the University of Warwick in 2009, Gregory Salmieri presented a paper comparing and contrasting Rand's thesis that perceptual awareness is always in a certain *form* with the idea of Bill Brewer and John Campbell that a "third factor" is essential to direct realism. We publish here a revised version of that paper.[1] At that same 2009 Warwick workshop, Bill Brewer commented on Salmieri's paper. He agreed to the publication of his original comments, with only light revision.

To round out the section on perceptual awareness, we invited Benjamin Bayer, an epistemologist sympathetic with Ghate's and Salmieri's views, to provide some reflections on these exchanges, and identify where, from his perspective, the issues lie at present.

We think this is an exciting volume, both for the freshness and breadth of the essays in part 1 and for the lively exchanges in part 2, and we would like to thank all of our fellow contributors for making it so. We think it will be rewarding both for those previously unfamiliar with Rand's epistemology and for those already quite familiar with it. As a volume of reflections, it breaks new ground both in the explanation of key elements of the Objectivist epistemology and in the application of it to central questions in philosophy of mind, epistemology, philosophy of science, and more.

We thank again our editorial board, for their assistance, especially Gregory Salmieri, now consulting editor for the series, who tirelessly supplied many valuable comments and suggestions throughout the process of preparing this volume. We would like to express our gratitude as well to Kathleen McLaughlin for outstanding copyediting, sensitive to our concerns; to Benjamin Bayer for another round of astute indexing; to

---

1. It should be said that both Le Morvan and Salmieri wrote their discussion pieces without knowledge of the content of the other's piece. Le Morvan addresses only Salmieri's main essay (along with Ghate's), and Salmieri does not address Le Morvan's (or Alston's) views.

Peter Kracht and Alex Wolfe and the production, design, and marketing team at the University of Pittsburgh Press for their creativity and helpfulness; and as always to Cynthia Miller, the outgoing Press director, for her support, her vision, and her wise advice beginning with our first conversations about the possibility of this series. We will miss working with Cynthia, but are delighted that Peter will be her successor.

As we said in the preface to our first volume, "Neither the editors nor the editorial board necessarily endorse the content of work published in the series, and we may on occasion publish writings one or more of us thinks 'gets it all wrong,' so long as these writings are respectful of Rand and her work and further the aims of the series. We intend to publish only professional work of a quality that seriously engages topics of importance philosophically in general and to Rand's work in particular."

It is with great pleasure, then, that we present the second book in this series, a collection of chapters and discussions aimed at exploring central aspects of Ayn Rand's Objectivist epistemology.

Part One
ESSAYS

Ayn Rand's Theory of Concepts
Rethinking Abstraction and Essence
ALLAN GOTTHELF

One notable change in the philosophical literature of the last thirty years has been the extent of attention to the nature of *concepts*. Although philosophers have been concerned with "conceptual analysis" and related issues since the early twentieth century (and in fact since Kant), sustained attention to what concepts are, to their "possession conditions," to their acquisition and—especially—to their epistemic role is quite recent. The problem of the nature of concepts is, of course, much more ancient, since the traditional problem of universals, today thought of as primarily a metaphysical issue, originally had as an important component the explanation of the universality of our knowledge. In this connection, I should say at the outset that I am using the term "concept" as Rand does, to refer not to an object of thought but to a retained grasp of objects of thought, where the grasp is of the appropriate unitary sort.[1]

---

1. Compare, for example, Geach (1957, 18–19), who cites for the former "Russell's use of [the term 'concept'] in *The Principles of Mathematics* and again . . . the use of it to translate Frege's '*Begriff*'; Russell's 'concepts' and Frege's *Begriffe* were supposed to be objective entities, not belonging to a particular mind." As Geach and others have pointed out, viewing concepts as "mental particulars," and thus your concept of electricity as a distinct existent from mine, does not preclude speaking of you and me as having the *same* concept of electricity. "Mental

A number of philosophers, including, for example, John McDowell in *Mind and World* (1994) (building especially on the writings of Wilfrid Sellars), have come to speak of the role of concepts in the justification of propositional knowledge.[2] Now, if one thought of perceptual awareness as preconceptual, and justification of perceptual judgments as noninferential, one would need, it seems to me, a normative theory of concepts as the bridge. On this view, the proper application of the subject and predicate concepts in a judgment would be crucial to the justification of perceptual judgments employing those concepts. McDowell, of course, does not think such a picture is plausible, and views the relationship of concepts to perceptual experience quite differently. He speaks of the picture of concept-formation I have just pointed to as "a natural counterpart to the idea of the Given," and argues that such a view would require the abstraction of "the right element in the presented multiplicity." But, he writes, "this abstractionist picture of the role of the Given in the formation of concepts has been trenchantly criticized, in a Wittgensteinian spirit, by P. T. Geach" (McDowell 1994, 7; referring to Geach 1957, §§ 6–11).

The view that Geach criticizes under the name of "abstractionism" involves, however, a crude, Lockean notion of abstraction.[3] Those of us disinclined to think that the "Given" is a myth should consider the possibility that a more sophisticated view of abstraction could provide just

---

particulars" is Jerry Fodor's term (see, for example, Fodor 1998, 23); Rand speaks (with some reservation) of "mental entities" (*ITOE* 10, 157–58). Throughout this essay, I follow Rand in putting terms for particular concepts in quotation marks.

2. In McDowell 1994, see, for example, Lecture I, sec. 2, where he refers to Sellars's "Empiricism and the Philosophy of Mind" in Sellars 1963; see also the index in McDowell 1994, s.v. "Sellars, Wilfrid." Both McDowell and Sellars acknowledge the Kantian source of their views on this topic (McDowell 1994, 1). Sellars is not explicit in "Empiricism and the Philosophy of Mind" about its Kantian roots, but, as McDowell observes at the opening of his 1997 Woodbridge Lectures, "In his seminal set of lectures, 'Empiricism and the Philosophy of Mind,' Wilfrid Sellars offers (among much else) the outlines of a deeply Kantian way of thinking about intentionality—about how thought and language are directed toward the world. Sellars describes *Science and Metaphysics: Variations on Kantian Themes* (1967), his major work of the next decade, as a sequel to 'Empiricism and the Philosophy of Mind.' (vii). The later work makes explicit the Kantian orientation of the earlier; Sellars now shows a conviction that his own thinking about intentionality (and, indeed, about everything) can be well expounded through a reading of Kant" (McDowell 2009b, 3).

3. "I shall use 'abstractionism' as a name for the doctrine that a concept is acquired by a process of singling out in attention some one feature given in direct experience—*abstracting* it—and ignoring the other features simultaneously given—*abstracting from* them" (Geach 1957, 18). Compare the accounts of *abstraction* and the coming to have a general idea in John Locke's *An Essay Concerning Human Understanding* (Nidditch 1979), e.g., II.iii.7, II.xi.9.

the bridge between preconceptual perceptual awareness and conceptually structured perceptual judgments (and in general between perceptual awareness and conceptual knowledge) that is needed to put knowledge on a perceptual foundation.[4]

It is my view that this is, in fact, the case, and that Rand has produced just such an account of abstraction, concept-formation, and knowledge. In this chapter I will not be focused on the issue of propositional justification per se, though I will say something about norms for the formation of concepts and definitions. My aim here is rather to sketch out Rand's theory of concepts and their formation, including its more sophisticated, non-Lockean view of abstraction, sufficiently to show its appeal and to provide a basis for further work.[5] I will take us through the theory of concepts and definitions, and the new view of essences that goes with the theory of definitions. The chapter will conclude with a brief account of the key normative concept in Rand's epistemology—*objectivity*—the concept that provides the bridge between Rand's theory of concepts and her views on issues of justification.

Rand (1905–82) presented her theory of concepts in a monograph titled *Introduction to Objectivist Epistemology (ITOE)*. It was first published in installments in 1966–67, then as a single volume later in 1967. An expanded edition, including edited transcripts of portions of several workshops on *ITOE* she held in 1969–71, was published posthumously in 1990.[6] The heart of the theory itself she had developed in the late 1940s (*ITOE* 307).

---

4. Recent work in the philosophy of science has suggested that a proper theory of concepts is important as well to the understanding of the process of discovering and justifying scientific theories. See, for example, the work on "exploratory experimentation" by Friedrich Steinle and Richard Burian, among others. A good place to start is Steinle 2006. (Thanks to Dick Burian for bringing work on this topic to my attention.) An understanding of the role of concept-formation in the reaching and justification of both propositional judgments and scientific theories helps one to see the unified epistemological character of issues (and work) that tend today to be divided among philosophy of mind, epistemology, and philosophy of science.

5. The implications of this theory of concepts for questions of justification will be discussed in detail in the next essay, by Gregory Salmieri, and to some extent in the chapter that follows his, by Onkar Ghate. See also Bayer 2011 and forthcoming.

6. "Introduction to Objectivist Epistemology," *The Objectivist,* July 1966–January 1967, reissued as a single volume by *The Objectivist* later in 1967. The monograph was reissued by Mentor Books in 1979 with a companion essay, "The Analytic-Synthetic Dichotomy," by Leonard Peikoff (first published in *The Objectivist,* May–September 1967). The 1990 expanded second edition was edited by Harry Binswanger and Leonard Peikoff, and was published by Meridian Books. All citations herein are from the 1990 edition (cited as *ITOE;* all italics in

The issue of concepts is for Rand primarily an *epistemic* issue. Concepts for her are cognitive vehicles, and more, are themselves cognitive grasps: they are *forms of awareness* of an indefinite number of individuals, and an account of them will be a crucial part of a general theory of the nature and means of knowledge. They are best understood by contrast with perceptual awareness, on which, she holds, they are built.

Her theory of concepts thus depends on a theory of perception, and both theories depend on a key proposition of her metaphysics, pertaining to the general relation between consciousness and existence, between mind and world. This is the thesis which has often been called "metaphysical realism," and which she calls "the primacy of existence." It is the thesis that existence has metaphysical priority over consciousness: that things exist and are what they are independent of consciousness, and that consciousness is a faculty of *discovery*—it neither creates its objects nor contributes in any way to their constitution. Consciousness, as Rand has put it, is *metaphysically passive*. It is, however, she says, *epistemologically active*.

"Consciousness, as a state of awareness," Rand writes, "is not a passive state, but an active process that consists of two essentials: differentiation and integration" (*ITOE* 5). This is true, she holds, at all levels of awareness: sensation,[7] perception, conceptual knowledge. But at each of these levels, consciousness is directed outward, at objects (or aspects thereof) that have an existence and a nature independent of that act of consciousness.

Perception is for Rand a distinct form of awareness, different from both sensation and conceptual awareness. It is a direct awareness of persisting things, of entities, discriminated from each other and from their backgrounds. The integration of sensory data into *perceptual* awareness, Rand holds, is done automatically by the brain and nervous system. Con-

---

quoted passages from this work are in the original. Peikoff's "The Analytic-Synthetic Dichotomy" will be cited as such, from *ITOE*, using the 1990 pagination. Peikoff's *Objectivism: The Philosophy of Ayn Rand,* especially chapters 3 and 4, is also an important resource for Rand's theory of concepts; it will be cited as Peikoff 1991.

7. Rand characterizes a sensation as "produced by the automatic reaction of a sense organ to a stimulus from the outside world; it lasts for the duration of the immediate moment, as long as the stimulus lasts and no longer" (*VOS* 19). She views it as a scientific, not philosophical, question whether human beings pass through a distinct sensory level of awareness prior to perception (as here explained). Even in the case of pre-perceptual sensory awareness, the sensory mechanism still isolates incoming stimuli from a background of stimuli and unites it into a single (if only momentary and sensory) awareness.

cepts are not required for perceptual awareness as such (though once acquired on the basis of prior perception, they may, of course, facilitate perceptual recognition).

There are various features of Rand's account of perception that should be underscored here. First, perceptual awareness is a form of *awareness*. Perception is the product of a causal interaction between perceiver and independent entity (with its attributes), but this product is irreducibly a state of awareness of the independent entity (not to be analyzed, for example, functionally or information-theoretically) and as such is a form of knowledge, a form of cognitive contact with the world. But—secondly—it is a *nonpropositional* form of awareness. Rand held that philosophers often confuse the character of the content of perceptual awareness with the character of our (inevitably conceptual) description of the content of perceptual awareness. Perception is not an awareness *that* (say) this ball is red, nor of a ball *as red* (which is to classify the perceived attribute), but is, rather (to the extent that one can describe a nonconceptual awareness conceptually), an awareness *of* the red ball, as discriminated from other objects in one's field of view and noticed perceptually as *different* from, say, the blue ball next to it.

Thirdly, such awarenesses, Rand says, are unerring: they are neither true nor false, they just are. But, as cases of awareness, they are forms of knowledge that provide evidence, once one has reached the conceptual level, for or against perceptual *judgments* (for example, *that* this ball is red), which do have truth values. On Rand's view, for instance, perceptually grasped similarities and differences between perceived entities (and their attributes), though nonpropositional, support the claims regarding those similarities and differences that are implicit in the formation of concepts such as "ball," "red," "blue," and of subsequent propositions such as "This ball is red." This understanding of perception will get further elaboration and defense in subsequent chapters in this volume, but part of the elaboration is precisely the theory of concepts that I go on to present in this essay.[8]

8. See the essays in this volume by Salmieri and, especially, Ghate. Rand's view of perception is outlined in Peikoff 1991, 37–48. See also Kelley 1986, who builds on her theory of perception. Robert Efron's Rand-influenced "What Is Perception?" (Efron 1969) builds an account of perception similar to Rand's upon a fascinating analysis of a case of visual object agnosia. Efron also discusses how attributes of consciousness are to be scientifically measured, and in that connection introduces the notion of the "specificity" of perceptual awareness, by reference to thresholds of perceptual discrimination. On perceptual awareness as a form of knowledge, see the opening portion of Salmieri's essay, which follows this one. On perception

All but the most primitive animals are not able to survive by isolated sensory data alone; they need the perceptual awareness that their brain's automatic integration of sensory data provides. Likewise, human beings are not able to survive by perceptual awareness alone. In order to live, we need to *integrate perceptual data into concepts,* and these concepts into a vast body of hierarchically structured, higher-order concepts, thereby permitting a correspondingly vast body both of propositional knowledge and of conceptually based skills.

It is worth seeing in simple terms some of the ways, according to Rand, in which concepts vastly expand our cognitive power and thereby our ability to deal with reality. With this in mind, we can ask what sort of mental entities, formed by what sort of process, makes these cognitive achievements possible. The answers will shed light on why Rand called a monograph on her theory of concepts an introduction to her *epistemology.*[9]

To start, concepts extend our cognitive reach well beyond perception to things not directly accessible to the senses. For instance, via concepts we can grasp things (and properties) that are too distant in space from us, too large or small in size, too many in number, to be perceived. Concepts also allow us to grasp differences that are too subtle, and similarities that are too remote, to be grasped perceptually. They give us cognitive access, in short, to an enormous range of things, attributes, actions, relationships, and so forth, not directly available to perception. In fact, a developed system of concepts allows a *classification* of the things, attributes, actions, relationships, and so forth, in the world, grouping these myriad particu-

---

as nonrepresentational and thus neither true nor false, see Ghate's essay and, among others, Brewer 2006; Brewer 2011a, chap. 5; Travis 2004; and, of course, Austin 1962, esp. 11. For discussion of the idea of nonpropositional justification, see, in addition to Ghate's essay, e.g., Pryor 2001 and 2005.

Central to Rand's view of perception is her insistence that what we perceive—both entities and their characteristics—is *particular.* Universality is not for her a feature of the objects of awareness, but of the form in which, on the conceptual level, we are aware of particular objects. This distinction between the object and the form of perceptual awareness, properly understood, provides the basis for a rejection of one of Sellars's main arguments against the "Given," as Ghate briefly discusses in the latter part of his essay in the present volume. On this distinction between the form and the object of perception see, in addition to discussion elsewhere in this volume, my *On Ayn Rand* (Gotthelf 2000), chaps. 6 and 7; Peikoff 1991, 44–55; and Kelley 1986, chap. 3.

9. See *ITOE* 1–3 and Salmieri's essay, following this one. In the next paragraph I draw on my presentation in Gotthelf 2000, 57. See also Peikoff 1991, 73–74.

lars into manageable cognitive units. And this classification allows us to organize and condense the vast amount of knowledge we acquire, according to the relevant subject matters and predicates; it is analogous, Rand says, to a complex file-folder system with extensive cross-references. This makes possible, among other things, specialized study; by studying some members of a properly conceptualized group, Rand observes, we are able to learn about all members of the group, and thus to apply that knowledge to new individuals of that group that we encounter.[10] That is, concepts make possible induction, and thus science and technology and, indeed, all rational action.[11]

The integration distinctive of concept-formation begins with multiple perceptual grasps of a small number of individuals (for example, a child's noticing of some tables similar to one another and different from some nearby chairs), and moves to an *open-end* grasp of all relevantly similar individuals, past, present, and future (for example, a grasp of *all* tables, past, present, and future) (*ITOE* 17–18, 26–28).[12] Later concepts will be formed from earlier ones. In some cases several earlier concepts will be integrated into a wider concept (for example, "furniture" from "table," "chair," "dresser"). In others, an initial concept will be subdivided into narrower ones (for example, when "beagle" and "greyhound" are formed from "dog"). In yet other cases a body of observation and theory, made possible by earlier concepts, establishes the existence of unobserved (or unobservable) particulars that need to be conceptualized (for example, "electron"). And so on. But the principle that the formation of a new concept is a move to a *single* grasp of all the relevantly similar particulars remains the same.

10. "The concept 'man,' for example, enables us to think and learn about all men (past, present and future) at once; and to call someone a man is to bring the whole of our knowledge about men (medical, psychological, philosophical, etc.) to bear on them" (Salmieri and Gotthelf 2005, 1996); see also *ITOE* 27–28. On the file-folder metaphor, see *ITOE* 66–67, 69.

11. This is a point that has also been stressed, to a greater or lesser degree, by "natural kind" theorists. See, for instance, Griffiths 1997, chap. 7, and the exchange between Ian Hacking and Richard Boyd at the Twenty-Ninth Oberlin Colloquium in Philosophy (Hacking 1991a, Boyd 1991, Hacking 1991b). See also note 4 above concerning recent work on "exploratory experimentation." Leonard Peikoff has developed an approach to induction based on Rand's theory of concepts. For references (and a brief discussion), see Salmieri's essay, which follows this one.

12. Rand typically uses "open-end" rather than "open-ended," perhaps because she has in mind a point that is more about the object (or content) of the grasp than about the grasp itself.

To understand this process, and the concepts that result, and the cognitive powers they make possible, we have to ask what is the nature of that integration. Indeed, says Rand, because concepts are *products of a certain kind of integration,* we will not understand the product—the concept—unless we understand the process—concept-formation. But, given the primacy of existence discussed above, to understand the process we will have to understand the *basis in reality* for the groupings that concepts ought to supply us with. Because conceptual groupings start from a grasp of *similarity,* we need an understanding of the nature of similarity, and this is where we will start, contrasting Rand's distinctive account of similarity with those of traditional realism and nominalism. This will address the heart of her view of the metaphysical basis of concepts, from which we will be best able to see her distinctive theory both of the process by which concepts are formed, and the nature of a concept once formed. This will be the subject of my first section: "Nature, Basis, and Formation of Concepts."

The process of concept-formation is not complete, Rand maintains, without proper definitions, and such definitions must specify the essential distinguishing characteristic(s) within the conceiver's context of knowledge. Understanding Rand's view of definitions and essences (including their contextual character) is thus crucial to understanding her theory of concept-formation and its implications for understanding the development both of human knowledge in general and of science in particular. This will be the subject of my second section, "Definitions and Essences," which will provide an account of Rand's views on these matters.

Rand's theory of concepts has both descriptive and normative dimensions—the theory not only seeks to identify how concepts are formed, but also, where there is choice, how (and when) they ought to be formed. This normative dimension of Rand's theory will be the focus of my final section—"Norms of Conceptual Activity"—in which I show how the character and basis of conceptual norms point us toward Rand's general theory of objectivity, which is at the center of her epistemology.

Nature, Basis, and Formation of Concepts

Traditional realists have held that the basis of proper conceptual grouping is a mind-independent universal or abstract element—an identical Form or essence or property which the individuals of a group somehow share (or otherwise stand in the same relation to). Conceptual groups come, in effect, ready-made.[13] Similarity is *identity within difference*. On this view, a concept is essentially a retained intuitive gaze at, or grasp of, that identical element. The acquisition of that grasp (or reacquisition, in Plato's version of realism) might involve a complex process of dialectic, or even a scientific discovery of causes, but at its final stage is the successful direction of cognitive attention to that preexistent identical element.

Traditional nominalists have held that they can find no such mind-independent universal or abstract element, nor is any such universal necessary to explain the groupings required for knowledge of general truths. Reality is through and through particular and determinate. Conceptual groupings, most nominalists hold, are based on *resemblances*—primitive, unanalyzable similarities, which we select arbitrarily or pragmatically from the myriad of similarities we find in experience. A concept for nominalism is either the *word* we select to represent the class of resembling individuals (or a capacity to use such a word), or some sort of mental image or images (or construct thereof) of a typical (or prototypical) instance, or small set of instances, with which we associate the word. The formation of such a concept is often viewed as a psychological and not a philosophical matter. On that view, the only thing of philosophical significance is the alleged fact that the selection of which resemblance-classes will serve as cognitive units is arbitrary, or merely pragmatic.[14]

Rand agrees with realists that there is a basis in reality that determines conceptual groupings, but disagrees that this basis is any sort of mind-independent universal or abstract element. Similarity is not, for her, shared identity within difference. She agrees with nominalists that reality is irreducibly particular and determinate, and that members of a proper conceptual grouping might vary in every particular respect. But she rejects their view that similarity is unanalyzable and that conceptual groupings are either arbitrary or merely pragmatic. In a given context, how groupings are to be made is, in most cases, mandatory, if our knowledge is to be retained, organized, and systematically expanded.

13. Such mind-independent kinds are often referred to as "natural kinds," although this terminology is sometimes used by those who do not subscribe to realism as here defined. See the discussions of natural kinds by Paul Griffiths and Ghate in part 2 of this volume.

14. Analytic metaphysicians have taken to defining "nominalism" as the thesis that denies that universals exist—that is to say, as *anti-realism*. I do not follow this practice because it packages together under "nominalism" theories that are radically different from one another both in their metaphysical and epistemological dimensions. There is a very good argument against this practice in Salmieri 2008, 52–55.

Rand begins by observing that we can detect similarity only against a background of difference. For example, we can detect that two tables are similar to each other only against the background of other, different objects, such as chairs. Or, to take another example, once a child has reached the stage of isolating colors, two shades of blue will be experienced as different, until put up against something red, in contrast to which the blue shades can now be experienced as similar. Some philosophers have claimed that similarity cannot be grasped without concepts (and in particular without the concept "similarity"). This is untrue: similarities and differences at the first levels of conceptualization are perceived directly, and at very early ages.[15]

As to the nature of the similarity relationship itself, in looking back and forth from one table to another and from each to the chairs, the child is not, Rand holds, responding to some identical, *universal* element shared by the tables. Each table has a particular shape, for instance, that in most cases will differ detectably from table to table. Likewise, there is no identical "blueness" shared by, for example, the light blue and royal blue shirts. But the similarity experienced is not an unanalyzable primitive either, she says. Rather, the similarity of the tables relative to the chairs, or the blues relative to the red, is a matter of *lesser difference* along some quantitative, or more-and-less, axis.[16] The tables experienced as similar are perceived to be less different from one another than any is from the chairs, the blues to be less different from one another than any is from the red.

The similar items must therefore share with the contrasting items a *commensurable* characteristic, "such as shape in the case of tables, or hue in the case of colors" (*ITOE* 15). In connection with its role in concept-

15. See Kelley and Krueger 1984. The assumption that similarity can be perceived without the use of previously acquired concepts for the respects in which the items are perceived to be similar seems widespread in the cognitive science literature, though the thesis is rarely argued in precisely those terms; see, e.g., Quinn, Eimas, and Rosencrantz 1993; Quinn and Eimas 1996; and Smith et al. 1996. A valuable survey by D. H. Rakison and Y. Yermolayeva (2010) is somewhat more explicit on this front. The articles just cited contain extensive references to other work by these authors as well as useful scholarship by other authors. For a broad representative survey of the range of psychological study of early category and concept development, see Rakison and Oakes 2003. Thanks to David Rakison for providing many of these references.

Of course, as will be made clear shortly, the grasp of similarities at a more abstract level does require concepts of various sorts (including, in some cases, the concept "similarity").

16. The explanation of similarity by reference to "lesser difference" is clearly implied in *ITOE*, but this terminology may have first been used in print to explain Rand's view of similarity in Kelley 1984.

formation, Rand calls this commensurable characteristic "the Conceptual Common Denominator" (and abbreviates it as "CCD," a practice I will follow).

The grasp of similarity, Rand thus holds, is a matter of implicit *measurement*, a relating of existents along an axis of quantitative, or more-and-less, comparison: "The element of *similarity* is crucially involved in the formation of every concept; similarity, in this context, is the relationship between two or more existents which possess the same characteristic(s), but in different measure or degree" (*ITOE* 13; see also *ITOE* 143–47).[17]

17. Rand argues that this essential condition on similarity applies as well to the similarity that is the basis of higher-level concepts, although there the similarity must be grasped conceptually. For instance, tables, chairs, beds, and so on—*furniture*—will not be experienced as similar, prior to the formation of the concepts of "table," "chair," "bed"; they are too different for their similarity, against the background, say, of walls, floors, and windows, to be noticed perceptually. One would need first to form the lower-level concepts. But once one is positioned to notice the similarity of pieces of furniture, one can do so only against the background of other parts of a human habitation that vary in quantity or degree from them along one or more commensurable characteristics, one or more axes, such that the pieces of furniture are less different from one another than they are from the contrasting items. As this case illustrates, the grasp of the similarities that underlie the formation of a concept typically depends on the possession and use of other, already-formed concepts. This fact is the basis of Rand's thesis that concepts are *hierarchical*—that, for the most part, they must be formed in a certain order. For more on the hierarchical character of concepts, see the discussion later in this section.

The similarities involved in higher-order theoretical concepts, such as, for example, the concept "nominalism," will be able to be grasped only on the basis of substantial propositional knowledge, for example, about the problem of universals, about theories thereof, and about the fundamentality of that issue to epistemology, all held in terms of prior concepts. As a concept of a certain range of theories produced by a human consciousness, "nominalism" can be fully understood, on Rand's theory, only against the background of her general account of "concepts of consciousness" (*ITOE* chap. 4); but, we can at least note what the "Conceptual Common Denominator" (CCD) in the case of "nominalism" would be, and what range of measurements along that CCD is given to the distinguishing characteristic of nominalism. Thus, she would have us note that the grasp of the similarity across the range of particular nominalist theories (for example, Thomas Hobbes's or Hume's or Ludwig Wittgenstein's) requires identifying (conceptually) these theories as varying in quantity or degree along at least one commensurable characteristic shared by these theories such that the theories are less different from each other along that axis or axes than they are from, for example, the realist theories from which they are differentiated when we form the concept "nominalism." This CCD might be, for instance, *degree of resemblance of particulars in virtue of which they are (or are to be) grouped*. The range across that CCD is from zero degree of resemblance (in the case of wholly arbitrary Hobbesian nominalism) to multiple partial resemblances each shared by only some of the particulars (in the case of Wittgenstein's family-resemblance nominalism) to whole resemblances (in the case of Hume's resemblance-nominalism) to the sameness of qualitatively indistinguishable, numerically distinct essences (in the case of one interpreta-

This reference to "the same characteristic" is not an endorsement of realism about universals. Characteristics exist only as particular and determinate. Their sameness is real but is not itself a particular property or attribute, just as those who speak of *determinates* and *determinables* might insist that the ultramarine and the blueness of something are not two properties or attributes of it, sitting side-by-side, as it were, in the entity, even if (and indeed precisely because) the ultramarine is a determinate form of blueness. In the process of forming the concept "blue," starting from the light blue and the royal blue shirts against the background, say, of a red one, what one is aware of are the two noticeably different but similar hues, standing in a relation to each other *along an axis that allows one to relate them as each more or less close to the other.* It is the commensurability of the two blue hues that is perceived—their "sameness" (in Rand's sense) is something graspable only abstractly and subsequent to the concept-forming process. The bases in reality for the formation of concepts, according to Rand, are these commensurability relationships across particular, determinate attributes.[18]

---

tion of Aristotelian realism) to the sameness of numerically one and the same essence (in the case of another interpretation of Aristotelian realism). It is no accident, then, as Gregory Salmieri has pointed out to me, that we often view such theories as existing on a continuum, sometimes speaking of one theory of universals (e.g., Aristotle's) as *between* two others (e.g., nominalism and Platonic realism).

Each of the concepts of the actions and products of consciousness involved in there being such a thing as a nominalist theory, and each of the concepts of the particulars that are the object or content of those actions of consciousness, would likewise be formed from similarities analyzable in terms of commensurable characteristics possessed both by the particulars integrated by the concept and by the particulars from which those particulars are differentiated. For discussion of some of these issues, see *ITOE* 215, 217–22.

18. As this discussion suggests, Rand's view of the similarity relationship (and of the relationships both of lower-level concepts to particulars and of higher-level concepts to lower-level ones) has some parallels with (and differences from) the notion of similarity implied by the traditional accounts of the determinable-determinate relationship; however, those parallels are best examined after Rand's conception of "objectivity" is explained, and so I will not discuss them in this essay.

In thinking of Rand's account of the relation of lower-level concepts to particulars and of higher-level concepts to lower-level ones, and of the use she makes of this account to explain the abstractness of concepts, some readers will benefit (as I have) from a comparison of her views with Aristotle's conception of the similarity (or, as Aristotle says, "sameness") involved in things under the same *genos* (which I will translate as "kind"). In the opening lines of *History of Animals* (*HA*), where he is identifying ways in which the parts of animals can be the same or differ, Aristotle speaks first of *sameness in form,* and then of *sameness in kind.* In introducing the latter, he says of animal parts (and of the animals that possess them) that "others, while the same, differ with respect to the more and the less" (*HA* 1.1.486a21–23). At

How, then, is the perceptual (or prior conceptual) awareness of a small number of similars integrated into an "open-end" concept, one that subsumes all relevantly similar instances, past, present, and future? By a process, Rand says, of *measurement-omission*. She introduces this idea as follows:

> Let us now examine the process of forming the simplest concept, the concept of a single attribute (chronologically, this is not the first concept that a child would grasp; but it is the simplest one epistemologically)—for instance, the concept "*length*." If a child considers a match, a pencil and a stick, he observes that length is the attribute they have in common, but their specific lengths differ. *The difference is one of measurement.* In order to form the concept "length," the child's mind retains the attribute and omits its particular measurements. Or, more precisely, if the process were identified in words, it would consist of the following: "Length must exist in *some* quantity, but may exist in *any* quantity. I shall identify as 'length' that attribute of any existent possessing it which can be quantitatively related to a unit of length, without specifying the quantity." . . .
>
> The same principle directs the process of forming concepts of entities—for instance, the concept "*table*." The child's mind isolates two or more tables from other objects by focusing on their distinctive characteristic: their shape. He observes that their shapes vary, but have one characteristic in common: a flat level surface and support(s). He forms the concept "table" by retaining that characteristic and omitting *all* particular measurements, not only the measurements of the shape, but of all the other characteristics of tables (many of which he is not aware of at the time). (*ITOE* 11–12)[19]

Parts of Animals I.4644a14–20, he says, "those animals that differ by degree and the more and the less have been brought together under one kind. . . . I mean, for example, that bird differs from bird by the more or by degree (for one has long feathers, another short feathers)" (trans. Lennox 2001b). Aristotle's nonrealist but nonsubjectivist account of the unity of the instances under a kind is instructive here. On the Aristotle-Rand relationship, see Gotthelf 2013; and for a fuller discussion of Aristotle's views on the type of unity possessed by a *genos,* Salmieri 2008, 71–98, and Salmieri, unpublished. On these Aristotelian topics, including difference in the more and the less, see also Lennox 1987.

19. We may think of this reference to omitting measurements of characteristics of which the child is not yet aware, as a standing order that, as one discovers new characteristics shared, in different measure or degree, by tables, one will omit the measurements of these as well. To illustrate, let us imagine a child who has recently formed the concept of "table" by retaining the range of table shapes while omitting the measurements within that range. Rand is holding that, when he discovers that tables have a distinctive use, namely, to support objects

Concepts, for Rand, are thus open-end, not only in the sense that they include in their reference all relevantly similar instances, past, present, and future, but also in the sense that (contrary, say, to the view of Kant or the logical positivists) they include in their content all of the characteristics of their instances, known or unknown. We will return to this later.

After indicating what would be explicitly retained and what would be omitted in the context of an adult's grasp of the concept "table" (including how "the utilitarian requirements of the table set certain limits on the omitted measurements"), Rand writes the important paragraph:

> Bear firmly in mind that the term "measurements omitted" does not mean, in this context, that measurements are regarded as non-existent; it means that *measurements exist, but are not specified.* That measurements *must* exist is an essential part of the process. The principle is: the relevant measurements must exist in *some* quantity, but may exist in *any* quantity. (*ITOE* 12)

This "some but any" principle needs to be carefully understood. In lectures on Rand's theory of concepts, Harry Binswanger (1989, Lecture 3) calls attention to the crucial difference between the process described here and the realist account of concept-formation. Rand is not saying that attention is to be directed away from the quantitative variation and to an identical "length" or "table-shape." Measurement-omission is not an *insight* into a universal element. It is, rather, an *interrelating* of the commensurable determinate particulars. Measurement-omission, as Binswanger puts it, is *measurement-inclusion.* In retaining the attribute—length or table shape—one retains not some "universal" but a *range* along an *axis* of measurement. That is, one recognizes that the commensurability of the various lengths or table shapes allows for many more particular lengths or table shapes, indefinitely many along (the relevant portion of) that axis of measurement. It is precisely this grasp of the axis of measurement, and the relevant range along it, with all its available points or slots, that open-

---

of one sort or another, that newly discovered characteristic can be expected to take its place in the concept of "table" alongside the shape as one of the retained characteristics distinctive to tables, with the measurements omitted of the particular variations along this range of use. Rand's formulation is a way of emphasizing that inherent in integrating mind-independent units into a concept is the expectation that these existents will have numerous other characteristics of which one is as yet unaware, characteristics which will come in varying measure or degree. Both Gregory Salmieri and James Lennox discuss this issue as well in their essays in the first part of the present volume.

ends the awareness to include *all* lengths (or table shapes), past, present, and future, and creates the concept.[20]

Based on this account of concept-formation, Rand offers the following definition of a concept: *"A concept is a mental integration of two or more units possessing the same distinguishing characteristic(s), with their particular measurements omitted"* (*ITOE* 13).[21]

The process of integrating the particulars into the concept—into what I called earlier *a retained unitary grasp*—must be completed by attaching a word to the concept. Rand writes, "In order to be used as a single unit, the enormous sum integrated by a concept has to be given the form of a single, specific, *perceptual* concrete, which will differentiate it from all other concretes and from all other concepts. This is the function performed by language" (*ITOE* 10).[22]

A concept, for Rand, is thus the product of a certain mental process: "The uniting involved is not a mere sum, but an *integration,* i.e., a blending of the units into a *single,* new *mental* entity which is used thereafter as a single unit of thought" (*ITOE* 10).[23] It is a *relational* entity, inherently *of* the units—the existents integrated—which existents exist indepen-

20. As is well known, George Berkeley (and Hume, following him) condemns Locke's theory of abstraction for maintaining the existence of such things as "the general idea of a triangle, which is 'neither oblique nor rectangle, neither equilateral, equicrural nor scalenon, but *all and none* of these at once'" (Berkeley, *Principles,* Introduction, §13 [in Dancy 1998], quoting Locke from *Essay* II.iii.9; italics added by Berkeley; compare Hume, *Treatise,* 1.1.7 [in Selby-Bigge and Nidditch 1978, 17]). To put Rand's view in these terms, one might say that for her the concept of "triangle" is a concept of triangles as being equilateral *or* isosceles *or* scalene. (This is not strictly correct, since the concept "triangle" is formed by differentiating triangles from, for example, squares and circles and other plane figures, along the axis of *number of sides,* and the measurements omitted when the characteristic "three sides" is retained are a continuum of [among other things] side length and angle size. Nevertheless, offering the disjunctive picture in place both of the self-contradictory "all" and of the realist "none" is here a useful way of capturing the force of Rand's "some but any" principle.) Locke's famous question of what sets the boundaries of such ranges will be addressed in the final section of this chapter. At the beginning level of concepts, the boundaries are set by the *perceived* similarities, which themselves are determined in part by the closeness of the relevant physical features and in part by our perceptual mechanisms.

21. Various aspects of this definition are discussed in detail in the workshop transcripts (*ITOE* 153–58). On the usefulness but yet the limitations of the term "mental entity" to capture the idea that a concept is a new mental existent, the persisting product of a mental process, see, in particular, *ITOE* 157–58.

22. See also *ITOE* 19, 40, 163–75.

23. See also *ITOE* 157–58. I imagine Rand would say that two people have *the same concept* (paradigmatically) when their concepts have the same content, that is, integrate essentially the same sort of existents, notwithstanding the level of knowledge within which one distinguishes those existents from other existents (along a shared CCD) on the basis of the

dent of that act of integration. And that act—a uniting via measurement-omission into a single, abstract mental unit—is something that only human beings can perform. The concept produced by that process is not an "image" or "copy" of a sensory "impression," nor any sort of special percept. And, though it is a mental particular (even if inherently relational), it is a mental particular of a sort only human beings can form. Hume was thus wrong, Rand holds, to insist on "the . . . proposition, *that the mind cannot form any notion of quantity or quality without forming a precise notion of degrees of each.*" For, in support of this proposition, Hume writes, "But 'tis evident at first sight, that the precise length of a line is not different nor distinguishable from the line itself, nor the precise degree of any quality from the quality. These ideas, therefore, admit no more of separation than they do of distinction and difference. They are consequently conjoined with each other in the conception; and the general idea of a line, notwithstanding all our abstractions and refinements, has *in its appearance in the mind* a precise degree of quantity and quality; however it may be made to represent others, which have different degrees of both" (Hume, *Treatise* 1.1.7, "Of Abstract Ideas," in Selby-Bigge and Nidditch 1978, 18–19).[24] Hume's argument here presupposes his general thesis, stated at the very opening of the *Treatise,* that "ideas" are "the faint images of [impressions] in thinking and reasoning" and not a more radically distinct sort of mental phenomenon.[25]

But "'tis evident at first sight," Rand would insist, that this thesis is false, as is the claim that, in effect, we cannot separate in thought a line's being of "some length but any" from the precise length of that line. Surely, we are able to form the idea of lines (and other lengths) as being of some length but any, or as we might say, of being "*x* inches long." Of course, there is for Rand no object, "being *x* inches long"—the object of the concept is all the particular, determinate lengths; but what makes it possible for our thought to have the latter sort of object is there being a new mental entity *by means of which* we can grasp those (indefinitely) many particu-

similarities and differences between those groups of existents. See, e.g., *ITOE* 42–45, and the discussion of "conceptual change" below.

24. The italics in the several Hume quotations are all in the original text, except for "its appearance in the mind" here, which is my own emphasis.

25. I take this premise to be behind the following argument: "Now as 'tis impossible to form an idea of an object, that is possest of quantity and quality, and yet is possest of no precise degree of either; it follows, that there is an equal impossibility of forming an idea, that is not limited and confin'd in both these particulars" (Hume, *Treatise,* 1.1.7 [in Selby-Bigge and Nidditch 1978, 20]).

lars. If Hume were right about the nature of the "ideas" with which we think, Rand maintains, algebra would be impossible,[26] not to mention the endless discoveries of science and technology from which our lives benefit in so many ways.

In the title essay of *FTNI*, Rand remarks, "If it were possible for an animal to describe the content of his consciousness, the result would be a transcript of Hume's philosophy. Hume's conclusions would be the conclusions of a consciousness limited to the perceptual level of awareness, passively reacting to the experience of immediate concretes, with no capacity to form abstractions, to *integrate* perceptions into concepts" (*FTNI* 26). Hume, says Rand, is denying that we can *abstract,* and *form concepts* in the way that she thinks we can. What is that way? The present essay's subtitle suggests that Rand has "rethought" the traditional view of abstraction, but I have said hardly anything so far, in this exposition of her theory of concept-formation, about her view of abstraction per se. So let me ask: What is the process of abstraction for Rand? And what is its relation to concept-formation, as she understands the latter?

Let us start with Geach's characterization of traditional "abstractionism," as quoted earlier in this chapter: "I shall use 'abstractionism' as a name for the doctrine that a concept is acquired by a process of singling out in attention some one feature given in direct experience—*abstracting* it—and ignoring the other features simultaneously given—*abstracting from* them." Notice that "abstractionism" for Geach designates a theory of *concept-formation.* The process of abstraction, on the traditional view, "singles out in attention some one feature given in direct experience"; once one has that feature in a selective attention that excludes the other features, one essentially *has the concept.*[27]

---

26. "The basic principle of concept-formation (which states that the omitted measurements must exist in *some* quantity, but may exist in *any* quantity) is the equivalent of the basic principle of algebra, which states that algebraic symbols must be given *some* numerical value, but may be given *any* value. In this sense and respect, perceptual awareness is the arithmetic, but *conceptual awareness is the algebra of cognition*" (*ITOE* 17).

27. I say "essentially" here because advocates sometimes speak of a distinct act of intuiting, or *grasping,* the feature that has been isolated by abstraction. But that "grasp" is understood to be intuitive—passive—and not a further processing comparable, say, to Rand's "process of measurement-omission," to which we will return shortly. Locke, for example, writes,

> This is called ABSTRACTION, whereby ideas taken from particular beings become general representatives of all of the same kind; and their names general names, applicable to whatever exists conformable to such abstract ideas. Such precise, naked appearances in the mind, without considering how, whence, or with what others they came there, the understanding lays up (with names commonly annexed to

Rand's view of concept-formation, by contrast, has, as we have seen, two stages, both involving distinct, active processes: isolation and integration—the *isolation of similars from differents sharing a CCD* and the *integration of the similars via measurement-omission*. Which of these is or involves the process of abstraction? One might reasonably think it is the former—the *isolation* stage. After all, Rand introduces her discussion of concept-formation by saying,

> A *concept* is a mental integration of two or more units which are isolated according to a specific characteristic(s) and united by a specific definition.
>
> The units involved may be any aspect of reality: entities, attributes, actions, qualities, relationships, etc.; they may be perceptual concretes or other, earlier-formed concepts. The act of isolation involved is a process of *abstraction:* i.e., a selective mental focus that *takes out* or separates a certain aspect of reality from all others (e.g., isolates a certain attribute from the entities possessing it, or a certain action from the entities performing it, etc.). The uniting involved is not a mere sum, but an *integration,* i.e., a blending of the units into a *single,* new *mental* entity which is used thereafter as a single unit of thought (but which can be broken into its component units whenever required). . . .
>
> Words transform concepts into (mental) entities; *definitions* provide them with *identity.* (Words without definitions are not language but inarticulate sounds.) We shall discuss definitions later and at length. (*ITOE* 10)[28]

------

them) as the standards to rank real existences into sorts, as they agree with these patterns, and to denominate them accordingly. Thus the same colour being observed to-day in chalk or snow, which the mind yesterday received from milk, *it considers that appearance alone, makes it a representative of all of that kind; and having given it the name whiteness, it by that sound signifies the same quality wheresoever to be imagined or met with;* and thus universals, whether ideas or terms, are made. (Locke, *Essay* II.vi.9, in Nidditch 1979; my emphasis)

See also III.iii.6–9 on the coming to have a general idea, and note 20 above. Peter Coffey, perhaps the best of the early twentieth-century scholastic epistemologists, writes, "Why are manifold individuals classified under a common or universal concept? . . . because they are *similar.* . . . Similarity is a partial *conceptual* or *logical* identity: each individual of the manifold is so constituted that *some factor of each, isolated by the abstractive power of the intellect from the other factors, appears to intellect as one definite self-identical object, and is apprehended as universal or as "common to all"* (Coffey 1917, 277–78; my emphasis).

28. Because Rand has not yet introduced the phenomenon of measurement-omission, she speaks here, in the initial definition of a *concept,* of the uniting as taking place at the stage at which the concept being formed is *defined;* but it is already clear by the end of this excerpt

One might suppose that it is the act of *mentally separating out,* or *isolating,* the units that are then to be integrated into the concept that is called "the process of abstraction"—and this would appear to be true of every case in which Rand speaks of *the process of* abstraction in *ITOE.*[29]

But, in fact, Rand distinguishes the isolation of the units from the process of abstraction per se. Note that in the passage just quoted, the units may be entities, as they would be in the case of the concept "table."[30] But the items said to be abstractable, listed immediately afterward, do not include entities (e.g., the tables that are differentiated from the chairs in the isolation process).[31] It appears that Rand would not speak of "tables" as being abstracted from their background when they are isolated from chairs and other items of furniture. If abstraction is involved anywhere in that process, it would have to be in the perceptual detection of the common range of shape that tables but not chairs or other items of furniture share. But in another passage, Rand distinguishes that process *from* abstraction.[32] So there is a question as to whether for her abstraction is inherent in the isolation stage of every process of concept-formation.

---

that the uniting, or integration, is part of the very process that forms the concept, while the definition of that concept completes the process of integration. Once she has introduced the phenomenon of measurement-omission, later in the chapter, she can, and does, clarify that point. See also her comment on this matter in the workshop discussion (*ITOE* 167).

29. For example: "But what an animal cannot perform is the process of abstraction—of mentally separating attributes, motions or numbers from entities" (*ITOE* 15). Or, again: "To form concepts of consciousness, one must isolate the action from the content of a given state of consciousness, by a process of abstraction. Just as, extrospectively, man can abstract attributes from entities—so, introspectively, he can abstract the actions of his consciousness from its contents, and observe the *differences* among these various actions" (*ITOE* 30). See also *ITOE* 55.

30. "The units involved may be any aspect of reality: entities, attributes, actions" (*ITOE* 10).

31. "The act of isolation involved is a process of *abstraction:* i.e., a selective mental focus that *takes out* or separates a certain aspect of reality from all others (e.g., isolates a certain attribute from the entities possessing it, or a certain action from the entities performing it, etc.)" (*ITOE* 10). Note, too, that the isolation is said to *involve* (not to *be*) a process of abstraction.

32. "In the process of forming concepts of entities, a child's mind has to focus on a distinguishing characteristic—i.e., on an attribute—in order to isolate one group of entities from all others. He is, therefore, aware of attributes while forming his first concepts, but he is aware of them *perceptually, not* conceptually. It is only after he has grasped a number of concepts of entities that he can advance to the stage of abstracting attributes from entities and forming separate concepts of attributes" (*ITOE* 15).

At the same time, however, Rand frequently uses "abstraction" to designate a *product,* and in each such use it is a virtual synonym for "concept." It is a product not just of the isolation stage (if it is a product of it at all) but of the entire process of concept-formation. For instance, in her very first statement of the problem *ITOE* is addressing, on the first page of its foreword, she writes, "The issue of concepts (known as 'the problem of universals') is philosophy's central issue. Since man's knowledge is gained and held in conceptual form, the validity of man's knowledge depends on the validity of concepts. But *concepts are abstractions* or universals, and everything that man perceives is particular, concrete" (*ITOE* 1; my emphasis). And a little bit later she writes, "Observe that the concept 'furniture' is an *abstraction* one step further removed from perceptual reality than any of its constituent concepts. 'Table' is an *abstraction,* since it designates *any* table" (*ITOE* 22; my emphasis). This usage of "abstraction" as a near synonym of "concept" pervades her writing and speaking (e.g., *Journals* 700, 702; *AOF* 53; *AON* 28). Its pervasiveness may explain her occasional use, outside of *ITOE,* of the phrase "the process of abstraction" to include the integration stage, so that it is a characterization of the process behind concept-formation as a whole. Thus, in *FTNI* she writes, "sensations are integrated into perceptions automatically, by the brain of a man or of an animal. But *to integrate perceptions into conceptions by a process of abstraction* is a feat that man alone has the power to perform—and he has to perform it by *choice.* The process of abstraction and of concept-formation is a process of reason, of *thought;* it is not automatic nor instinctive nor involuntary nor infallible. Man has to initiate it, to sustain it and to bear responsibility for its results" (8; my emphasis, except for *choice* and *thought*).

I do not have a full explanation of Rand's varied use of the term "abstraction," both as process and as product. However, I would like to show that there is a way in which, given Rand's theory, the expression "process of abstraction" can naturally apply to the isolation and integration stages together. From that perspective, we will be able to see how radically Rand has, as my subtitle suggests, rethought the traditional idea of "abstraction" (and why this new conception is not subject to the sorts of objections that have been raised, by Geach and others, to an abstractionist account of concept-formation).

Let us start by considering why Rand would say that each concept is an abstraction, and let us illustrate with "table." As Rand often says, "table" does not exist in the world as such, only *tables* do. How do we reach the concept "table"?

Suppose the concept is "table," and the units being integrated are a number of tables in one's field of view, which one has mentally isolated from some chairs, which share a CCD with the tables. While Geach's abstractionist would hold that one is selectively attending to an identity running through the tables, an identity which, in virtue of that act of abstraction, one now has before one's mind as the concept "table," Rand holds that one does not yet have the concept. To reach it, one needs to perform "an *integration,* i.e., a blending of the units into a *single,* new *mental* entity which is used thereafter as a single unit of thought (but which can be broken into its component units whenever required)" (*FTNI* 8). This integration takes place via a process of "measurement-omission." It is the process of measurement-omission that abstracts out "table" by permitting the integration of individual grasps of tables into a single grasp "table." While Geach's abstractionist finds the identical core by separating it out from its background in the entity, Rand takes out, as we might say, tables qua tables, by regarding the entities as the same by virtue of falling within the same range within the CCD. This is a very different separation process from that done in the abstractionist account, and it occurs at a later stage of the concept-formation process. As we have discussed, it is the measurement-omission process (and not the mere gaze at an identical "tableness") that gives one the concept—the open-end grasp of the indefinitely many tables, past, present, and future. So there is a sense in which the integration that follows the isolation stage *extends and completes* the abstraction process. It is therefore not unreasonable to speak of the entire process of isolation and integration as *a process of abstraction,* and its product, the concept table," as *an* abstraction.

Because Rand is not a realist, she has had to rethink the second part of the process of concept-formation, both as an active integration in its own right *and* as an extension of the isolation process (and of any abstraction involved in that process). And because the integration is via measurement-omission, she has had to rethink the nature of the similarity grasped in the first part of the full abstraction process—the isolation of the tables in one's field of view. In order for them to be integrated into a concept via measurement-omission, they have to be regarded as falling in a range within a conceptual common denominator, *shape,* by contrast to other objects (e.g., chairs) that share that CCD but fall outside that range.

This conception of the overall process of abstraction, and of the overall process of concept-formation, is radically different from the traditional abstractionist one. We will also see at the end of this section how this new conception of abstraction is *not* subject to the criticisms Geach has brought against traditional abstraction, and, subsequently, how it enables Rand's approach to justification to get off the ground.

In *ITOE* Rand shows how the theory of concepts I have outlined applies to a wide range of concepts beyond the first level of concepts of things and of attributes we have already discussed. In chapter 3, for instance, she addresses "abstraction from abstractions," that is, the process by which lower-level concepts are integrated and a wider concept formed (for instance, "furniture" from "table," "chair," "bed," "dresser," etc.), or a previously formed concept is subdivided and one or more narrower concepts is formed (for instance, "beagle," "poodle," "greyhound," etc., from "dog"). She explains how measurement-omission (and abstraction in our broader sense) is involved in the formation of these sorts of concepts as well.[33]

The implication of Rand's presentation in this chapter on "abstraction from abstractions" is that, for the most part, concepts must be formed in a certain *order*. Concepts are, as Rand puts it, *hierarchical*. Concepts are formed on the basis of grasped similarities along commensurable characteristics, and we have already seen in the case of the concept of "furniture," the relevant similarities in the case of most concepts can be grasped only with the aid of already-formed concepts. The hierarchical character of concepts was already adumbrated in Rand's discussion of lower-level concepts in *ITOE*, chapter 2, where she observes that concepts of attributes (as well as of materials, motion, relationships, and so forth) can be formed only after some concepts for the entities they characterize have been formed.[34] This fact about our concepts—that they are hierarchi-

33. "When concepts are integrated into a wider one, the new concept includes *all* the characteristics of its constituent units, but their distinguishing characteristics are regarded as omitted measurements, and one of their common characteristics becomes their distinguishing characteristic. When a concept is subdivided into narrower ones, its distinguishing characteristic is retained and is given a narrower range of specified measurements or is combined with an additional characteristic(s) to form the individual distinguishing characteristics of the new concepts" (*ITOE* 84).

34. "It is only after he has grasped a number of concepts of entities that he can advance to the stage of abstracting attributes from entities and forming separate concepts of entities" (*ITOE* 15, best read in its surrounding context, 15–17). On "furniture," see my discussion of higher-level similarities above, note 17.

cal—is of great epistemological importance, according to Rand, because it leads to norms for the formation and validation both of concepts and of the propositions composed from them—and thereby leads to a distinctive conception of the discipline of epistemology. It also has profound consequences in her metaethics (and in much else in her philosophical thought).[35]

The complexities of Rand's theory, including the role of hierarchy, are especially evident in her treatment of concepts of consciousness (*ITOE,* chap. 4) and of what we might describe as "theoretical concepts." Though the methods and standards of measurement in the case of concepts of consciousness are somewhat different from those involved in conceptualizing material entities and their attributes, concepts of consciousness, she shows, are formed by a process of measurement-omission. This is made possible by the fact that phenomena of consciousness share commensurable attributes:

> Two fundamental attributes are involved in every state, aspect, or function of consciousness: content and action—the content of awareness, and the action of consciousness in regard to that content. These two attributes are the fundamental Conceptual Common Denominator of all concepts pertaining to consciousness. . . . In the realm of introspection, the concretes, the *units* which are integrated into a single concept, are the specific instances of a given psychological process. The measurable attributes of a psychological process are its object or *content* and its *intensity.* (*ITOE* 29–31)

35. Rand's presentation of this thesis is spread throughout *ITOE:* see its index, s.v. "hierarchy." Along with "hierarchy," Rand treats as a fundamental to concepts the fact that they are *contextual,* i.e., formed within a certain context of knowledge, and integrated to one's other concepts; her presentation of this thesis—one that must carefully be distinguished from various other theses in contemporary thought that go under that name—is also spread through *ITOE;* see index, s.v. "context." One aspect of this complex thesis—namely, the role of context in producing objective definitions—is discussed in the next section of this chapter. On the bearing of the thesis that concepts are contextual on the development of *scientific* concepts, see Lennox's essay in this volume, "Concepts, Context and the Advance of Science." On hierarchy and context, and their place in Rand's epistemology, see also Peikoff's (1991) excellently systematized account in his chapter 4, "Objectivity." On the implications of these aspects of Rand's theory of concepts for the discipline of epistemology, see Salmieri's chapter in this volume. For very brief accounts of the way the hierarchical nature of concepts bears on Rand's metaethics, see Gotthelf 2000, 22, 79–81, and Salmieri and Gotthelf 2005. Rand first presented her view that the concept of "value" (and thus all ethical concepts) rests hierarchically on the concept of "life" in John Galt's speech in *Atlas* 1012–13. Her fullest presentation is in "The Objectivist Ethics," the first chapter of *VOS.*

Rand's intriguing discussion of different measures both of content and of intensity (with respect to the various sorts of conscious phenomena) is too complex to summarize here. With respect to the intensity of a particular cognitive process, for instance, she speaks of the *scope* of its content and the length of the conceptual chain—the extent of the *hierarchy* of concepts—required to perform that process. In the case of "concepts pertaining to evaluation (including 'value,' 'emotion,' 'feeling,' 'desire,' etc.)," she speaks of a hierarchy of a different kind, and also of a form of measurement unique to concepts of evaluation, which she calls "teleological measurement." In general, phenomena of consciousness, she holds, are all of them particular and determinate and exist along measurable axes. Forming concepts of consciousness thus also involves, in their distinctive ways, *measurement-omission* (see esp. *ITOE* 38–39).[36]

Rand's view of the hierarchical character of concepts of consciousness is nicely illustrated in the case of concepts of consciousness. These concepts are formed by differentiating the actions (or reactions) of consciousness from their content, which requires concepts for "some aspect[s] of the external world." Rand includes among concepts of consciousness "concepts pertaining to the *products* of psychological processes, such as 'knowledge,' 'science,' 'idea,' etc.," and "a special sub-category of these, concepts of *method*."[37] Concepts of method necessarily depend for their formation on the possession of concepts for the goals, actions (psychological and/or physical), tools, and products of the method. And the "integrations of existential concepts with concepts of consciousness" obviously presuppose the formation of concepts of the two types integrated: "The

36. The notion that conscious phenomena are subject to a type of measurement is not entirely unfamiliar to analytic philosophers. See, for example, the extensive contemporary discussion of the commensurability of *values*. See also the discussion by Robert Efron, in his Rand-influenced 1969 paper on perception, of how the specificity (or degree of determinateness) of perceptual awareness can be measured—and, in this connection, the more recent literature about the fine-grainedness of perception (some of which could benefit by taking into account Efron's discussion).

37. She includes in this subcategory of concepts of consciousness not only purely psychological methods ("such as a method of using one's consciousness") and methods involving "a combination of psychological and physical actions (such as a method of drilling for oil), but also concepts for (normative) disciplines devoted to the discovery of methods, such as logic, epistemology, ethics, medicine, and the applied sciences." "The concepts of method," Rand goes on to say, "are the link to the vast and complex category of concepts that represents integrations of existential concepts with concepts of consciousness, a category that includes most of the concepts pertaining to man's actions." As examples, she cites "marriage," "property," "law," and, later, "justice."

concept 'marriage' [for instance] cannot be formed or grasped merely by observing the behavior of a couple: it requires the integration of their actions with a number of concepts of consciousness, such as 'contractual agreement,' 'morality,' and 'law'" (*ITOE* 34–38, 70).

Another aspect of Rand's thesis that concepts are hierarchical is illustrated by her treatment of what are often called "theoretical" concepts (such as "electron," which she mentions in passing on *ITOE* 47). In a portion of the workshops not transcribed for the expanded second edition of *ITOE*,[38] Rand briefly discusses the transition from a concept of a type of entity hypothesized by scientific researchers to the same concept when the existence of such entities has been established (the example is "archaeopteryx"). But neither there nor anywhere in *ITOE* does she identify a special category of concepts that depend for their formation on a complex body of scientific theory as philosophers who speak of "theoretical concepts" sometimes mean to do. (Nor does she isolate a corresponding sort of existent, a "theoretical entity.") She does not do so, I suspect, because she holds that all concepts beyond the simplest ones depend for their formation on a complex, hierarchical body of *knowledge,* itself connected to a complex hierarchy of concepts. In that sense, the difference between theoretical concepts of science and other higher-order concepts probably did not seem a fundamental one to her—not, one might say, because she underestimated the cognitive complexity of scientific concepts, but because she understood the cognitive complexity of concepts which one might think of as outside the realm of theoretical science.[39]

Nonetheless, a closer look at the implications of her theory for the formation of such concepts will bring out the way in which later concepts depend on propositional knowledge expressed in terms of earlier concepts, and not just the earlier concepts themselves. First, note that Rand would certainly hold that concepts such as "electron" are also formed by a

38. Folder A, L, H, P–18 in the Special Collections of the Ayn Rand Archives (Irvine, CA).

39. See, in this regard, *ITOE* 48, and the passages cited above on the hierarchical character of concepts of consciousness. A remark of Lennox's, in his essay in this volume, is pertinent. Lennox identifies five types of changes in an existing conceptual structure to which new discoveries might lead, "each of which is acknowledged at some point by Ayn Rand in *Introduction to Objectivist Epistemology.*" After doing so, he states, "Since I am focusing on the philosophy of science, I will refer to these as *developments in the conceptual structure of a science.* It is worth noting, however, that such conceptual advances—the introduction, replacement, reclassification, or subcategorization of concepts, or the generation of a wider concept—are not peculiar to the sciences. They are a pervasive aspect of cognitive development."

process involving measurement-omission, in essentially the same way as the other sorts of concepts we have examined.[40] The difference between this sort of concept and most of the concepts we have discussed would lie in the *basis* for knowing (or, perhaps first, hypothesizing) that their units—the things they integrate (e.g., electrons, in the case of the concept "electron")—*actually exist,* with similarities that warrant their being conceptualized. As an example of such an "existence proposition," as I like to call it, consider the following from J. J. Thomson: "the experiments just described, taken in conjunction with previous ones on the value of *m/e* for the cathode rays . . . , show that in gases at low pressures negative electrification, though it may be produced by very different means, is made up of units each having a charge of electricity of a definite size; the magnitude of this negative charge is about 6 x 10^{-10} electrostatic units, and [in light of Townsend's results] is equal to the positive charge carried by the hydrogen atom in the electrolysis of solutions" (qtd. in Dahl 1997, 187–88). This basis for knowing (or, perhaps first, hypothesizing) that such and such things exist would not be perceptual awareness alone (as in the initial formation, e.g., of "table"), or perceptual awareness plus a few simple cognitive steps therefrom (as in the initial formation of, say, "furniture"), but a complex body of propositional, and indeed theoretical, knowledge, itself built on prior concepts and propositions—which concepts and propositions are themselves ultimately built up from perception.[41]

In his critique of "abstractionism," referred to at the opening of this essay, Peter Geach says that "the supposed process of abstraction" (1957, 18) cannot explain our acquisition of (to use his terms) (1) concepts of sensible things (including material stuffs) (19–20), (2) psychological concepts (20–22), (3) logical concepts (22–27), (4) arithmetical concepts (27–32), (5) relational concepts (32–33), or even (6) color concepts (not to mention concepts of other sensible qualities) (33–38); in short, Geach concludes, "no concept at all is acquired by the supposed process of abstraction" (18).

This is all true enough, if abstraction is what Geach and his abstractionists take it to be, but, as I have already suggested, I do not believe his arguments against abstractionism have any force against Rand's theory

40. That electrons might not vary *at all* in the basic characteristics that distinguish them from other particles does not count against this; see *ITOE* 142–44 and Dahl 1997, 187–88.

41. Note, then, that on Rand's view, although all concepts (e.g., "electron") are built hierarchically *from* perceptual awareness, the units of a concept need not be directly discernible *in* perceptual awareness (as, e.g., "electron" is not).

of abstraction and concept-formation. For reasons of space, I can only be brief on this matter, but let me at least indicate the direction a fuller response would take. To start, the view being criticized in (1) and (6) holds that, for example, particular instances of red have an identical core of *redness,* and particular color ranges (*red, blue,* etc.) an identical core of *hue;* but we have seen that Rand rejects this, holding that the instances need only be commensurable, i.e., comparable along a scale of more and less. Geach's argument in regard to (2) depends, among other things, on a primitive view of introspection, overanalogized to perception; this is not Rand's view, since for her introspection typically involves the use of previously formed concepts (*ITOE* 225–29). In regard to (3), Geach's abstractionists, incredibly, take concepts such as "and" and "or" to be formed from things like feelings of hesitation. Rand much more sensibly looks to their role in capturing, and facilitating, "relationships among thoughts" and indicates what sort of measurement-omission is involved in their formation (*ITOE* 37–38). Finally, given the priority in Rand's theory of the formation of concepts of kinds of entities, she has no difficulty accounting for the kind-relative dimensions of both (4) and (5). Indeed, Rand's general account of mathematics and mathematical concepts, though by no means fully developed, is well worth further study.[42]

In this section, I have only been able to outline Rand's theory of concepts. My aim has been to lay down the elements of the theory, to aid readers in the study of her work, and to provide a platform from which students of her theory (myself included) could go on to expand on this presentation and to develop its implications for a host of epistemological issues. But even an outline of Rand's theory would not be complete without an account of the place of definitions in concept-formation, and of their relation to essences as she conceives them.

Definitions and Essences

In the formation of a concept, as we have seen, the units (for example, tables) are first *isolated* from certain other objects (for example, chairs) by focusing on a distinguishing characteristic or characteristics (for ex-

---

42. Cf. *ITOE* index, s.v. "numbers," "mathematics." In a book-length project, Pat Corvini draws on the Objectivist theory of concepts to explore the nature of number and related mathematical concepts. Preliminary results have been presented in lectures delivered at Objectivist summer conferences; see esp. Corvini 2007, 2008.

ample, a specific shape, and, later, also a use).[43] Then, the units are *integrated* by retaining those characteristics, with their axes of measurement, while implicitly omitting all particular measurements (of that shape, that use, and of all the other common characteristics of tables). The integration is turned into a retainable mental unit by being assigned a word. To complete the process the concept is given a *definition*. "A definition," says Rand, "is a statement that identifies the nature of the units subsumed under a concept. . . . The purpose of a definition is to distinguish a concept from all other concepts and thus to keep its units differentiated [in one's mind] from all other existents" (*ITOE* 40).[44] I quote from her discussion:

> The rules of correct definition are derived from the process of concept-formation.
>
> The units of a concept were differentiated—by means of a distinguishing characteristic(s)—from other existents possessing a commensurable characteristic, a "Conceptual Common Denominator." A definition follows the same principle: it specifies the distinguishing characteristic(s) of the units, and indicates the category of existents from which they were differentiated.
>
> The distinguishing characteristic(s) of the units becomes the *differentia* of the concept's definition; the existents possessing a "Conceptual Common Denominator" become the *genus*.
>
> Thus a definition complies with the two essential functions of consciousness: differentiation and integration. The differentia isolates the units of a concept from all other existents; the genus indicates their connection to a wider group of existents. (*ITOE* 41)

A definition thus both *differentiates* a concept from other concepts and *integrates* it to them, allowing us, as our knowledge expands, to retain the hierarchical structure of our concepts and to keep our knowledge integrated into a single whole.[45]

The units of a concept normally have many distinguishing character-

---

43. In this section I borrow heavily from my presentation in Gotthelf 2000, chap. 7. See also Lennox's discussion of definition in his essay in part 1 of this volume, which, as he says, builds on and elaborates the material presented here.

44. The only concepts that cannot "be defined and communicated in terms of other concepts . . . are concepts referring to sensations, and [axiomatic concepts, such as *existence* and *consciousness*]." These must be defined ostensively (*ITOE* 40–41, 55–61).

45. On the importance for Rand of the hierarchical (and contextual) nature of concepts, see my discussion in the previous section of this essay. On both hierarchy and integration, see also Salmieri's discussion in the next essay.

istics, however, and to specify them all in its definition would defeat the purpose of a definition: it would make it impossible for a mind to hold the concept as a single unit, clearly grasped. What is needed is a single distinguishing characteristic, or a very small number of them, that can be held as a single mental unit and yet can bring readily to mind all the other characteristics. It is here that Rand introduces her conception of *essence*.

She observes that the distinguishing characteristic(s) of a concept's referents that readily bring to mind the referents' other characteristics will be the ones on which those others, or the greatest number of them, depend. The distinguishing characteristic(s) on which the others depend are *essential* to the concept's referents: without those characteristics (and the others that depend on them), the referents would no longer be the kind of things they are (*ITOE* 42). This is the Aristotelian rule of *fundamentality* put to epistemological use. The essential characteristic is the *fundamental* distinguishing characteristic—that is, the distinguishing characteristic or characteristics that are *responsible for* (and thus explain) the greatest number of other distinguishing characteristics.[46]

Thus, in the familiar example of the definition of *man*—where we observe that man is the only animal that can tell time with a watch, catch a joke, speak a language, experience certain complex emotions, grasp things conceptually, and so on—it is the ability to reason, to grasp

46. At *Topics* I.5 101b38, Aristotle says that "a definition is a phrase (*logos*) that signifies the essence (*to ti ên einai*)." *Topics* VI is devoted to ways of evaluating proposed definitions. In VI.4 Aristotle argues that the candidate for essence should be *prior* to and *more intelligible* than the other features universally predicable of the subject whose essence is being sought (i.e., prior and more intelligible not just *to us*, but *absolutely*, i.e., in nature [141b15–142a16]). He says that such a definition is "more scientific" (*epistêmonikôteron*) than one that is the reverse (141b16), but in the *Topics*'s usage of that term, there is no clear evidence that the priority in question is meant to be causal or explanatory. From the beginning of the *Posterior Analytics* (*APo.*), by contrast, a definition's requisite priority is *causal* (whatever else it might be). Scientific knowledge is *demonstrative* in form, and we have a demonstration when "we are aware both that the cause because of which the object is is its cause, and that it is not possible for this to be otherwise." (*APo.* I.2 71b10–11). The cause appears as the middle term of the demonstration: All *S* is *P*, for instance, because *S* is (by definition) *M*, and *M* (qua cause of being *P*) necessitates being *P*; definitions are among the first principles of a demonstration (*APo.* I.2, 10, 13, 19, II.1–2, 8–11, and elsewhere). "So, as we say, to know what it is is the same as to know why it is" (*APo.* II.2 90a31–33).

There is an excellent discussion of Aristotle's theory of definition in Charles 2010a. (I express a reservation about one aspect of Charles's view in Gotthelf 2012c, 76n34, but it only reinforces the point of the centrality of causality to the notion of essence.)

Aristotle's essences are clearly "metaphysical" in Rand's sense, but in Gotthelf 2012a, 394–96, I point to passages that show at least an in-principle receptivity on Aristotle's part to epistemological essences in Rand's sense, even if he has not explicitly reached the idea.

things conceptually, that makes the others possible and explains them. And so, by defining man as *a rational animal,* one brings readily to mind the other characteristics one knows to follow from the capacity to form concepts and to reason. Were we to define man as *the time-telling animal,* the mental effort of moving up and down the causal chain to hold one's knowledge of man's distinguishing characteristics as a single whole would be stultifying.

Two facts about this account of definition have significant implications, Rand observes. First, a concept is an integration of *existents,* not just of selected aspects of them, so that the meaning of a concept is not exhausted by its definition.[47] Second, knowledge about the units of a concept is acquired over time, and new knowledge may call for a revised definition. Both facts are best seen in the context of Rand's general approach to concepts, discussed in the previous section of this chapter.

A concept, as I have said, is an integration ultimately of perceptual (or introspective) data, an integration of particular existents either discernible in perception or inferable therefrom. It is not an awareness of special "abstract objects," but a distinct and powerful form of awareness of particular existents—past, present, and future—with all their attributes, known and unknown. The concept is formed by a certain *means* (isolation and integration via measurement-omission) and held in a certain *form* (an integration of retained characteristics with measurements omitted, fixed by a word and specified by a definition). But neither the means by which conceptual awareness of existents is achieved nor the form in which it is held is the *object* or content of conceptual awareness. The object or content is the units, the *existents* grouped together, with all of their attributes.

The concept's content is thus not to be equated with its definition.

47. The concept of "meaning" does not play a central theoretical role in Rand's theory of concepts, but she does occasionally make use of it, as I do here, to contrast her view with the view (held by Locke and Gottlob Frege, in different forms) that a concept (in Rand's sense) is a grasp of a small number of *known* attributes of the units, which then determines which existents fall under the concept. In that context she would typically say that "the meaning of a concept consists of the units—the existents—which it integrates, including all the characteristics of these units." (See Peikoff's discussion in "The Analytic-Synthetic Dichotomy," *ITOE* 97–106, esp. 98, from which I have just quoted, and Rand's own remarks in response to questions about meaning in the workshop discussions [*ITOE* 165–66, 174–77, 235–38].) Why Rand holds that the notion of "meaning" should not have the sort of theoretical role in philosophy that it has had at least since the early twentieth century is a complex matter that requires more discussion.

As one comes to discover additional distinguishing characteristics of the units of a concept, one's knowledge of those units changes—it expands. But, except in special cases, *one's concept does not change.* The concept still integrates essentially the same units, the same existents.[48] However, if one should discover a more fundamental distinguishing characteristic of the existents integrated into a concept, the definition will need to change to reflect that new knowledge. In the new context of knowledge, the old defining characteristic is *no longer essential* and falls out of the definition. The earlier definition is still a true statement, and the earlier essential characteristic (and its causal relationship to the other earlier known distinguishing characteristics) is still included in the content of the concept, but it is replaced in the definition. Our knowledge has *expanded* and our definition reflects that.[49]

The essential characteristic of a concept, then, is that distinguishing characteristic of its units, *from among those known,* which is *known* to be responsible for (and thus explanatory of) the greatest number of other *known* distinguishing characteristics.

Definitions are thus *contextual.* They depend in part on the definer's context of knowledge. But within a given context of knowledge they are, Rand says, *absolute*—that is, determined by the *actual* causal-explanatory relationships between the distinguishing characteristics known within that context. "An objective definition, valid for all men," says Rand, "is one that designates the *essential* distinguishing characteristic(s) and genus of the existents subsumed under a given concept—according to all

48. The concept itself will change—or, strictly, be replaced—only in those cases where new information, or a newly established scientific theory, so modifies our understanding of the similarity relationships as to require a reclassification of the relevant existents. (The abandonment of the concept of "humours," or of the concept of "phlogiston," is an example of that.) Much of what philosophers of science today call "conceptual change" does not in fact involve an actual replacement of one concept with another. See Lennox's essay for an extended discussion of these issues. Rand sometimes makes this point by saying that the concept's meaning does not change. (See again Lennox's discussion, in the second section of his essay.)

49. See, for instance, the historical move from defining chemical elements in terms of atomic weight to defining them (after subatomic particles had been discovered and the understanding of chemical interaction had advanced) in terms of atomic number. The move is described in Scerri 2006, chap. 6, and in Hendry 2006, 867 (forthcoming, 59–60); see also Hendry 2010, 145–47. Thanks to Michael Weisberg for first pointing me toward this very interesting literature in history and philosophy of chemistry. For other examples, see Peikoff 1991, 96–105; and Lennox's essay in this volume.

the relevant knowledge available at that stage of mankind's development" (*ITOE* 46).[50]

Definitions are also *factual statements*. "*A definition is the condensation of a vast body of observations*" (*ITOE* 48)—observations of similarity-and-difference relationships, observations of which characteristics distinguish a particular group of existents from others, and observations that establish which of those characteristics are in fact responsible for the rest. They are neither stipulations nor conventions.

If definitions are contextual for Rand, so are essences. Or, as she puts it, essences are *epistemological,* not metaphysical. (Here she differs from those in the realist tradition.) A distinguishing characteristic that is caus-ally prior to other distinguishing characteristics is not more "real" than those other characteristics, nor more what an existent integrated by the concept "really is," nor is it the sole or primary referent of the concept.[51] The concept refers to the existents it integrates, including all of their characteristics, known and unknown. But the characteristic designated "essential" does perform a distinct *epistemological* function. Its ability to perform this function, then, depends in part on the factual (causal) relations between the characteristics, but also in part on the way a conceptual consciousness must function if it is to acquire, retain, and expand its knowledge.[52]

It is clear from this discussion that, as I suggest in the subtitle of this essay, Rand has radically rethought not only the traditional notion of abstraction as discussed earlier, but also the traditional notion of "essence," replacing metaphysical essences with epistemological essences.[53] Has she

50. Jim Bogen, in his discussion in this volume, objects to the universality of Rand's thesis. See his interesting comments, and my response, in part 2 of this volume.

51. Nor is a causally prior distinguishing characteristic any sort of deep identity running through the concept's referents: it too typically varies within a range. (Thanks to Gregory Salmieri for this point.)

52. Fodor et al. 1999, among others, insist that any theory that identifies concepts with definitions must fail because there are no definitions of that type, or at least very few. So, it is important to underscore two things that may be clear already: first, Rand does not identify concepts with their definitions, and second, Rand's definitions are not "analytic" definitions of the sort Fodor and colleagues denigrate. See Peikoff, "The Analytic-Synthetic Dichotomy," in *ITOE* 88–121, and Griffiths's discussion in this volume of Rand's view of definition. Also relevant, more generally, are remarks by Ghate's in his reflections on Griffiths's commentary, in part 2 of this volume.

53. Rand's replacement of metaphysical with epistemological essences is nicely elaborated by Lennox in his essay below, in his section on "The Cognitive Role of Definitions," where he makes good use of the important *ITOE* 52. See also Ghate's account of Rand's position on "natural kinds" in part 2 of this volume.

rethought essences out of existence? I think not. From its inception in Greek philosophy, from at least the time of Socrates, through its development in Aristotle, the root idea of a thing's essence, as we have already discussed, has been that which makes it to be what it is.[54] While Rand rejects the notion that a particular thing or existent, as such, has a metaphysical essence—some single feature or subset of features that is more truly what that thing is than any other features of it—there is an important sense in which, for her, a thing's epistemological essence makes it to be of the *kind* of thing it is.[55]

Norms of Conceptual Activity

Our focus in regard to concepts per se has been, so far, on their nature and formation, and their basis in reality. In speaking of their basis in reality, we have been speaking of a necessary condition of their formation: concepts can be formed only by an active process of *differentiating* (similars from differents along shared commensurable characteristics) and *integrating* (those isolated similars into a unitary, open-end grasp). Similars can be integrated *only* if they share a commensurable characteristic (*ITOE* 13).

This condition on concept-formation is a condition from the side of reality: the quantitative relations that underlie commensurability are mind-independent facts about the world, and as such provide what I have called a "basis in reality" for conceptual integrations.[56] (The causal relations crucial to the determination of essential characteristics are, of course, another part of that basis.)

---

54. See, for example, the essays on Socrates, Plato, and Aristotle in Charles 2010, and my note 46 on essence in Aristotle.

55. As I have explained, an essence in Rand's sense is a *condensation*. It integrates all the known distinguishing characteristics. As such, short of listing every known distinguishing characteristic, it thus most fully distinguishes the concept—and the kind the concept captures—from everything else. For clarification of Rand's view of the relationship of a thing to the kind of thing it is, see Ghate's reflections on Griffiths's discussion in part 2. See also the discussion in the next section of this chapter of the norms of concept-formation, and the role of essential characteristics in that process, as well as the brief note there on the *objectivity* of kinds.

56. Actually, the commensurability of the units to be integrated is a condition only because our conceptual apparatus is such that our mode of conceptual integration involves measurement-omission. In that sense, this condition, though from the side of reality, involves a coordinate condition from the side of consciousness (a point to which we will return later). Still, *given* our apparatus, the relevant quantitative relations required for integration are themselves mind-independent and should be classified as a *basis in reality* for our concepts.

However, though this condition sets limits on what concepts we *can* form, it does not by itself tell us what concepts we *should* form. Existents are similar (even in Rand's sense) in myriad ways and can be grouped in myriad ways. Yet we do not have concepts for all these groupings. We often identify unconceptualized groups by descriptive phrases; for example, someone might speak (to use Rand's example) of "beautiful blondes with blue eyes, 5′5″ tall and 24 years old." But we can easily see that an attempt to form a new concept (with a single word) for each such a grouping would clutter our consciousness and stultify our thinking (or those so-called concepts would fall out of use).

We spoke at the beginning of this chapter of the role of concepts both in organizing our knowledge and in facilitating its expansion. Forming a concept every time we notice a similarity would do neither. What else, then, is involved in proper concept-formation, and what normative principles should guide our conceptual faculty in deciding what integrations to make and what concepts to form? Rand observes that "one of that faculty's essential guiding principles" is "the principle of *unit-economy*." She explains that "the range of what man can hold in the focus of his conscious awareness at any given moment is limited. The essence, therefore, of man's incomparable cognitive power is the ability to reduce a vast amount of information to a minimal number of units" (*ITOE* 63; see also 172–73).

This is a pattern throughout successful conceptual activity. We have seen some of the ways in which concepts themselves expand our knowledge by radically reducing the number of units: "A concept substitutes one symbol (one word) for the enormity of the perceptual aggregate of the concretes it subsumes" (*ITOE* 64). And we have seen the principle of unit-economy at work in guiding the formation of definitions: the *essential* characteristic (or characteristics) of a concept condenses into a single mental unit our knowledge of all the many distinguishing characteristics (*ITOE* 65).[57] Think too of how *outlining* a complex argument, or an article or a book, facilitates understanding the argument or article or book: the larger whole, which one cannot hold in mind as a whole, is reduced, via the outline, to relatively few manageable units. That is the principle of unit-economy at work.

This principle, Rand holds, plays a crucial role in determining which concepts should be formed and (as a direct consequence) what, in Locke's

57. Likewise, the definition's genus enables condensation of the many characteristics in common with nearby groupings.

term, their "boundaries" should be (see Locke, *Essay,* III.vi.27, among many other passages). In her discussion of "The Cognitive Role of Concepts," in *ITOE,* chapter 7, Rand lists some cases where the principle of unit-economy makes it mandatory that we form concepts. Among the types of concepts that it is mandatory to form, says Rand, are:

> such categories as: (a) the perceptual concretes with which men deal daily, represented by the first level of abstractions; (b) new discoveries of science; (c) new manmade objects which differ in their essential characteristics from the previously known objects (for example, "television"); (d) complex human relationships involving combinations of physical and psychological behavior (for example, "marriage," "law," "justice").
>
> These four categories represent existents with which men have to deal constantly, in many different contexts, from many different aspects, either in daily physical action or, more crucially, in mental action and further study. The mental weight of carrying these existents in one's head by means of perceptual images or lengthy verbal descriptions is such that no human mind could handle it. The need of condensation, of unit-reduction, is obvious in such cases. (*ITOE* 70)

Later, in discussing her response to the nominalist "borderline case argument," Rand stresses the role of unit-reduction in regard to the issue of specialized study. Speaking of black swans, she explains that it is mandatory to classify them as *swans,* and not as a separate, coordinate group, because "virtually all their characteristics are similar to the characteristics of the white swans, and the difference in color is of no cognitive significance" (*ITOE* 73). I take her remark that "the difference in color is of no cognitive significance" to refer to the fact that black swans do not need separate, specialized study. They don't need it because they do not have anything *essential* to them as such—that is, they don't have any distinguishing characteristics that bring along many other distinguishing characteristics, such that there is a wealth of unique information to be condensed by a concept.[58] Forming a separate, coordinate *concept* for black swans, therefore, "would lead to senseless duplication of cognitive effort (and to conceptual chaos)" (*ITOE* 71; see 70–73).

Were we, however, to discover that a group previously classified among the swans actually has essential similarities among themselves in this way—that is, has characteristics, not possessed by the other birds

---

58. I owe the formulation in the latter part of this sentence to Gregory Salmieri.

with which it has been grouped, that bring along many others, requiring specialized study—then a new, coordinate concept would have to be formed. It is the principle of unit-economy that mandates, in such cases, the forming of a separate major grouping, and a concept integrating it. (This was presumably the case with regard to the formation, probably first by Aristotle, of the concept *cetacean,* incorporating whales, dolphins, and porpoises.)[59] And because the principle mandates the formation of new concepts in order to integrate *certain ranges* of things, the norms it provides for when concepts should be formed also serve as norms for the "boundaries" of the kinds of things (e.g., swans, fishes) to be recognized by these concepts.

Generalizing on this discussion, Rand identifies a broad norm for the formation of concepts, a kind of "epistemological 'razor'": "The requirements of cognition determine the *objective* criteria of conceptualization. They can be summed up best in the form of an epistemological 'razor': *concepts are not to be multiplied beyond necessity*—the corollary of which is: *nor are they to be integrated in disregard of necessity*" (*ITOE* 72).[60]

These brief illustrations of the role of the principle of unit-economy in determining when new concepts need be formed (and when not) and what existents these concepts need to integrate illustrate a wider fact about Rand's theory of concepts, and indeed about her philosophy in general. They show that the nature and formation of a concept depends in part on *reality* (for instance, mind-independent commensurability and causal relationships) and in part on *the requirements of a conceptual consciousness* (for instance, the need to integrate via measurement-omission and the need of unit-economy). Concepts, then, are neither products of subjective conscious choices, as nominalism claims, nor intuitive grasps of *intrinsic* universals or essences, as realism claims. They are, on Rand's view, essentially distinct from what both of these theories take concepts to be. And because grasping their nature is central to our understanding of human cognition and to the establishment of norms thereof, we need a new concept—and term—for the actual relationship between concepts and the world. Rand's term for this third status is "objective." As she writes, "None of these schools regards concepts as *objective*, i.e., as

---

59. Aristotle, *History of Animals* I.6 490b8–9, VII.2 589a31–590a18. Interestingly, in the almost certainly earlier work, *Parts of Animals* (*PA*), Aristotle has not yet separated off such a wider kind (*PA* IV.13 697a14–b1 and Lennox 2001b, 343).

60. The allusion is to Ockham's metaphysical "razor."

neither revealed nor invented, but as produced by man's consciousness in accordance with the facts of reality, as mental integrations of factual data computed by man—as the products of a cognitive method of classification whose processes must be performed by man, but whose content is dictated by reality" (*ITOE* 54).[61]

"Objectivity" here can refer both to the status that a properly formed concept achieves, when it is formed in accordance with a process based on facts of mind-independent reality, and to that process when it is guided according to a systematic body of norms (i.e., to a *method*) required for such a process to adhere to mind-independent reality. For Rand, then, as Peikoff (1991, 117) summarizes, "To be objective in one's conceptual activities is volitionally to adhere to reality by following certain rules of method, a method based on facts *and* appropriate to man's form of cognition."[62] And, to simplify a large issue, on Rand's view a conceptual consciousness will be *justified* in its conclusions if and when it has followed such a method.[63]

This status—*objective*—in the context of its distinction from *intrinsic* and *subjective*—and the general conception of *objectivity* that underlies

---

61. See also Salmieri and Gotthelf 2005, especially the concluding paragraph; Gotthelf 2000, chap. 7; and especially Peikoff 1991, chap. 4. The same point will apply to Rand's view of *kinds:* they are neither intrinsic (or "natural") nor subjective, but *objective*. See Ghate's discussion of kinds in his reflections on Griffiths, in part 2 of this volume. In response to Locke's question as to whether the boundaries of the kinds of existents we recognize are set by "nature" or by "the workmanship of the understanding," Rand's answer is (in effect): "Both, jointly"—understanding that that workmanship must be in accordance with an objective method (as we are about to discuss).

62. Peikoff continues:

People often speak of "objective reality." In this usage, which is harmless, "objective" means "independent of consciousness." The actual purpose of the concept, however, is to be found not in metaphysics, but in epistemology. Strictly speaking, existents are not objective; they simply are. It is minds, and specifically conceptual processes [including their products], that are objective—or nonobjective.

The concept of "objectivity" is essential to a rational epistemology; it is a requirement of the proper development of human consciousness and, ultimately, of human survival. . . . A conceptual consciousness must focus on reality by a deliberate resolve, and it must discover and then choose to practice the method required to implement this resolve. Such is the fundamental state of mind that the concept of "objectivity" identifies and upholds. (Peikoff 1991, 117)

63. Various implications of Rand's view of conceptualization and objectivity for the familiar problems of contemporary epistemology are discussed at length by Salmieri in the next essay.

it—is central to Rand's philosophy. It characterizes not only her view of concepts and definitions, but also her view of knowledge generally, and of values, and much more. Its centrality is one reason why she called her philosophy *Objectivism*.[64]

64. For important further discussion of Rand's conception of "objectivity," see the closing pages of Salmieri's essay.

Conceptualization and Justification

GREGORY SALMIERI

iven its title, one might expect Ayn Rand's *Introduction to Objectivist Epistemology* (*ITOE*) to outline her positions on the issues normally covered in introductory courses and texts on epistemology. In particular, one might expect to find discussions of epistemic justification—i.e., "our right to the beliefs we have" (Dancy 2005, 263). Justification and the nature of knowledge are widely regarded as the essential subject matter of the field, and, as we will see, Rand effectively agrees with this consensus.[1] Yet her monograph says little directly on these subjects. Rather, it is devoted entirely to the presentation of a theory of concepts. My subject in this essay is how a theory of concepts can be an introduction to an epistemology. More specifically, I will show how Rand's theory and the view of consciousness that it embodies relate to some concerns about justification that are familiar from the contemporary, analytic literature on epistemology.

---

1. In his contributions to two standard reference works, Moser (1999, 273; 2002, 1) defines the field as "the study of the nature of knowledge and justification." Similarly, the introduction to Pojman's (2002, 1) popular epistemology reader begins by telling us that the field "inquires into the nature of knowledge and justification of belief."

Though I will present some exegesis of Rand and some arguments in support of her positions and related theses of my own, this essay is not primarily exegetical or argumentative. My aim is, rather, to sketch the outlines of an epistemology in a way that brings out the relations between a seldom studied theory of concepts and some much debated questions about justification. I hope in doing so to shed light both on the theory and on the questions.

I hope this paves the way for others to argue in greater detail for (or against) the theses I sketch here, and to do so in a way that engages more substantially with the analytic literature. In my view, the chief obstacle to work of this kind has been the lack of a big-picture account of the relation between the subject matter of *ITOE* and the central concern of analytic epistemology. This is the lack that I aim to remove.

Epistemology and the Nature of Awareness

Rand defines epistemology as the "the science devoted to the discovery of the proper methods of acquiring and validating knowledge" (*ITOE* 36). She describes the facts that give rise to such a science as follows.

> Man is neither infallible nor omniscient; if he were, a discipline such as epistemology—the theory of knowledge—would not be necessary nor possible: his knowledge would be automatic, unquestionable and total. But such is not man's nature. Man is a being of volitional consciousness: beyond the level of percepts—a level inadequate to the cognitive requirements of his survival—man has to acquire knowledge by his own effort, which he may exercise or not, and by a process of reason, which he may apply correctly or not. Nature gives him no automatic guarantee of his mental efficacy; he is capable of error, of evasion, of psychological distortion. He needs a *method* of cognition, which he himself has to discover: he must discover how to use his rational faculty, how to validate his conclusions, how to distinguish truth from falsehood, how to set the criteria of *what* he may accept as knowledge. (*ITOE* 78–79)

We can see in this passage (and in Rand's definition) a concern with the set of issues that motivates contemporary discussions of epistemic justification. Rand emphasizes that our putative knowledge is not *unquestionable*: it may be mistaken and is open to challenge. Therefore, it must be *validated* before we *accept* it as knowledge. Since, to accept something as knowledge is to believe it, Rand's question of whether we *may accept* something as knowledge is equivalent to asking whether we have a right

CONCEPTUALIZATION AND JUSTIFICATION ▪ 43

to believe it—i.e., whether belief in it would be *justified*. I will discuss Rand's conception of "validation" later, but it should be evident from what we have seen already that it is a normative concept and that she means by it something broadly similar to what contemporary epistemologists call "justification."

The function of epistemology is to define a method by which we can discover new knowledge and validate putative knowledge. The need for such a method arises, says Rand, because man is "a being of volitional consciousness" whose knowledge is obtained by an effortful process that he can fail to perform correctly (or indeed to perform at all). But these considerations only apply "beyond the level of percepts": perception is a more primitive form of knowing that is automatic and does not require a method. As the language of "levels" indicates, the volitional forms of knowing that do require a method are founded on the primitive form that does not—i.e., conceptual knowledge is founded on perceptual knowledge. Thus, to understand Rand's view of conceptual knowledge and of the role of validation in it, we will need first to understand something about her view of perception and about the broader conception of knowledge or consciousness that embraces both perceptual and conceptual awareness.[2]

In speaking of consciousness, we can distinguish between the faculty of consciousness and the state of being conscious of something. The latter is the primary sense of the term for Rand, with the former being understood in terms of it. "Consciousness" in this primary sense is synonymous with "awareness," or with "perception" or "knowledge" in the widest senses of these terms. It subsumes sense-perception, propositional knowledge, and any other form in which an organism might be aware of the world.

Crucially, though, what it denotes is an awareness *of an external world*: "A consciousness with nothing to be conscious of" (or that was

---

2. On this view knowledge is not to be understood fundamentally as a type of belief. Rather, we begin with a sense of knowledge broader than propositional knowledge—one that includes knowledge by acquaintance with objects—and we understand propositional knowledge as a species of this. A similar position is taken by McGinn (1984). His account of knowledge (and indeed many externalist accounts) has an affinity with Rand's insofar as it emphasizes the relation between knowledge and *discrimination*. However, for Rand the notion of discriminating is not, as McGinn implies (and as many information-theoretic accounts of consciousness hold), more primitive than that of knowing; quite the reverse. Moreover (as will become clear in the second section), the implications of Rand's view for the role of differentiation in propositional knowledge make her position quite unlike McGinn's.

"conscious of nothing but itself"), Rand wrote, "is a contradiction in terms" (*Atlas* 1015). Rand called this dependence of consciousness on external objects the "primacy of existence," and she regarded it as a self-evident axiom that is contained in and presupposed by all knowledge.[3] She was thus contemptuous of radical skeptical worries to the effect that we might not have any knowledge of an external world. All mental content, she held, must have its basis in an awareness of real objects.

Of course, not all conscious states are awarenesses of real objects, nor is it always obvious to a subject which of his states constitutes awarenesses. (It is precisely because this is not obvious that a method of *validating* one's knowledge is necessary.) In addition to the state of being aware, there is also the faculty of awareness (which is what Rand most often means when she speaks of "consciousness").[4] Not all states or exercises of the faculty of consciousness are aimed at awareness: there are other sorts of conscious states—e.g., desires, dreams, intentions to act, imaginings, etc. All these states derive their contents from awareness of the world, but are not awarenesses in themselves (even if some may occasionally be mistaken for such). In addition to such states, there are also *errors*—states that aim at awareness and purport to be knowledge, but are not.

For our immediate purposes, however, we can limit our attention to genuine awareness. Here is how Rand characterizes it in *ITOE*'s opening sentence: "Consciousness, as a state of awareness, is not a passive state, but an active process that consists of two essentials: differentiation and integration" (*ITOE* 5). As an illustration of what it means to call a *state* of awareness an *active process,* consider the state of seeing a ball roll across the floor. The seeing is a complex activity of discriminating the ball from the background and tracking it over time as it moves (or as the perceiver moves through the environment).

In Rand's view, the various processes in the eyes and brain by which this is accomplished are not merely causal antecedents of the seeing, but parts of the seeing itself. The state of seeing is an activity the subject engages in. This is true even when it is experienced introspectively as passive, as it would be if the person is not intentionally following the ball, but

3. Thus, Rand did not think that the primacy of existence could be proved. Instead its axiomatic status is established by a process of reaffirmation through denial. On this issue, see Peikoff 1991, 17–23.

4. Thus Rand's characterization of consciousness as "the faculty of perceiving that which exists" (*Atlas* 933).

simply notices its motion. The example of a moving ball helps to highlight the fact that perception involves tracking objects over time, but the state of seeing the ball would be no less active if the ball were stationary: as long as the subject sees the ball, he is engaged in a process of *differentiating* it from its background and of *integrating* the sensory information required to discriminate and track the ball *as a whole*.

In the case of vision, the processes involved are primarily physiological. In describing seeing as an activity consisting largely of these processes, I do not mean to *reduce* seeing to these processes. Indeed, I think (and Rand seems to have thought) that conscious states cannot be reduced to physical ones and that awareness is a sui generis category of action that includes an irreducibly experiential component.[5] The physiological processes are *parts* of the action of seeing, not the whole of it. I emphasize them, however, to call attention to the integral role that processes play in being aware of something, even when the awareness is experienced as a passive reception. As we will see, there are corresponding processes in the case of conceptual knowledge, but these must be consciously initiated and sustained.

Each state of awareness, for Rand, is an active process of differentiating its object(s) from other existents and integrating information about it. Elsewhere, she refers to this as *identifying* the objects—saying that "consciousness is identification"—and she often speaks of it as a "grasp" of an object. The analogy to physical grasps is apt: though physical grasps can be described as states, they are more accurately described as activities we engage in. Thus, for someone to have a grasp of an apple is for that person to be *grasping it*—something that involves continual (though minimal) action over time.

The analogy to physical grasps is useful for introducing another feature of awareness. There are different forms of grasping an object— different grips. For example, physiologists distinguish between the "power grip" and the "precision grip"; in the former the object is "held in a clamp formed by the partly flexed fingers and the palm, counter pressure being applied by the thumb lying more or less in the plane of the palm," whereas in the latter the object is "pinched between the flexor aspects of the fingers and the opposing thumb" (Napier 1956, 903). And, of course, there are many subtypes of grips within these two broad categories. Similarly there

5. For a useful discussion from an Objectivist perspective of the sui generis nature of consciousness, see Binswanger 1998.

are many different forms in which we can consciously grasp an object—
many different forms of awareness.

Propositional knowledge differs from the perceptual awareness of an
object, and, within the category of perception, the sense modalities differ.
To be aware of the shape of a ball visually is different from being aware of
it tactilely. The point applies also within the same sense modality. For example, one can see the same object from different vantage points or with
different acuities of vision. Because these cases may involve differences
in what parts or aspects of the object the subject perceives in addition to
differences in how he perceives it, considering a more fanciful example
may help to focus our attention on differences of perceptual form: suppose that someone's visual spectrum became inverted while he was looking at an object, but that his visual acuity was in no way affected. Before
and after the event, the man was aware of the same objects and attributes,
but in very different forms.

"Form" denotes the identity of the state of awareness as distinguished
from the identity of its object; it is *how* one is aware, in distinction from *what*
one is aware of.[6] Similar distinctions have been drawn by other thinkers.
Most notably Aquinas distinguishes between the *id quod* and the *id quo*
of a cognitive power.[7] However, these distinctions have rarely been maintained consistently. Considering the history of thought from the perspective of Rand's distinction, there has been a pervasive tendency to conflate
the form and object of awareness and to treat the result either as an object
of which one is aware formlessly, or as an objectless state of consciousness.

These two positions and Rand's alternative can be illustrated by considering the case of a myopic man looking at a tree with and without his
glasses. In both cases he sees the same object, the tree, but he sees it differently. The blurriness of his vision when he is not wearing his glasses
is an attribute of the perception rather than of the object; it is part of the
form. We can capture this by saying that "he sees the tree blurrily," using
a noun to denote *what* he sees and an adverb to denote *how* he sees it.

If we use the grammar this way, then one of the views with which
Rand's should be contrasted can be represented by saying that "the man

6. On Rand's "form-object" distinction, see Peikoff 1991, 44–52; Binswanger 1989; Gotthelf 2000, 55–57; and Salmieri 2006, Lecture 1.

7. See *Summa theologica* 1a85.2c. There is some scholarly debate over how to interpret
this distinction, with some versions of it being nearer to Rand's than others. For discussion of
competing views, see Pasnau 1997, chap. 6. Another distinction that is sometimes interpreted
in a way that is broadly similar to Rand's is Frege's between sense and reference, though there
are important differences, which I discuss in my other contribution to this volume.

sees a blurry tree." This suggests that the blurriness is a feature of the *object seen*. An especially naïve realist would take the blurriness to be a feature of the very tree in front of which the man is standing. It is doubtful whether anyone has held this position, but a great many thinkers have held that there is some blurry tree-like object internal to the man (be it an image on his retina or an idea or sense datum in his mind), which is the immediate object of his awareness.[8] From the standpoint of Rand's theory, both versions of the "blurry tree" view make the same error. They ascribe to an object of awareness a feature that belongs, rather, to the form in which we are aware of it. Such ascriptions are motivated by the premise that awareness itself must be *featureless*.[9]

The second view to be contrasted with Rand's would ascribe the features of the perceived object to the act or state of perception. It would hold, in effect, that the man sees blurrily and "treely."[10] On such a view, the state of awareness has features but lacks an object. For Rand, such a position would amount to denying that the perception is a state of awareness at all, since the subject would not be aware *of* anything.

On the first of these two views, consciousness has an object but no identity; on the second, it has an identity but no object. Both views, thus, "regard *identity* as the *disqualifying* element of consciousness" (*ITOE* 80), holding that a state of awareness must have no identity of its own in order to succeed at being an awareness of an object as it actually is. On this premise, any characteristics of the cognition would constitute parts of the cognized content, with the result that we could be aware only of objects constituted by our own means of cognition. This last is the Kantian position, which Rand regards as amounting to the claim that "man is blind, because he has eyes—deaf, because he has ears—deluded, because he has a mind—and the things he perceives do not exist, *because* he perceives them" (*FTNI* 32).[11]

8. Examples of this sort of position include Locke's theory of ideas and the sense-data theory maintained by Russell (1912, chap. 1), among many others.

9. Thus, Moore (1903, 446, 450) famously describes consciousness as "transparent" and "diaphanous."

10. My language here is deliberately evocative of adverbial theories of perception such as that advocated by Chisholm (1957), but the broad view of awareness I am discussing is not limited to such views of perception. It includes any view on which the awareness does not have objects, and where the things that ordinarily would be taken for such objects are constituted by the mind's own activities or states.

11. This is not intended, of course, as a literal statement of Kant's position, but a vivid characterization of his view that having a specific and limited means of awareness prevents us from knowing "things in themselves."

Rand rejects this shared premise and so rejects the dichotomy between these two positions. For her, to be aware is to be aware of *something somehow*. Just as when we physically grasp an object that grasp has a certain form, which is distinct from its object, so too does a mental grasp. She holds that this is the only position that is consistent with what each of us knows implicitly in each state of awareness—namely, that there is an *object* of which we are aware, and that we are *aware* of it.

Conceptual knowledge is the distinctively human form of awareness, but it is based on sense-perception, which is shared with the lower animals and is man's *basic* form of consciousness—his only *direct* contact with reality (*ITOE* 5).[12] In sense-perception we are immediately acquainted with objects in our environments, and this acquaintance constitutes knowledge of them.

As noted above, the objects of perception are entities, which we grasp perceptually as wholes.[13] This grasp includes many of the entities' attributes, actions, and relations (though it does not isolate and focus on them in the way one can in thought). Importantly, it also includes an awareness of the causal roles played by some of the entity's perceptible characteristics in its actions. For example, the role of roundness in rolling is perceptible, as is the role of legs (and their specific shape) in walking. This point will become significant later, when we discuss concept-formation and induction.[14]

12. A qualification is necessary here. Rand distinguished between perception and sensation in the same manner as William James (1890, chaps. 17 and 19). A sensation is an atomic and transient response by a sense organ to a stimulus, whereas a perception is a retained awareness of entities, formed physiologically by the integration of sensations. Sensations as such are never experienced by adults, and considerable conceptual sophistication is required to isolate individual sensory qualities within their experience. However, Rand (like James) thought that infants and certain animals do experience isolated sensations rather than perceptual wholes. This last point (which, in the case of infants, has been refuted) is a psychological theory of little relevance to epistemology and was regarded by Rand as such.

13. I follow Rand and Peikoff in reserving the term "entity" for "solid things with a perceivable shape, such as a rock, a person or a table" (Peikoff 1991, 13).

14. Rand did not herself say that such causal connections are directly perceptible, but it can be inferred from her positions on causality and on the objects of perception. For statements and defenses of this position from an Objectivist point of view, see Peikoff 2005, Lecture 2; Salmieri 2006, Lecture 1; and Harriman 2010, 21–25. A similar position was earlier maintained by Harré and Madden 1975, 49–67. Their discussion is valuable both for the arguments they present in favor of the view and for the useful historical context they provide. Psychological research supporting the perceptibility of causal connections includes Michotte 1963, Leslie and Keeble 1987, and Scholl and Tremoulet 2000 (all of whom are cited by Bayer 2011, 372n21).

Rand regarded perception as infallible in the sense of not being able to err. On her view, the many errors that are possible in identifying what one perceives are all posterior to the perception itself. An illusion, for example, is a case in which one object looks just like another object would in a more familiar circumstance, such that the first object is liable to be mistaken for the second. When such mistakes are made, however, the fault lies not in the perception, but in the judgments made about the perceived object.[15]

Perception always occurs in a form. The form may be unfamiliar because of unusual conditions (as is the case in many illusions) or because of damage to the sense organs. Such perceptions might be less detailed, less useful, or more apt to be misinterpreted than others, but they remain awarenesses of objects in the subject's environment, and there is no standard in accordance with which their *veridicality* can be impugned. And, however prone to misinterpretation by a given subject a given perception may be, it contains potentially valuable information about the object as well as information about the circumstances of perception and about the subject's own faculties. With attention, and given time, the subject can learn to utilize this information and judge correctly. But whether his judgments are correct or incorrect, they are no part of the perception itself. Perception is a direct encounter with objects and does not have the kind of content that could be true or false. The senses are, as Charles Travis (2004) (echoing J. L. Austin) puts it, *silent*.

Rand sometimes makes this point by saying that man's "senses tell him only that something is, but *what* it is must be learned by his mind" (*Atlas* 934). This formulation can be misleading, however, if it is taken to suggest that what we are acquainted with in perception is bare particulars. There is a great deal of content to the perceptual awareness of an entity—content that can be identified conceptually and expressed in propositions. However, unlike the perception itself, the process of conceptually identifying it is fallible. It is impossible to capture the full content of any perception in conceptual terms or to conceptually describe a perception without assuming material that is not part of the perception itself, because in bringing the perceived material under concepts one relates it to other knowledge that is not part of the episode of perception being described.

---

15. For a more detailed discussion of this position and responses to some common objections to it, see Onkar Ghate's chapter in part 1 of the present volume.

Rand's view of perception and its infallible character can be further clarified by differentiating perception itself from the perceptual level of consciousness as a whole. I mentioned earlier that the faculty of consciousness performs activities other than being aware. Most significantly, it directs action, which requires such states as projecting scenarios and forming values (which are experienced in the form of emotional responses). There is also memory, which (when veridical) is, like perception, a form of awareness. And there are dreams and other such states, the function of which in human life is less clear. All of these conscious functions are distinct from perception, and they depend on it for their content. They take place *at the perceptual level of consciousness* when this content is held in *perceptual form,* rather than in the form of concepts or propositions. Even for a human being it is possible to fantasize about something (or to fear it or remember it) wordlessly, in the form of visual images or associations between them. It is also possible to manipulate mental content held in perceptual form so as to project possible future scenarios and to form rudimentary plans. Presumably such abilities account for much of the behavior exhibited by the higher animals. All of these functions are distinct from perception, even when they are carried out at the perceptual level. Some of these states aim at awareness (e.g., of the future or past or of objects not immediately in view). We can call all states that have this aim cognitive (whether at the perceptual or conceptual level).

Perception's infallibility consists in its inability to miscognize—to present the world as being other than it is. It is in this way that perception is necessarily veridical. Other cognitive states, however, including those at the perceptual level, can be nonveridical, in that they can represent the world as being other than it is. This is possible because perception's more basic presentation of the world forms a standard against which these other cognitions can be impugned.

Perception is our basic form of awareness, and as such qualifies as *knowledge,* in the widest sense of that term. As the basic form of consciousness, it serves as the paradigm and foundation for knowledge (including, as we will soon see, propositional knowledge). Every other state of consciousness is based on perception and will qualify as knowledge only if it stands in the sort of relation to external objects that is exemplified by perception. This is the very relation of awareness or *consciousness* that Rand regards as axiomatic.

In the Objectivist literature, one often finds the point made that the senses cannot err or deceive us because they are deterministic physical systems, and that reason can err because it is volitional (*Atlas* 1041; Peikoff 1991, 39–40). I agree entirely with this contrast between the senses and reason; however, I do not think that it is being deterministic *alone* that makes the senses infallible. The consciousness of a cat or dog is likely entirely deterministic, yet both animals clearly form *expectations* based on their past experiences about how the things around them will behave, and these expectations can be mistaken. (When their expectations are frustrated, cats and dogs show signs of surprise or confusion.) Perception, however, cannot be mistaken because, in addition to being deterministic, it is also basic. The basicness removes the possibility of any standard against which a perception can be judged erroneous (either by the perceiver or by a third party), and so renders the idea of an erroneous perception incoherent.

Because there is nothing that the contents of a perception might contradict that is not itself built on perception, in the case of conflict it is never the perception which is to be rejected. One might think that two perceptions can contradict each other, but this is not so. Perception is an awareness only of the present, so two differing perceptions of the same object on different occasions are not a contradiction; rather, this is how one is aware of change. We cannot have two conflicting perceptions at the same time because perception provides us with a single, integrated field of awareness rather than with multiple discrete perceptions. The belief that perception can err (or "deceive" us) stems from the confusion of perception with perceptual judgment, from the form-object confusion, or from failing to grasp the essential difference between perception and such states as dreams or hallucinations (on which see Ghate's essay in part 1 of this volume). Once we have differentiated these states from perception and grasped the relation between perception and other forms of cognition, we can see that there is nothing left to be meant by the phrase "erroneous perception."

Though error of a sort may be possible with some deterministic, perceptual-level processes in animals, the point remains that, for man, the crucial distinction is between perception itself, which is deterministic and infallible, and thought, which is up to us and fallible. The sorts of projecting and expectation-forming processes that are deterministic in animals are, in human beings, largely under the control of thought, and, even where they are not, our thinking determines how much credence to give them. More importantly, though occasional errors may be possible with these deterministic processes, it is only the advent of thought that makes error pervasive and something that we need to be concerned about.

Because the conceptual form of awareness is not automatic and can easily drift into error, we need to perform the activities in which conceptual knowing consists in self-conscious adherence to certain *methods,* and we need to *validate* our conclusions, tracing them back step by step to their roots in the infallible foundation of knowledge—in the direct contact with reality that is sense-perception. We will not be in a position to discuss these methods and the need for validation until we have considered the nature of conceptual knowing.

The Process of Conceptualization

We turn now from the perceptual level of consciousness to the conceptual—to reason: "the faculty that identifies and integrates the material provided by man's senses" (*VOS* 22). I have already remarked on Rand's general view that to be conscious of something is to identify it by differentiating it from other things and by integrating information about it (over time and across sense modalities). Reason identifies objects by *conceptualizing* them. I quote Rand at some length:

> A *"concept"* is a mental integration of two or more perceptual concretes, which are isolated by a process of *abstraction* and united by means of a specific definition. Every word of man's language, with the exception of proper names, denotes a *concept,* an abstraction that stands for an unlimited number of concretes of a specific kind. It is by organizing his perceptual material into concepts, and his concepts into wider and still wider concepts that man is able to grasp and retain, to identify and integrate an unlimited amount of knowledge, a knowledge extending beyond the immediate perceptions of any given, immediate moment. Man's sense organs function automatically; man's brain integrates his sense-data into percepts automatically; but the process of integrating percepts into concepts—the process of abstraction and of concept-formation—is *not* automatic.
>
> The process of concept-formation does not consist merely of grasping a few simple abstractions, such as "chair," "table," "hot," "cold," and of learning to speak. It consists of a method of using one's consciousness, best designated by the term "conceptualizing." It is not a passive state of registering random impressions. It is an actively sustained process of identifying one's impressions in conceptual terms, of integrating every

CONCEPTUALIZATION AND JUSTIFICATION ■ 53

event and every observation into a conceptual context, of grasping relationships, differences, similarities in one's perceptual material and of abstracting them into new concepts, of drawing inferences, of making deductions, of reaching conclusions, of asking new questions and discovering new answers and expanding one's knowledge into an ever-growing sum. The faculty that directs this process, the faculty that works by means of concepts, is: *reason*. The process is *thinking*.

It is a faculty that man has to exercise by *choice*. Thinking is not an automatic function. In any hour and issue of his life, man is free to think or to evade that effort. (*VOS* 21–22)

Rand's theory of concepts is a theory about the process by which percepts or prior concepts are integrated to form new concepts, in terms of which we can then identify objects. It is a process that is sustained and iterated over the course of one's life so as to constitute a complex and ongoing activity of conceptually knowing the world. Unlike perception, the activity is volitional, and must be initiated, sustained, and directed by choice. Thus, as Rand puts it, "*man is a being of volitional consciousness*" (*Atlas* 1012; *ITOE* 78). It is the volitional character of reasoning that makes error an ever-present possibility and gives rise to the need for methods and standards of cognition. I will discuss these methods and standards in the final section of this essay. In the present section I will discuss the nature of the process in which conceptual knowing consists, making little reference to the need for this process to be chosen and directed.

A concept is a unitary form in which we are aware of a (potentially infinite) group of similar existents.[16] To conceptually identify something is to treat it as a *unit*: "an existent regarded as a separate member of a group of two or more similar members" (*ITOE* 7). For Rand, similarity is a relationship of comparatively slight difference in some measurable characteristic, which Rand calls the "Conceptual Common Denominator" (CCD). For example, two greens are similar insofar as the differences between them are dwarfed by the larger difference between either and red. And all of these colors are compared along the CCD of hue.

To view items as similar is to take a complex, comparative perspective on them. A unit is an existent *regarded* as one of a number of existents that stand in this complex relation. It is an object insofar as it is cognized

---

16. I follow Rand and Peikoff in using the term "existent" to denote anything that exists, regardless of metaphysical category.

in a certain form on the basis of certain (putative) knowledge about the relations in which it stands to other objects.

It is possible to regard something as a unit without forming a concept for the group of similars to which it belongs. We often group items transiently, based on similarities that are significant only in some momentary context. For example, in the process of deciding what to order from a restaurant menu, someone might group together certain entrées on the grounds that they fall within a certain price range, are comparatively light, and are complemented by a certain wine. He might decide to order *one of* these entrées, without deciding which, and on the basis of this decision he might decide on an appetizer, before making up his mind among the grouped entrées. A detective investigating a murder or a director casting a play might similarly group people in ad hoc manners based on similarities that are relevant to the purpose at hand—whether the actors are within a certain range of heights, for example, or whether the suspects have enough upper body strength to strangle a man in his prime.

Regarding things as units is a complex mental activity, which, in cases like the ones just described, is experienced as effortful. A concept integrates our awareness of a group of similars into a single "mental entity"—a unitary and enduring awareness of the units as units. This is accomplished by the process that Rand calls "measurement-omission" and by the introduction of a word to stand for the concept.

"Measurement," writes Rand, "is the identification of a relationship—a quantitative relationship established by means of a standard that serves as a unit" (*ITOE* 7). To grasp that existents are similar is already to measure them in a crude form, establishing their nearness by a series of pairwise comparisons (in which each of the compared items serves as a standard against which the other is measured). To omit measurements is to despecify them, projecting from a set of discrete quantities on a CCD to a *range* along it.[17] The result is a unity encompassing the several units with which one started along with an infinity of additional ones. Prior to the process of measurement-omission, one regards the units as similar by pairwise comparisons, whereas afterward one has a holistic awareness of a range in which one sees each as falling.

By associating a word with this range and automatizing the policy of using the word indifferently for anything that falls within it, one effec-

---

17. In some cases, as in the concept "length" or "hue," one omits all the measurements along the range to reach an awareness of the CCD as a whole, rather than a range along it.

tively institutionalizes the unit perspective on the similar objects, making this perspective a stable and enduring feature of thought. The result is a new form of awareness—the concept, a unitary mental grasp of all of the units.

Notice that this new form of awareness is a way of *regarding* things. Though we can speak of it as a "mental entity" (as we can speak of a "*state of awareness*"), it is not a static item, but an *institutionalized policy* of considering things in a certain manner. Like perception, concept-formation consists in differentiating material jointly from a wider context and integrating it into a whole, and, like perception, it is a process of integration that must be maintained over time. Unlike perception, however, conceptual integration is performed consciously and is *based on prior knowledge*. To be more exact, it is based on the putative knowledge of relations of similarity and difference in which the units stand to one another and to the foils from which they are differentiated.

If this putative knowledge is incorrect, then we are mistaken to regard the relevant existents as units, and the resulting concept is (to use Rand's term) invalid. We will discuss invalid concepts in the next section. Since our immediate purpose is to understand successful cognition, we can set aside temporarily the possibility of error and think of concepts as a form of awareness based on prior knowledge. Because the foundation of conceptual knowledge is perception, we will need to consider how the first concepts could be formed on the basis of perceptual knowledge.

The first things to be conceptualized are perceptible entities. Entities are measured by measuring their attributes, most obviously shape and motion. These characteristics can be reduced to a set of linear measurements geometrically, but it is not necessary to do this to make the sort of coarse and implicit measurements that are inherent in noticing similarities and differences. One notices, for example, that one entity is *more* or *less* round or thin or tall than another. This can be done without any concepts, simply by comparing things pairwise.[18]

In forming a concept, measurements are omitted not only along the CCD, but also along all the axes along which the entities can be mea-

---

18. Indeed, we generally form new attribute concepts by first noticing such more-and-less differences among entities. For example, in explaining the concept of a wine's "body," a popular wine-tasting site asks us to "Think [of] how a milkshake seems different than water, how a ginger ale seems different from cough syrup. All of these are liquids, but all have different bodies" (see http://wineintro.com/glossary/b/body.html) The site then elaborates on the concept by discussing examples of wines with light, medium, and full bodies.

sured. That is, one omits the measurements of all the known characteristics of the entities, and one institutes a policy of omitting measurements of new characteristics as they are discovered. Thus, for example, a child who forms the concept "man" along the CCD of shape and/or motion may already have noticed variations in skin or hair color, and she omits these measurements as well. When the child later learns of professions and marital statuses, she will omit these measurements also, retaining the axes along which the measurements are made and the ranges (if she can determine them) in which men fall along them. For example: every man must somehow produce (or otherwise attain) the material goods he needs to live, and the ways in which a man can do this fall within a range that includes countless occupations but excludes the process of photosynthesis.

The result of the process of concept-formation, thus, is a new form of awareness of all entities within the relevant range along the CCD with whatever other characteristics they may have (in whatever degrees along whatever axes they may be measured). Essential to this form of awareness is a commitment to maintaining it by continuing to regard the units as units and all of their characteristics as measurements falling within ranges that are characteristic of the kind as a whole.

The holistic and future-looking character of measurement-omission is essential to the function of the concept, which is to allow what is learned about each unit to be applied to all the others. This function also determines which features can serve as CCDs and which ranges along them can be integrated. Rand calls the range along a CCD in which the units of a concept fall its "distinguishing characteristic" (DC), and the DC must be causally related to ranges along other axes of measurement so as to render the units of the concept globally similar to each other rather than merely similar in some isolated respect; otherwise, there will be nothing of interest to be learned by grouping the units together. The formation of a concept requires an awareness in some form that the DC is *fundamental*—that it causes and/or explains a host of other facts.[19]

Such an awareness is directly available in perception for the types of concepts that children form first. These are concepts of perceptible entities, especially ones that move on their own. The ways in which such entities move (or can be moved by others) are perceptibly underwritten by their shapes. Walking, for example, is perceptibly a leg-involving activity;

---

19. A characteristic that is nonfundamental (such as color) can, of course, be properly conceptualized, but the units of the concept will be the instances of the characteristic itself, rather than the entities possessing it.

rolling perceptibly requires roundness (which perceptibly excludes top-pling); and the shapes of tools, toys, and items of furniture play a percep-tible role in the uses made of them. It is for this reason that shape and/or motion serves as the CCD for our first concepts.[20] Each of these concepts denotes entities that are perceived to be similar in respects that percepti-bly have consequences, and it is this body of perceptual knowledge that is leveraged to form the concept.

Just as the first-level concepts we have been discussing can be formed directly on the basis of perception, perception also supplies all the evi-dence necessary for many applications of these concepts. Having formed the concept "dog" by integrating a range of similarly shaped creatures based on their perceptibly similar shapes and the perceptible role of this in activities such as running, barking, biting, and the like, the child can then apply the concept to Lassie by noticing how her shape falls within that range. In looking at her and exclaiming "Dog!" the child forms the *judgment* we would express by saying, "This is a dog," and this judg-ment serves to identify Lassie by relating her to all the other dogs the child has observed and to everything from which he has differentiated dogs in the past. It thus applies all of the child's knowledge about dogs (much of which still may be held in a largely perceptual form) to Lassie. The identification is based directly on the child's present perception and on the prior acts of perception and integration required to form the concept. (I will discuss later the respects in which the child is and is not conscious of what he is doing in making his claim and of what his basis is for doing so.)

The primary value of such first-level concepts as dog, however, lies not in the ability it affords a child to deem that various animals are dogs and to apply his observations about past dogs to them. He could do al-most as much without the integration of the concept, because he has the

20. Of course, as one learns more about the units of these concepts one will come to understand more deeply the causal relations among their characteristics. One may discover deeper causes underlying what was fundamental in one's initial context, or one may discover a respect in which what one initially saw as a derivative is, in fact, a fundamental. (To choose an obvious example, the actions of animals are evidently causally dependent on their shapes insofar as only creatures with those shapes could move in those ways, but the evolution and maintenance of the shape through natural selection is caused by its enabling that activity, so viewed from another perspective the activity could be said to be the cause of the shape.) On how the discovery of such new knowledge factors in the development of a concept, and how this is reflected in changes in the concept's definition, see *ITOE*, chap. 5; the section on definitions and essences in Gotthelf's essay and Lennox's essay, both in part 1 of this volume; and Salmieri 2006, Lecture 2.

perceptual-level abilities to notice similarities and differences among things and to associate them with each other and imagine how they might act in different scenarios. The concept's main value lies in the *unit economy* it provides. That is, it allows the child to regard all dogs as constituting a single kind of thing that can now function as a single unit in thought. This makes "dog" a subject about which he can accumulate general knowledge.

In order to accumulate such knowledge, a child needs to conceptualize not only dogs themselves, but also their *characteristics*. I use this term quite generally to include attributes, actions, relations, etc.[21] Though an awareness of some characteristics is utilized in the formation of one's initial entity concepts, one is not yet aware of them in *isolation* from the entities they characterize. It is entities that are isolated for us in perception, and we are aware of characteristics only as parts of these wholes. Having conceptualized the entities, however, we are then in a position to abstract and conceptualize their perceptible characteristics.[22]

Though the formation of concepts of characteristics requires that one has already formed concepts for some perceptible entities, all of the concepts we have discussed so far can be described as "first-level" for three related reasons: the knowledge on which they are based is available directly in sense perception; they are the first form in which their units are conceptualized; and the combination of such concepts of entities and characteristics enables the formation of first-level propositions (e.g., "Dogs bark" or "Balls roll"), which can be validated directly on the basis of perception without the mediation of other concepts or propositions.[23]

21. A characteristic, in this sense, is anything that *characterizes*. Thus, the term subsumes everything in every ontological category other than entity. Though I will discuss only characteristics of entities, characteristics can themselves have characteristics. An action, for example, can be quick or slow.

22. It is clear from *ITOE* 15 that Rand thinks that this is the necessary order of learning, and this order has been borne out in developmental studies (Anglin 1977, Rosch 1978, Sloutsky 2003; for discussion, see Bayer 2011, 379n31). I attribute the necessity of this order to two related factors. First, a concept of a characteristic involves omitting the measurements of the characteristic's subject and thinking of it as a characteristic that can hold of *any* subject of a relevant sort; this requires seeing the subject as the unit of a concept. Second, the function of concepts of characteristics is to *characterize* entities by being predicated of them in propositions; thus, there can be no need for such concepts until one has concepts of entities to serve as subjects in these propositions. (I discuss the first of these reasons in Salmieri 2006, Lecture 3.)

23. In Objectivist lectures, the term "first-level concept" has sometimes been reserved for first-level concepts of entities, which are the only concepts that in no way presuppose prior

All of these first-level concepts can be contrasted with "higher-level concepts" (or "abstractions from abstractions"), which are based on earlier conceptual knowledge. These concepts come in several varieties.

Some higher-level concepts are formed by integrating several earlier-formed concepts into a wider genus (as "organism" might be formed from "plant" and "animal" or "perform" from "sing" and "dance"). Such "widenings" presuppose the narrower concepts because the similarities on which these new concepts are based are too remote to be grasped without the unit-economy provided by the prior concepts. Whereas a parrot is perceptibly similar to a pigeon, the similarities between a lion and a linden can only be grasped by first regarding the linden as a plant and the lion as an animal.

Other concepts, "narrowings," are formed by isolating a narrower group among the units integrated by an earlier concept. For example, "bird" would be narrowed to form "parrot" or "pigeon," and "sing" would be narrowed to form concepts like "croon" and "chant." A narrowing depends on the concept from which it is narrowed because the similarities between the narrowing's units (e.g., between two parrots) as opposed to the other units of the wider concepts (e.g., to a pigeon or a finch) are too slight to be noticed (or seen as causally significant) in a context in which the units of the wider concept have not yet been isolated from more different things (e.g., cats, cars, chairs). The scale of similarities that can be noticed directly is, in part, a function of the nature of our senses.

Many narrowings also require the prior formation of concepts to identify the distinguishing characteristic of the new, narrower concept. This is particularly true of "cross-classifications": concepts that are formed not by specifying a narrower range along the same CCD on which the initial concept was differentiated but rather by introducing a DC along an independent CCD, such as when tables (or other items of furniture) are subdivided not on the basis of their overall shape and function (into concepts like "kitchen table," "end table," etc.) but along some CCD such as style, material, or age to yield concepts like "rococo table," "claw-foot table," etc.

The higher-level concepts discussed thus far all stand for existents, which one can be aware of perceptually but which cannot be grasped as *similar* and integrated into a concept without the intervention of previ-

---

concepts. I used the term this way occasionally in Salmieri 2006. I follow Peikoff 2005 and Harriman 2010 in adopting the wider usage here.

ous conceptual knowledge. Other, higher-level concepts, like "disease," "germ," "element," "electron," or "charge" denote existents that cannot even be discovered without prior conceptual knowledge.

The advent of these various sorts of higher-level concepts gives rise to a complex system of concepts that is hierarchical in two respects. First, certain concepts are presupposed by others, in the sense that the prior concepts are made use of in the processes by which the units of the posterior concepts are isolated and integrated. Indeed, most concepts presuppose complex chains of prior concepts (and often propositional knowledge, to which we will come shortly). As an example of this sort of complex hierarchy, consider Rand's discussions of the presuppositions on which the concept "justice" is based:

> What fact of reality gave rise to the concept "justice"? The fact that man must draw conclusions about the things, people and events around him, i.e., must judge and evaluate them. Is his judgment automatically right? No. What causes his judgment to be wrong? The lack of sufficient evidence, or his evasion of the evidence, or his inclusion of considerations other than the facts of the case. How, then, is he to arrive at the right judgment? By basing it exclusively on the factual evidence and by considering all the relevant evidence available. But isn't this a description of "objectivity"? Yes, "objective judgment" is one of the wider categories to which the concept "justice" belongs. What distinguishes "justice" from other instances of objective judgment? When one evaluates the nature or actions of inanimate objects, the criterion of judgment is determined by the particular purpose for which one evaluates them. But how does one determine a criterion for evaluating the character and actions of men, in view of the fact that men possess the faculty of volition? What science can provide an objective criterion of evaluation in regard to volitional matters? Ethics. Now, do I need a concept to designate the act of judging a man's character and/or actions exclusively on the basis of all the factual evidence available, and of evaluating it by means of an objective moral criterion? Yes. That concept is "justice."

> Note what a long chain of considerations and observations is condensed into a single concept. And the chain is much longer than the abbreviated pattern presented here—because every concept used in this example stands for similar chains. (*ITOE* 51–52)

The second respect in which conceptual knowledge is hierarchical is that the integration and subdivision of concepts to form genera and species give rise to a taxonomic structure—a hierarchy of generality.[24]

The significance of this structure becomes clear when we recall certain general points about the nature of concepts. The concept is a *form of awareness*—a perspective taken on an open-ended grouping of existents. As such it is an "active process" rather than a "passive gaze." Earlier I described the concept as a *policy,* and a policy exists only so long as it is enacted. Thus, a concept's possession requires its use. To have the concept "man" requires always regarding men as men—never considering any characteristic of any man as an isolated concrete with no bearing on other men, but rather subsuming each characteristic under a concept (forming new concepts as necessary in order to do this) and recognizing that this concept applies (sometimes or always) to men.

For these same reasons, one must never regard a man merely as a man, but always also as an animal, an organism, an entity, and an existent. We must conceptualize each of man's attributes at varying levels of abstraction and bring all the knowledge held at all these levels to bear on each man, and indeed on each concrete that we encounter. The very policy of integration inherent in the formation of even a single concept commits each of us ultimately to integrating his every observation with the sum total of his knowledge. Insofar as a given concept ceases to function in the growth and maintenance of this system, it ceases to be a concept at all.[25]

These last points can be illustrated by reflecting on the analogy Rand drew between concepts and file folders. Consider what it is for a professor to have a file of receipts pertaining to expenses for which he expects to be reimbursed from his research account. He could start such a file by putting the relevant receipts he has on hand into a folder, labeling the folder "expenses pending reimbursement," and initiating a policy of putting all other relevant receipts in the folder when he receives them and

24. It should be clear from the preceding that the hierarchies of presupposition and of generality are not identical. A more general concept might either presuppose or be presupposed by a narrower one.

25. Though I will not take the space to discuss them here, central to the process of holistic integration are "axiomatic concepts," which Rand describes as "the constants of man's consciousness, the *cognitive integrators* that identify and thus protect its continuity" (*ITOE* 56). Rand singles out "existence," "identity," and "consciousness" as the "first" and "primary" of these concepts and devotes a chapter of *ITOE* to the topic of their formation and their role in knowledge.

of removing receipts from the folder once he is either reimbursed or else determines that the expenses cannot be reimbursed. It is only insofar as the professor maintains this policy that his file of "expenses pending reimbursement" continues to exist. If he ceases to add or remove receipts when necessary, the folder ceases to be the file it was and becomes a motley collection of loosely related documents. The folder's being the file that it is is inseparable from the relevant policy of filing. Moreover, the professor's ability to carry out this process depends on other concurrent policies by which he keeps track of such things as how much money remains in the research account and the university's (perhaps changing) policies concerning which expenses are eligible for reimbursement. Thus, the file's continued existence as the file it is depends not only on the specific policy by which items are directly filed into the relevant folder, but also on the wider bookkeeping policies of which this policy is a part. So, too, with a concept: its continued existence depends both on the continuance of the process of integration and differentiation by which it was formed and on one's whole conceptual hierarchy and method of functioning.[26]

In the first section of this essay, I observed that, for Rand, to be conscious of something is to identify it, and that, at the perceptual level, this means discriminating it from the rest of one's perceptual field. Conceptualizing is the process of identifying objects by differentiating them from everything else in existence, and this is accomplished by a complex series of *integrations*, which enable one to grasp progressively more remote or more nuanced relationships, which then ground further integrations. As a result, one is able to identify each existent by relating it not just to the other things perceived at the moment, or other objects that one happens to remember, but also systematically to the whole of existence. This process does not take place automatically. One must perform it by choice; and, especially at the higher levels, it requires self-conscious adherence to norms—it requires the methods that it is epistemology's charge to discover. We will turn to these norms in the next section. First it is necessary to consider the nature of judgment and inference.

Rand did not write at any length on the topic of propositions or judg-

---

26. Though I do not have space to explore it here, it is worth noting the connection between this position and the concerns of the recent "virtue epistemology" movement, some of whose proponents have argued that, because of the complex relations between beliefs and the processes by which they are formed and maintained, the primary objects of epistemic assessment should not be individual beliefs considered as such, but epistemic agents and their stable cognitive habits (see Grecco and Turri 2011 for a helpful introduction to this movement).

ment as such, so what I say here is my own extension of her theory. But if she is right that concepts are not objects themselves (nor identityless apprehensions of objects) but are an active form of being aware of objects, then judgments and the propositions that are their contents must be understood accordingly as active processes of concept–application.

A judgment is the (attempted) identification of an existent by means of a concept(s). To judge is to identify an existent of which one is already conscious in some form, by the application of a concept (or a complex description composed of concepts).[27] The existent identified is the subject of the judgment, and the concept by which it is identified is the predicate.

The subject can be held in mind perceptually (as when a child points at a dog and says "Dog!") or conceptually (as when we say "Dogs are animals" or "Dogs bark").[28] Judging consists in either subsuming the subject as a unit of the predicate (as in "Dogs are animals") or isolating one of the subject's characteristics and subsuming it under the predicate ("Dogs bark").

Consider the judgment as a state of awareness. The object of this state is the existent being identified—namely, the judgment's subject or some aspect thereof. Typically this subject will be held in conceptual form, in which case the objects are the units of the subject concept (or some aspect thereof) *regarded as units*. For example, the object of "Dogs are animals" is the many dogs in the world (past, present, and future), and the object of "Dogs bark" is their (many and varied) abilities to bark. However, in both cases, the dogs are the object qua dogs—that is, not severally, but insofar as they are units of the concept "dog." The dogs are available to serve as the object of the act of judging by being grasped unitarily in the form of the concept "dog." The same goes for propositions about "a dog" or "some dogs," except that the objects of these propositions are not all dogs but certain dogs, regarded as dogs.

A proposition is the content of a judgment, but not its object. The object exists independent of the judging, whereas the proposition does not. To continue with our previous example, both the many dogs and the con-

27. In the remainder of this discussion I will omit this qualification, but it should be understood. In the interest of space I pass over the question of how phrases are composed out of concepts, except to suggest that the processes involved in forming different sorts of phrases are essentially the same as those involved in the formation of different sorts of higher-level concepts except that no word is introduced to integrate the result into a single enduring unit.

28. Cases of definite descriptions (e.g., "The dog barked" or "That dog barked") are slightly more complex. They denote perceived individuals qua units of a concept.

cept "dog" (by means of which the dogs are available for judgments about dogs) exist prior to and independently of any judgments about dogs.[29] The proposition "Dogs bark," however, does not exist prior to or independent of the act of judging. Though the fact that dogs bark, of course, exists prior to and independent of the judging, the proposition is not this fact, but a *form* in which someone can be aware of it. And the form of the act of judging no more exists independently of the act of judging than the perfect form with which an Olympic figure skater performs a particular maneuver on a particular occasion exists independently of the act of skating.

Just as there are mental acts other than perceiving whose contents can be perceptual in form (e.g., imagining), there are mental acts other than judging whose content is (or can be) propositional in form. These are the various acts that are commonly referred to as "propositional attitudes"—for example, hoping, wondering, expecting, intending, etc. In all cases, the proposition involves the application of a predicate concept to identify or specify a subject, but the way in which the predicate is applied is different in the different acts.[30]

Because we will discuss the justification of beliefs later, it is worth saying a word at this point about what beliefs are. I take them to be the same mental states as judgments, but whereas the concept "judgment" conceptualizes these states in terms of their cause in the act of judging, "belief" identifies them in terms of their effects—of the role they go on to play as premises for inferences and actions. The concept "belief" is formed as a widening that integrates "knowledge" and "error," on the grounds of their common effects.

So far we have discussed only simple judgments. There are also more complex ones that involve conjoining or disjoining simple propositions, asserting them conditionally, or qualifying their assertions in various ways (via what are commonly called "modal operators"). These all involve

29. Two qualifications are necessary here. First, judgments involving a concept can (and often do) come into being simultaneously with a concept, but cannot precede it. Second, concepts (especially sophisticated ones) can be formed in confused or approximate manners. It is often possible in such cases to form some variant or approximation of a concept and then to make judgments on the basis of this that help to refine one's grasp of the units and their relations, thereby contributing to the correction or re-formation of the concept. Such subtleties can be set aside for our present purposes, however.

30. I think that all of the acts other than judging that have propositional contents are instances or derivatives of a second activity, supposing, which is the conceptual-level equivalent of the perceptual-level activity of imagining. However, this topic is too far afield of our present concerns to be pursued here.

more complex acts of asserting, which I will not treat here.[31] What I have said already will be sufficient to let us see how Rand's theory of concepts leads to a view of propositional knowledge.

We have already discussed the simplest judgments, which predicate first-level entity-concepts of perceived entities (e.g., "dog" of Lassie). Such judgments are performed by perceiving that the subject possesses the distinguishing characteristic (i.e., falls within the relevant range along the CCD). The same applies for judgments predicating characteristics that can be directly observed. One perceives in the subject a characteristic within the concept's CCD and applies the concept to it. Thus, "Brown!" or "The dog is brown" can both be formed directly on the basis of perceptual knowledge (as can "The dog barks"). When so formed, these judgments are propositional knowledge.

Moreover, Lassie's barking will be immediately conceptualized as a *dog's* barking, so that someone who has formed the relevant concepts can judge directly on the basis of perceiving Lassie bark that (at least some) dogs bark. In many cases, universal generalizations about the units of a concept can also be formed directly from perception (given that the relevant concepts are in place). Specifying which cases will require a brief discussion of induction more generally.

Inherent in the conceptual perspective on the world is regarding every characteristic of an individual unit of a concept as a measurement that falls within a range occupied by corresponding characteristics in the other units. Thus, if I know that Lassie is sable, and I regard her as a dog, I will think of sable as situated on a continuum along which each dog will have some characteristic—each dog will have *some* color, and I may or

31. One point about such judgments is worth noting, however. If what I have said about them is correct, then the difference between categorical and conditional judgments consists not in *what* is judged, but in *how* it is judged. The judgment "If you build it, they will come" judges the same thing as "They will come," but it does so *conditionally*—that is, from within a context established by supposing that you build it. It follows from this that there are no *material* conditionals, and I think it follows that conditional and disjunctive judgments cannot, strictly speaking, be true or false. In fact, I do not think that they are normally regarded as such, except by logicians (who view them materially) or when the conditional language is taken to represent a causal relationship. There are a number of implications of this in such fields as the metaphysics of causality, which, if I am right, cannot be ultimately analyzed into counterfactuals formulated in terms of material conditionals. However, I cannot pursue such issues here, except to opine that such accounts of causality have yielded no great insights into nature and are essentially an outgrowth of a Humean view of causation, which we would do well to abandon in favor of an Aristotelian account in terms of natures and powers (see Harré and Madden 1975, chap. 2). "Causality" itself, I think, is an unanalyzable, axiomatic concept.

may not know what range of colors are possible for dogs, but if I did not yet know that sable was in it, my observation of Lassie has settled that question at least.

A generalization is an (attempted) identification of the range within which the units of the subject concept fall along some axis. Thus, for example, if someone were to judge that all bananas are yellow, he would be identifying (or misidentifying), by means of the concept "yellow," the range within which bananas fall along the axis of color. The problem of induction is that of how such identifications can be made—how it can be established that all of the units of a concept have a certain characteristic. The remarks that I will go on to make on the subject are based largely on Leonard Peikoff's theory of induction, which is itself based on Rand's theory of concepts.[32]

One is able to grasp, from observation of a small number of a concept's units, that all of the units possess a characteristic when one grasps a causal relationship between falling under the concept and possessing the characteristic. (Typically this will be grasping that the characteristic is an effect of the concept's essence, though there may be more complex causal relations as well.) As was discussed earlier, some cause-effect relations between particulars can be perceived, and a perceptual-level grasp of causal relations between characteristics is involved in forming even our first concepts.

Though I do not think they are the only examples, the relationships between entities' shapes and their motions are the clearest case of perceptually available causal relationships. When one sees a man walk, for example, his shape is perceptibly involved in his moving in the way he does. I refer here not only to the fact that he needs to be two-legged to walk as human beings do, but also to the specific measurable features of

---

32. Peikoff's theory was originally presented in the summer of 2002 in a lecture series called "Induction in Physics and Philosophy." Related lectures were given the following summer, and recorded material compiled from both occasions was released as *Induction in Physics and Philosophy* (Peikoff 2005). The theory has now been given a fuller presentation (with Peikoff's support and endorsement) by David Harriman in *The Logical Leap: Induction in Physics*, which appeared in the summer of 2010. My essay is a revised version of material I delivered in 2006 and 2007, so the opinions on induction expressed herein are the result of my reflection on Peikoff's lectures, without the benefit of Harriman's book, but I have had the book in mind when revising the essay. There are some points of detail on which I am not certain whether what I say is consistent with Harriman's book, and, if it is not, which position is correct.

his particular walk that are perceptibly dependent on the specific measurable features of his shape. Consider, for example, whether the rotund comedian John Candy could have performed John Cleese's "silly walks": Cleese's lanky build is perceptibly necessary for his peculiar motions. The same applies for some less dramatic differences in build and gait. What is available to perception itself is not the role played by the general human (bipedal) shape in our walking as we do, but the role played by some particular man's shape in his particular motion on some occasion. When we omit the measurements that distinguish one man's shape from another's, and those that distinguish one instance of walking from another, we also omit the measurements of the causal relation to reach an awareness of the role of the human shape in human walking.

Because of this, there are cases where we can, from a single observation of an entity of a certain kind performing a certain action, grasp that all entities of that kind are capable of that sort of action, or even that they will necessarily act that way in certain circumstances. The most straightforward example here is Peikoff's of pushing a ball and observing it roll. As I noted earlier, the round shape perceptibly makes possible the rolling and excludes other actions, such as toppling, that would result when differently shaped objects are pushed, and the perceived solidity of the ball makes it perceptibly necessary that motion of some sort must result from the push. Thus, someone who has the relevant concepts can grasp from a single observation of a ball rolling in response to a push that *all balls roll when pushed*.[33] And a child could grasp this generalization, when initially conceptualizing the observed event as a *ball rolling* when *pushed*. Peikoff calls such generalizations, which can be grasped directly from perception by someone who has the relevant first-level concepts, *first-level generalizations*.

Many first-level generalizations are conceptual identifications of relationships whose grasp in a perceptual form was crucial to forming some of the concepts involved, but this need not be the case with all first-level generalizations. It is unlikely for someone to form the concept "ball"

---

33. I take it that it is understood that the concept "ball" includes a range of sizes, materials, etc. Neither a soap bubble nor Jupiter is a ball, for example, so their behaviors when pushed are not relevant here. Likewise, the concept of "pushing" includes ranges and presupposes certain circumstances, so the proposition should be understood to allow for the possibility of exceptions in unusual circumstances—e.g., if the ball is hovering in a vacuum or held in place by a magnet.

without having noticed (and made some use of) balls' ability to roll, but there are other features perceptibly caused by balls' shapes that might have gone wholly unnoticed prior to the formation of the concept—for example, that balls can be spun. And even in the cases where the relationship grasped in a first-level generalization was earlier grasped perceptually, the conceptualization of this material marks a cognitive advance.

Before leaving the topic of first-level generalizations and the conceptualization of causal connections, it is worth noting that some of our most important and most basic causal knowledge concerns not how entities *must* act in certain circumstances, but the ways in which they *can* act. Though I think that, having formed the relevant concepts, we can directly grasp from a single observation that balls must roll when pushed, I do not think we can similarly grasp the circumstances in which dogs must run or bark or just what things will burn in a fire under just what conditions, but we nonetheless grasp that *fire burns* and that *dogs bark* and *run*—that is, we identify fire in general as capable of igniting other objects, and we identify dogs in general as capable of barking and running. This knowledge is of great value both in its own right and as a foundation from which one can then go on to specify the conditions in which these capacities are actualized, noting any exceptions there may be to them.

All of the judgments that I have discussed thus far are first-level in that they are identifications formed directly on the basis of perception by a subject who has the relevant concepts—concepts that do not themselves presuppose any judgments.[34] I turn now to the topic of higher-level judgments and the processes by which they are performed.

The application of predicates known to hold generally of a concept's units to a particular unit is deduction, and is well understood.[35] The subsumption of a perceived object under a concept that was formed by widening or narrowing presupposes the subsumption of it under the relevant first-level concept. Only by regarding a particular table as a table can you regard it either as furniture or as a drop-leaf table. Thus, the application

34. Concepts of characteristics do presuppose concepts of entities, as discussed above, but they do not presuppose judgments.

35. It is worth making explicit, however, something that may already be clear. I am conceiving of deductive logic along the lines of traditional Aristotelian term logic, rather than the Fregean logic that dominated the twentieth century. Though that logic surpasses traditional logic in terms of completeness, I think it is deeply misleading about the structure of thought, language, and knowledge. The remedy is a more robust incarnation of traditional logic, such as that provided and defended by Sommers 1982.

of these higher-level concepts is quasi-deductive, with the first-level concepts playing the role of the middle term. Generalizations that cannot be grasped directly from perception are induced when new causal connections are identified.[36]

I close this section with some general remarks about the nature of judgment and inference. If a judgment is an act of applying a concept, then, when that application is inferential in character, the judgments that are the premises partially constitute the act of judging that is the conclusion. One can, of course, also look at the judgment as the product of the action, but just as a concept is not detachable from the act of integration that produces (and sustains) it, so a judgment (considered as a product) is not detachable from the act of judging, and this act can include complex chains of inference.[37]

Those judgments that constitute knowledge are awarenesses of objects in the world, and though the *form* of this knowledge is propositional, the *objects* are not. Rather, the object of any given item of propositional knowledge is the subject of the proposition, and the knowledge consists in the identification of this object by subsuming it (or an aspect of it) under the predicate concept. This is accomplished by a process of observation and (in some cases) inference.

36. The topic of how causal connections are identified is too large for me to broach here. For Peikoff and Harriman's views of the process, including the roles in it of concept-formation, experiment, measurement, and mathematics, see Harriman 2010, especially chapters 2 and 3.

37. There are a number of semantic implications of this view, which have ramifications in epistemology and related fields. For example, Rand holds that assertions made in defiance of the need for evidence become literally meaningless. This follows from the view of a concept as a form of awareness that exists only insofar as one maintains the relevant cognitive policies of subsuming existents as units only when one has identified (even if tentatively or provisionally) them as standing in certain relationships. To the extent that one abandons this policy and attempts to subsume existents under the concept without evidence (or in defiance of the evidence), the concept ceases to be a concept, with the result that there is no longer any judgment or proposition. This semantic thesis leads to the epistemic rule that such arbitrary assertions must be dismissed on principle without consideration. This rule, in turn, leads to responses to certain arguments for skepticism, theism, and a number of other positions (see Peikoff 1981 and 1991, 163–71; on the role of this view of the arbitrary in Rand's politics, see Wright 1999). The view of judgments discussed above also leads to interesting questions about the nature of truth. Rand's view is, broadly speaking, a correspondence theory, and she describes it as such ("Philosophical Detection," *PWNI* 19), but there is a sense in which there is no mental item to do the corresponding. Propositions do not represent reality in the sense of exhibiting any sort of isomorphism to it; rather, they *identify* existents by interrelating them via concepts. This is perhaps why Rand defined truth as "the recognition of reality" rather than as correspondence with it (ibid.; see also *Atlas* 1017; "Apollo 11," *VOR* 174).

Validation and Epistemic Criteria

Because conceptualization does not take place automatically but must be initiated, sustained, and directed by choice, much of what I have said above about the process must be recast into standards for how it *ought* to be performed. This brings us at last to the relation between Rand's theory of concepts and the topic of epistemic justification.

Let us begin by considering what some of the standards for conceptualization are, and then turn our attention to the relation between satisfying these standards and knowledge.

Among the criteria for what may be accepted as knowledge will be standards for deductive and inductive inference. I will say nothing further about these, because the idea that there are standards for inference is quite familiar, and the standards for deduction are too well understood to require discussion, while those for induction are too difficult and controversial a subject to be discussed briefly.[38] In addition to the standards for assessing inferences, there is the foundationalist principle that, in order to support a conclusion, premises must be known prior to and independently of it. This is also familiar, and requires no elaboration. There are also some less familiar standards concerning the formation and use of concepts.

Rand describes the central norm concerning the formation of concepts as "an epistemological razor": "*concepts are not to be multiplied beyond necessity, nor are they to be integrated in disregard of necessity*" (*ITOE* 86, reformulating an earlier statement from 72). The content of the necessity involved is given by the theory itself. The integration of a concept depends on the observation of a fundamental similarity, one from which many things follow such that there is a wealth of information to be economized by the introduction of the concept and reason to think that there is more to be learned by further study. It is necessary to form a concept in precisely those cases where such a fundamental exists and where one needs to deal with the relevant information frequently enough in thought and/or action.[39]

---

38. See Harriman 2010, 184–88 (compare 238–39) for Harriman's summary of the criteria that an inductive proof must satisfy (according to Peikoff's theory of induction) and the relation of these criteria to some of the criteria with reference to which concepts are validated (according to Rand's theory).

39. See also Gotthelf's discussion of this matter in the last section of his essay in part 1 of this volume.

In various articles, Rand discusses several types of invalid concepts that violate this razor. The most common are "package deals"—attempts to integrate existents based on superficial similarities in disregard of fundamental differences between them.[40] There are also concepts that have no basis in perception because they arise from mystic fantasies or false theories. (She regarded "duty" in the Kantian sense and "analytic" and "synthetic" as applied to propositions as examples of such concepts.)[41]

The basic grounds for applying concepts to perceived objects were discussed in the last section, and it is straightforward to recast them as norms. One should identify a perceived object by predicating a concept of it when it or one of its characteristics perceptibly falls within the concept's CCD. In addition to the basic principle of applying a concept to all and only the things known (perceptually or otherwise) to fall within its CCD, and the various inference rules alluded to above, there are some further standards for the proper use of concepts.

First, because some concepts presuppose other concepts (and propositions), with the chain of presuppositions terminating ultimately in first-level concepts, it is necessary to take cognizance of these dependency relationships in one's thinking.[42] Failing to do so results in "floating abstractions" and worse, "stolen concepts." A floating abstraction is a concept that has become detached in one's mind from its basis in perception and has therefore lost its meaning (Peikoff 1991, 96). People use the words that denote floating abstractions as tokens in a sort of social game, but Rand thinks that this kind of manipulation of words is not genuinely meaningful.[43] A stolen concept is one that is used in a manner that contradicts its presuppositions (*Atlas* 1039; Peikoff 1991, 136). For example the concept "orphans" in the proposition "There is no such thing as parents, all people are orphans," is stolen; and the concept "theft" is stolen in the slogan "property is theft." Rand thinks that any concept is stolen when it is used in an effort to deny sense-perception's status as an awareness of a

---

40. Rand identified a number of such concepts in political discourse, including "isolationism," "extremism," and "polarization" (in the sense in which it is used in politics). See her "'Extremism,' or the Art of Smearing," *CUI*; and "Credibility and Polarization," *ARL* I.1.1.

41. On "duty," see "Causality vs. Duty," *PWNI*; on "analytic" and "synthetic," see *ITOE* 77 and Peikoff's "The Analytic-Synthetic Dichotomy" (*ITOE* 88–121).

42. For elaboration, see Peikoff 1991, 129–41.

43. The notion of language as a game is most associated with Ludwig Wittgenstein. Rand (*ITOE* 78) writes that his "theory that a concept refers to a conglomeration of things vaguely tied together by a 'family resemblance' is a perfect description of the state of a mind out of focus."

mind-independent world, because all concepts are based on perception (*ITOE* 3).

Because of the holistic character of conceptualization and the nature of a concept as an integrative policy, Rand's theory also demands that a thinker always work to discover new connections and integrate each newfound conclusion into the whole of his knowledge.[44] This is a requirement on conceptualization, insofar as to abandon this forward-looking approach is to renounce the essence of conceptual cognition itself. The result is "a fallacy which may be termed 'the fallacy of the frozen abstraction' which consists of substituting some one particular concrete for the wider abstract class to which it belongs" ("Collectivized Ethics," *VOS* 94).[45]

In sum, the conceptualizer must bear in mind the basis for his concepts and judgments and actively pursue the expansion of his knowledge.[46] If he neglects either task, he compromises his concepts. Their meanings become progressively indeterminate and the frontier of his knowledge is

---

44. For elaboration, see Peikoff 1991, 121–28.

45. By a "particular concrete" here, Rand does not mean only perceptible entities. She discusses the fallacy in connection with people who, having formed the concept "ethics" in a social context dominated by altruism, have difficulty conceiving that there could be an alternative code of ethics or understanding how such a code would apply to issues: "Thus, a man may reject the theory of altruism and assert that he has accepted a rational code—but, failing to integrate his ideas, he continues unthinkingly to approach ethical questions in terms established by altruism" (*VOS* 94).

46. Insofar as someone does not do these two things, he has an "anti-conceptual mentality":

> It is a mentality which decided, at a certain point of development, that it knows enough and does not care to look further. What does it accept as "enough"? The immediately given, directly perceivable concretes of its background—"the empiric element in experience."
>
> To grasp and deal with such concretes, a human being needs a certain degree of conceptual development, a process which the brain of an animal cannot perform. But after the initial feat of learning to speak, a child can perform this process almost automatically, by memorization and imitation. The anti-conceptual mentality stops on this level of development—on the first levels of abstractions, which identify perceptual material consisting predominantly of physical objects—and does not choose to take the next, crucial, fully volitional step: the higher levels of abstraction from abstractions, which cannot be learned by imitation. . . .
>
> The anti-conceptual mentality takes most things as irreducible primaries and regards them as "self-evident." It treats concepts as if they were (memorized) percepts; it treats abstractions as if they were *perceptual* concretes. To such a mentality, everything is the given: the passage of time, the four seasons, the institution of marriage, the weather, the breeding of children, a flood, a fire, an earthquake, a revolution, a book are phenomena of the same order. (*PWNI*, 51–52)

driven back toward the perceptual level. (He remains able to use more so-phisticated language only by aping.) Both of these tasks are facilitated by definitions. By explicitly situating concepts in a hierarchy, definitions indicate the processes by which they were formed and facilitate inference.[47] For example, the definition of "man" as "the rational animal" makes it clear that knowledge about men should be applied with its measurements omitted to animals in general and that general knowledge about animals should be applied in a specialized way to man, with the relevant measurements specified to reflect his rational nature.[48]

Rand regarded definition as the final step of concept-formation.[49] There have, of course, been rules for defining since Aristotle, and Rand endorses many of these, including the propriety of the genus-differentia form and the rule that the differentia express a fundamental characteristic, as well as (of course) the more mundane rule that the definiens cannot be narrower or wider than the definiendum. Rand also had distinctive views on how definitions must sometimes be refined in light of new knowledge. Since Gotthelf and Lennox treat this issue at length in their respective essays in part 1 of this volume, I will say no more about it here except to note that making such refinements when necessary is an extension of the initial act of concept-formation. Such refinements are part of the policy one adopts in forming a concept, and to fail to make these refinements when the context demands it is to compromise (and ultimately

47. Definitions indicate the process by which a concept was formed in that the genus is the wider class from which the units are differentiated and the differentia is the fundamental distinguishing characteristic. However, the concepts of which a definition is composed are not always prior to the definiendum. Indeed, they are often posterior to it, for a number of reasons. First, often the genus concept was formed by widening from the definiendum. Second, concepts for characteristics are normally not formed until one has a concept for the things characterized by them, so very often (especially in the case of low-level concepts) the differentia will be posterior to the definiendum. Third, as our context of knowledge grows it is sometimes necessary to replace the differentia (and occasionally the genus) with something newly discovered to be fundamental; thus, though a child might initially define man in terms of his shape or motions, the mature definition of the concept has "rationality" as the differentia, even though the child would not have been initially aware of this characteristic when forming the concept. When using a definition to retrace the concept-forming process, what one needs to consider is in what form one would first grasp the difference indicated by the differentia between the units and the other members of its genus.

48. See VOS 16–23, where Rand argues for the fundamental principles of her ethics by applying general biological principles to man in a distinctive way because of the distinctive (volitional) character of reason.

49. However, she thought that definition is neither necessary nor possible with axiomatic concepts and concepts designating sensations; and in the case of lower-level concepts, definition is possible, not always necessary.

to abandon) the concept. The same holds for all of the other norms discussed in this section: following them is part of the process of conceptualizing and is essential to the continued existence of all the concepts involved.

With some of these criteria for conceptualization in mind, let us turn now to some of the questions concerning justification that are familiar from the contemporary literature.[50] I have already discussed the alternative between foundationalism and coherentism. It should be clear by this point that Rand is a foundationalist: she takes sense perception to be a basic form of knowledge on which all other knowledge is based, and she thinks other knowledge is validated by tracing back the steps by which it was derived from these perceptual foundations. Much of this essay has been about how her theory of concepts provides an answer to the most common twentieth-century challenge to the thesis that perception can be a foundation for propositional knowledge. Donald Davidson (2001, 143) poses the challenge as follows: "The relation between a sensation and a belief cannot be logical, since sensations are not beliefs or other propositional attitudes. What then is the relation? The answer is, I think, obvious: the relation is causal. Sensations cause some beliefs and in *this* sense are the basis or ground of those beliefs. But a causal explanation of a belief does not show how or why the belief is justified." Thus, as John McDowell (1994, 8) puts it, "the idea of the Given offers exculpations where we wanted justifications."

If what I have been saying up to this point is correct, then this challenge has already been met. If Rand's theory of concept-formation and my application of it to the issue of judgment are correct, and if perception does include an awareness of the similarity and causal relations on which I said the formation and application of concepts is based, then we have seen how judgments can be based on non-conceptual knowledge given in perception. And if the processes of concept-formation and application are subject to the norms discussed above, then this basing or grounding of beliefs in perception is not merely causal and exculpatory, but logical and justificatory.[51] As Gotthelf discusses in the introduction to his piece, it is

50. For discussion of further epistemic norms given rise to by Rand's approach to epistemology, see Peikoff 1981, 1987, 1991, chap. 5; 1993, 1994, 1996, 1998, 2005; Salmieri 2006, Lecture 4; and Harriman 2010.

51. The objection rests on an unduly narrow view of logic: the idea that logic includes standards for definition and abstraction is not new to Rand; it has long been part of the Aristotelian tradition.

precisely the lack of a plausible theory of abstraction that has made this sort of grounding for knowledge seem to many to be impossible.[52] Thus, if Rand's theory of concepts is viable, a perceptual foundationalism is possible and unproblematic.

The foundation of knowledge is not, for Rand, any set of foundational beliefs, but perception itself, which is infallible. There are first-level concepts and judgments that are based directly on this foundation and upon which subsequent concepts and judgments are based.[53] However, Rand takes quite seriously the task of integrating knowledge into a consistent whole. To form even a first-level concept or judgment is to integrate knowledge that one already possesses, and the meaningfulness of any integration (not to mention its status as knowledge) is dependent on its continued functioning as part of a systematic whole. So although there are first-level beliefs, they are not self-sufficient atoms of cognition. Neither are they infallible and immune from correction in light of counterevidence. Only perception is infallible; we can incorrectly perform the processes by which any subsequent knowledge is formed, and there are unusual circumstances (e.g., cases of cunning deception) in which, despite following a proper method, we can reach a false conclusion.[54] However, such mistakes are rare in the case of first-level judgments, which in normal circumstances qualify as knowledge.

This point brings me from foundationalism and coherentism to a second alternative that looms large in the epistemology literature, that between internalism and externalism. According to traditional internalist views, justification is the self-conscious adherence to epistemic standards or at least one's being in a position to see that the grounds for his beliefs conform to such standards. This is analogous to the senses of justification in other areas: in each case talk of justification presupposes that we are subject to prescriptive guidance when issues of justification arise, and

52. For a more detailed argument along these lines that includes a survey of the literature, see Bayer 2011.

53. Also part of the foundation are axioms (and their corollaries), such as the primacy of existence, the law of identity, and the principle of noncontradiction. As indicated earlier, Rand held that this content is implicit in all states of awareness, though conceptualizing it and (later) recognizing its role in knowledge is a sophisticated achievement (see *ITOE*, chap. 6).

54. There are several such cases in Rand's fiction, the most dramatic of which is Hank Rearden's condemnation of Francisco d'Anconia, to which the latter responds, "Within the extent of your knowledge, you are right" (*Atlas* 641). In courses, Peikoff has lectured on situations in which, because of unforeseeable factors, it is possible to be rationally certain and yet wrong.

that someone is justified insofar as he complies with the relevant prescriptions. Thus, when epistemic justification is understood along internalist lines, definitions of knowledge in terms of justification (such as the classic "justified true belief" definition) treat compliance with certain prescriptive norms as a necessary condition for knowledge.

"Externalist" accounts of justification understand it in terms of a causal or statistical relation between the belief and the facts that would make it true (such as the belief's being formed by a mechanism that reliably produces beliefs like it only in those circumstances in which they are true), and the relation need not be within the subject's ken. The externalist sense of "justification" stretches the word far outside the bounds of the sense established by analogous uses in other fields, and happily some externalists have chosen to abandon it in favor of more suitable terms.

A difficulty in relating Rand's views to either of these views is that she would not accept any analysis of knowledge in terms of justification. "Knowledge," for her, as we have seen, is either the axiomatic concept of "awareness" or a narrowing of it to include only propositional awareness. In neither case is there any room or need for a justification condition. She does, however, accept something like the traditional internalist conception of justification in her discussion of the need for epistemology (quoted above), and she speaks of the need to "validate" knowledge.

A difference is worth noting between the family of words related to the verb "validate" and the corresponding family related to "justify." "Validate" corresponds to two adjectives, "valid" and "validated," and to the nouns "validity" and "validation," whereas "justify," as it is used in most contexts, only corresponds to "justified" and "justification" because "just" and "justice" are reserved for their specifically ethical meanings.

I take it that to validate something is to establish that it is valid or to certify it as valid, and that things are often valid prior to having been validated. For example when the clerk at a shop validates my parking, he is not making my claim that I am entitled to park valid, but simply certifying the validity of this claim. The claim is already valid by virtue of my having made a purchase at the store.

Because "just" and "justice" are not used in some of the contexts where the verb "justify" is, the word "justified" (or "justification") can sometimes be ambiguous between a sense that would correspond to "valid" (or "validity") and a sense that would correspond to "validated" (or "validation"). This is significant because, if we take epistemic validity to be a matter of satisfying certain epistemic standards, then there is a difference between speaking of a "valid belief" and a "validated belief," which can be obscured by using the language of "justification." A valid belief would simply be one that satisfies the standards, whereas a validated one would be one that has been somehow *certified* as having satisfied them. Thus, someone who says that a belief must be valid to be knowledge is saying something much more modest than someone who contends that it must be validated.

The fact that conceptualization is volitional (and, therefore, prone to error) gives rise to a crucial need for validation—that is, for self-conscious knowledge that one's concepts and judgments conform to the relevant standards and so may be accepted as knowledge. Moreover, I think there are many cases in which such validation is required for a judgment to constitute knowledge; that is, there are cases where validity requires validation.

In writing on the purpose of epistemology, Rand distinguishes between stages in one's intellectual development. Discussing a child who has already learned many concepts, she writes:

> His full, independent conceptual development does not begin until he has acquired a sufficient vocabulary to be able to form sentences—i.e., *to be able to think* (at which time he can gradually bring order to his haphazard conceptual equipment). Up to that time, he is able to retain the referents of his concepts by perceptual, predominantly visual means; as his conceptual chain moves farther and farther away from perceptual concretes, the issue of verbal definitions becomes crucial. It is at this point that all hell breaks loose.
>
> Apart from the fact that the educational methods of most of his elders are such that, instead of helping him, they tend to cripple his further development, a child's own choice and motivation are crucial at this point. There are many different ways in which children proceed to learn new words thereafter. Some (a very small minority) proceed straight on, by the same method as before, i.e., by treating words as concepts, by requiring a clear, first-hand understanding (*within the context of their knowledge*) of the exact meaning of every word they learn, never allowing a break in the chain linking their concepts to the facts of reality. Some proceed by the road of approximations, where the fog deepens with every step, where the use of words is guided by the feeling: "I kinda know what I mean." Some switch from cognition to imitation, substituting memoriz-

ing for understanding, and adopt something as close to a parrot's psycho-epistemology as a human brain can come—learning, not concepts nor words, but strings of sounds whose referents are not the facts of reality, but the facial expressions and emotional vibrations of their elders. And some (the overwhelming majority) adopt a precarious mixture of different degrees of all three methods. (*ITOE* 20–21; see also 75–76)

It is only after someone's "independent conceptual development" has begun that he needs the sort of criteria that epistemology is devoted to discovering, and then his need for such criteria arises by degrees. Before considering how it arises, however, let us consider the state of the child prior to this need, when he is forming his earliest concepts and judgments directly from perception.

For his concepts to be valid he must know in some form that the units share a fundamental similarity. I wrote earlier about how this can be perceived in the case of first-level concepts. Though the fundamental similarity can be perceived, the fact that this makes conceptualization valid cannot. But this does not matter. All the child needs to consciously grasp in order to form a concept is the similarities themselves. He does not need to know *what he is doing* in forming the concept; he may simply find himself regarding the units as interchangeable and, as a result, he may be able to catch on to and partake in his parents' practice of referring to these objects by a word, which word will then enable him to complete the process of integrating the units into a concept.[55]

In addition to being able to form first-level concepts without reflecting on how or why he is doing so, the child can also apply these concepts. To see that a given table is a table, he just notices its table-look. This look consists in its visibly falling within the range of shapes which (in the child's context) serves as the distinguishing characteristic of tables. In a similarly non-self-conscious fashion the child may form some simple higher-level concepts. Now in the habit of thinking of tables as tables, he is in a position to notice their similarities (in shape and use) with chairs and beds, thus forming the concept "furniture" (*ITOE* 21). In like fashion, the child can, from the vantage point of the earlier knowledge encoded

---

55. Rand discussed this issue in response to a question in one of a series of workshops on epistemology, which are transcribed as an appendix to the current editions of *ITOE*. The relevant material is on 150–52.

in his rudimentary concepts and propositions, see the truth of certain other propositions. That is, he can make simple inferences without knowing that this is what he is doing or being able to articulate his grounds for doing it.

Here then we have knowledge being built upon knowledge, all un-self-consciously. At each step the child knows enough (in some form) to grasp the necessity or propriety of the succeeding step, though not articulately. The child knows the inferred propositions to be true by knowing the premises, and he knows the premises on the basis of the perceptual knowledge that enables him to form and apply his concepts. His concepts and judgments satisfy all of the criteria for conceptualization discussed above that are applicable to his situation, but he has not yet identified these criteria or their applicability to his situation. His knowledge is valid, but not validated.

It is not long, however, before this manner of knowing becomes impossible. In advancing past the perceptual level the mind soon reaches a point at which it can no longer retain in a perceptual form the relation of its conceptual content to the perceptually given or take further steps with the clarity and confidence that have so far been possible. As we have seen, Rand thinks that, after the initial stages of concept-formation, very few people proceed "by requiring a clear, first-hand understanding . . . of the exact meaning of every word they learn, never allowing a break in the chain linking their concepts to the facts of reality" (i.e., to perception). Those people who do proceed in this manner only do so with great effort, and even they reach a point after which they cannot do this without an explicit understanding of *how it is done*. It is at this point—the point after which one only "kinda knows" what one means—that one needs knowledge of method.[56] This is a knowledge that too many men never acquire:

56. She makes a similar point regarding the need for verbal definitions:
    In fact and in practice, so long as men *are* able to identify with full certainty the perceptual referents of simple concepts, it is not necessary for them to devise or memorize the verbal definitions of such concepts. What *is* necessary is a knowledge of the rules by which the definitions can be formulated; and what is *urgently* necessary is a clear grasp of that dividing line beyond which ostensive definitions are no longer sufficient. (That dividing line begins at the point where a man uses words with the feeling "I kinda know what I mean.") Most people have no grasp of that line and no inkling of the necessity to grasp it—and the disastrous, paralyzing, stultifying consequences are the greatest single cause of mankind's intellectual erosion. (*ITOE* 50)

The result is a mentality that treats the first-level abstractions, the concepts of physical existents, as if they were percepts, and is unable to rise much further, unable to integrate new knowledge or to identify its own experience—a mentality that has not discovered the process of conceptualization in conscious terms, has not learned to adopt it as an active, continuous, self-initiated policy, and is left arrested on a concrete-bound level, dealing only with the given, with the concerns of the immediate moment, day or year, anxiously sensing an abyss of the unknowable on all sides. (*ITOE* 75–76)

There comes a point, then, after which it is impossible to proceed in the manner of a child. One cannot perform complex feats of conceptualization without knowing how one is doing it and deliberately adhering to explicit criteria. There is a point after which it is impossible to think validly without validating one's thinking.[57]

But, though I speak of this as a point, I do not think there is a sharp binary division between not needing any methodological guidance at all and not being able to get along with a full-fledged method, nor is self-conscious knowledge of how to think something that could be acquired all at once. Rather, the further one gets from perception, the more room there is for error, and the harder it is to (literally) know what one is talking about—i.e., to have one's concepts function as concepts integrating kinds of entities rather than as mere words. Thus, it becomes necessary by degrees to become conscious of how one is proceeding and why.[58] One

---

57. Part of what one needs to make self-conscious in formulating a method is what the ultimate basis of one's knowledge is and why this is fit to serve as a basis. Thus, what a mature thinker needs to validate is not only his conceptual knowledge, but sense-perception and the axioms as well. These are validated not by proving them to be true (that would be question begging), but by a process of reaffirmation through denial, which makes clear their status relative to other knowledge (see Peikoff 1991, 8–12).

58. Rand praised Montessori education for teaching children to conceptualize. It does this by exposing children to a "prepared environment" that highlights fundamental similarities and differences, making it easier for children to form new concepts and reach new conclusions in cases where this requires effort. The materials are designed to enable the student to tell for himself when he has mastered them, and new materials are introduced in a logical order, so the students learn at firsthand what proper thinking is like. (See Beatrice Hessen, "The Montessori Method," published under Rand's editorship in *TO* [May–July 1970]; Rand's editorial policy in that periodical was such that her inclusion of a piece represents an endorsement of its content, and she referred favorably to that article on several occasions both in print [in "The Comprachicos," *VOR*] and in public appearances.)

can meet this growing need by progressively identifying different aspects of the activity of conceptualizing, in different forms and with different degrees of precision.

For example, people (and cultures) are able to understand and assess complex inferences by analogizing them to simpler ones well before they abstractly grasp the forms of inference involved and formulate abstract standards against which to assess individual inferences. The process of conceptualizing the means by which we acquire knowledge is something that an active-minded person continues with ever-increasing detail and scope over the course of his life. And it is something that mankind continues over the course of centuries. Thus, the practitioners of the various sciences continue to refine the specialized methodologies appropriate to their disciplines; and, if Rand's theory of concept formation is correct, it represents a recent philosophical discovery about conceptualization in general, which points the way toward future work to be done in applying the theory to different issues.[59]

The idea that self-conscious knowledge of method becomes possible and necessary by degrees provides a ready answer to a common challenge to internalism—namely, that it sets standards for knowledge that are too demanding to be met by unsophisticated subjects whom we nonetheless take to have knowledge. Validation does require a good deal of sophistication, and there are many judgments that cannot constitute knowledge without being validated, because the processes of judging are so intricate that we cannot be rationally confident in them unless they are performed (or checked) methodically. In these cases, validation (i.e., self-conscious monitoring) is part of the very process that makes the judgments valid. However, there are also forms of cognition—perception and low-level concepts and judgments—that can be valid without being validated, because they do not involve intricate, fallible processes. Thus, some knowledge is available to the unsophisticated. And if, as I suggested, the need for validation arises gradually over time, and there are more and less sophisticated ways to meet it (not all of which will be sufficient for all types

59. For both individuals and cultures there can be regress as well as progress. I indicated how Rand thought our culture was intellectually distintegrating due proximately to progressive education, but more remotely to philosophical trends going back ultimately to Kant, who she saw as undermining all the essentials of a proper epistemology (and ethics, for that matter). On these issues, see "For the New Intellectual," "Kant vs. Sullivan" (in *PWNI*), and "The Comprachicos" (in *VOR*).

of knowledge), then we are in a position to understand a wide variety of cases intermediate between those of a young child and a sophisticated scientist or philosopher, and we are able to understand how the latter could develop from the former.

Though in the sense I have been discussing, there is a smooth continuum between the child's way of knowing and that of a philosopher or scientist, there is another respect in which there is a binary division, which Rand stresses:

> The day when [a child] grasps that the reflection he sees in a mirror is not a delusion, that it is real, but it is not himself, that the mirage he sees in a desert is not a delusion, that the air and the light rays that cause it are real, but it is not a city, it is a city's reflection—the day when he grasps that he is not a passive recipient of the sensations of any given moment, that his senses do not provide him with automatic knowledge in separate snatches independent of context, but only with the material of knowledge, which his mind must learn to integrate—the day when he grasps that his senses cannot deceive him, that physical objects cannot act without causes, that his organs of perception are physical and have no volition, no power to invent or to distort, that the evidence they give him is an absolute, but his mind must learn to understand it, his mind must discover the nature, the causes, the full context of his sensory material, his mind must identify the things that he perceives—*that* is the day of his birth as a thinker and scientist. (*Atlas* 1041)[60]

What the child described in this passage grasps is that knowledge is not a passive revelation, but something that must be achieved and for which he must take responsibility. Part of grasping this is grasping that errors are possible, and that they are *his* errors rather than deliverances of faculties over which he has no control. This implies that he must work to reach the truth and avoid error, and therefore that he must discover and adhere to the proper method. Rand's term for purposeful adherence to a proper method is "objectivity":

---

60. In this passage Rand is reserving the word "knowledge" for conceptual knowledge, rather than using the term in its broadest sense, as I have been doing in this piece and as she sometimes does (e.g., in "The Objectivist Ethics," where she says that "an animal has no choice in the knowledge or skills that it acquires" and refers to the sensations of the most primitive animals as "an automatic form of knowledge" (*VOS* 20).

Objectivity begins with the realization that man (including his every attribute and faculty, including his consciousness) is an entity of a specific nature who must act accordingly; that there is no escape from the law of identity, neither in the universe with which he deals nor in the working of his own consciousness, and if he is to acquire knowledge of the first, he must discover the proper method of using the second; that there is no room for the *arbitrary* in any activity of man, least of all in his method of cognition—and just as he has learned to be guided by objective criteria in making his physical tools, so he must be guided by objective criteria in forming his tools of cognition: his concepts.

Just as man's physical existence was liberated when he grasped the principle that "nature, to be commanded, must be obeyed," so his consciousness will be liberated when he grasps that *nature, to be apprehended, must be obeyed*—that the rules of cognition must be derived from the nature of existence and the nature, the *identity,* of his cognitive faculty. (*ITOE* 82)[61]

In order to be objective, a person need not know a perfectly precise method that articulates in detail every element of proper conceptualization. He need not understand, for example, Rand's theory of measurement-omission. What objectivity does require, however, is that one be explicitly committed to truth and clarity, and that one know in broad terms what is required to attain knowledge. It requires working to define one's terms when they are unclear and checking one's premises when they feel floating or when one encounters a contradiction. Thus, instead of assuming uncritically whatever one is in the habit of believing, one comes to attend to the chains of prior concepts and judgments by which each of one's higher-level cognitions is based on perception. Finally, objectivity requires that one strive to integrate one's knowledge into a consistent whole.

Past the first primitive steps into the conceptual level, objectivity is a requirement for knowledge. Objectivity is possible to someone who has only a rudimentary grasp of the nature and methods of conceptualization, but the better his grasp of these things, the more he will be able to really *know.*

61. For elaboration of Rand's view of objectivity, see Peikoff 1991, chap. 4.

One can raise questions about whether various people who are on the cusp of grasping some of the above points have knowledge or not, or about what degree of methodological sophistication is needed to know a given conclusion. Rand says little on such issues, because for her the point of epistemology is not to assess claims to knowledge third-personally.[62] It is to determine for *oneself* what to accept as knowledge.

62. She does make one remark that is especially interesting in this connection, however. Speaking of the dividing line after which ostensive definitions are no longer sufficient and explicit definitions are necessary for knowledge, she writes, "Most people have no grasp of that line and no inkling of the necessity to grasp it—and the disastrous, paralyzing, stultifying consequences are the greatest single cause of mankind's intellectual erosion. This suggests that the determination of when a method is necessary is itself a methodological achievement, with the result that methodologically impoverished people are not in a position themselves to differentiate between those cases in which their means of knowledge is sufficient and those in which it isn't. To recognize this difference would be the crucial step in becoming objective" (*ITOE* 50).

Perceptual Awareness as Presentational

ONKAR GHATE

L et me begin by describing a brief episode of perception.
I enter my apartment from the outside. I can feel the smooth key as I take it from my pocket and the slight resistance of the lock as I use the key to turn the bolt. I open the door and feel its handle slide away from me and watch the door as it swings open. I enter, and as I do I feel how the surface underneath my feet has changed, from a hard concrete to a more yielding carpet. Before me lies a spread of entities. In the entrance of the apartment are shelves on which rest numerous pairs of shoes; atop the shelves are some keys on a key ring, a pad of paper and a pen. As I walk through the entrance into the living room, I see shelves that contain innumerable CDs and a leather couch the surface of which is catching the light in different ways. I see fish swimming in an aquarium in the corner of the room and hear the trickle of the water as the filter pumps. I see the spider plant hanging over the aquarium, its leaves, shades of green and white, moving in the breeze. I can smell the scent of meat cooking; I walk to the screen of the balcony, and down below by the pool I can see a person grilling hamburgers, smoke rising from the barbecue. All this, and indeed much, much more am I aware of in a relatively short span of perceptual awareness.

Pre-philosophically, one takes one's perception to be a relation between oneself (one's faculty of consciousness) and existents in the (external) world; in an episode of perceptual awareness like the one described above, external existents (the aquarium, the spider plant) are components of the conscious experience. Parts of the (external) world are present, given to one, in perception. But in philosophy, at least since the arguments of the ancient skeptics and especially since the publication of Descartes's *Meditations on First Philosophy*, this pre-philosophical view is all too often rejected.

Modern philosophical accounts of perception usually describe perception in terms of one or both of the following general elements: (1) a *sensory impression* (or a sensation, a sensory qualia, an objectless way of sensing characterized in adverbial terms, etc.) and (2) a *representational mental experience* (*being aware* of a mental image, of an idea, of a sense-datum, etc., or *having* a type of propositional attitude, a type of mental state with satisfaction conditions, a type of mental state with propositional content, a belief, a tendency to believe, a judgment, etc.).

Typically, sensory impressions are thought of as aspects or properties of the perceiver, produced by his causal interaction with the world, as a small stone dropped from an overpass will leave an impression on the hood of the car passing underneath. Some accounts of perception maintain that if an impression has an appropriate causal genesis, that is sufficient for the perceiver to be aware of, to be cognizing, the world. But most will not. No matter how it is caused, these accounts maintain, a sensory impression is not cognition, anymore than the impression left by the stone is the car's awareness or cognition of the stone.

Like all cognition, perceptual awareness, these accounts maintain, requires *representation*: the perceiver must be undergoing an experience that represents the world as being a certain way. A necessary condition of (successful) perceptual cognition will be that the world *is* as the perceiver's mental experience represents it to be. (A particular causal genesis of the representational mental experience or of the sensory impression may also be a necessary condition.)

In some theories of perceptual cognition of the (external) world,[1] one and the same thing can be both a sensory impression and an essential part of a representational experience. For instance, an image or idea or

---

1. I leave aside phenomenalist or idealist accounts of perception, which discard the idea of perceptual cognition of the *external* world.

sense-datum can be characterized as the product of a perceiver's causal interaction with the world; from this perspective, it is an impression. But the perceiver can also attain an (inner) awareness of this image or idea or sense-datum, and from this perspective the impression is part of a representational mental experience: in becoming aware of the image or idea or sense-datum, the perceiver is now undergoing an experience that *represents* the world to be a certain way.

In other theories of perceptual cognition, the sensory impression and the representational experience are more separate. In some of these theories, although impressions must be part of or accompany the representational experience, the impressions do little to nothing to help make the experience representational. In other theories of perceptual cognition, there are no sensory impressions, only representational experiences.[2]

But all these theories are in error. It is an error to analyze perceptual awareness in representational terms. Perceptual awareness is not the *representation* of the world being a certain way, it is the *presentation* of (a part of) the world (as that part of the world in fact is). In this regard, the pre-philosophical view is correct: in an episode of perceptual awareness one is not representing external objects to oneself; the external objects are themselves present—this is what it means to say one is directly aware of them.[3]

Presentationalism, however, is usually equated with naïve realism and consequently quickly dismissed. The naïveté in naïve realism, supposedly, is its thesis that the external world *is* as it is presented. In other words, according to naïve realism it is incorrect to maintain that *perceptual* awareness itself can be incorrect, mistaken, or nonveridical. But, so it is held in most philosophical circles, perceptual awareness obviously can be incorrect, mistaken, or nonveridical; indeed, it is identification of this (supposed) fact, raised at least since the writings of the ancient skeptics, that first motivates representational accounts of perception. The switch from presentationalism to representationalism occurs because a *representation* of objects can correctly or accurately represent those objects,

2. When the representational mental experience is characterized in broadly conceptual terms, William Alston (1998a, 64–69) classifies the first type of representational account (impressions accompanying representational experiences) as moderate conceptualism and the second type of representational account (representational experiences without impressions) as extreme conceptualism.

3. See Alston 1999 and 1998a. In Alston 2005a, especially 180–87, Alston calls this kind of theory not a theory of appearing, as he did in his earlier work, but the "presentational view" or "presentationalism," which I contend is the better term and is the term I will use.

or incorrectly or inaccurately do so; a *presentation* of the objects cannot. Only a representational account of perception, therefore, has the tools to conceptualize the fact of perceptual errors. The question then becomes which *version* of representationalism best accounts for all the facts about perceptual cognition.

But presentationalism I think has been dismissed too quickly, and current philosophical debates are the poorer for it.[4] There are two fundamental errors in the reasoning leading to the switch from presentationalism to representationalism, or so I will argue here. First, it is wrong to equate presentationalism with naïve realism. Second, the naïveté in naïve realism is *not* that this account maintains that perceptual awareness cannot be incorrect, mistaken, or nonveridical. This is actually the attractive, plausible element in the account. The naiveté of naïve realism lies elsewhere: not in its idea that external objects (as they are) are components of perceptual awareness, but in its (implicit) idea that this is all there is to the nature of perceptual awareness.

To argue for these two points, I will sketch some of the features and reasoning behind Rand's account of perceptual awareness, which is a non-naïve version of presentationalism;[5] in doing so, I will contrast her version to a more standard and well-known description of presentationalism, that given by William P. Alston. How Rand's version of presentationalism differs from naïve realism and how her version of presentationalism handles traditional examples of perceptual errors (the kinds of examples that first motivated representational accounts of perception) will be crucial. I will end with brief remarks concerning some implications of Rand's version of presentationalism for the relation of conception to perception, for the issue of infallibility, and for the so-called Myth of the Given.

Presentationalism versus Representationalism

Unlike representationalism, presentationalism maintains that perceptual awareness of the (external) world exists and is a primary, which cannot be reduced to the causes that generate it or to other forms of cognition, whether awareness of an (inner) image, an idea, a sense-datum, or possession of a belief, of a tendency to believe, etc. As Alston writes,

---

4. It is therefore good to see an explicit move toward presentationalism in the current literature. See, in particular, Brewer 2006, 2011a; Campbell 2002, 2009; Travis 2004, and, in this volume, the discussion pieces by Brewer, Le Morvan, Salmieri, and Bayer.

5. For Rand's account of perceptual awareness see *ITOE*, especially 29–39, 75–82, and 279–82; *FTNI* 174–75; and Peikoff 1991, 37–54.

TA [the theory of appearing, a supposedly non-naïve version of presentationalism] does not deny that perceived objects stand in causal relations with perceptual experience, but it denies that those causal relations are constitutive of *what it is* for X to look so-and-so to a subject, S. TA construes the appearing (looking) relation as *irreducible* to theoretically more fundamental factors. X's looking a certain way to S is a bottom line concept in TA, not to be construed in terms of allegedly deeper, ontologically more fundamental concepts, such as causality, conceptualization or tendencies to belief. . . . When one speaks . . . of objects being *presented* or *given* to . . . S, TA takes this to be just another way of speaking of objects *appearing* to S. And if we speak of S's being *directly aware* of certain objects in perceptual experience, we are still reporting the same relation of appearing, or, strictly speaking, its converse. (Alston 1999, 183)

In this sketch I am not going to argue for this fundamental point; to do so properly would require examining the concept of consciousness and the basic relation of consciousness to existence. All accounts of perception and all epistemological theories I think rest in the end on one's basic view of the relation of consciousness to existence, a view that a full account of perceptual cognition must explicitly state and validate.[6]

But it is worth pointing out that what is distinctive to presentationalism is *not* the claim that some type of awareness is basic and irreducible, in which something is *present* to the perceiver. Representational accounts of perception assume this too, at least implicitly. A sense-datum theory, for instance, actually posits an irreducible, inner awareness of sense-data to explain perceptual cognition of external objects; in other words, sense-data are themselves *present* to the perceiver. One finds this kind of notion in all representational accounts of perception, even when they are discussing not sense-impressions but propositional content: appeals to *representational* experiences presuppose experiences in which something is *present*. James Pryor, for example, talks of our perceptual experiences "presenting propositions to us" (not representing propositions to us); in other words, perceptual experience represents the external world to us

---

6. In *FTNI* 138–40, 168–76, and 24–28, and in *ITOE* 55–61 and 75–82, Rand argues that the concept of consciousness is axiomatic and argues for her fundamental approach to consciousness as awareness. See also Peikoff 1991, 4–54. Kelley 1986 seeks to apply Rand's account of consciousness and perceptual awareness to many of the issues in the philosophy of perception, and to show how alternative approaches depend upon alternative accounts of the fundamental relation of consciousness to existence.

because within our perceptual experience propositions about the external world are presented to us (Pryor 2000, 547n37). More fundamentally, I would argue that to conceptualize representational experiences, experiences of the world as if it is a certain way, presupposes prior conceptualization of presentational experiences: experiences of the world actually *being* a certain way. But in any case, what is distinctive to presentationalism is that (1) it explicitly states that it regards a type of presentation—a type of awareness—as basic and, especially, (2) that what is presented in this basic form of awareness is not a sense-impression or a proposition or other type of representational content, but objects—i.e., a part or aspect—of the *external world*.

This crucial point is often stated in a different way. According to presentationalism, perception is an inherently relational phenomenon between mind and external world. In an episode of perception, I see pairs of shoes, hear the water trickling into the aquarium, and feel the resistance of the lock to the key. I perceive parts or aspects of the external world: "TA takes perceptual consciousness to be ineluctably *relational* in character. . . . TA is distinguished from both [the sense-datum and adverbial theories] by insisting that perceptual consciousness *is* an *awareness of* objects, which are, in normal cases, *physical objects in the environment*" (Alston 1999, 182–83).

Of course, in a way many theories claim that perception is relational. What is distinctive to presentationalism is that objects in the world are literally components of an episode of perception. If we use the term "content," the content of perceptual awareness is some part of the external world. Take away the pairs of shoes I am seeing, and my perceptual awareness is eliminated, and not just in the sense that a part of the cause of the experience is eliminated. It is not that my perceptual experience's so-called representational content fails to be satisfied; it is that its content is literally gone.

Within the representational approach to perception, proponents "put their positions in terms of 'representational content'" and then argue whether this content is "always conceptual or propositional." But a proponent of presentationalism "rejects this whole way of thinking of content because she does not take perceptual experience to be inherently representational." She does not "take perceptual experience to be in itself objectless and wholly within the subject's mind-brain." Rather, "in normal perception the external world is already, so to say, 'in' the experience." So, "the difference between the views goes deeper than a disagreement over the nature of content. It is rather a disagreement over how to think of what makes an experience the experience that it is" (Alston 1998a, 66–67; see also *ITOE* 29–31).

Even if a representational account of perceptual awareness maintained that a perceptual experience's representational content is always satisfied—that in perception the world always is the way it is represented as being—it still would be a radically different account of perception. For part of what is essential to calling a perceptual experience representational is the idea that the (purported) objects it is representing are not components of the experience. This is precisely what presentationalism denies.[7]

Any plausible account of presentationalism will, I think, maintain that perceptual awareness is the awareness not of an object but of *objects* in the world, of a spread of entities. Alston does not elaborate on this in his discussion of presentationalism, but it is worth doing so briefly.

To say that we perceive objects or entities is to say that we perceptually discriminate things that are singular and unitary from other things that are singular and unitary.[8] I see the pen resting on, and each of the shoes resting in, the shelf. Each of these things stands out from the others as a unified thing, which I could explore further. To perceive a thing is to perceive some of its characteristics—as inseparable aspects of the thing (see *ITOE* 264–66, 277–79). In seeing the pen on the shelf, I see that it has a long, cylindrical shape, a smooth surface, a combination of blue, gray, and black colors. But it is not exhausted by the characteristics of which I am presently aware: I experience it as something that I could learn more about.[9] I could walk around it to see whether there is anything printed on its other side. I could pick it up and feel its cylindrical shape and just how

7. As Alston (1998a, 61) notes, this understanding of perceptual awareness "does not bear the usual marks of an intentional relation." That S is perceptually aware of X entails that X exists; and if S is perceptually aware of X, and X = Y, then S is perceptually aware of Y. So "S's being *directly aware* of X . . . is not a mode of intentionality on the currently most popular criteria for this." But as Alston also notes, on the traditional understanding of intentionality, the sense "of being *of* or *about* something," perceptual awareness remains intentional. These issues are not independent. If perceptual awareness is better accounted for in presentational rather than representational terms, then the traditional sense of intentionality is likely superior to the current sense.

8. Crucial to the issue of what we are aware of in perception is what we can discriminate from what and at what point we can detect gradual variations in an object's characteristics. See Kelley 1986, 146–47 and 157–64.

9. There is no reason to accept the idea that because we do not perceive the whole object, we do not perceive the object as a whole (see Kelley 1986, 169–71).

smooth its casing is and detect its weight. I could shake the pen to see if it makes any noise. I could put it close to my nose to detect if its plastic gives off any odor. I could put it in my mouth to discover if it has any taste. (Toddlers, of course, regularly perform such actions, with almost everything they encounter, as they explore the world.)

In the primary sense, the objects or entities we perceive are things like pens, shoes, shelves, sofas, potted plants, fish swimming in an aquarium. But one can extend the notion to things like the water in the aquarium or the smoke rising from the barbecue.[10] In each case, it is experienced as something singular and unitary, which can be further explored. I see the slightly greenish-blue color of the water; I could swish my hands through the tank to feel the water's temperature and put my nose close to it to determine if it smells like it needs to be changed with fresh water. The smoke I see has a certain color; I can watch how fast it rises, how long it takes to dissipate, in what direction it travels.

As the discrimination of some singular and unitary things from other singular and unitary things, as the awareness of a concrete world of entities, perceptual cognition is to be distinguished from conceptual cognition.

An adult, of course, automatizes the application of many concepts to what he perceives. Pen, shoes, shelf, sofa, carpet, aquarium, fish—as I enter my apartment I automatically subsume many of the things I perceptually discriminate under some of the concepts I possess. Concepts also often help direct one's perceptual attention. Is that a fish hiding in the plants of the aquarium? This thought helps me to focus selectively on aspects of the concrete world before me.

But however intertwined perception and conception become, the two forms of cognition remain distinguishable. My concepts help me direct my *perceptual* attention. Moreover, to conceptualize the thing I am seeing as, say, a fish, I must be discriminating the thing and some if its characteristics from the other things in the aquarium—and this is the perceptual awareness of the thing. As Alston states, "The nonconceptual awareness of the objects gives me something to conceptualize, form beliefs about, and, more generally, think about in various ways" (Alston 1998a, 82).[11]

10. See Leonard Peikoff, "The Philosophy of Objectivism" lecture series, 1976, question period, Lecture 3, quoted in *ARL* 146.

11. Of course, in describing my perceptual awareness of the fish, I must do so in conceptual terms: that is what a description is. But this does not mean that the perceptual awareness is partially conceptual in nature. When a biologist dissects a frog to discover its anatomy, he

It is important to note that, in maintaining that perceptual awareness is distinguishable from conceptual cognition, presentationalism is
not committed to a view of perceptual experience as a chaotic flux of sensations, in which everything is loose and unconnected; perception is not,
as perhaps Hume held, a bunch of separate "impressions," which we must
somehow figure out how to put together.[12]

I do not perceive, in separate snatches, blue, cylindricality, and
smoothness: I see a blue, cylindrical pen. I do not perceive triangularity,
black stripes, and swimming: I perceive a black-striped, triangular-
shaped fish swimming in the aquarium. Characteristics—attributes, actions, relations—are given in perception *as* the characteristics of entities.
Their "separateness," presentationalism holds, is a result of a selective act
of thought (which is a plausible reading of the Aristotelian account of abstraction; see also *ITOE* 277–79, 264–66).

On this approach, perception is not propositionally structured; it
does not predicate a characteristic, P, of some subject, S. But nor does it
give you, in separate snatches, Ps, which you must unite in a judgment.
Perception gives you the S and P already united; S's perceptual characteristics are just aspects of S, which we can selectively focus on and abstract
out in thought. Perceptual awareness gives you particular entities with
some of their particular perceptual characteristics. It gives you some individual referents of the concepts being used to conceptualize S and P,
already united, referents that you can learn to separate out and conceptualize, subsume under the different concepts for S and P, and then (re)unite
in a judgment. On this approach, the unity of the judgment "That fish is
swimming" reflects the unity found in perception; it does not in any sense
help produce that unity.

Thus, a plausible version of presentationalism would be a sophisticated version: in maintaining that we perceive a world of entities, including many of their characteristics, it would hold that we perceive particular facts or particular states of affairs (this does not imply that every fact

---

describes that anatomy in conceptual terms; but that does not show that the frog's anatomy is
partially conceptual in nature.

12. Another line of argument to maintain that perception is partially conceptual in
nature is that the physiological processing of man's sensory systems must be understood in
terms of the deployment of concepts or the making of inferences. At the very least, I think
one should be initially suspicious of any position that attributes concepts or inferences to
nonconscious processes, but this issue is outside the scope of this essay. For critical analysis of
the arguments, see Kelley 1986, 44–80.

or state of affairs is perceivable). I can *perceive* the fact that this pen is resting on this shelf, the fact that this fish is swimming in this aquarium, and
the fact that this carpet is soft. There is no difference between perceiving
these facts and perceiving this pen resting on this shelf, this fish swimming in this aquarium, and this soft carpet.

Presentationalism, Naïve Realism, and Perceptual Error

Presentationalism maintains that perceptual awareness is relational
and that external objects are components of perceptual awareness: eliminate the external objects and the objects (the "content") of the episode
of perception are eliminated. Naïve realism is a version of presentationalism; its naïveté, however, lies in the fact that it (implicitly) maintains
that the external objects are not just necessary components of perceptual
awareness, they exhaust the nature of an episode of perceptual awareness.
Two episodes of perception differ only if the external objects presented
differ. Any plausible version of presentationalism must reject this (implicit) premise. It must distinguish between (1) the *nature* of the *objects*
that the perceiver is aware of and (2) the *nature* of the perceiver's *awareness* of those objects.[13]

The objects presented exist; they are something; they have a nature,
an identity, characteristics. To be aware of external objects is to be aware
of some of their characteristics. But the perceiver's *awareness* of the objects also exists; it too is something; it has a nature, an identity, characteristics, which cannot be reduced to the natures, identities, or characteristics of the objects being perceived.

The identities of the external objects are *determined* by what those
objects are. The identity of the cognizer's *awareness* of those objects is determined by what those objects are *and* by the cognizer's specific means
of awareness, operating in definite conditions. In the case of perception,
the identity of the perceiver's perceptual awareness of some external objects is determined by the specific nature of the perceiver's sensory systems causally responding to the objects' natures, in definite conditions of
perception.[14]

13. Rand insists on this distinction and its fundamental importance. See *ITOE* 75–82
and also Peikoff 1991, 48–52.
14. For similarities and differences between the view I am defending here and the "third
factor" theories of Bill Brewer and John Campbell, see, in part 2 below, Gregory Salmieri's
"Forms of Awareness and 'Three-Factor' Theories," Brewer's response, and Benjamin Bayer's
"Reflections."

Perceptual awareness is a relational phenomenon, and, like any relation, it is affected by changes in *either* item standing in the relation: the objects (of awareness) and the subject's means of perception operating in definite conditions of perception. If, for instance, I am one hundred meters away from Tom, I can alter this spatial relation by taking a step backward; but Tom can alter it, too, by taking two steps forward. In perception, obviously, if the objects change, the perceiver's perceptual awareness of those objects can change. I can feel the pot on the stove getting warmer. There is a change in my perceptual awareness of the objects because the objects of which I am aware are changing. But the perceiver's perceptual awareness of the objects can also change, even if the objects themselves are not changing; if the perceiver's means of awareness or the conditions in which they are operating change, the nature of his awareness of the same unchanging objects can change. Such a change in the nature of the perceiver's awareness does *not* imply that the perceiver is no longer aware of the same unchanging objects (including some of their same characteristics).

Perhaps the most vivid type of example to illustrate the point is the case of objects and characteristics perceivable in more than one sense modality. Consider again the pen that was on the shelf. I can *see* it and its long, straight, cylindrical shape, the smoothness of its encasing, its tip extended, ready to write. If I now close my eyes and pick the pen up, I can *feel* its straight, cylindrical shape, its smooth encasing, its extended tip. There is something very different between my current awareness of the pen and my previous awareness, a difference not explained by a change in the object of awareness. Of course, in vision I am aware of some characteristics of the pen, such as its color, that I am not aware of by touch; and through touch I am aware of the pen's weight, of which I am not aware in vision. But there remains overlap: I am aware of the pen and many of its same characteristics in vision and in touch. The object is the same, yet the nature of the perceptual awareness is different. External objects are necessary components of perceptual awareness, but they do not exhaust the nature of an episode of perceptual awareness.

The difference in the nature of the perceptual awareness between seeing the pen and touching it is explained by the fact that different sensory systems are operating. In one episode of perceptual awareness, I am *visually* aware of the pen; in the other episode, I am *tactilely* aware of it. The difference in "sensory qualities" or "sensory qualia" in the two episodes is not a difference in *what* is being perceived, but a difference in *how* it is being perceived. As characteristics of a relation, namely as perceiver's perceptual awareness of some external objects, sensory qualities are not properties or characteristics of the perceiver (nor of his consciousness). They are not impressions, as the dent on the hood of the car is a property of the car; they are not objectless ways of sensing, etc. But sensory qualities are also not properties of the external objects (properties that are or could be presented to the perceiver in perception). Rather, as characteristics of a *relation,* sensory qualities are the object-as-it-is-being-perceived-by-the-subject.[15]

Presentationalism is not to be equated with naïve realism. Naïve realism amounts to the view that only the objects of awareness can affect the nature of the awareness of those objects. This *is* naïve. In effect, naïve realism holds that the (perceptual) awareness of the pen has no identity, other than it being the awareness of that pen. This means that the only way naïve realism can explain the difference between my visual and tactile awareness of the cylindrical pen, is to claim that I am aware of two different objects.

Since presentationalism does not account for perception in terms of judgments or representational experiences, the distinctions of veridical and nonveridical, and of being satisfied and failing to be satisfied, do not apply. But a non-naïve version of presentationalism should also reject the idea that perceptual awareness can "match" or "fail to match" the objects of awareness (Alston, as we will see, uses this terminology). From one perspective, there can be no match because sensory qualities are not characteristics of an object but of a relation; they are (aspects of) the object-*as-it-is-being-perceived-by-the-subject.* From another perspective, they always match because they are (aspects of) the *object*-as-it-is-being-perceived-by-the-subject.

This is why the terminology of "appearances" is misleading when used to describe perceptual awareness. First, appearances are often reified into objects of awareness—into that which is presented. But second, even if appearances are not reified into objects, "appearance" is normally used in a context where one seeks to distinguish something from fact: the person sitting over there in the bleachers appears to be Tom but is, in fact, Harry. In a consistent, non-naïve version of presentationalism, *no* such distinction is applicable to perceptual awareness.

---

15. In this essay's brief sketch I do not have space to address the nature of sensory qualities further. But see *ITOE* 279–82 and Peikoff 1991, 41–48, for some discussion.

Perception is awareness of some external objects, including some of their (actual) characteristics. Whatever the specific forms of a perceiver's perceptual awareness of those objects, and however those forms vary from episode of perception to episode of perception as the perceiver's means of perception or his conditions of perception change, it is perceptual awareness *of those objects*. There is no standpoint from which one could declare that, say, visual awareness of the cylindrical pen presents the pen "as it really is," but tactile awareness of the cylindrical pen fails to presents the pen "as it really is"—or vice versa. And when one rejects naïve realism, when one recognizes that perceptual *awareness* itself has a nature, there is no need to privilege one form of awareness over another, as presenting the way the object "really is." Every form of perceptual *awareness* of some objects is a form of perceptual awareness of those *objects* (see Peikoff 1991, 50–51).

Alston thinks that a non-naïve version of presentationalism can reject this conclusion, but it is not clear why he thinks this. He writes, "TA, as I understand it, is not saddled with the thesis that objects only appear perceptually as what they actually are. It is not that "naïve" a direct realism. . . . It is a familiar fact of life that perceived objects are not always what they perceptually appear to be. . . . The directness and givenness [of perceptual awareness] has to do with the absence of any mediation in the awareness, not with any guaranteed match between how X appears and what it is" (Alston 1999, 183).[16] Recall that, according to Alston, the converse of "a perceiver is perceptually aware in a certain way of external objects" is "those external objects appear in a certain way to the perceiver." A particular appearance, a particular presentation, of the external objects to the perceiver has a specific nature, an identity. What would it mean for a presentation of external objects to "fail to match" what those objects are? "Failure to match" cannot mean that the characteristics of the presentation are not the same as the characteristics of the objects. Presentation and objects presented are not comparable in this way. The presentation is a relational phenomenon: the objects are presented in a specific way to the perceiver, but the external objects themselves are not relational phenomena. To make sense of the notion of "failure to match" in this way is to abandon presentationalism and substitute some version of represen-

16. Presumably the evidence supporting the "familiar fact of life" are the traditional examples of illusions and perceptual relativity, which Alston (1998a, 74) thinks are easily handled by TA since it can say that "things can appear perceptually to be other than they are." I address illusions and perceptual relativity in the next section.

tationalism—where one does ask whether the representation matches or fails to match the objects being represented.

Perhaps what "failure to match" is meant to capture is the idea that external objects and their characteristics should be presented in only one way to the perceiver. If they are presented in more than one way to the perceiver, then at least in one presentation the objects do not appear perceptually as what they actually are. But why make this assumption? Why assume that objects can be presented in only one valid way to the perceiver? And which presentation do you privilege over which, as the way of presenting the object "as it really is"? Notice that this requirement for presentation "matching" object would rule out that we can be perceptually aware of the cylindrical pen through vision and through touch, since we would have two presentations of the same object and characteristics. Either the visual awareness or the tactile awareness must "fail to match" the way the pen is.

To be sure, if a perceiver's means of perception and his conditions of perception are the same, the same objects will be presented in the same way to the perceiver. Otherwise, perceptual awareness would be non-causal. But if the perceiver's means of perception or his conditions of perception change, there are no a priori grounds from which to declare that the objects must be presented in the same way to the perceiver—and that if they are not, the presentation "fails to match" the objects.

No doubt what motivates Alston's claim of "failure to match" are situations (such as illusions) where objects (like straight and bent sticks) with perceptually distinguishable characteristics are presented in the same or in a similar way to the perceiver. In such circumstances, a perceiver is liable to make mistakes in his conceptual judgments about the perceived objects. But presentationalism should explain this phenomenon by appeal to the distinction between perception and judgment, not by trying to resurrect the representational notion of "failure to match."

At the level of *perceptual awareness,* if external objects are presented in a specific way to the perceiver, then given the specific conditions (the perceiver's specific means of perception operating in the specific conditions of perception), *that* is what such objects appear like. The objects necessarily appear—that is, are necessarily presented—*as they actually are* (there are no *objects as they actually are not* that could appear or be presented). This may sound strange, but that is because "appearance" is usually used in a context where one is distinguishing a mistaken judgment from what actually is. When the same point is put in terms of per-

ceptual awareness, the incongruity disappears. If a perceiver is perceptually aware in a certain way of external objects, then given the specific
conditions (the perceiver's means of perception operating in the specific
conditions of perception), that is the specific form in which the perceiver
is aware of the objects. Any episode of *perceptual awareness* of objects, no
matter the specific and differing nature of that awareness, is an episode of
perceptual awareness *of the objects.*

Perceptual Relativity, Illusions, and Errors of Judgment

Because the essence of naïve realism has been taken to be the thesis
that perception is always the awareness of external objects (rather than
the thesis that the nature of the external, perceived objects is all there is to
the nature of the perceptual awareness of those objects), presentationalism has been equated with naïve realism. And so the facts that sink naïve realism—the traditional examples of perceptual illusions and of perceptual relativity, like that of a straight stick partially immersed in water
looking as if it is bent, and that of warm water feeling hot to one of your
hands but warm to the other—have been thought to sink presentationalism as such. But this is not the case.[17]

According to naïve realism, (1) the natures of two episodes of perceptual awareness can be similar to each other only if the external *objects* of
the episodes are similar to each other, and (2) the natures of two episodes
of perceptual awareness can differ from each other only if the external
objects of the episodes differ from each other. Traditional examples of illusions violate the first condition; traditional examples of perceptual relativity violate the second condition.

Consider the example of the straight stick looking as if it is bent when
it is partially immersed in water. The nature of the perceiver's perceptual
awareness in this episode of perception is similar to his perceptual aware-

17. Another fact that is thought to sink naïve realism and any version of presentationalism is the existence of hallucinations. Hallucinations, allegedly, are cases where an object
is present but the object does not exist in the external world. So presentationalism is mistaken when it characterizes the objects of perceptual awareness as external objects; what is
instead present to the perceiver is an inner object, such as a mental image or a sense-datum.
The perceiver's cognition of the external world, if and when there is such cognition, must
be understood in representational terms because representational accounts can hold that in
hallucinating a person is having an experience the content of which is that "the elephant is
in the closet" (where the elephant is considered to be an object in the external world), but the
experience's content fails to be satisfied (because the elephant does not even exist). I address
hallucinations briefly in the next section.

ness of a bent stick when it is seen out of water, resting on the ground. Yet the external objects of the two episodes of perceptual awareness are *not* similar to each other: in one case the external object is a straight stick, in the other it is a bent stick. Now consider the example of tap water feeling hot to one's left hand (which was handling items from the freezer) and warm to one's right hand. The nature of the perceiver's perceptual awareness when he places his left hand under the running water is different from the nature of his perceptual awareness when he places his right hand under the running water. Yet this difference cannot be explained by a difference in the objects being perceived: the tap water is at a constant temperature.

But presentationalism is not the same thing as naïve realism. Presentationalism need not assume that the nature of the perceiver's perceptual awareness is exhausted by the nature of the objects he is perceiving. In fact, as I have argued, it should not assume this: in maintaining that perceptual awareness is a relation between perceiver and the external objects he is perceiving, it should maintain that both the nature of the external objects *and* the nature of the perceiver (operating in specific conditions of perception) determine the nature of the resulting perceptual awareness. A similarity or a difference in two episodes of perceptual awareness may be explained by a similarity or difference in the natures of the external objects that the perceiver is aware of, *or* by a similarity or difference in the nature of the perceiver (operating in specific conditions of perception). The traditional cases of perceptual illusions and of perceptual relativity just reinforce this fact.

Given a normally functioning visual system, when you see a straight stick partially immersed in water, in those conditions of perception *that is what a straight stick looks like.* You the perceiver are directly aware of the stick *and* its straight shape. Evidence of this is the fact that you can perceptually discriminate the straight stick from bent ones. To see this, place a second, bent stick alongside the straight one, both sticks partially immersed in water. The second stick *looks* different from the first one (because it is different). *That is what a bent stick looks like to you the perceiver in those conditions of perception.* To be sure, when the two sticks are partially immersed in water, the nature of your perceptual awareness of the sticks and their shapes is different from the nature of your perceptual awareness of the two sticks and their shapes when the sticks are seen on dry ground. But so what? There is no a priori reason why the nature of one's perceptual awareness of the same objects and characteristics must remain unvarying even though the conditions of perception have changed.

From where, then, does the sense of illusion arise? From a perceiver's comparison and conceptualization across many episodes of perceptual awareness—i.e., from a perceiver's powers to classify and judge. Suppose a perceiver has learned to discriminate perceptually straight sticks from bent ones and separately groups the former together and the latter together. In each case, he does so on the basis of the grouped items' perceived similarity. And he does so in conditions where he is observing sticks (and the like) on dry ground, not partially immersed in water. He can now point to sticks and judge, "That is straight" and "That is bent." When he sees a straight stick partially immersed in water, there is a similarity between his visual awareness of the straight stick, and his prior visual awareness of bent sticks. It is natural for a perceiver to take this similarity to be a similarity between the objects he is visually aware of. And so he judges of the stick he sees partially immersed in water: "That is bent."

When he discovers that the stick is not bent—by, say, touching (i.e., perceiving) the stick with his hands when it is partially immersed in water, or by noticing that when he immerses his arms in the water, no force is exerted that could be bending the straight stick as it is immersed, he needs to reclassify and reconceptualize. The similarity in his perception of straight sticks partially immersed in water and his perception of bent sticks on dry ground is not a product of a similarity between the objects— between their physical shapes. The similarity in these episodes of perception is a product of the conditions of perception. It is not the *nature* of the *objects* of which he is visually aware that is similar; it is the *nature* of his *awareness* of the (dissimilar) objects that is similar. Normally, a perceiver will reconceptualize the facts that he now grasps by saying that the straight stick partially immersed in water *looks* or *appears* bent but *is* straight.[18]

The perceiver in this instance draws a conceptual distinction, which requires introspection, comparisons across episodes of perceptual awareness, and background (conceptual) knowledge; it is not a perceptual distinction. At the perceptual level of awareness, there is no way to distinguish or discriminate between the object one is aware of and the nature of one's awareness of the object. One does not *perceive* the nature of one's perceptual awareness of the external objects. One simply perceives the

18. Thus, I think it is better to leave the terminology of appearances for contexts in which the perceiver is making judgments about what he perceives.

external objects (and some of their characteristics), and one's perceptual awareness of the objects *has* a nature. (A fortiori, there is no way to perceptually discriminate the contribution the external objects make to the nature of one's perceptual awareness and the contribution one's means of perception and the conditions of perception make.) A perceiver does not perceive the nature of his perceptual awareness of the stick and its straight shape. He simply perceives the stick and its straight shape, and his perceptual awareness *has* a nature—a nature that can vary not only as the object varies, but also as the conditions of perception vary.

A similar analysis applies to the case of a cold hand feeling the warm water to be hot—except that in this situation it is not the conditions of perception that vary, it is the means of perception, a variation in the perceiver's sensory systems. Imagine putting water of sixty degrees Fahrenheit and of eighty degrees Fahrenheit into two sinks. Plunge your right hand into the freezer for a minute. Stick both hands in the water of the first sink, then of the second. The sixty-degree water feels cool to your left hand, warm to your right hand. The eighty-degree water feels warm to your left hand, hot to your right hand. In none of the cases is the object felt to be other than it is. In each case, all there is to say is that that is the nature of your awareness of sixty-degree/eighty-degree water when perceived by means of a cold/room-temperature hand. In each case, you are aware of the water and its temperature. In each case, you can discriminate between different temperatures of water—to both hands, for example, the eighty-degree water feels warmer than the sixty-degree water.[19]

If there is any sense of illusion here, it occurs because of classification and conceptualization. Our initial concepts for temperature—cold, warm, hot—are formed on the basis of differentiations made with hands (and bodies) that are usually at room temperature. The similarity between the perceptual awareness of the cold hand feeling the sixty-degree water and the room-temperature hand feeling the eighty-degree water is, naturally enough, taken to rest on the side of the objects of awareness. If felt with just a cold hand, one may well judge that the eighty-degree water is hot (if felt simultaneously with a cold and a room-temperature hand, one would be puzzled and would have to think of how to conceptualize what is going on). When one identifies (say, by using a thermometer) the fact that the water is not hot—that the water is not similar to other things one

---

19. It may be true that by means of a hand at room temperature one can detect smaller variations in temperature, but that is not relevant here.

has classified as hot—one reconceptualizes. The eighty-degree water *feels* or *appears* hot but *is* warm. The similarity in the nature of the perceptual awareness in the two episodes of perception is caused not by a similarity in the objects of awareness, but by a difference in the specific means of awareness.

Again, this is a conceptual distinction, not a perceptual one. One cannot distinguish perceptually between the nature of the object of one's perceptual awareness and the nature of one's perceptual awareness of the object. The perceiver does not perceive the nature of his perceptual awareness of the water and its temperature. He simply perceives the water and its temperature, and his perceptual awareness *has* a nature—a nature that can change not only as the object of awareness changes, but also as the perceiver's means of perception change.

The Red Herring of Hallucinations

The phenomenon of hallucination is thought to pose a special difficulty for presentationalism, which holds that we are perceptually aware of objects in the world—that perceptual consciousness is a real relation between subject and external object. But the worry is unwarranted.

Why is it thought to arise? Because of two alleged facts: (1) hallucinating is indistinguishable from perceiving, and (2) it is "obvious" that we are not aware of external objects in hallucination (of course it is equally "obvious" that we are aware of external objects in perception). What is supposed to follow from these two alleged facts? It is claimed that hallucinating and perceiving therefore fall into the same category of experience and must be given the same account. Since hallucinating is not awareness of external objects, perceiving is also not.

But as is widely recognized, nothing actually follows from the fact, if it is a fact, that hallucinating is phenomenologically indistinguishable from perceiving.[20] A counterfeit dollar bill may be perceptually indistinguishable from a real dollar bill, but they do not therefore belong in the same category of legal tender. And whatever hallucinations turn out to be, a non-naïve version of presentationalism can accommodate the findings.

---

20. A real possibility is that hallucinating and perceiving are phenomenologically distinct, but that an individual, when hallucinating, loses the capacity to attend to the difference. A drunk may declare that he is sober and fit to drive, but this does not show that his mental state is the same as when he is sober, even phenomenologically; in his drunkenness, he may have lost the capacity to distinguish between the phenomenologically different states of being drunk and being sober.

For instance, if it were discovered that hallucinating is the result of stimulation of a perceiver's perceptual systems, then it would be an episode of perceptual awareness. The perceiver *would* be aware of objects in the external world. But the nature of the person's awareness of those objects would be unusual, because of a drastic change in the perceiver's means of perception (caused by the drug or whatever is causing the person to hallucinate).[21] If hallucinating is not an episode of perception, then it may turn out to be an episode of interoception, in which the person is aware of the effects the drug is having on his body and nervous system. Or it may turn out that hallucinating is more akin to dreaming, in which the person is reexperiencing, perhaps in rearranged forms, things previously perceived. In none of these scenarios is there reason to think that an account of hallucination must dictate one's account of perception (or vice versa).

Perception and Conception

According to presentationalism, perceptual awareness does not involve impressions or representational experiences, such as an experience in which propositions are presented to the perceiver in a certain way. In perception, what is present to one are existents in the external world. Further, as we have seen, perception is regarded as a basic form of awareness.

Part of what is meant by "a basic form of awareness" is that other processes of consciousness are dependent on perception and are experienced as such. Memory, for instance, is experienced as a form of reexperiencing what one has previously perceived (or introspected or conceived). Imagination is experienced as a form of rearranging one's perceptual or conceptual awareness; the sense of what might be in imagination takes place against one's sense of what is—of facts one has attained awareness of by perceptual or conceptual means. Introspection is experienced as a form of turning inward, of self-consciousness, distinguished from consciousness, from one's outward, perceptual (or conceptual) awareness. Dreaming is experienced as a form of rearranging what one has previously perceived or conceived, and seems akin to imagination, and so on (see *ITOE* 29–32).

The same goes for conception. According to presentationalism, conception is dependent on perception and is experienced as such. Concep-

---

21. Alston accounts for hallucinations in terms of air or something else in S's environment appearing to S (though Alston thinks the appearance does not match the object) and in terms of visual images (see Alston 1999, 189–92).

tion is experienced, at least at its beginning stages, as a form of being aware, of classifying and categorizing, the things in the world that one is aware of in perception (and then in introspection).[22] Let me explore this dependence very briefly.

In perceptual awareness one discriminates particular entities from others. I see, for instance, the many pairs of shoes as I enter my apartment. I see many differences among the shoes: they have different shapes, sizes, colors, laces, treads, they are made of different materials, they exhibit different degrees of wear, etc. But I also experience the shoes as being similar to one another, when contrasted to, say, the hat that is also resting on the shelf. These similarities seem relevant to the fact that I classify all these things I am seeing as shoes. But what exactly is the nature of this similarity? How is it grasped? And how is it relevant to my conceptualization?

Moreover, in conceptualizing the various different pairs of shoes as shoes, I am not simply regarding them as similar. I am regarding them as identical. Each is equally, interchangeably, a shoe. The judgment "that is a shoe" as I point to each shoe is essentially the same in each case. Conceptual cognition abstracts from perceptual differences among similar things. And this is as true for our concepts of objects, like that of "shoe," as for our concepts of characteristics of objects, such as concepts of attributes. Our concepts "bent," "green," and "hot" subsume perceptually distinguishable things. How is this possible? And why is it legitimate to treat perceptually different (but similar) existents as identical? What identity among the existents do we grasp at the conceptual level of cognition, which we are unable to grasp at the strictly perceptual level? How do we explain the fact that concepts range over perceptually distinguishable concretes?

When I conceptualize the thing that I am seeing as a shoe, I am grouping it not only with the other shoes in the room, but also with all shoes, past, present, and future. Or, when I judge that shoes are manufac-

22. Thus one might say that in contrast to (present-day) representationalism, presentationalism speaks of "perceptual content" and "nonperceptual content" instead of "conceptual content" and "nonconceptual content." For the latter terms may suggest that the basic notions of content and intentionality are found at the conceptual level of cognition; if there are such things as perceptual content and intentionality, these are to be understood in comparison and contrast with the conceptual. Presentationalism reverses this and suggests that conceptual content and intentionality are to be understood in comparison and contrast with the perceptual. But I will not use the term "content" in what follows because I think it is important to always distinguish between what a perceiver is aware of and how the perceiver is aware of it, and I think many current uses of "content" blur this crucial distinction.

tured products, my judgment extends to all shoes, not just to those I am perceiving. My judgment is *universal*. Perceptual cognition is of the here and now, but conceptual cognition extends across the universe. What about the nature of concepts makes this possible?

These—the nature of similarity and universality—are some of the principal issues an account of conceptual awareness must address, according to presentationalism. And these features of conception are grasped in contrast to the discriminative cognition involved in perceptual awareness; an account of conceptual awareness must show what its exact connection is to perception.[23]

Perceptual Awareness, Fallibility, and the Given

Perception, according to presentationalism, is a form of awareness of the external world, with no possibility of nonveridicality or even of a "failure to match" the way the world is. Given such a position, it would be plausible to go on to hold that all the rest of one's cognition of the world must be based on some episode(s) of perceptual awareness and be consistent with the entirety of one's perceptual awareness.[24] To hold such a view would not require that there be some type of judgment that is infallible or unrevisable.

To subsume what one is perceiving under a concept is to relate the perceived existent to existents one is not perceiving. I walk down the street and see a thing moving up ahead on the sidewalk; I judge, "That's a cat." In subsuming what I am perceptually discriminating under the concept "cat," I am asserting that, despite the perceivable differences between this thing and other cats, there exists a specific identity among all of them. This judgment is fallible and revisable. I watch the creature a bit longer, and judge, "No, that's not a cat, that's a small dog." That my initial judgment was mistaken, however, does not show that I was not all along perceptually aware of the dog and some of its characteristics—anymore than when I mistakenly judge that a stick partially immersed in water is bent shows that I was not perceptually aware of the stick and its straight shape all along.

23. For the fundamentals of Rand's account, see *ITOE*, Peikoff 1991, and Allan Gotthelf's exploration of some of these issues in the present volume. Of course, on the basis of accounts of similarity and universality, a theory of conceptual awareness should go on to address further issues about conceptual cognition.

24. "Based on" and "consistent with" are notions that epistemology would have to spell out, and to do so would require a theory of concepts and conceptual awareness.

As the example of the stick indicates, fallibility enters not just for judgments categorizing objects, but also for judgments categorizing an object's characteristics. I judge, "That shirt is green—no, actually, it's blue"; "That serving plate is circular—no, actually it's elliptical"; "That curry tastes like it has cashews in it—no, actually, it tastes like it has pistachios in it." Conceptualization of what one is perceiving is not a simple translation of an episode of perceptual awareness into conceptual form. Conceptual awareness extends beyond a particular episode of perception because it is universal in nature.

Even if one considers a supposedly minimal judgment, namely, judgments about how an object appears, such judgments are not simple translations of an episode of perceptual awareness. In fact, I think such judgments are even more sophisticated than those already considered.

As I have indicated in the discussion of illusions, a non-naïve version of presentationalism suggests that "is" precedes "appears." When one conceptualizes how things look, feel, taste, smell, and sound, one does so against the background of one's knowledge of how things *are*. One is distinguishing the *nature* of one's perceptual *awareness* of objects from the (known) *nature* of the *objects* of which one is perceptually aware. This distinction is not available to perceptual awareness. One does not perceive the nature of one's perceptual awareness of the objects—one perceives the objects, and one's perceptual awareness *has* a nature. To isolate that nature requires introspection and a relatively sophisticated process of comparison and conceptualization. A non-naïve version of presentationalism suggests, in other words, that a perceiver first grasps: "This stick is straight; that stick is bent." Then a perceiver grasps: "This stick is straight but looks bent." And then a perceiver grasps: "This stick is straight and looks straight." So if "minimal" is meant to suggest that the judgment presupposes less knowledge or is less sophisticated or commits the perceiver to less, I do not think the proposed judgments are minimal judgments.

Further, judgments about how things look, feel, taste, smell, and sound do not "simply reproduce the content of appearance," as Alston and many others suggest (see Alston 2005a, 185). Like all judgments, these judgments are forms of conceptualization, of classification and identification. They extend beyond a single episode of perceptual awareness (and a single episode of introspection). To use Alston's example, I am perceptually aware of a tree—and my visual awareness of the tree has a specific nature. I reflect on this episode of perception and try to classify the nature of my visual awareness of the tree. I think to myself, "Whatever the object I'm perceiving *is*, it *looks* like a maple tree." What does this mean? It means that I judge that the nature of my present visual awareness of the world is sufficiently similar to past episodes of visual awareness of the world in which I was perceiving maple trees, and therefore they should all be classified together. Such a judgment is fallible and revisable. Indeed, revisions here are common occurrences. "It looks like a maple tree—no, actually, it looks more like an oak tree." "It looks green—no, actually, it looks more bluish than green." "The stick looks bent—no, actually, it only sort of looks bent, and sort of looks like it is disjointed." Conceptual judgments about the nature of our perceptual awareness of objects, just as much as conceptual judgments about the nature of the objects we are perceptually aware of, are universal.

Nor does one need "minimal" judgments about how things appear in order to possess justification for how things are. One need not hold that in order to possess justification for the judgment that that is a maple tree, one must *first* judge that that *looks* like a maple tree. One could hold that the perceptual awareness itself gives one (some) justification for the judgment that that is a maple tree.[25]

But if one endorses the idea that an episode of perceptual awareness can stand in a justificatory relation to a judgment, does it follow that one endorses the "Myth of the Given"? Probably.

It is not clear, I think, to what cluster of views the Myth of the Given is meant to refer.[26] But let us take Pryor's characterization of anti-Given arguments and see where (a non-naïve version of) presentationalism might fit into the debate. In a footnote in which Pryor mentions Sellars's "Empiricism and the Philosophy of Mind," Davidson's "A Coherence Theory of Truth and Knowledge," Bonjour's "Can Empirical Knowledge Have a Foundation?" and *The Structure of Empirical Knowledge*, and Michael Williams's *Groundless Belief*, Pryor writes,

> These anti-Given arguments deserve a re-examination, in light of recent developments in the philosophy of mind. The anti-Given arguments pose a dilemma: either (i) direct apprehension is not a state with propositional

25. Alston seems to argue this; see Alston 1999, 198. See also Pryor 2005 and 2000.
26. Alston (1998b, 1), writes of Sellars's critique: "I will concentrate here on his complaints about 'the given.' But I must admit at the outset that it is not easy to pin down the target to which Sellars applies that title." And Bonevac (2002, 1) writes, "Sellars initially addresses the Myth in the form of sense data theory, a theory long dead; though he intends 'a

content, in which case it's argued to be incapable of providing justification for believing any specific proposition; or (ii) direct apprehension is
a state with propositional content. This second option is often thought
to entail that direct apprehension is a kind of believing, and hence itself
would need justification. But it ought nowadays to be very doubtful that
the second option does entail such things. These days many philosophers
of mind construe perceptual experience as a state with propositional content, even though the experience is distinct from, and cannot be reduced
to, any kind of belief. Your experiences represent the world to you as being a certain way, and the way they represent the world as being is their
propositional content. Now, surely, it's looking to you as if the world is
a certain way is not a kind of state for which you need any justification.
Hence, this construal of perceptual experience seems to block the step
from 'has propositional content' to 'needs justification.' . . . It should at
least be clear that the second horn of the anti-Given argument needs
more argument than we've seen so far. To be fair, most of the founda-
tionalists who appealed to a notion of 'direct apprehension' understood
this notion along the lines of horn (i); and that is where their critics have
focused most of their attention. (Pryor 2001, 101n10)

A non-naïve version of presentationalism seems to fall under the first
horn of the dilemma, since it speaks of perception as direct awareness
of the external world, which is not representational in form (it does not
have "propositional content"). From this perspective, a non-naïve version
of presentationalism would have to explain how a state without propositional content can provide justification for a judgment. But when one
thinks about what kind of explanation a non-naïve version of presentationalism would offer, it seems more natural to regard it as rejecting the
second horn of the dilemma.

Presentationalism considers an episode of perceptual awareness to be
superior to a representational experience: it is a presentational experience.
If representational experiences that are not beliefs can justify conceptual
judgments, so can presentational experiences that are not beliefs. Moreover, if it is plausible to hold that "it's looking to you as if the world is a
certain way" is not a kind of state for which you need any justification,

general critique of the entire framework of givenness,' how much of the argument applies
more generally is not immediately clear. Sellars never specifies precisely what the Myth of the
Given *is*. Tracing Sellars's dialectic, the reader gets the sense that the target repeatedly shifts."

then it is also plausible to hold that "the world looking to you a certain way" (namely, the way that it is) or "you being perceptually aware in a certain way of the world" is also not a kind of state for which you need any justification. From this perspective, a non-naïve version of presentationalism rejects the second horn of the dilemma. It, like some other views today, advocates the existence of conscious states that can provide justification for judgments but are themselves in no need of justification. In particular, of course, episodes of perceptual awareness are such states. In this sense, a non-naïve version of presentationalism denies that the given is a myth.

Another way of approaching this issue is by asking what it is about episodes of perceptual awareness that make them capable of providing justification for judgments. Pryor writes elsewhere (also in a footnote):

> we would certainly *like* to have a more informative story about why our perceptual experiences offer us the justification they do. One such story would appeal to the fact that our perceptual beliefs are *irresistible*. . . . A different story would make it constitutive of our concept of justification, or of our perceptual concepts, that having such-and-such experiences counts as good reason to believe that certain perceptible properties are instantiated. I am not attracted to any of these stories. In my view . . . it's the peculiar "phenomenal force" or way our experiences have of presenting propositions to us. Our experience represent propositions in such a way that it "feels as if" we could tell that those propositions are true—and that we're perceiving them to be true—just by virtue of having them so represented. (Of course, to be able to articulate this "feeling" takes a high grade of reflective awareness.) I think this "feeling" is part of what distinguishes the attitude of experiencing that *p* from other propositional attitudes, like belief and visual imagination. Beliefs and visual images might come to us irresistibly, without having that kind of "phenomenal force." . . . It is difficult to explain what this "phenomenal force" amounts to, but I think that it is an important notion, and that it needs to be part of the story about why our experiences give us the justification that they do. I will have to develop these suggestive remarks elsewhere. (Pryor 2000, 547n37)

On a non-naïve version of presentationalism, perception is capable of justifying because it is a form of awareness, a form of cognition—indeed, a basic, nonfallible form—and is experienced by us as such. This, according to the approach, is the "peculiar 'phenomenal force'" of perception: it presents the world to us—the world "as it is." The grasp of this fact is one of the roots of the concept of objectivity.

But to fully articulate and defend this would require more than is allowed by a sketch of Rand's presentational approach to perception. In particular, a full account of perceptual awareness would have to establish and validate its fundamental framework by explaining its approach to awareness, representation, consciousness, and the basic relation of consciousness to existence in more depth.

Concepts, Context, and the Advance of Science

JAMES G. LENNOX

One central theme running through Ayn Rand's *Introduction to Objectivist Epistemology* (*ITOE*) is that the objectivity of concepts is not threatened by, and in fact is a precondition for, the growth of knowledge. Crucial to her defense of that view is her argument that a proper account of definitions must reflect the fact that we learn more over time about the nature of the units—the cognized referents—a concept subsumes. At the same time, she stresses that a properly formed concept retains its identity—remains the same concept—as our information about its referents expands.

Understanding how her views about definition and about concept identity are related to each other not only highlights a number of distinctive features of the Objectivist approach to concepts; it also points to a distinctive response to the claim that the "conceptual change" that is evident in the history of science, and particularly in so-called scientific revolutions, undermines the belief that science provides an ever-expanding body of knowledge about the world in which we live.

In her discussion of these issues, Rand tends to treat the cognitive development of individual human beings and the historical development of the sciences as governed by similar principles.[1] On a contextual view of concepts and definitions such as Rand's, objectivity is determined by the widest epistemological context available at a given point of history: "If definitions are contextual, how does one determine an objective definition valid for all men? It is determined according to the widest context of knowledge available to man on the subjects relevant to the units of a given concept" (*ITOE* 46).

An Ambiguity in the Idea of Conceptual Change

In the late 1950s and through the 1960s, N. R. Hanson (1958), Stephen Toulmin (1961, 1972), Thomas Kuhn (1962), and Paul Feyerabend (1962) introduced into philosophy of science what is now commonly referred to as "the problem of conceptual change." Part of the problem stems from an unfortunate ambiguity in the term "conceptual change," so I need to begin with some disambiguation. On the one hand, "conceptual change" is sometimes used as a highly abstract notion that subsumes a variety of different sorts of change in *the conceptual structure of a science*. On the other hand, it has also been used to refer to a process whereby a concept undergoes a change in its meaning.

Let me begin by noting five types of change in the conceptual structure of science, none of which obviously entail "conceptual change" in the second sense, and each of which is acknowledged at some point by Rand in *ITOE* (the locations of the acknowledgments are indicated parenthetically).

1. The introduction of a new concept to designate a class of newly discovered (or hypothesized) entities, processes, relations—for example, "electron," "gene," "natural selection," or "mitosis" were all introduced at a certain point in time for this reason (*ITOE* 46–47).

2. The development of subcategories of a concept in response to more intensive study of the objects identified by the initial concept. A glance through the glossary of a recent advanced textbook in genetics (Levin 1990), for example, reveals regulatory genes, reporter

---

1. This is a point that is being increasingly stressed in the literature on scientific concepts and theories. As one example: "Indeed, we believe the most fascinating thing about science may be its connection to human learning in general, and in particular, to the rapid, dramatic, learning that takes place in early childhood" (Schulz, Kushmir, and Gopnik 2007, 67).

genes, structural genes, suppressor genes, constitutive genes, extra-nuclear genes, luxury genes, oncogenes, and pseudogenes (*ITOE* 25).

3. The development of more general concepts designating wider categories, based on recognition of fundamental similarities among the entities grouped by less abstract concepts. Often this process goes hand in hand with a new conceptual differentiation—for example, the categories "vertebrate" or "eukaryote" group together narrower biological taxa, but were coined in part to differentiate those taxa from others lacking, on the one hand vertebral columns, on the other cell nuclei (*ITOE* 24, 28).

4. The rejection and/or replacement of a concept deemed problematic on the basis of new information—"phlogiston," "miasma," "epicycle," "nervous fluid," or "sublunary." In these cases certain observed phenomena suggested a hypothetical entity or attribute, for which a new concept was formed; while further investigation of these and related phenomena invalidates the original concept (*ITOE* 239).

5. The reclassification of a class of entities on the basis of a deeper understanding of them. To cite an example I will discuss in some detail later: members of Cirripedia (the class to which barnacles belong) were, until early in the nineteenth century, thought of either as an unusual form of mollusk or as a distinct class of invertebrates. Comparative and developmental investigation led to them being reclassified as a subclass of Crustacea, that is, placed in a different phylum (today referred to as a subphylum of arthropod) (*ITOE* 239).

Since I am focusing on the philosophy of science, I will refer to these as *developments in the conceptual structure of a science*. It is worth noting, however, that such conceptual advances—the introduction, replacement, reclassification, or subcategorization of concepts, or the generation of a wider concept—are not peculiar to the sciences. They are a pervasive aspect of cognitive development.

All of these developments in the conceptual structure of the sciences deserve serious attention. It should be noted, however, that none of the above changes requires that an already formed concept changes its identity or undergoes a change in meaning. Yet in the writings of historians and philosophers of science the term "conceptual change" is often used to refer to the idea that concepts themselves, after being formed, undergo changes in their identity as a consequence of changes in the theoretical structure of a science—a view often expressed in terms of changes in the *meanings of concepts* associated with that science.[2] What this idea implies is clearly going to depend on how one understands both a concept's identity and its meaning. On certain very influential views, one implication is that the key concepts of scientific theories are unable to retain their identity, or their meaning, through significant changes in those theories.

It is, I think, important to keep this idea of change in a concept's identity, and the corresponding idea of change in a concept's meaning, distinct from the other forms of conceptual development mentioned above.[3] It is the claim that the act of integrating new information about the referents of a concept with what was previously known about it will lead to significant changes in its meaning that has been thought to present a challenge to the notion of scientific objectivity and scientific progress.[4] By investigating the themes in Rand's *ITOE* that were outlined in my introduction and their implications for the identity and meaning of concepts, I will point the way to a powerful and distinctive theory of cognitive progress. I will then conclude the discussion by indicating how that theory can be mobilized in clarifying the fifth sort of conceptual development noted above, that which Rand refers to as "conceptual reclassification."[5]

Ayn Rand on Concepts and Cognitive Context

Concept-formation for Rand involves two interrelated processes: *differentiating* a group of entities similar with respect to a number of attributes (where similar means falling within a specifiable, measurable range on a continuum) from others that share one or more of those attributes

2. Thomas Kuhn (1996, 102), for example, talks about the "need to change the meaning of established and familiar concepts" as a key element in scientific revolutions; but in the same paragraph says that the transition from Newtonian to Einsteinian mechanics "did not involve the introduction of additional objects or concepts."

3. As an example of research that seems to blur this distinction, see Carey 2000, 459–87.

4. And it is worth noting that, on certain views about meaning, the distinction I am making here is intentionally blurred. For example, if the meaning of a scientific concept is thought to be determined primarily by its place in a network of concepts, then conceptual reclassification directly implies a change of meaning. For a detailed presentation of the ways in which Paul Feyerabend's (1962) and Kuhn's (1996) views about concepts lead to this conclusion, and one of the earliest, and best, systematic critiques of their presuppositions and arguments, see Shapere 1966, 41–85.

5. I am assuming here that questions regarding the identity of a concept and questions about a concept's meaning are closely related. I have done so because the question of conceptual change is typically discussed in contemporary philosophy of science (as in the authors referred to in the previous note) in terms of changes in meaning. Nevertheless, it is not the way in which Rand typically discusses the issues with which we are concerned.

but outside that range; and *integrating* those entities by focusing on the shared characteristics/ranges and omitting from focus their measurable differences. The characteristic(s) shared with the items from which the group is being distinguished is referred to as the conceptual common denominator, or CCD. For example, in forming the concept "porpoise" you note that certain cetaceans share many of that group's general characteristics, but in specific ways that distinguish them from other cetaceans and allow them to be united conceptually. To acquire the concept "porpoise" is to acquire the ability to differentiate the members of this subcategory from other aquatic mammals with the characteristics shared by all cetaceans, and to integrate them into a unit by focusing on the specific range of those characteristics that is distinctive to porpoises. In this example, one or more of the characteristics shared by all cetaceans (e.g., the many special aquatic adaptations of their mammalian characteristics) would be the CCD. The genus—the wider group with these shared characteristics—is, then, "cetacean." Forming a concept such as "porpoise" involves distinguishing groups with significant, measurable differences in those shared characteristics.[6]

Most scientific concepts are, like these, higher order abstractions, in which case, on Rand's view, the "units"—the referents of the concept—to be differentiated and integrated are previously formed concepts. The distinguishing characteristics of the lower level concepts become the range of measurements to be omitted. In forming the concept "cetacean," for example, we would treat the distinguishing characteristics of whales, dolphins, and porpoises as the omitted measurements. Every cetacean must have a mammalian respiratory system adequate to an aquatic lifestyle, but may have any of the features of such a system within the range found among the units of the concepts being integrated (e.g., the blowholes of the different genera are positioned differently, the "windpipes" leading to the lungs vary in length and width, etc.). Rand stresses that the process of forming more abstract concepts inevitably involves an increasingly complex network of interrelationships among concepts (*ITOE* 23).

Rand's is a normative theory of concepts, and she has much to say about the value of conceptual thought for human beings. In her discussion of "The Cognitive Role of Concepts" in *ITOE*, she stresses the importance of the fact that concepts are open ended: "a concept is an 'open-end'

6. This is a very brief sketch of the theory. For much more detail, see the essays in part 1 of this volume by Gotthelf and Salmieri.

classification which includes the yet-to-be-discovered characteristics of a given group of existents. All man's knowledge rests on that fact" (*ITOE* 66).[7] There are two aspects to her view that concepts are open-end classifications. The first aspect of open-endedness—that concepts refer to a potential infinity of entities similar in the relevant ways to those on the basis of which the concept was first formed—is emphasized by her insistence that it is critical to actually possessing the concept that one is able to apply it to *all* the entities of a certain kind, not just to those with which one is familiar. If you encounter a typical cat that you have not seen before and you do not recognize it *as a cat,* that failure is clear evidence you have not yet grasped the concept (*ITOE* 147).

The second aspect of open-endedness is emphasized in the above quotation; a concept includes reference to the yet-to-be-discovered *characteristics* of the entities it subsumes. A child's concept of "man" includes the attribute "capable of learning geometry," though the child does not yet know that fact about human beings. Similarly, the concept of "electron" imbedded in current physical theory includes any facts about electrons we may discover in the future.[8]

A critical question for Rand's theory of concepts, then, is: What does it mean for a concept to "include" attributes of the referents that have yet to be discovered?[9] I suggest that we understand this notion of inclusion in line with Rand's general understanding of concepts as products of a norm-guided cognitive process. The concept provides a cognitive grasp of all entities sharing an interrelated set of similarities falling within certain measurable ranges along a set of axes.[10] The *meaning* of the concept is all those entities *as grasped by that process.* Though a concept may initially be formed, and associated with a term, on the basis of the awareness of only a small number of distinguishing features, to possess a concept is to commit oneself to a long-term process of constant integration of new

---

7. Also: "Concepts stand for specific kinds of existents, including *all* the characteristics of these existents, observed and not-yet-observed, known and unknown" (*ITOE* 65).

8. I am still trying to work out the connection between Rand's notion of the open-end nature of concepts and what Burian (2005, 136–37) refers to as "open reference." The two ideas have at least this much in common: concepts must have a way of accommodating the input of new information without them somehow transforming into new concepts with each new input. They are not "closed" (Burian) or "frozen" (Rand) at the time of their initial formulation.

9. This question is also addressed by Salmieri's and Gotthelf's essays in this volume.

10. I specify "entities" here because of the areas of science on which I will focus my discussion; however, one should keep in mind that Rand indicates in *ITOE* the way in which her theory applies to concepts in other categories, such attributes, actions, or relations.

information. As Rand herself writes shortly after introducing the idea of "open-end" classification, "The implicit principle guiding this process is: 'I know that there exists such an entity as man; I know many of his characteristics, but he has many others which I do not know and must discover.' The same principle directs the study of every other kind of perceptually isolated and conceptualized existents. A concept, then, is a cognitive tool for integrating everything you learn about its referents; that is the sense in which it 'includes' the yet to be discovered" (*ITOE* 66).[11]

Note that the last sentence in the above quotation claims that the open-ended character of concepts is epistemologically fundamental. Human knowledge is acquired and held in conceptual form, and the primary cognitive function of our conceptual faculty is "to reduce a vast amount of information to a minimal number of units." This function implements what Rand refers to as "the principle of unit-economy." "A concept substitutes one symbol (one word) for the enormity of the perceptual aggregate of the concretes it subsumes" (*ITOE* 64). Concepts thus expand our cognitive range enormously, and in two distinct ways. First, they allow us to apply what we have learned about the units we *initially* investigated in forming the concept to the unlimited number of relevantly similar entities to be encountered in the future, and are thus critical to inductive reasoning.[12] Second, they are tools for the ongoing integration of newly discovered information as we carry out more extensive and intensive investigations of these, and related, entities. Note that this entails that new information about the units subsumed by a concept is an aspect of that concept's identity.

The principle of unit-economy also lies behind the importance Rand attaches to concepts being *defined* in terms of their units' *essential* characteristics. She reinterprets the classical Aristotelian understanding of definition *per genus et differentiam* in terms of the Objectivist epistemology: the *differentia* corresponds to that which, in a given context of knowledge, is the fundamental distinguishing characteristic(s) of the concept's units; the *genus* corresponds to all the entities that share this concept's conceptual common denominator. As opposed to others in the Aristotelian tradition, Rand argues that what are identified as the *essential* characteristic(s) of a concept's units may change as more is learned

---

11. I owe this way of formulating the issue to discussions with Greg Salmieri and Allan Gotthelf.

12. Richard Boyd stresses the importance of this role for concepts (Boyd 1991, 129–33); compare Griffiths 1997, 173–74, 187–88.

about their nature. As she liked to put it, her view of essence is *episte-mological* while Aristotle's is *metaphysical*. In her view the designation of certain characteristics as essential is *context sensitive*—an essential characteristic of the units subsumed by a concept is, *within the context of one's knowledge*, the one that is fundamental, that is, the one upon which the largest number of their other distinguishing features depend. Additional information about them may include previously unknown information about such relations of dependence, and this may, in turn, require one to change one's definition.

However, while the integration of new information about a concept's referents may lead to changes in what should be identified as their essential attributes, and thus to changes in the *definition* of the concept, it does not follow that the identity or the meaning of the concept has changed. Using the growth in our knowledge of human beings as an example, she comments:

> the concept "man" has not changed: it refers to the same kind of entities. What has changed and grown is the knowledge of these entities. The definitions of concepts may change with the changes in the designation of essential characteristics, and conceptual reclassifications may occur with the growth of knowledge, *but these changes are made possible by and do not alter the fact that a concept subsumes all the characteristics of its referents, including the yet-to-be-discovered.* (ITOE 66; emphasis added)[13]

The last sentence, which I have emphasized, reflects the second aspect of her view of the open-end nature of concepts mentioned earlier. Not only are concepts open ended for her in including within their scope of reference all the relevantly similar existents, known and unknown, but also in being centers of integration for all of their yet-to-be-discovered attributes. Since their reference-scope includes these yet-to-be-determined attributes, the later acquisition of such knowledge does not imply *change* in reference. Provided the concept is formed according to the appropriate process initially and new information is integrated according to the same process, that concept subsumes all requisitely similar entities of the kind, known and unknown, with all their characteristics, whether we are currently aware of them or not. Even a massive amount of new information does not change the concept's meaning—in fact, it is a critical part of her

13. Since conceptual reclassification is precisely the issue I will focus on in the second half of this essay, I here simply want to highlight the fact that Rand is aware of it as a special case.

view that such growth in knowledge *depends on* the concept retaining its identity through constant integrative updating. Near the close of her discussion of higher-order abstractions, she puts the point this way:

> The formation of a concept provides man with the means of identifying, not only the concretes he has observed, but all the concretes *of that kind* which he may encounter in the future. Thus, when he has formed or grasped the concept "man," he does not have to regard every man he meets thereafter as a new phenomenon to be studied from scratch: he identifies him as "man" and applies to him the knowledge he has acquired about man (which leaves him free to study the particular, individual characteristics of the newcomer, i.e. the individual measurements within the categories established by the concept "man"). (*ITOE* 27–28)

A more intensive study of the units subsumed by a concept, in other words, presupposes the background knowledge of those entities already possessed. But that background is available *as background* only if the new units to be investigated have been identified *as* units of the kind denominated by the concept. Developing an analogy between concepts and file folders, Rand insists that under ordinary circumstances, even a vast expansion in our knowledge of a concept's referents does not change the meaning of the concept itself: "The content of such folders varies from individual to individual, according to the degree of his knowledge—it ranges from the primitive, generalized information in the mind of a child or an illiterate to the enormously detailed sum in the mind of a scientist— *but it pertains to the same referents, to the same kind of existents, and is subsumed under the same concept.* This filing system makes possible such activities as learning, education, research—the accumulation, transmission and expansion of knowledge" (*ITOE* 66–67; emphasis added).[14] She saw quite clearly the importance of insisting, as Paul Griffiths (1997, 192) has put it, that "concepts can retain their identity across radical changes in theory." Griffiths put this forth as a claim about the phenomena of science for which a proper theory of concepts ought to be able to account.

---

14. Though I won't be able to explore it in this essay, here Rand also is clearly concerned to deal with the issue that Georges Rey refers to as the "stability function" of concepts, their role in permitting communication between people with very different levels of knowledge of the units of a particular concept (Rey 1983; repr. in Margolis and Laurence 2000, 279–99; see esp. 282). Jessie Prinz (2001, 14) states the issue this way: "Concepts must be capable of being shared by different individuals and by one individual at different times"; compare Peikoff 1991, 104.

But of course there are many who would insist that at the heart of radical changes in theory are radical *changes in the meanings of concepts,* and who would therefore *deny* that concepts are able to retain their identity through significant theory change.[15] To quote one presentation of the point: "the meaning of a term or concept is given, at least in part, by the network of assumptions with which it is associated. Thus, the meaning of 'point' or 'line' in Euclidean geometry is different from the meaning of those same terms in Riemannian geometry" (Laudan 1990, 124). This is the view that Richard Burian (2005, 127–29) refers to as the assumption of holism about theoretical concepts.[16] It is, perhaps, views such as this that Ayn Rand had in mind in the following comment: "it is precisely the 'open-end' character of concepts, the essence of their cognitive function, that modern philosophers cite in their attempts to demonstrate that concepts have no cognitive validity" (*ITOE* 67).

Their error, as she saw it, lies in a tendency to identify the meaning of a concept with what is currently known about its referents (or worse, with its current definition), rather than with the referents themselves. If the meaning of a concept is specified by reference to what we know at a given time about its referents, then any significant new information about those referents changes its meaning. As she puts it, "This view implies . . . that concepts are not a cognitive device of man's type of consciousness, but a repository of closed, out-of-context omniscience—and that concepts refer, not to the existents of the external world, but to the frozen, arrested state of knowledge inside any given consciousness at any given moment" (*ITOE* 67). At the level of scientific domains, this means that the historical development of a science consists in a series of disconnected bodies of ideas: in some cases the terms may remain the same, but this merely disguises an underlying conceptual discontinuity.[17]

15. This is a claim about the possibility of conceptual continuity during such changes, not about its necessity. Many genuine cases of scientific revolution require the replacement (sometimes the wholesale replacement) of concepts. And as a matter of scientific history, it has sometimes been the case that the same word is retained for what, in fact, is a different concept, and this can lead to confusion. But, to cite one example, the gradual acceptance in the nineteenth century of the idea that taxonomic relationships reflected historical relationships of descent added illuminating information to our understanding of every taxon, but it would be wrong to say that by itself it changed any of the concepts in the biological hierarchy of concepts. I will have more to say on this point later.

16. The idea can be traced back to Quine 1951 and in a quite different form to Duhem 1906.

17. The problems with semantic holism are nicely laid out by Michael Devitt (1996) in the first chapter entitled "A Critique of the Case for Semantic Holism."

Her view, by contrast, is that if we understand the meaning of a concept as the entities cognitively integrated by the relevant process (and their attributes, of course, since on her view that integration is based on omitting measurements of specific attributes), and if the very nature of that integration requires that concepts be open ended, then changes, even significant changes, in our scientific understanding of those entities are no threat to the growth of scientific knowledge. Indeed, to form a concept is to make a commitment to a constant process of integrating and differentiating its units as we learn more about them; there is no mysterious latching on to kinds or essences given in nature, as some have held.[18]

By contrast, developments in the conceptual structure of a science, of the kind I discussed in section two of this essay, are common in the history of science, and it is important to understand such developments and integrate that understanding with one's theory of concepts. I will take one modest step in that direction by looking at a historical example of conceptual reclassification, after discussing Rand's distinctive understanding of the cognitive role of definitions in a scientific context.

The Cognitive Role of Definitions

On the view of concepts that Ayn Rand developed, definitions have an extremely important cognitive role to play, a role that becomes increasingly important as our knowledge of the world expands. Their role is both to identify in fundamental terms the nature of a concept's referents *as currently understood,* and to summarize their relationships to other things in the same domain of knowledge. They are able to do so because "a definition complies with the two essential functions of consciousness: differentiation and integration. The differentia [of a definition] isolates the units of a concept from all other existents; the genus indicates their connection to a wider group of existents" (*ITOE* 41). Note that the stress is on the role of definitions in providing us with a means of seeing how the *items* subsumed by the concept are related to one another and to other, similar things, rather than how *concepts* or *terms* are interrelated. No-

---

18. The classic statement of such a view is Putnam 1977. A valuable presentation and critical analysis of Putnam's account of meaning and essence, in the context of comparing it with Aristotle's, can be found in Charles 2000, 5–19. Suffice it to say that since Rand argues that essences are established within the context of what is known, and thus may change as our knowledge expands, and since she has a complex account of how perceptual awareness of similarity underwrites concept and language acquisition, her views about both meaning and essence differ fundamentally from Putnam's. These aspects of her thought are discussed in great detail in the previous three essays.

tice too, that the primary activity of concept-formation is the integrating of similars against a background of difference—definition by means of identifying essential characteristics becomes increasingly important as our knowledge of the units of a concept widens and deepens. It is a highly economical way of *compressing* that knowledge.[19]

To illustrate these ideas in a scientific context, allow me to quote from one of the best-written advanced textbooks in the biological sciences, Scott Gilbert's (1997) *Developmental Biology*:

> The life of a new individual is initiated by the fusion of genetic material from the two gametes—the sperm and the egg. This fusion, called fertilization, stimulates the egg to begin development. The subsequent stages of development are collectively called embryogenesis. Throughout the animal kingdom an incredible variety of embryonic types exist, but most patterns of embryogenesis comprise variations on four themes:
>
> 1. Immediately following fertilization, cleavage occurs. Cleavage is a series of extremely rapid mitotic divisions wherein the enormous volume of zygote cytoplasm is divided into numerous smaller cells. These cells are called blastomeres, and by the end of cleavage, they generally form a sphere known as a blastula. (Gilbert 1997, 3)

Gilbert goes on to develop themes 2–4, wherein gastrulation, germ layers, ectoderm, endoderm, mesoderm, organogenesis, germ cells, somatic cells, and gametogenesis are defined in the same clear, crisp manner. It is interesting to review the above passage with an eye on the way in which it accomplishes the cognitive roles that Rand stresses.

So: Fertilization is the fusion of the genetic material of sperm and egg. That is to say, it is *similar*, along various measurable dimensions, to other sorts of (biological) fusion, but it is *fundamentally distinguished* from other, similar fusions in that it involves the fusion of the genetic material of the two gametes that initiate (sexual) biological development.

"Embryogenesis" is the concept that *integrates* all concrete cases of (sexual) biological development begun by such a fusion, and these are then *differentiated* from developmental processes *not* so initiated. Blastomeres are defined as cells created by the process of cleavage at the beginning stages of embryogenesis—which identifies them as *similar* along various dimensions to other cells, but *differentiates* them by reference to the causal process by which, and temporal point of development at which, they are created. And so on.

19. There is a nice discussion of this point in Peikoff 1991, 97, 101, 108.

One of the most admirable features of the material quoted, typical of this author, is that it is written in a pleasing, narrative form that almost makes you forget that it has provided you with an elegant, economical snapshot of the hierarchical network of concepts referring to the entities, processes, and relationships at the basis of the science of embryology. The foregoing example illustrates three distinctive features of definitions highlighted by the Objectivist account.

1. Definitions are *contextual,* and a definition formulated at one stage of scientific advance can cease to play its proper role as new knowledge of the field is acquired. Most of the concepts in the above passage were formed decades before the field of genetics developed, and therefore before it was known that the fusion of gametes that constitutes fertilization is, more deeply, the fusion of the genetic material in the nuclei of the gametes. But since (as we are now aware) it is *this* fusion that is critical in initiating the complex processes now subsumed by the concept of embryogenesis, reference to genetic material is correctly included, in the current context of knowledge, in the differentia.

2. This passage exemplifies Rand's point that more advanced definitions do not contradict earlier ones, if those earlier ones were formed properly—it is not *false* to say that fertilization involves the fusion of gametes, but today it would be a case of defining by nonessentials.

3. By introducing "genetic material" into the definition of fertilization, an explicit link to a related but distinct domain of the biological sciences is made. One can think of this as a "flag" to ask questions such as "What *is* the genetic material?," "How is genetic material fused?," "In what way does this fusion play a causal role in initiating development?," and on and on.

As Rand notes, "A definition is the condensation of a vast body of observation. As a legal preamble (referring here to *epistemological* law), every definition begins with the implicit proposition: 'After full consideration of all the known facts pertaining to this group of existents, the following has been demonstrated to be their essential, therefore defining, characteristic'" (*ITOE* 48).

It is critical for the objectivity of concepts that they retain their identity through the growth of knowledge about the units that they subsume. This is so *despite* the fact that "all conceptualization is a contextual process" and that "the content of [an individual's] concepts is determined and dictated by the cognitive content of his mind" (*ITOE* 43). It is Rand's account of definitions as contextual that allows for a concept to retain its identity while its definition changes in response to the process of integrating new discoveries with our current knowledge—reflecting in particular the way in which expanding information about the objects of investigation may suggest a change in which distinguishing characteristics of those objects are taken to be causally fundamental. These two central strands of her theory intersect in her understanding of essence—essences are neither metaphysically given, intrinsic features of the units subsumed by a concept, nor are they merely "nominal," selected without regard for the nature of those units. Here is the crucial passage in full:

> Objectivism holds that the essence of a concept is that fundamental characteristic(s) of its units on which the greatest number of other characteristics depend, and which distinguishes these units from all other existents within the field of man's knowledge. Thus the essence of a concept is determined *contextually* and may be altered with the growth of man's knowledge. The metaphysical referent of man's concepts is not a special, separate metaphysical essence, but the *total* of the facts of reality [about their referents] he has observed, and this total determines which characteristics of a group of existents he designates as essential. An essential characteristic is factual, in the sense that it does exist, does determine other characteristics and does distinguish a group of existents from all others; it is *epistemological* in the sense that the classification of "essential characteristic" is a device of man's method of cognition—a means of classifying, condensing and integrating an ever-growing body of knowledge." (*ITOE*, 52)[20]

There is a distinctive metaphysics and epistemology behind this quotation, most of which I will have to set aside here. But I do need to take note of the fact that in this passage, by contrast with much of the chapter from which it is quoted, she is discussing essence *not* from the standpoint of what is identified by the differentia of a definition but as a feature of *concepts,* a feature which "may alter with the growth of man's knowledge." Now in one respect this is unremarkable—concepts involve an ongoing process of integrating an open-end set of similar concretes (or, at higher levels, sets of sets of concretes), including an open-end set of their distinguishing characteristics and characteristics that can serve as conceptual

---

20. The relation of her theory of concepts to her views about definition and essence are further discussed in the section of Gotthelf's essay headed "Definitions and Essences."

common denominators. As such this *must* include those characteristics that, in a given epistemic context, are designated as essential and defining.

But it also means that which features play the role of the distinguishing characteristic(s) and the conceptual common denominator(s) of the concept in a given context may change. In particular, new information about the entities to which the concept refers may well require processes of *redifferentiation* and *reintegration*. What implications might this have for the identity of the concept itself? I want to explore this question by examining the process of scientific reclassification. As I proceed I hope it will be clear why exploring this question is vitally important for the conceptual foundations of science.

Within the general category of learning additional information about the entities subsumed by a certain concept, I will focus on learning additional information that may cause us to rethink which attributes are most fundamental and/or from which entities the units referred to by this concept ought to be most immediately differentiated. On the view of concepts I have been articulating, it is of critical importance to the advance of science that concepts retain their identity through knowledge expansion, and it is the open-end nature of concepts that makes this possible—once a valid concept is formed, its content must be thought of as including the full range of requisitely similar entities and their unknown, yet-to-be-discovered, attributes. To use Rand's metaphor, if we are to put newly discovered information into the correct file folder, we had better have a means of determining in which folder it belongs.

The special case of context expansion I want to focus on, however, raises interesting and important questions about this process—it is the fifth sort of *conceptual development* mentioned in the second section of this chapter—that involving *conceptual reclassification*. To continue the metaphor, in such cases the file folder may need to be moved to a new drawer, and with that move the "labeling" may also need to change in order to differentiate it from and interrelate it to the contents of the new drawer.[21] Moreover, as the example I am going to discuss indicates, such reclassification may allow us to identify and correct errors regarding the *nature* of the attributes that were used to form the concept originally.

To avoid the ambiguity in the term "conceptual change" that I noted at the beginning of this essay, I am adopting the language of conceptual *development* used by Rand in the context of discussing the growth

21. Compare Griffiths 1997, 189–96, on conceptual revision.

of knowledge. For example, in her discussion of the contextual nature of definitions, she qualifies her account of changes that might take place in a person's definition of "man" as follows: "The specific steps given in this example are not necessarily the literal steps of the *conceptual development of every man* . . . but this is the *pattern of development which most concepts and definitions undergo* in a man's mind with the growth of his knowledge" (*ITOE* 45; "pattern" is emphasized in the original, the remaining emphasis is mine). The sort of case I am going to focus on is one in which conceptual reclassification takes place, but without any significant change of reference for the reclassified concept. Many important advances in the natural sciences produce significant changes in the way we *differentiate* the referents grouped under a concept from other, similar things, and thus in the way we hold or integrate those units. We will look briefly at the historical example I mentioned earlier to provide a concrete illustration of such a change. It represents in dramatic fashion a pattern that I believe is common, and commonly misinterpreted, in the history of science.

Conceptual Reclassification: A Biological Case Study

In the late eighteenth and early nineteenth century, the barnacles, or "cirripeds,"[22] were treated as a subclass of sessile mollusks by Georges Cuvier and as a class unto themselves by Jean-Baptiste Lamarck, the leading invertebrate zoologist in France at the time. But with the publication of a series of papers by John Vaughn Thompson in the 1830s, arguing, based on painstaking studies of their life cycle from larval to adult stages, that cirripeds were a subclass of Crustacea, a controversy arose over their classification. Against their reclassification to the Crustacea, even after these developmental homologies with crustaceans were known, were facts that pointed to how different they were from all known crustaceans—for example, there were many hermaphrodite species of Cirripedia, while there were no known hermaphrodite crustaceans.

The details of the debate are fascinating, but we must ignore many of them here. What is interesting from the standpoint of the philosophical issue with which we are concerned is the clear *referential stability*, among zoologists of this period, of the concept "Cirripedia" before, during, and

22. Like most popular terms for groups of organisms, "barnacle" refers to the most familiar organisms grouped together by systematists in the subclass Cirripedia. It is a very large subclass of Crustacea, consisting of hundreds of species grouped by Darwin into three orders consisting of many suborders, families, subfamilies, and genera. Many species were only known in a fossilized form.

after their reclassification, a reclassification based on the discovery of a great deal of new information about them. Knowledge of their anatomy, development, and reproduction was expanding rapidly and was absolutely fundamental to the decision to reclassify them as crustaceans—a decision more or less solidified by Charles Darwin's massive, four-volume *A Monograph of the Sub-class Cirripedia*, the product of over ten years of work examining virtually every known species, both fossil and extant. What "in the world" the debate was *about* was never in question; and indeed the shared, stable concept (and the hierarchy for which it stood) was critical to the ultimate resolution of the debate.[23]

Nevertheless, a significant part of the debate over their reclassification had to do with whether the new evidence of their clear similarities to other crustaceans in early stages of development should be taken to be *fundamental* to their nature, or rather whether greater emphasis should be placed on their adult forms.[24] There is a clear answer to this question in favor of development, which is reinforced once the group can be considered in the light of its evolutionary relatedness to the other crustaceans. In fact, many of the attributes of mature barnacles that originally led to them being grouped with mollusks are shown to be both historically and developmentally related to their crustaceous nature.[25] The key

23. This example has wider historical significance than might be imagined, in two different though related respects. Over the past two decades there has been a systematic rethinking of Charles Darwin's intellectual development, based on his sustained focus on the invertebrates, from his early passion for insect collection, to his late teen years working with Robert Grant in Edinburgh on the anatomy, behavior, and classification of marine invertebrates, through the publication of his monumental four-volume study of Cirripedia, completed in 1854 (Darwin 1851–54). The influence this focus had at every level on his thinking about the origin of species has been argued most persuasively by Jonathan Hodge (1985, 207–24); by Philip Sloan (1985, 71–120); and, most recently and extensively, by Alan Love (2002, 251–89). More broadly, the reorganization of classification in these fields was closely bound up with questions of how to integrate fossil species into systems of classification and the extent to which classifications should reflect our understanding of the *evolutionary* relationships among groups of organisms.

24. I say "a significant part" because Darwin begins his monograph by reviewing six reasons for *not* reclassifying cirripeds based on their alleged fundamental differences from crustaceans—Darwin then shows that these alleged differences are based on various sorts of errors in previous research. Thus, in debates about conceptual reclassification of this kind, eliminating or correcting previous errors can play an important role.

25. Here is a beautiful example, from Darwin, concluding a painstaking description of the development of the organ that produces the "cement" that attaches barnacles to their surfaces:

> I am well aware how extremely improbable it must appear, that part of an ovarian tube should be converted into a gland, in which cellular matter is modified, so that

point philosophically is that the integration of this previously unknown developmental and historical information about the organisms grouped conceptually as Cirripedia served as the basis for them being reclassified as crustaceans.

Historically, the growth of knowledge about the referents of the concept "Cirripedia" had no significant impact on scientists' *referential* behavior toward them, but *did* make a significant difference to their *understanding* of the referents of the concept. They had not only learned more about barnacles, they had learned more about *the nature* of barnacles, what they are *actually* similar to and what their "nearest neighbors" are, those animals from which they most need to be differentiated. The phylum within which this class of organisms is to be placed, and thus the animals with which it should be grouped, and from which it should be differentiated, had changed. This, of course, does not mean that the *cirripeds* have changed, nor does the large amount of new, sometimes startling, information, some of which is relevant to their reclassification, contradict the information (insofar as it was accurate in the first place) about the typical adult forms, on which the original classification was based.[26]

Such changes are the stuff of scientific progress; it is with realizations like this one that *systematic advances* take place in a field. And, though it would be another essay to explore this subject, this example also shows the impact that wider theoretical changes can have on conceptual advance. Here, the decision to treat information about embryological de-

---

instead of aiding in the development of new beings, it forms itself into a tissue or substance, which leaves the body in order to fasten it to a foreign support. But on no other view can the structure, clearly seen by me both in the mature cirripede and in the larva, be explained, and I feel no hesitation in advancing it. I may here venture to quote the substance of a remark made by Professor [Richard] Owen, when I communicated to him the foregoing facts, namely, that there was a new problem to solve—new work to perform—to attach permanently a crustacean to a foreign body; and that hence no one could, *a priori*, tell by what singular and novel means this would be effected. (Darwin 1851a, 38–39)

Here, and throughout these four volumes, Darwin is encouraging the reader to think about such changes in evolutionary terms (he had written out a draft of a book outlining his theory of descent with modification by natural selection just before he began his investigation of the cirripeds).

26. Though it is entirely possible, and I believe actually occurred in this case, that the deeper understanding of the group can lead to a reinterpretation of earlier observations. Following this thought systematically takes us too far afield, but it is worth noting that the "tests" or "shells" of the familiar "Balanomorphic" barnacles are, in fact, the calcareous excretions that Darwin was referring to in the passage quoted in the note just above.

velopment as central for classification is closely tied to arguments that development provides evidence for the evolutionary relationships among groups of organisms.

This example is a paradigmatic case of what Rand refers to as "conceptual reclassification." Recall the context in which she introduces this idea: "The definitions of concepts may change with the changes in the designation of essential characteristics, and conceptual reclassifications may occur with the growth of our knowledge, but these changes are made possible by and do not alter the fact that a concept subsumes all the characteristics of its referents, including the yet to be discovered" (*ITOE* 66). In a series of workshops on *ITOE* that took place shortly after its publication, some contributions to which are reprinted as an appendix to the expanded second edition published in 1990, this passage provoked a request for an example. The first example Rand gives is a case in which a medical subclassification of human beings based on humoral physiology was replaced by a different set of categories. A second example, the reclassification of whales from fish to mammals, is also discussed. The historical details in this case are far more complicated than is typically realized,[27] but I believe the philosophical lessons are similar to the case presented above. The actual referents of the concept "whale" would not, or at least need not, change. So, the units integrated by the concept—the referents— need not change, even if what they are to be grouped *with* at the wider level of abstraction, and what they are to be immediately differentiated *from* within that new wider group, and the *basis* of that differentiation, must be rethought.

The crucial issue here is that such reclassifications do not *require* a change in the reference of the concept "whale" or "Cetacea"—these concepts might well subsume the same referents before and after the conceptual reclassification, and in that sense retain their identity. And this

---

27. It is unclear which, if any, important figure in the history of biology thought cetaceans were fish. The first systematic biologist in history, Aristotle, was fully aware of the (as we would say) "mammalian" characteristics of the cetaceans, despite their aquatic way of life, and thus does not refer to them as fish. (In the *History of Animals* I.6, 490b7–9, where he lists, among the three "large kinds" of blooded animals already recognized, birds, fish, and cetaceans.) Nor could they be placed in the category under which he placed most animals with these characteristics, since that category was *four-legged* live-bearing animals. I have not systematically investigated the subsequent history, but I suppose most scientific anatomists in the Renaissance would have followed Aristotle. It is certainly the case that Fabricius ab Aquapendente and William Harvey did; see Wear 1990, 8.

could be so despite the fact that the other kinds of animals with which they share their conceptual common denominators, and from which they must now be distinguished, *have* changed. In these cases the file folders have been moved to new drawers, and with that move must come a process of reintegration and interrelating with the contents of other files in that new drawer.[28] The price of (conceptual) liberty is eternal vigilance.

Behind such reclassifications lies a fundamental epistemological truth: not all new knowledge discovered about the units of an existing concept has the same epistemological status. Rand was emphatic that there is no *metaphysical* distinction between those attributes of a group of similar entities that are designated "essential" and those that are not. Moreover, it was by stressing that the notion of "essence" is *epistemological* that she was able to allow for the attributes so designated to change with advances in our knowledge.

But an implication of this important step is that we may discover new information about the beings subsumed by a concept that alters not only our understanding of which attributes are the most fundamental differentiating attributes, but also of which attributes should play the role of conceptual common denominators relative to these beings. In cases like those discussed briefly in this section, the wider group of entities from which the units of the target concept should be immediately distinguished has changed. There is a fundamental shift in our understanding of how the wider set of attributes are related to one another, and which of those attributes are most central to establishing the place of the concept in the wider hierarchy of biological concepts.

In such cases, reclassification is mandated without leading to any need to reject the original integration represented by the concept. The new understanding of the development and life cycle of the cirripeds simply adds to the list of attributes in virtue of which they are integrated as

28. The analysis of reclassification in Peikoff 1991, 104, does not consider this possibility. He writes: "Occasionally, a process of reclassification—a change in the filing system itself—is necessitated by advancing knowledge. Even in such a case, which is rare, a concept does not change, or vary from one man to another. The old concept is simply dropped outright and replaced by a new one." It is correct to see such cases as I have discussed, metaphorically, as a change in the filing system. But such changes do not necessarily imply that old concepts are replaced. Rather, reclassification may represent a reconsideration of the wider group with which the units of the concept should be placed, based on new information that may lead to a reconsideration of the question of which attributes are most fundamental to their classification.

units of the concept. But that new understanding also leads to a reconsideration of the place of the concept within the hierarchy represented by biological systematics. And part of that change involves learning to differentiate Cirripedia from a systematically different group of organisms by treating different attributes as the relevant conceptual common denominators.

Making such decisions about the bases of integration and differentiation are key processes in concept-*formation,* and thus one might expect that such conceptual reclassifications would require the formation of a new concept. In these and many similar cases, however, the concepts retain *referential stability* and the new information is integrated with everything we previously knew about the referents. How is that possible? I suggested earlier that if we see concepts as tools of cognition, as ways of "holding" a group of referents together as a single unit, concepts retain their hold on their referents through the process of acquiring new information about them. But in some cases the new information acquired produces not merely an *additive* change in the content of the concept, but a *qualitative* change in those aspects of its content that are most important to the classificatory role of the concept. Concepts are open-end classifications, and this very fact may lead, as in the case we have been exploring, to significant *reclassification.* Notice too that a significant role in the decision to reclassify the Cirripedia is based on changing views about the relative explanatory importance, especially within an evolutionary framework, of information about their developmental life history. This was not just new information, but explanatorily fundamental new information.[29]

Conclusion

I have briefly considered an example from the history of biology in order to make concrete the idea of conceptual reclassification, in which a concept, in virtue of being open-ended, may continue to refer to the same kind of existents, through a systematic process of reintegration and differentiation. Such cases constitute a kind of conceptual reclassification that is *intermediate* between advances in knowledge without the need to con-

29. Relatively speaking, even in the history of science, such cases are rare. But they are also extremely important, since they are a subclass of the cases that can lead to allegations of "meaning incommensurability" resulting from scientific change. More positively, they are also among those cases that can be cited as examples of the systematic nature of scientific progress.

sider conceptual development or revision, and advances that require rejecting and/or replacing a previously formed concept. My aim has been to show that the Objectivist theory of concepts provides the machinery we need to understand how such concepts retain their identity and meaning through systematic advances in scientific knowledge, including systematic rearrangements in the network of concepts in a particular scientific domain.

Part Two
DISCUSSION

Concepts and Kinds

Rand on Concepts, Definitions, and the Advance of Science

Comments on Gotthelf and Lennox

PAUL E. GRIFFITHS

yn Rand's theory of concept-formation plays an important role in her
broader program of Objectivist epistemology. Some of the themes in
her work correspond to core themes in what Ian Hacking calls the
"tradition of natural kinds" in mainstream Anglo-American philosophy
(Hacking 1991c). In particular, Rand's theory converges on the idea that
concepts are intellectual tools forged by human beings in order to allow
them to recover elements of the structure of the world around them and
thus to achieve pragmatically successful action.

It is not clear to me, however, that Rand's existing body of work addresses the major current problems facing this strand of philosophical
thought. This should hardly surprise us, as mainstream analytic philosophy only started to discover these problems in the 1980s. The interesting
question is whether these problems pose any fundamental challenge to
Rand's theory of concept-formation.

The Tradition of Natural Kinds

Hacking has, correctly in my view, located the beginning of the modern discussion of natural kinds in early-nineteenth-century discussions
of the relationship between scientific taxonomies of nature and inductive

inference. The vital importance of taxonomy to reliable induction was one of the few points on which John Stuart Mill and William Whewell could agree. In his review of Mill's *Logic,* Whewell wrote, "I consider also that the recognition of *Kinds* . . . as classes in which we have not a finite but an *inexhaustible* body of resemblances amongst individuals, and as groups made by nature, not by mere definition is very valuable, as stopping the inroad to an endless train of false philosophy" (Whewell 1860, 290). Mill's and Whewell's point was that if a science can only hit upon a good taxonomy of the objects in its domain, then the road to inductive inquiry lies wide open. Until that time, however, no amount of careful data gathering will avail. Perhaps the most famous example of this fact in the history of science is the fruitless (but rigorous!) nineteenth-century attempt to determine the atomic weights of elements that preceded the realization that naturally occurring samples of those elements contain arbitrary combinations of isotopes of differing weight.

Rand's use of the term "definition" to refer to a temporary stopping point in our attempts to understand nature, with its implication that definitions are defeasible by empirical facts seems odd to analytic philosophers but is, in reality, very much in the spirit of Mill and Whewell. This way of thinking about definitions is so much a part of the practice of the inductive sciences that it is not hard to find scientists speaking explicitly in these terms. Here are two emotion researchers: "Definitions in science are really working definitions. They provide an orientation but they are subject to change when anything relevant is discovered" (Oatley and Jenkins 1996); "We all recognize that nature is complex . . . we must sharpen our conceptual tools as best we can and have faith that in using them to untangle the complexity we shall see how to fashion better ones" (Hinde 1985, 990). Nevertheless, in philosophical discourse, "definition" is more typically used to refer to a description associated with a term by stipulation, any change of which reduces the terms on either side of that change to mere homonyms. This notion of "definition" has its uses, especially in the formal sciences, but in the tradition of natural kinds it has no obvious use and we can usefully adopt Rand's usage and regard a definition as a temporary resting place in our ongoing search for knowledge. Whewell himself was notably dismissive of the value of traditional "definitions." In his day, biological species were among the most successful examples of natural kinds, as they remain today, and Whewell noted that, although everyone knows what a dog is, few people could even attempt an adequate definition. Nor should they try, since the history of science is littered with strictly defined categories of no scientific value. "Superlunary object," for example, is that rare thing, a category defined by necessary and sufficient conditions, but since Galileo it has been recognized as one of the most arbitrary categories anyone could dream up. Whether a category is worth having has little to do with how strictly we can define it and everything to do with whether it captures, however vaguely, some set of nomic relationships between phenomena.

In the mainstream tradition of thought about natural kinds, the idea has two important aspects. Natural kinds are associated with a vision of *naturalness* and also with a picture of *conceptual dynamics*. The "naturalness" of kinds is the idea that they are constructed by nature and not by our intellect, discovered and not invented, and are "mind-independent." The dynamic associated with the natural kind idea is that of progressively refining our definition in the light of our growing empirical knowledge of nature. It is on this picture of conceptual dynamics, and which I believe is fundamentally correct, that Rand converges. It is less clear that she converges on the conception of "naturalness."

A useful way to strip the vision of conceptual dynamics away from the vision of naturalness so as to consider their merits independently is to adopt for the former the term "investigative kind," which Ingo Brigandt (2003) suggests as a replacement for "natural kind." An investigative kind concept is a concept that it *makes sense* to seek to clarify through empirical inquiry. Thus, it makes sense to try to clarify what we mean by "inflation" or "teenage depression" through an inductive investigation of prototypical samples of these things. It makes no sense to attempt this for "triangle" or "act legal in Pennsylvania." Brigandt's idea converges in some respects with Hans-Jorg Rheinberger's term "epistemic object." Epistemic objects enter scientific discourse not through being clearly defined but by being introduced as targets of research—*putative* entities that are discussed and investigated through certain experimental practices (Rheinberger 1997, 2000). "Gene" and "species" would be prime examples. As in Rand's theory of concept-formation, the idea of an investigative kind assumes that we have certain *goals* that can be served by adjusting the definition of that kind. In the tradition of natural kinds these goals have usually been assumed to be those of induction and explanation, but, as we will see, this is no longer undisputed.

The other aspect of the tradition of natural kinds is a vision of *natu-*

ralness. Thus, for some contemporary philosophers, notably Brian Ellis, "natural kind" implies fundamental kinds in the most fundamental sciences, kinds whose stability and inductive utility is underpinned by the most fundamental laws of nature. Genes and species are too parochial to be truly natural. For others the term "natural kind" can be extended to the special sciences, but still implies a single best taxonomy of nature independent of any particular human purposes. This conception of "naturalness" has been the focus of John Dupré's (1993) well-known rejection of the natural kind concept. While I make no pretense to Rand scholarship, it seems to me, guided by Allan Gotthelf's and James Lennox's readings, that Rand has a much more human conception of what we should aim for in forming a concept. Concepts are for *life* in all its aspects and we need criteria for judging them in many domains besides the fundamental sciences. The objective aspect of Rand's theory of concept-formation seems to me to come down to a very strong form of intersubjectivity, as embodied in her slogan that a correct definition is one "good for all men." Rand tries to enforce this strong intersubjectivity via the condition that a definition-at-a-time must reflect the complete body of knowledge at that time and must achieve maximum cognitive efficiency. I will now consider three phenomena that feature in contemporary discussion of natural kinds and that I think suggest that requirements of this sort may not yield a unique solution to the question of which definition we should adopt (I mean definition *sensu* Rand, and the term is used below only in this sense). These phenomena are multiple dimensions of efficiency, multiple epistemic projects, and nonepistemic projects.

Multiple Dimensions of Efficiency

The first problem is that there are multiple dimensions of efficiency that must be traded off against one another. Unless these dimensions can be reduced to a common metric, which seems highly unlikely, considerations of cognitive efficiency will at best produce a partial ordering of definitions. Useful scientific categories need to produce *reliable* predictions (force) in a *large domain* of properties (scope) (Griffiths 1999). The classic examples of natural kinds, chemical elements and biological species, achieve both desiderata to a high degree, but there is no intrinsic link between the two. I have argued that, in some biological domains, categories defined in terms of shared adaptive function achieve scope at a very considerable cost in force and that we should not adopt them for certain scientific purposes because for *those specific purposes* force is more valuable (Griffiths 1997; see also Lawrence and Calder 2004). For other purposes, these "ecological" categories with high scope and low force may have value. There is also a third consideration to take into account when choosing a definition—theoretical fruitfulness. Scope and force must both be assessed relative to our current knowledge, but we are also interested in which schemes of categorization will open up new projects of scientific inquiry that have not yet been explored. This dimension is obviously much less open to any precise treatment than the other two.

My first worry about the idea of a definition "good for all men," then, is that there are several, apparently orthogonal, ways of being good.

Multiple Epistemic Projects

It is surely uncontroversial that different scientists may have different legitimate scientific projects. It is perhaps less obvious that these projects may involve the very same concept and may drag it in different directions. Let me take an example from my own research to illustrate this. The majority of molecular biologists are interested in using genes as epistemically powerful entry points to the molecular pathways that underlie developmental and physiological processes. Regions of nucleic acid molecules stand in identifiable linear correspondences to one another and to proteins and the consequent ability to locate the "image" of a molecule in DNA or RNA is the key to many of the techniques of molecular bioscience (Waters 1994, 2000). Molecular biologists who work in molecular systematics or comparative genomics, however, have a different and very specific set of interests. They are interested in identifying the corresponding parts of genomes across species so as to reconstruct evolutionary history and also as a way make inferences about gene function. In a recent study, my collaborator Karola Stotz and I asked biologists to rate the extent to which they took their work to have "a comparative focus" and then asked them to comment on the transcription event shown in figure 1.

Whether the biologists classified the five exons illustrated in figure 1 as parts of a single gene reflected whether their research had a comparative focus (figure 2). This makes perfect sense, since a comparative biologist would regard the wheat sequences as *the same thing* as the corresponding sequences in mosses and mammals that are unproblematic examples of a single gene (technically, these sequences are "orthologous" to those in wheat, meaning that they are derived from a common ancestral

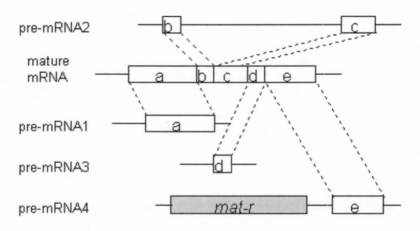

FIGURE 1. Subunit 1 of the respiratory chain NADH dehydrogenase is encoded by NAD1, which in the mitochondria of flowering plants is fragmented into five coding segments that are scattered over at least 40kb and interspersed with other unrelated coding sequences. In Wheat, the example shown here, the five exons together encoding a polypeptide of 325 amino acids, require one cis-splicing event (between the exons b/c) and three trans-splicing events (between exons a/b, c/d and d/e) for assembly of the open reading frame (ORF). In addition, RNA editing is required, including a C to U substitution to create the initiation codon for this ORF. In some mosses and in mammalia the homologous (orthologous) ORF for NAD1 is transcribed from an uninterrupted stretch of DNA.

sequence). The other molecular biologists, however, relied on the actual facts in wheat to make their decision and here *NAD1* looks very unlike a single gene. In fact, it fails most of the standard criteria for being a single gene, such as having a single promoter and being transcribed from a single open reading frame.

A much more general version of the idea illustrated by this example, namely that there are different sets of identity conditions for the concept of the gene depending on the research context, can be found in the work of Lenny Moss (2001, 2002).

The case of the gene illustrates that a set of objects (DNA sequence elements) can be unquestionably real and yet not impose any clear requirements for how we should define them until we specify *very specific* epistemic goals. The general goals of gaining knowledge and achieving pragmatic effectiveness as we act in the world are simply not sufficient to

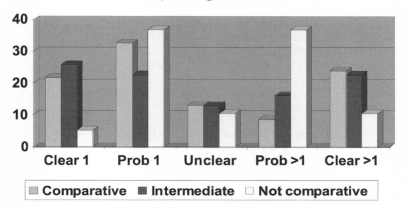

FIGURE 2. Answers to the question "Would you describe this case as one in which *one* or *more than one gene* is involved in generating the final transcript(s) and/or the polypeptide(s) that result from the process described?" asked with respect to the transcription event in figure 1.

guide us in trying to decide how to define "gene." My second worry about the idea of a definition "good for all men," then, is that several different definitions may be good, depending on exactly what those people are trying to achieve.

Nonepistemic Projects

It has been suggested that the "naturalness" of natural kind concepts is a matter of the purposes they are used for. Classic natural kinds are used for epistemic purposes, whereas many other concepts are used for pragmatic or normative purposes (Hacking 1992, 1995, Griffiths 2004). This leads naturally to the idea that there are "pragmatic kinds" and "normative kinds" in addition to the better-known natural kinds.

In defense of "pragmatic kinds," as opposed to classically natural (e.g., scientific) kinds, John Dupré (2004) writes, "Some scientific terms strike me as probably lower on the scale [of utility] than many artefact terms. 'Reinforced concrete beam' is a very useful term in explanations of how a wide variety of buildings stand up, but it would be odd to call it natural. 'Gonadotropin-releasing hormone antagonist' is only useful for an extremely narrow range of explanatory functions, though it's very good when you do need it, and plausibly very natural. Perhaps a bit more needs to be said about the nature in natural kinds." His point, I take it, is that if we consider human purposes and values more generally, a robust scientific understanding of the basic principles underlying phenomena needs supplementing by many approximate but facile ways of classifying nature that let us get by in the real world, in real time, and at a realistic cognitive cost. In itself, this is not in conflict with Rand's notion of achieving maximum cognitive efficiency, for it certainly does not seem part of her project to exalt the realm of the theoretical above that of the practical. However, as with the different scientific purposes discussed in the last section, pragmatic considerations can pull the same concept in different directions from purely scientific concepts, so that what is "good for all men" depends on what they need to achieve.

Of all the ideas found in contemporary discussions of natural kinds, perhaps the least sympathetic with the spirit of Rand's theory of concept-formation is the suggestion that *normative* considerations might be relevant to how to classify nature and draw the boundaries of our concepts. As an example of a "normative kind," Stephen Stich and Dominic Murphy have suggested "mental illness"—psychopathologies have little in common neurologically or psychologically, but are all "ways of going wrong" relative to some socially defined conception of normal functioning (Brown et al. 1999, 25). Similarly, John Doris (2000) has responded to my claim that vernacular emotion terms do not name natural kinds by arguing that, for example, anger may form a unified kind for the purposes of assessing whether anger is *warranted*. More generally, if Doris is right, emotion categories function in our language not as part of our theory of mind, but as part of normative social practices. More radically still, Hacking has argued that some concepts, child abuse for example, exist in large part as elements of a project of ameliorative social reform (Hacking 1991a, 1992). The boundaries of the category are altered in step with changing conceptions of human flourishing and of the rights and responsibilities of parents and offspring.

My third worry about the idea of a definition "good for all men," then, is that we do many things with our concepts and that some of these do not apparently fit comfortably within the framework of Objectivist epistemology.

To conclude, the account of conceptual change found in Rand's theory of concept-formation is strikingly prescient with respect to some aspects of the mainstream "tradition of natural kinds." If, however, Rand's ideas are to make a significant contribution to contemporary philosophy they will have to deal with some of the difficulties that this tradition has recently encountered. I have tried to sketch some of these, inevitably inadequately in this small space, and hope that those who wish to carry Rand's work forward will take these remarks in the spirit of constructive challenge.

Natural Kinds and Rand's Theory of Concepts
Reflections on Griffiths
ONKAR GHATE

In his commentary on the essays in the present volume by Allan Gotthelf and by James G. Lennox, Paul Griffiths raises a number of interesting issues about (1) how to situate Rand's theory of concepts, particularly with regard to recent debates about natural kinds, and (2) whether her theory has the resources to address some recent findings about the nature of concepts. I will address a few of the issues he raises in my brief, exploratory comments.

Natural Kinds and a Complete Taxonomy

Griffiths in his comments writes,

In the mainstream tradition of thought about natural kinds, the idea has two important aspects. Natural kinds are associated with a vision of *naturalness* and also with a picture of *conceptual dynamics*. The "naturalness" of kinds is the idea that they are constructed by nature and not by our intellect, discovered and not invented, and are "mind-independent." The dynamic associated with the natural kind idea is that of progressively refining our definition in the light of our growing empirical knowledge of nature. Rand converges on this picture of conceptual dynamics, and I believe it is fundamentally correct. It is less clear that she converges on the conception of "naturalness."

It is definitely correct that Rand's theory of concepts maintains that it is often mandatory to revise our definitions of concepts in light of our growing knowledge of nature (*ITOE* 40–54; Lennox in the present volume). I think it is also correct to say that Rand would *reject* the mainstream conception of naturalness described by Griffiths.

Although Rand argues that a properly formed concept has a basis in the facts of a mind-independent reality, she also argues that mind-independent reality does not come preclassified or presorted into kinds. The abstractness and universality of (valid) concepts—the facts that a concept ranges over qualitatively and perceptually different things that count as instances or units of the concept (the concept's abstractness) and that a concept encompasses all instances or units, whether past, present, or future, which obviously includes existents the knower has never personally encountered (the concept's universality)—are a product of the mind *processing* the facts of a mind-independent reality. Absent this mental processing, neither abstractness nor universality nor groups nor kinds exist.

Here is the key passage from *ITOE* where Rand makes this point (the rest of *ITOE* is in essence an explanation of her point):

> *The ability to regard entities as units is man's distinctive method of cognition,* which other living species are unable to follow.
>
> A unit is an existent regarded as a separate member of a group of two or more similar members. (Two stones are two units; so are two square feet of ground, if regarded as distinct parts of a continuous stretch of ground.) Note that the concept "unit" involves an act of consciousness (a selective focus, a certain way of regarding things), but that it is *not* an arbitrary creation of consciousness: it is a method of identification or classification according to the attributes which a consciousness observes in reality. This method permits any number of classifications and cross-classifications: one may classify things according to their shape or color or weight or size or atomic structure; but the criterion of classification is not invented, it is perceived in reality. Thus the concept "unit" is a bridge between metaphysics and epistemology: units do not exist *qua* units, what exists are things, but *units are things viewed by a consciousness in certain existing relationships.* (*ITOE* 6–7)

Griffiths writes, in the first section of his discussion, that one way of capturing the mainstream idea of natural kinds is that the notion "implies a single best taxonomy of nature independent of any particular human purposes." Given what has been said above, I think Rand would argue that *her* theory has no such implication—and that it would be defective if it did; this further suggests that she rejects the mainstream notion of naturalness.

The notion of a "single best taxonomy" seems to be the idea of identifying the unique, correct place of each existent in one's "conceptual scheme." And this smacks of the idea that each existent in reality has a metaphysical essence that we must discover, a metaphysical essence that makes the existent the kind of thing that it "really" is and fixes its single and proper place in the "best taxonomy" of reality. Rand argues, however, that essences are not metaphysical but epistemological (*ITOE* 40–54). One implication of her theory is that an existent can be subsumed validly under many different concepts, no subsumption being more "real" or "correct" than the others; John Smith, say, is both a unit of the concept *male* and of the concept *doctor*. Loosely speaking, on Rand's view an existent like John Smith can have many different essences qua being a unit of different concepts (strictly speaking, no existents have essences according to Rand: only concepts do).

None of this is meant to suggest, however, that there cannot be specialized, delimited contexts in which the idea of a taxonomy has meaning and where one might want to create a single, best taxonomy. But I do not think that this should be taken as the goal of all science or of concept-formation as such.

Consider, for instance, the case of chemical elements and the periodic table. When, after much observation, experimentation, and thought, scientists reached the point of grasping that there are many elements in nature and that the subject of chemistry is, in fact, the study of these elements and their interactions, they saw the need to catalog the elements. They could do so as a simple list, perhaps putting the elements in alphabetical order. But because they also knew that there are many similarities and differences among the properties of the elements, and that some of the properties seemed fundamental, others derivative, they naturally searched for a causal organization of the elements. Such an organization would achieve unit-economy, making possible further integrations and discoveries. The search culminated in the periodic table and the full causal explanation provided by the atomic theory. It might be correct to view the periodic table as a single, best taxonomy of the elements (of course one must allow that a new element could be discovered, which must then be integrated into the taxonomy). But the need for the taxonomy arises in a specialized context.

Here I think are at least a few of the factors that generate such a specialized, delimited context. First, one has identified a significant number of coordinate items, the elements, which form the foundation of a whole field of investigation, chemistry, and which one needs to organize and catalog conceptually. Second, one observes many similarities and differences among the items' properties, some of which seem fundamental and others, derivative. This suggests that a causal organization of the items is possible, and by the nature of the quest, what one is seeking to create is a single, best taxonomy in that context.

(Compare this to the organization of the alphabet: the alphabet consists of coordinate items, the individual letters, which form the foundation for the whole field of visually encoding spoken language. One needs to organize these items, but since they all are roughly coordinate items with no (or few) causal relationships, one just establishes a list: a, b, c, d, e, . . . x, y, z.)

Similar considerations to those in chemistry in regard to the elements perhaps apply in the generation of a biological taxonomy. Living organisms are the foundation of biology: the science of biology (roughly put) studies living organisms. Biologists face a sprawling number of coordinate items, which need to be cataloged. And as biological knowledge advances, as many similarities and differences are noted among living organisms, some of which appear fundamental and some derivative, the idea of a causal organization, a scientific taxonomy, occurs to some genius(es). And here perhaps the theory of evolution plays the role that the atomic theory did for the periodic table of elements, in that the theory cements an organism's unique place in the evolutionary chain, thereby generating a single, best taxonomy in that context.

But the fact that certain sciences in certain contexts and for certain reasons need to generate a single, best taxonomy of a multiplicity of items does not suggest that the validity of man's concepts rests on discovering a single, best taxonomy of all existents in reality.

In fact, Rand stresses precisely the opposite. Man's concepts, she writes, "represent a system of mental filing and cross-filing, so complex that the largest electronic computer is a child's toy by comparison. This system serves as the context, the frame-of-reference, by means of which man grasps and classifies (and studies further) every existent he encounters and every aspect of reality" (*ITOE* 69). Notice her term "cross-filing." She is well aware that conceptualizing the same existent in different ways and from different perspectives is crucial to our identifying and understanding the facts of reality. Our system of concepts is not like a two-dimensional biological taxonomy, rising from species to genera to families, but a three-dimensional, complex network that contains many existents that are cross-filed. And there are optional elements within the overall system. But it is a system, which means that it must integrate logically. She writes:

> A scientist could not specialize in a particular branch of study without a wider context, without the correlation and integration of his work to the other aspects of the same subject. Consider, for example, the science of medicine. If the concept "man" did not stand as the unifying concept of that science (if some scientists studied only man's lungs; others, only the stomach; still others, only the blood circulation; and still others, only the retina of the eye), if all new discoveries were not to be ascribed to the same entity and, therefore, were not to be integrated in strict compliance with the law of non-contradiction, the collapse of medical science would not take long to follow. (*ITOE* 68)

The crucial epistemological task of philosophy, on her view, is precisely to guide this integration. "The highest responsibility of philosophers is to serve as the guardians and integrators of human knowledge" (*ITOE* 74). They should not do so, however, by attempting to create a single, best taxonomy of nature, in which the phenomenon of cross-filling has been eliminated.

Investigative Kinds and Nominal Kinds

Since Griffiths suspects, rightly as I have argued, that Rand does not accept the mainstream conception of "naturalness," he suggests that it would be useful to separate the issue of conceptual dynamics from that of naturalness.

> A useful way to strip the vision of conceptual dynamics away from the vision of naturalness so as to consider their merits independently is to adopt for the former the term "investigative kind," which Ingo Brigandt . . . suggests as a replacement for "natural kind." An investigative kind concept is a concept that it *makes sense* to seek to clarify through empiri-

cal inquiry. . . . As in Rand's theory of concept-formation, the idea of an
investigative kind assumes that we have certain *goals* that can be served
by adjusting the definition of that kind. In the tradition of natural kinds
these goals have usually been assumed to be those of induction and explanation, but, as we will see, this is no longer undisputed.

In contrast to investigative kind concepts would be concepts for which it
does *not* make sense to seek to clarify them through empirical inquiry,
sometimes termed "nominal kind" concepts. The concept "uncle" is often regarded as a nominal kind concept, for which there is no project of
further clarification through observational study. No further research is
needed on what makes uncles uncles. Once one grasps the kinship relationship (in the narrow sense, an uncle is the brother of a person's mother
or father), there is nothing more to grasp. The extension and intension
are fixed. This is not so for an investigative kind concept like "species"
or "zinc": further research is needed, after we form the concept, on what
makes a species a species or on what makes zinc zinc; neither the concept's extension nor its intension is fixed.

I think it is unlikely that Rand would accept any such classification of
different types of concepts. To be sure, she does argue, as Griffiths notes,
that concepts are tools made by man to advance his life: "While I make
no pretense to Rand scholarship, it seems to me, guided by Allan Gotthelf
and James Lennox's readings, that Rand has a much more human conception of what we should aim for in forming a concept. Concepts are for *life*
in all its aspects and we need criteria for judging them in many domains
besides the fundamental sciences." Here is the crucial passage in Rand
where she makes this point:

> Many kinds of existents are integrated into concepts and represented by
> special words, but many others are not and are identified only by means
> of verbal descriptions. What determines man's decision to integrate a
> given group of existents into a concept? The requirements of cognition
> (and the principle of unit-economy).
>
> There is a great deal of latitude, on the periphery of man's concep-
> tual vocabulary, a broad area where the choice is optional, but in regard
> to certain central categories of existents the formation of concepts is
> mandatory. This includes such categories as: (a) the perceptual concretes
> with which men deal daily, represented by the first level of abstractions;
> (b) new discoveries of science; (c) new man-made objects which differ

in their essential characteristics from the previously known objects (e.g., "television"); (d) complex human relationships involving combinations of physical and psychological behavior (e.g., "marriage," "law," "justice").

These four categories represent existents with which men have to deal constantly, in many different contexts, from many different aspects, either in daily physical action or, more crucially, in mental action and further study. The mental weight of carrying these existents in one's head by means of perceptual images or lengthy verbal descriptions is such that no human mind could handle it. The need of condensation, of unit-reduction, is obvious in such cases. . . .

The descriptive complexity of a given group of existents, the frequency of their use, and the requirements of cognition (of further study) are the main reasons for the formation of new concepts. Of these reasons, the requirements of cognition are the paramount one. (*ITOE* 69–70)

But the fact that Rand argues that there are different reasons for why concepts should be formed does not imply that the resulting products are different, that is, that different *types* of concepts are formed. There is nothing in her theory to suggest that she would accept a distinction between investigative kind concepts and nominal kind concepts, and much to suggest that she would not.

There may be a distinction to be made between an individual's reasons in forming the concept "uncle" and his reasons in forming the concept "zinc." But that does not mean that the process of forming the two concepts, or the nature of the resulting concepts qua concepts, is different. Rand's theory of concepts, I think, would explain both concepts by reference to the processes of differentiating, grasping similarities, and omitting measurements (for the details of the theory, of course, see *ITOE*). And the resulting mental products in each case would be essentially the same: "a mental integration of two or more units possessing the same distinguishing characteristic(s), with their particular measurements omitted" (*ITOE* 13).

In other words, it may well be that the primary reason one forms the concept of zinc is that one wants to engage in further study of the new material one thinks one has discovered, whereas the primary reason one forms the concept of uncle is not that one wants to engage in further study of uncles. Further, it may be true that as knowledge advances one learns a great deal more about the units of the concept of "zinc" than one does about the units of the concept of "uncle." And it may be true that the growth in one's knowledge about the nature of zinc and of surrounding facts of reality causes one to change one's definition of zinc, but that the growth of one's knowledge does not cause one to change one's definition of uncle. But as far as I can see, on Rand's theory none of this suggests that the processes of forming the concepts, or the resulting concepts that are formed, are different. Stating it in terms of the metaphor that Rand uses of concepts as mental file folders, none of the factors mentioned suggest that we have two different *types* of file folders.

Note that on Rand's theory, the fact (if it is a fact) that as knowledge advances we find the need to change the definition of "zinc" but not of "uncle," does not imply that we do not learn more about the units of the concept "uncle" (including of what makes uncles uncles, if this kind of phrase has any real meaning). For instance, discoveries in biology explain why one observes more physical similarities between one's uncles and one's (biological) parents than between one's parents and their friends. Further, discoveries in biology explain what it means to be biologically related to someone, such as being their brother or sister, and shed light on what it means to be a brother and therefore on what makes an uncle an uncle.

In comments on a previous draft of this response, Griffiths asked me to clarify whether, if the above account of Rand's theory is correct, she has some distinction corresponding to that between knowledge that is constitutive of a concept and knowledge that is incidental. And if she does not, how does she find a basis for the traditional idea that some things are true a priori? These are large topics, and I can only indicate here what her theory maintains, but not really why.

Rand rejects both the division of truths into those that are a priori and those that are a posteriori and the division of a concept's meaning into its extension and its intension. She rejects both because she rejects the whole analytic-synthetic dichotomy (Peikoff, "The Analytic-Synthetic Dichotomy," *ITOE* 88–121). According to her theory, a (valid) concept is a mental integration of (metaphysically similar) existents—an integration that includes *all* of the characteristics of the existents that are being regarded as units, whether or not those characteristics are presently known and whether or not those characteristics are specified in the (current) definition. There is no knowledge about the units that is incidental to the concept. (This does not change the fact, however, that there must be valid reasons for forming a concept in the first place. And if one later discovers that one's reasons were not valid ones, one might delete or drastically revamp the mental file folder, since what one has discovered is that it is defective *as* a mental file folder.)

Rand, it is important to note, rejects any equation of a concept with its definition (another point for which Griffiths asked for elaboration on my earlier draft). On her theory, a concept is a mental integration of existents that are being regarded as units. A definition is a device to enable us properly to retain and use our concepts. As Peikoff explains her view,

> When a man reaches a certain level of conceptual complexity, he needs to discover a method of organizing and interrelating his concepts; he needs a method that will enable him to keep each of his concepts clearly distinguished from all the others, each connected to a specific group of existents clearly distinguished from the other existents he knows. (In the early stages of conceptual development, when a child's concepts are comparatively few in number and designate directly perceivable concretes, "ostensive definitions" are sufficient for this purpose.) The method consists of *defining* each concept, by specifying the characteristic(s) of its units upon which the greatest number of their other known characteristics depends, and which distinguishes the units from all other known existents. The characteristic(s) which fulfills this requirement is designated the "*essential*" characteristic, in that context of knowledge. . . .
>
> On the objective, contextual view of essences, a concept does *not* mean only the essential or defining characteristics of its units. To designate a certain characteristic as "essential" or "defining" is to *select,* from the total content of the concept, the characteristic that best condenses and differentiates that content in a specific cognitive context. Such a selection presupposes the relationship between the concept and its units: it presupposes that the concept is an integration of units, and that its content consists of its units, including *all* their characteristics. It is only because of this fact that the same concept can receive varying definitions in varying cognitive contexts. . . .
>
> The nominalist view that a concept is merely a shorthand tag for its definition represents a profound failure to grasp the function of a definition in the process of concept-formation. (Peikoff, *ITOE* 102–3)

Three Worries

Griffiths raises three specific worries about Rand's theory of concepts, in particular for her view that a proper definition must be "good for all men." As Rand herself writes, an "objective definition, valid for all men, is one that designates the *essential* distinguishing characteristic(s) and genus of the existents subsumed under a given concept—according to all the relevant knowledge available at that stage of mankind's development. (Who decides, in case of disagreements? As in all issues pertaining to objectivity, there is no ultimate authority, except reality and the mind of every individual who judges the evidence by the *objective* method of judgment: logic)" (*ITOE* 46).

Griffiths's basic worry is that there will not be a "unique solution to the question of which definition we should adopt" because there are competing factors relevant to the formulation of a good definition. Among these factors are that there exist multiple dimensions of (epistemic or cognitive) efficiency, multiple epistemic projects, and nonepistemic projects.

If we keep in mind that Rand does not equate a concept with a definition, does not argue that there is a single, best taxonomy of the existents in reality, allows that there can be more specialized definitions of a concept for the purposes of a science (*ITOE* 46–47, 233–35), and recognizes that there must be valid reasons for forming a concept in the first place, I think we can see that Griffiths's worries can be addressed by Rand's theory of concepts.

In regard to the issue of multiple dimensions of efficiency, I think what is crucial to note is that on Rand's theory this would primarily be an issue of which concepts we should form, not of what definitions we should adopt. Griffiths writes, at the start of his second section, "Multiple Dimensions of Efficiency": "Useful scientific categories need to produce *reliable* predictions (force) in a *large domain* of properties (scope). . . . There is no intrinsic link between the two. I have argued that, in some biological domains, categories defined in terms of shared adaptive function achieve scope at a very considerable cost in force and that we should not adopt them for certain scientific purposes because for *those specific purposes* force is more valuable. . . . For other purposes, these 'ecological' categories with high scope and low force may have value." This seems to be a point about our categories and concepts, not their definitions. The point seems to be that we should form two sets of concepts in the given contexts. This presumably would violate the idea of a single, best taxonomy of reality, but as we have seen, Rand's theory is not committed to this idea. Far from being a problem, the formation of multiple categories and cross-classifications is essential to human knowledge on her view.

If, however, the point is not that there should be two sets of concepts but rather two definitions of the same concept, this too could be accommodated by Rand's theory. If we are really dealing with the same concept integrating the same units, but two specialized sciences each requires its own specialized definition, this would be proper so long as there is a more generic definition of the concept that both agree on and are in effect subdividing.

Similar things on behalf of Rand's theory, I think, should be said for the issue of multiple epistemic projects. One either would have two (or more) sets of concepts carving up the world differently, which represent cross-classifications of existents, or one would have two (or more) specialized definitions that subdivide a more generic definition shared by all. Not being a specialist in biology, however, I am in no position to determine what should be said about the interesting example of the concept "gene" that Griffiths presents. It could be that there is more than one concept at work here; it could be that it is the same concept at work but one that requires varying specialized definitions; it could be that there is more than one concept at work and all the concepts are subdivisions of a more global concept, a global concept that is in play but that has not been formally identified.

Finally, in regard to the existence of nonepistemic projects, we have seen that although in Rand's theory the requirement of further study is the primary factor in deciding whether a concept needs to be formed, it is not the only factor. Concepts are tools to aid both thought and action. The frequency of our interactions with some similar existents, for instance, may lead to the need to integrate those existents into a new concept. If we keep this in mind, I think we will see that the issue is again similar to that contained in the earlier worries: the need for multiple concepts and the rejection of a single, best taxonomy of reality. For instance, although scientific concepts grow out of our prescientific concepts, it need not be the case that the scientific concepts (always) replace the earlier concepts.

Griffiths seems most worried about nonepistemic projects that are normative. But in Rand's philosophy a normative subject, such as ethics, is a complex cognitive, epistemic subject, which suggests that she would not share this worry (see *VOS* and *RM*).

As a last example to illustrate his third worry, Griffiths notes that "more radically still, Hacking has argued that some concepts, child abuse for example, exist in large part as elements of a project of ameliorative social reform. . . . The boundaries of the category are altered in step with changing conceptions of human flourishing and of the rights and responsibilities of parents and offspring."

But on Rand's view a conception of human flourishing is an epistemic, philosophic, and scientific matter, about which we do and will learn more over time. On her approach, there is nothing radical in the suggestion that this new knowledge may lead us to improve our concepts or our definitions of, say, moral values or moral virtues. The same holds for our conceptions of the rights and responsibilities of parents and children. Rand regards the whole issue of individual rights as an aspect of a proper understanding of the conditions of human flourishing, knowledge of which can again expand over time. So I do not think she would consider this kind of example to be problematic for her theory. (None of this is to imply, of course, that a notion of, say, "child abuse" that basically stands in a person's mind as "any form of parenting that I dislike and want to outlaw" would be a valid conceptualization according to Rand's theory of concepts. Any cognitive subject can be approached noncognitively.)

Definitions

Rand on Definitions—One Size Fits All?

Comments on Gotthelf

JIM BOGEN

R and's normative discussion of definitions and concepts assumes that all definitions are of the same kind, do the same kinds of cognitive work, and should be evaluated against the same standards. This gives rise to troubles reminiscent of the ones Edouard Machery exposes with regard to concepts in cognitive psychology. Machery argues that the phenomena uncovered by cognitive psychologists are too various to account for without appeal to significantly different kinds of concepts (Machery 2010, 195–202). By the same token I think that, contrary to Rand, specific cognitive performances in scientific reasoning are too various to benefit from, let alone require, the same kind of definitions. My second and third sections below discuss examples from epidemiology and neuroscience of definitions that serve their cognitive purposes perfectly well even though they do not measure up to Rand's standards.

Rand's File-Folder Concepts and Definitions

Rand says concepts are "mental integrations" of individuals, characteristics and other sorts of things "isolated according to a specific characteristic[s] and united by a specific definition" (*ITOE* 10). As Gotthelf explains in his introduction, she thinks concepts are analogous to file folders; we rely on them to classify and group the "myriad" "things, attributes, actions, relationships (and so forth) in the world" that we think about together "into manageable cognitive units. . . . This makes possible, among other things, specialized study; by studying some members of a properly conceptualized group, Rand observes, we are able to learn about all members of the group, and thus to apply that knowledge to new individuals of that group which we encounter. That is, concepts make possible induction, and thus science and technology and, indeed, all rational action."

I will call the concepts Rand talks about *file-folder concepts* and the definitions she associates with them *file-folder definitions*. Without them, she holds, it would be cumbersome if not unworkable to think about more things than we can hold in mind as individuals all at one time, and impossible to think about items we have not experienced even if they resemble things we have. (Gotthelf explains this in his section on definitions; see also *ITOE* 27–28, 45, 66–67, 69.)

Things falling under one concept are isolated in our thinking from items falling under others by our ascription to them of distinguishing characteristics. Rand maintains that things belong to natural groups by virtue of shared characteristics they possess independently of what we know or think about them (*ITOE* 45–47). The degree to which a concept facilitates cognition and the quality of the cognition it facilitates depends in part upon how well what we take to be the distinguishing characteristics of a group of things approximate to the characteristics that actually set its members apart from members of other natural groups.

This brings us to Rand's ideas about definitions. A file-folder concept, Gotthelf writes, "is turned into a retainable mental unit by being assigned a word. To complete the process the concept is given a *definition*. 'A definition,' says Rand, 'is a statement that identifies the nature of the units subsumed under a concept. . . . The purpose of a definition is to distinguish a concept from all other concepts and thus to keep its units differentiated [in one's mind] from all other existents.'" That is a hard saying. If we need file-folder definitions to understand the words that turn concepts into "retainable mental unit[s]" and we can't cognize without concepts retained as mental units, then we can't cognize without definitions. Rand thinks well-conducted scientific reasoning is a good example of epistemically acceptable human cognition. The trouble is that many spoken and written expressions of good scientific reasoning do not explicitly use definitions.[1]

1. And it is worth noting, as Clark Glymour reminded me in conversation, that people often demand definitions for rhetorical rather than epistemic purposes.

Perhaps Rand would disagree, but historical and present-day examples are easy to find. Perhaps she thinks definitions play tacit roles in cognition whose results are expressed without overt appeal to them. Perhaps she thinks that even when definitions play no role in a specific course of reasoning, acceptably good cognition depends on a grasp of fundamental characteristics available for incorporation into definitions with which to understand bits of language that refer to concepts. The examples I discuss below feature explicitly stated definitions, but what I say about them should be applicable to Rand under all of the alternatives just sketched.

Rand does not explicitly say whether she thinks "human cognition" is one basic, widely used mental function, or a family of different functions. In either case, the generality of her discussion suggests that "human cognition" is exhibited in the performance of all of the scientific and nonscientific theoretical and practical cognitive tasks we engage in to learn about and deal with ourselves and things in the world we live in. The point of asking whether one size fits all is that Rand appears to think that no matter how many different cognitive tasks we engage in their satisfactory performance always requires concepts and definitions that contribute by doing the same jobs. One job is to group things, characteristics, etc. so that we can think about them without experiencing or having to bring to mind every member of the relevant group all at once, or one by one (*ITOE* 70). A second job is to unify knowledge in such a way as to facilitate cognitive access to what we know about individuals and their distinguishing characteristics (*ITOE* 70).

Things falling under typical concepts have so many distinguishing characteristics, Gotthelf states, that "to specify them all in its definition would defeat the purpose of a definition: it would make it impossible for a mind to hold the concept as a single unit, clearly grasped. What is needed is a single distinguishing characteristic, or a very small number of them, that can be held as a single mental unit and yet can bring readily to mind all the other characteristics." Rand calls the one or very few distinguishing characteristics that bring the others readily to mind "fundamental" or "essential" (*ITOE* 42, 45–46). This is possible because the characteristics they bring to mind "depend upon" or are "explained by" them, as Gotthelf says. Good definitions hold concepts together and enable us to grasp them clearly by invoking fundamental distinguishing characteristics to describe the things that fall under them. Thus, a good definition of obesity should incorporate distinguishing characteristic(s) responsible for and explanatory of such things as obesity's contribution to certain health risks, and its connections to poor nutrition, lack of exercise, and other lifestyle factors. Similarly, an adequate definition of the nerve impulse should specify features responsible for and explanatory of the influences it exerts on a variety of physiological and psychological states and processes, its causal relations to membrane potentials, a variety of inhibitory and excitatory influences, and so on. (These are my, not Rand's, examples.) Choices of which characteristics to treat as fundamental and include in definitions are crucial to the integration of knowledge by virtue of which concepts promote cognitive access to information about the things they are used think about.

If all concepts and definitions serve the same cognitive purposes, Rand thinks, they should all be evaluated according to the same standards.[2] I will call one of Rand's standards *comprehensiveness*. A good definition is satisfied by members of a single natural group—the more the better. An ideal definition is satisfied by all and only members of a single natural group. A second standard has to do with *unification*. The more distinguishing characteristics of members of the relevant group depend upon or are explained by the fundamental characteristic(s) specified in the definition, the better the definition. As said, I question whether definitions and concepts that meet these standards are important to nearly as many kinds of cognitive tasks as Rand believes.

Non–File-Folder Definitions of Obesity

Epidemiologists and other medical scientists and practitioners use different definitions of obesity. None of them measure up very well to Rand's standards. According to the World Health Organization (WHO), obesity is "a disease in which excess body fat has accumulated to an extent that health may be adversely affected" (Stevens 2003, 287). Investigators can't study how widespread obesity is, its contribution to health risks in different populations, the effectiveness of specific preventative measures and medical treatments, and so on without effective procedures with which to decide which individuals to classify as obese, and which data points and data distributions are statistically indicative of facts about obesity. The WHO definition does not even pretend to provide an effective decision procedure. Investigators, policy makers, and health practitioners must rely instead on *operational definitions* that specify test or measurement results with which to distinguish obese from nonobese subjects and classify data points and statistical patterns with regard to obesity.

2. Ignoring a few special concepts such as "existence" and "identity" (*ITOE* 55–56).

According to a commonly used operational definition, men or women whose BMI (body mass index, i.e., the proportion of weight in kilograms to the square of height in meters) is equal to or above (30 kg/m²) are obese. As Uljana Feest explains, operational definitions typically do not purport to specify the *meanings* of the terms they define. Thus, there is no logical contradiction or semantic incoherence in denying that someone whose BMI meets or exceeds the 30 kg/m² cutpoint is obese. Nor is there any a priori reason not to modify or replace the BMI definition in light of empirical findings or theoretical developments. Operational definitions do no more than to "partially and temporarily" specify one's use of the defined term or concept "by saying which kinds of empirical indicators are indicative of [their referents]" (Feest 2005, 133).

The WHO definition helps us to think about more instances of obesity than we can hold in mind all at one time, and to think about instances we have not yet experienced, but these are not the primary functions of the operational definitions. As said, their job is to facilitate testing for obesity and classifying data. If Rand's filing system analogy applies to operational definitions at all, they are more like filing instructions than file folders.

Investigators, policy makers, and health practitioners concerned with obesity employ different epistemic tactics to deal with different theoretical and practical issues involving statistical or causal connections between body fat and various health risks and quality-of-life issues. Excess body fat is implicated in diabetes, different kinds of heart and circulatory diseases including stroke, and other health and quality-of-life risks. But causal and statistical relations between these and other diseases and BMI levels vary across populations. Furthermore, obesity research, policy making, and the like, are subject to an impressive variety of constraints arising from economic and other pragmatic factors, and differences in background beliefs and assumptions. Differences between populations studied, investigators' interests, and pragmatic and theoretical influences raise various questions. It is not surprising that different operational definitions are epistemically appropriate to the performance of the cognitive tasks that must be performed to answer them.

One important alternative to the BMI definition is waist-hip ratio (WHR) obesity. WHR is obtained by measuring waist and hip circumference with a tape measure and dividing the former by the latter. The WHR cutpoint for obesity is 1.0 for men and 0.8 for women (World Health Organization 2011, 26).

BMI cutpoints correlate well enough with adverse health effects of interest to provide useful information with regard to a number of questions about obesity in many large populations. But the correlations vary quantitatively or even break down in certain subpopulations. For example, athletes whose muscle and bone mass is responsible for most of their weight have lower health risks than sedentary subjects with the same BMI. The cutpoints that predict cardiovascular disease in some ethnic groups are lower than cutpoints that deliver equally good predictions for others (Stevens 2003). BMI health-risk correlations are sensitive to still other factors, including age and gender. They also vary from person to person even if one corrects for ethnicity, physical fitness, and so on. Thus, even though BMI can be useful for studying large populations, some purposes are better served by the WHR definition, or variants using measurements of height, neck, belly at the level of the navel, and hip, or calculations from caliper rather than tape measure measurements. Because such measurement results correlate better than BMI with health risks in some individuals and populations, a health practitioner might well prefer to use WHR or one of its variants to evaluate the overall health of individual patients (Lafortuna et al. 2006). At the same time, the BMI definition is sometimes preferable to WHR because BMI measurements are immune to some errors that beset WHR measurements.[3]

Let us see how our obesity definitions fare with regard to Rand's norms.

WHO defines obesity functionally as an accumulation of body fat capable of affecting health adversely, and qualitatively as excessive accumulation. The only clue to what counts as excessive that the definition offers is its mention of increased health risks. These conditions are too vague to unify our knowledge of obesity by explaining as many as possible of its distinguishing characteristics. The WHO definition fares even worse with regard to comprehensiveness. For most practical and theoretical purposes, obesity is distinguished from being overweight. But overweight individuals also have excess body fat that raises the probability of the same health conditions as WHO obesity. Thus, the WHO definition is satisfied by nonobese as well as obese subjects. Heart disease, diabetes,

3. Rolls of fat can shift during measurement to produce significant disparities between tape measurements of the same subject. Caliper measurements are subject to similarly caused errors. I am indebted to Wendy King for telling me about this and helping me with the obesity literature.

and so on may be less probable for overweight than obese subjects, but this is a quantitative difference that does not prevent overweight (non-obese) subjects from satisfying WHO's qualitative standard for obesity. Whether this detracts from the WHO definitions' cognitive usefulness or to the quality of the performance of cognitive tasks in which it figures is another question.

In providing effective tests for obesity, the BMI and WHR cutpoints are not required to unify our knowledge or to mention (as they do not) the kinds of characteristics Rand calls fundamental, or to bring other distinguishing characteristics readily to mind. Like many other operational definitions, what the BMI and WHR definitions do to promote cognition is best described on a case-by-case basis in terms of the kinds of distinctions they support and the cognitive uses to which those distinctions are put.

The WHO definition looks like a mental file folder because it groups individuals together, but the operational definitions group things, too. The most important difference between them is that the WHO definition explicitly mentions the factors that make obesity a matter of concern. By defining obesity in terms of excess fat accumulation that increases health risks it constrains operational definitions by indicating what people who study and try to deal with obesity would like them to apply to, and what factors operational definitions should converge toward.[4] Neither comprehensiveness nor unification is required for this purpose. The BMI and WHR cutpoints also constrain obesity research, policy making, and health practices, but not in the same way. Their influence derives from the roles they play in classifying individuals, data, and data patterns for use in investigating and dealing with obesity.

To sum up, contrary to Rand's assumption that all adequate definitions support human cognition in the same way, the obesity definitions we have looked at are used for a variety of different purposes. Contrary to Rand's normative claims, the standards of comprehensiveness and unification by reference to fundamental features are not particularly relevant to the cognitive work these definitions do.

E. D. Adrian's Definition of the Nerve Impulse

In 1932, when E. D. Adrian published *The Mechanism of Nervous Action*, neuroscientists had not completely settled the question whether

---

4. Note, however, that even though the BMI and WHR definitions converge toward the conditions of the WHO definition, they do not classify exactly the same individuals as obese.

nerve impulses were identical to electrical currents. Adrian urged the need for a clear definition of the nerve impulse for use in addressing this issue. He himself believed the nerve impulse was an electrical phenomenon, but he could not define it as such without begging the question. Instead, he defined the nerve impulse as "the change which propagates itself down the [nerve] fibre and leads to the activity of other structures such as muscles and glands" (Adrian 1932, 17). This is a nonoperational definition that worked perfectly well even though it does not meet Rand's unification standard.

Adrian's purposes in formulating the definition were such that they could be served without distinguishing nerve impulses from all the members of every other natural group. All he needed was a definition that specified features sufficient to distinguish nerve impulses from "chemical and thermal changes which are still in evidence . . . after the impulse has done all it can in the way of activating other regions along with other things that go on in nerve fibers in response to a stimulus" (Adrian 1932, 17–18). For Adrian's purposes it made no difference that relatively few of the distinguishing characteristics of the nerve impulse he and his contemporaries knew about were explained by or depended upon the features he incorporated into the definition. The definition was used explicitly and implicitly to design and execute experiments and interpret their results. The cognitive tasks it helped the investigator perform had much more to do with obtaining new information relevant to deciding the nature of the nerve impulse than integrating and bringing to mind what was already known about its distinguishing characteristics. An experimental result that favored identifying nerve impulses with electric currents was that they are both produced by the same natural and artificial stimuli as the sensory and muscular responses the nerve impulses were known to cause. But their experimental results indicated that the electrical currents Adrian wanted to identify with nerve impulses were self-propagating, brief, and uniform in magnitude, while the muscular and sensory activities they initiated were continuous and variable in speed and magnitude (Adrian 1932, 17). In view of these differences, how could the former cause the latter? Adrian's definition played a role in experimental work undertaken in response to this difficulty. Adrian (1932, 17) used experimental results to argue that, like "succession[s] of dots in the Morse Code whose number and temporal pattern determines what message they carry," neuronal signals change over time with respect to the number and temporal pattern of their constituent electrical bursts. If the analogy holds, changing rates and temporal distributions of uniform spikes might account for changes in magnitudes and speeds of muscular and sensory activities. Muscles and sensory tracts like the optical nerve are bundles of fibers whose components take inputs from different neurons. Thus, a muscle could be made to contract continuously by discontinuous but temporally overlapping impulses from the nerves that innervate its constituent fibers, and similarly for a bundle of sensory neurons. Adrian's definition figured, sometimes implicitly and sometimes explicitly, in subsequent investigations of the merits of this solution. Its failure to specify fundamental characteristics, in Rand's sense, was no obstacle to the cognition that went into designing and executing the relevant experiments, and interpreting the data they produced. When investigators needed to explain and call distinguishing characteristics to mind they could rely on background knowledge that Adrian did not include in his definition.

Twenty-first-century textbook authors know enough about nerve impulses to define them to Rand's specifications. It is of interest that they do not. For example, Alberts et al. define nerve impulses functionally as "action potentials that occur in nerve cells and make possible long distance signaling in the nervous system" and the action potential as a "rapid, self-propagating electrical excitation in the plasma membrane of a cell" (2002, G1). These defining features (rapidity and self-propagation, location in the plasma membrane, and functioning to support long-distance signaling) do not explain nearly as many distinguishing characteristics of the nerve impulse as features of ion channel mechanisms that open and close to permit and damp cross-membrane flows of charged ions in response to changes in membrane potential. The latter are more fundamental or essential in Rand's sense than the former. Alberts and his coauthors understand the relevant mechanisms and their causal and dependency relations to other distinguishing characteristics of the nerve impulse well enough to discuss them in some detail. Thus, they could have used them to define the nerve impulse had they chosen. Their failure to do so argues that they do not evaluate definitions by the standards Rand would use.

Conclusion

Does the adequacy of scientific reasoning always depend on the use or availability of definitions that organize knowledge about members of natural groups and facilitate cognitive access to as many as possible of their distinguishing characteristics? Does a definition's epistemic worth always depend upon how well it measures up to Rand's standards?

The examples I have discussed argue that the answer to both questions is no.[5]

They illustrate two troubles with Rand's account. The first is that because definitions are used to perform different cognitive tasks, their epistemic value does not always depend upon whether they meet the same standards. Operational definitions of obesity allow investigators to sort individuals and data points as needed to serve their purposes. Different kinds of sorting are required for different purposes pursued under different theoretical, factual, and practical constraints. The epistemic adequacy of the sorting procedure typically does not depend on how well the relevant operational definition integrates or brings knowledge of obesity and its distinguishing characteristics to mind.

In defining the nerve impulse, all Adrian needed to specify were conditions with which to distinguish the nerve impulse from certain other physiological phenomena. A definition that specified fundamental features in Rand's sense would have defeated Adrian's purposes by begging the question he was using it to answer.

The WHO definition illustrates that, contrary to the requirement of comprehensiveness, a definition can be epistemically adequate even though it fails to supply sufficient conditions for membership in the relevant group. Rand may think this counts against the definitions I have discussed, but I see no evidence that their failure to meet her standards interfered with the performances of the relevant cognitive tasks.

The second trouble with Rand's account is that when scientists need to organize or call to mind what they know about the members or distinguishing characteristics of a group of interest, they can often do so by using background knowledge and other cognitive and psychological resources that are not incorporated into a definition. This exhibits a division of cognitive labor that Rand's account ignores. It is not always epistemically desirable, let alone necessary for definitions to do all the work she supposes they do.

5. I do not claim that scientists *never* use definitions congenial to Rand's account. The biological writings of Aristotle (whose work she draws from) illustrate that sometimes they do. My view is just that many scientific definitions do not and need not.

Taking the Measure of a Definition
Response to Bogen
ALLAN GOTTHELF

J im Bogen has provided us with a very thoughtful summary and critique of Rand's theory of definition, attending to its basis in her theory of concepts. Though I do not think he always gets Rand's views right, my disagreement is not primarily with his exposition but with his critique, and I will, in the body of this response, address such interpretative matters only when they bear directly on this.[1]

Bogen's main complaint, stated in his opening sentence, is that Rand incorrectly assumes that "all definitions are of the same kind, do the same kinds of cognitive work, and should be evaluated against the same standards." On Rand's account of definition, as he puts it in his title, "One size [i.e., type of definition] fits all [cognitive situations]." In fact, he argues, definitions perform many different functions in cognition and thus come in various types ("sizes"), and definitions of any sort are not as important for some cognitive tasks as Rand thinks.

I am going to argue that some of the things Bogen calls "definitions" are not actually definitions. For those that are, and perform cognitive

---

1. Two aspects of Rand's theory of concepts that I do not think Bogen gets quite right, which I will not discuss in the body of this response, are (i) his account of her file-folder

roles other than those emphasized by Rand, I will argue that they can do so *only because* they also perform the role that Rand identifies as fundamental to a definition. Let us review Rand's account of that role.

A concept, for her, is a retained unitary grasp of indefinitely many relevantly similar particulars. Its definition sharpens that grasp and facilitates its retention and use. As Rand puts it, the definition "is a statement that identifies the nature of the units subsumed by [that] concept. . . . [Its] purpose . . . is to distinguish [that] concept from all other concepts and thus to keep its units differentiated [in one's mind] from all other existents." It does this by "specif[ying] the distinguishing characteristic(s) of the units, and indicates the category of existents from which they were differentiated" (*ITOE* 40–41). This is a definition's primary cognitive function.

If only a few distinguishing characteristics of the existents subsumed by the concept are known, the definition would state those characteristics. As the number of known distinguishing characteristics multiplies beyond what could be held in conscious awareness all at once, what is needed is a way of condensing that knowledge into a graspable unit—a specification of a single (or small number of) distinguishing characteristic(s) that brings the others (and the knowledge associated with them) readily to mind. The characteristic(s) that does this is the one that is *fundamental* to the grouping in question, the one known to be responsible for, and thus explanatory of, the others. This is the characteristic Rand calls *essential*: the fundamental distinguishing characteristic. More precisely (as I wrote

---

analogy and (ii) his reference to her theory as holding that concepts aim to capture "natural groups."

> (i) Bogen treats Rand's file-folder analogy as though it is the referents of the concepts that are being filed; Rand instead speaks of the concept as "a file folder in which man's mind files his knowledge of the existents it subsumes" (*ITOE* 66–67). On this point, see the quotation from Salmieri and Gotthelf 2005 in note 10 of my essay in part 1 and the discussions of the file-folder analogy in the essays in the same part of this volume by Salmieri and James Lennox.
>
> (ii) Bogen's references to "natural groups" correctly suggest that Rand thinks conceptual groupings are not *subjective*, but he appears to attribute to her a realism regarding concepts which she rejects in favor of the view that concepts are objective in the sense I discuss in the last section of my essay. Because of this, the standard of "comprehensiveness" that Bogen attributes to her would need to be reworded, in accordance with the norms of concept-formation I discuss in that same section. For further discussion of Rand's position on "natural groups" in (what I take to be) Bogen's sense, see Onkar Ghate's "Natural Kinds and Rand's Theory of Concepts: Reflections on Griffiths" in part 2 of this volume.

in my essay), the essential characteristic of a concept is that distinguishing characteristic(s) of its units, *from among those known,* which is known to be responsible for (and thus explanatory of) the greatest number of other *known* distinguishing characteristics.[2] An essence in Rand's sense, as I explained, is an *epistemic device* and may change as our knowledge of the distinguishing characteristics and their causal interrelationships expands.

Whatever else definitions do, according to Rand, they must specify the (epistemologically) essential characteristic(s) of the units grouped by the concept—and virtually every well-formed concept, above the simplest, will have such a definition, explicitly or implicitly.[3] I will seek to illustrate this in what follows.

In the course of our discussion, we will see (in outline at least) that while all such concepts must be defined by essential characteristics in Rand's sense, just what is required to specify an essential characteristic will be different for different sorts of concepts at different stages in the development of knowledge. Playing on Bogen's title, then, we may say that, while all concepts must wear the relevant item of clothing (i.e., have essence-specifying definitions), these will need to be *precisely tailored* to the cognizer's situation. Definitions, that is, must be *made to measure* for the particular sort of concept involved, and for the precise level of knowledge the cognizer possesses for these concepts. (Thus *my* title.) I will seek to illustrate this as well with the sorts of concepts Bogen focuses on and the examples he cites of actual definitions of such concepts as given by professionals: medical and biological concepts. The point of his examples is to show that none of these actual definitions satisfies Rand's standards. We shall see.[4]

Let us start with the concept (and definition) of "obesity." Bogen begins with the World Health Organization (WHO) definition of obesity as "a disease in which excess body fat has accumulated to an extent that health may be adversely affected." This definition, he observes, "does not even pretend to provide an effective . . . procedure" with which "to decide which individuals to classify as obese," and thus cannot support fur-

---

2. This is the source of what Bogen calls Rand's standard of "unification."

3. For elaboration, particularly with regard to the earliest concepts, see *ITOE* 49–50, 231.

4. Since Rand's theory is a normative one, if a proffered definition fails to live up to Rand's standards, this could be a failing of the definition. This will, in fact, be the case for one category of "definition" Bogen considers, though for the rest I will argue that they do indeed satisfy her standards.

ther medical, clinical, or epidemiological study. Those engaged in or who make use of the results of this "must rely *instead* on operational definitions" (my emphasis), which specify such a decision procedure. And here, several different such definitions are possible, depending on the precise cognitive need; there are, for instance, the body-mass index, the waist-hip ratio, and others.

I will return to these indexes and ratios—and with them to Bogen's notion of an "operational definition"—shortly. But first I would like to consider his claim that, decision procedure apart, the WHO definition, though medically useful in its own way, does *not* specify fundamental features of obesity or unify very well our knowledge about it—because I think it *does* do those things, for the level of knowledge in which (or for which) it is introduced.[5]

I will build my case on two facts, one about the particular sort of concept we are dealing with, and one about the general relationship between concepts and their definitions.

I start from the fact that the concept of "obesity" is a *medical* concept. It is to be distinguished from any concept that designates bodily appearance, weight, size, or proportions per se. To be obese is not merely to be *fat*. The definition reflects the concept's tie to health in two ways. First, its genus is given as *disease,* and second, its full differentia does not just specify the condition in question—an accumulation of excess body fat—but also identifies that condition by reference to a likelihood of its having *an adverse effect on health.*[6]

Indeed, any thought about this medical condition must begin with a grasp of the difference between it and such physical conditions as being fat (say, big and loose around the waist, hips, face and arms) or heavy (having significantly above-average weight) or portly (having a certain character-

5. Because I am neither a medical theorist nor a philosopher of medicine, I am not in a position to certify the validity of particular medical concepts or definitions; the same applies in regard to the neurobiological concepts and definitions I briefly discuss later in this response. My focus is, rather, on the proper methodology to be used by such specialists in the development of concepts and definitions in their fields, and any evaluations I offer of concepts and definitions developed by specialists must be seen in that light.

6. I put aside as not relevant to our concerns here exactly how we are to understand the term "excess" in the definition. There is, by the way, some serious question as to whether obesity should be classified as a *disease* or merely a *medical condition*. I myself find persuasive the arguments for the latter in Heshka and Allison 2001, but this issue does not matter for our purposes either, since obesity's status as a medical condition (i.e., as a condition viewed from the standpoint of its bearing on its possessor's health or disease) itself makes "obesity" a medical concept.

istic shape), and so on. One's initial grasp of this concept, whether one is a young physician or a concerned ordinary citizen, requires just the sort of sharpening of the concept—just the sort of *definition*—that the WHO definition provides. We may call this an *introductory* definition. It assumes a minimal context of knowledge, namely, that there is a physical condition closely connected with being fat or heavy or portly (and so on), that in many such cases there is an above-average accumulation of body fat, and that this condition frequently has adverse effects on health.[7] The context addressed by the definition does not involve detailed knowledge either of the ways excess body fat may adversely affect health or of the causes of excess body fat, even if it is commonsense lore that excess body fat may slow one down, cause early windedness, and so forth, and is in some way due to or at least correlated with the eating of larger-than-average amounts of certain foods. And no matter to what extent medical science subsequently comes to understand the causes and health-damaging effects of obesity, and whatever advanced definitions such understanding results in, a WHO-like introductory definition is where every new student of obesity must start.

Does such an introductory definition capture what is (in Rand's sense) *essential* to obesity in such an introductory context? Here is where the second fact I mentioned enters, a fact concerning the relation between concepts and their definitions: "A definition is not a description; it *implies*, but does not mention all the characteristics of a concept's units. . . . [A] definition implies *all* the characteristics of the units, since it identifies their *essential*, not their *exhaustive*, characteristics; since it designates *existents*, not their isolated aspects; and since it is a condensation of, not a substitute for, a wider knowledge of the existents involved" (*ITOE* 42). The health-problematic condition shared by the individuals we group together as obese involves various physical characteristics or dimensions, in addition to a larger-than-average accumulation of body fat. It is the perceptible condition of being "fat" (again, big and loose around the waist, hips, face, and arms) and portly (again, having a certain characteristic

7. The WHO definition is, in fact, more sophisticated than I make out here. As Gregory Salmieri has pointed out to me, it involves a knowledge of the difference between body tissues (in this definition, "fat" does not just mean excess flesh of any sort), and some knowledge of the role of body fat in particular in other bodily processes. In calling it an "introductory definition," I do not mean that it captures the state of knowledge when the concept of "obesity" was first formed (a state at which it might have been characterized, as Salmieri put it to me, as "so fat that it's unhealthy"); I mean, rather, that it reflects what is a relatively limited state of knowledge today, so far as sustained medical study is concerned.

shape) and slow-moving and quicker to get winded, and so on (all in some combination or other). Obesity is that *joint* set of features viewed together as being health problematic. Of that set of features, the causally fundamental one, which explains the others, is the having of an excess accumulation of body fat, insofar as that condition may adversely affect health. That is precisely the *essential* characteristic, in Rand's sense. The genus is "medical condition"; the differentia specifies the known basis of the condition in question and its particular bearing on health. Together they constitute what I have called an *introductory* definition of obesity, appropriate for the context of knowledge with which someone enters the study of that condition. Further study of obesity will bring a greater knowledge both of the causes of the excess accumulation of body fat, and the way in which such excess accumulation leads both to other associated features and especially to adverse effects on health.[8] That greater knowledge may well call for a change in the definition, but a WHO-like definition of obesity, satisfying as it does Rand's standards for definition, is indeed made to measure for that medical condition in the context of knowledge for which it was devised.

What then of the indexes and ratios that are used in the determination of the presence or absence (or degree) of obesity? If Rand is right in her rejection of realism in regard to universals, then concepts will typically group together units that differ in measurement along one or more ranges within one or more "Conceptual Common Denominators." If the borderlines are clear enough, definitions that capture the relevant range(s) in general terms will be sufficient (see Rand's definition of "table," for instance). But for further, sustained study—whether for scientific or craft-oriented purposes—those ranges will need to be specified quantitatively in some appropriate way, and units of measurement will need to be established. In medical contexts, the range will pertain to the effect on health. Thus, in the case of obesity, we need to ask what the unit of measurement is (or units are) for accumulations of body fat and what range would indicate an excess level. Since treatment is a central concern, easily accessible diagnostic criteria will be a desideratum.

---

8. Both directions are relevant, if only because medicine involves both theoretical (causal-explanatory) and practical (treatment-focused) dimensions. How the character of medicine as treatment-focused—i.e., as ultimately a *healing* art—affects the conceptualization of medical conditions is an important matter for the understanding of medical concepts, and for the philosophy of medicine more generally, but not a matter I am in a position to discuss as yet beyond the brief remark I go on to make at the end of the next paragraph.

We know that weight range is not sufficient, because the same weight can come with very different accumulations of fat, and thus can affect health in very different ways. Study shows that one accessible way toward measuring body-fat accumulation is a certain complex mathematical relationship of two attributes—the proportion of the individual's weight to the square of his height. Expressed in the relevant units (typically, as Bogen cites, in kilograms to meters squared), this allows a quantitatively determinate specification of a feature usefully correlated with body-fat accumulation. As such, it is an *index* of such accumulation, and a range along that feature—a range which is correlated with the likelihood of adverse accumulations of health—can provide a working measure of obesity (say, "equal to or above 30 kg/m^2"). But the body mass index (BMI) is not as such a definition of anything. It is a measurement of a specific relational attribute of a particular human body. Nor is any *range* along the scale of measurement in which body mass indexes are given a definition of anything. Having a BMI of, say, equal to or above 30 kg/m^2 is not as such *what it is to be obese*. It does not specify the nature of the phenomenon or of the concept and should not be called its definition. An index range is simply a *specification of the concept's differentia*, necessary for further study, a specification that makes sense only by reference to that differentia. Bogen is right that such specifications play a central role in the application, and myriad uses of, the concept, but he is wrong to view them as being used *instead* of the WHO definition. They get whatever connection they have to *obesity* in conjunction with, and as an application or specification of, a WHO-like definition, a definition that, in its context, as I have shown, fully satisfies Rand's standards.[9]

I can be briefer with Bogen's second example, the definition of *nerve impulse* offered by E. D. Adrian in 1932, and then modified by him and subsequent researchers as their knowledge expanded, since there is a very good discussion of this matter by Corinne Bloch, in a 2011 essay, written independently of Bogen's, in which she applies my characterization of Rand's notion of an epistemological essence to those very definitions (Bloch 2011).

Referring to Adrian's exclusion of electrical changes from the definition, Bogen suggests (1) that his definition does not distinguish nerve impulses "from all the members of every other natural group," only from

9. I put aside for now any discussion, in the light of Rand's theory of concepts and definition, of the general notion of an "operational definition." That notion, and various premises that structure the standard discussions of it, need to be rethought.

associated "chemical and thermal changes" (Adrian 1932, 17; qtd. by Bogen) that remained after the mentioned activity; (2) that "relatively few of
the [known] distinguishing characteristics of the nerve impulse . . . were
explained by or depended upon" the defining features; and (3) that the
latter remains true of more recent definitions of nerve impulse. But Bloch
explains why Adrian excluded the associated electrical change from his
1932 definition of "nerve impulse," given the context of knowledge in
which the definition was offered, *and* how the functional component of
his differentia contributed centrally to explaining the other distinguishing characteristics of nerve impulses known at the time (thereby satisfying the "unification standard" that Bogen says Adrian's definition failed
to meet). She also shows how, as a result of an increased understanding
of the processes involved, the electrical change came to be viewed as essential to nerve impulses—and how the later definitions, while expanding the specification in the definition of the material process involved in
nerve impulses, retain a functional component, because together these
two components are explanatorily fundamental in these later contexts of
knowledge.

The definitions of biological concepts must, then, as we have already
seen for medical concepts, also be tailored to the kind of phenomena conceptualized. In this case it is especially their teleological character that
is relevant. Biological phenomena that have functions must have in their
definitions a reference to those functions as they are understood at the
level of knowledge in question.

In this part of his discussion, Bogen makes two other points I want
to question. First, he puzzlingly dissociates a definition's role in condensing knowledge already acquired from its role in facilitating the "obtaining [of] new information." But, as Rand has explained, and as I indicate
at several places in my essay, it is precisely the condensation of existing
knowledge which a definition provides that makes possible the growth of
knowledge of the phenomenon in question.[10]

Second, supporting his claim that there are some cognitive tasks for
which definitions are not as important as Rand thinks, Bogen, at the close
of his comments, refers to the role of background knowledge: "when scientists need to organize or call to mind what they know about the mem-

10. See, for example, *ITOE* 45, speaking of the pattern of defining in terms of what is
contextually fundamental: "It is this pattern which makes intensive study and, therefore, the
growth of knowledge—and of science—possible." There is an extensive discussion of this issue in James Lennox's essay in part 1.

bers or distinguishing characteristics of a group of interest, they can often do so by using background knowledge and other cognitive and psychological resources that are not incorporated into a definition." This is, of course, correct, if "incorporated" means explicitly stated. But, as I have indicated, it is precisely the grasp of the essential characteristic (in Rand's sense) that enables the bringing of that background knowledge to mind.

Rand's theory, then, survives Bogen's criticism, and that theory's rich implications for our understanding of concepts and definitions in science invite further study.[11]

11. My thanks to Jim Lennox and especially Greg Salmieri for very helpful comments.

Concepts and Theory Change

On Concepts that Change with the Advance of Science

Comments on Lennox

RICHARD M. BURIAN

These comments represent the first round in print of an ongoing dialectic between James Lennox and me over the proper understanding of concepts and conceptual change in science, with a particular focus on the example of changing concepts of the gene. Further rounds are in the offing. I hope that our ongoing debate will clarify (and perhaps reduce) our differences, but also that it will help others to improve their accounts of the ways in which concepts change both in science and in daily life.

I wish to acknowledge, with gratitude, the amount that I have learned from Jim Lennox, Allan Gotthelf, and many other colleagues in three meetings bearing on conceptual change sponsored by the University of Pittsburgh's Fellowship for the Study of Objectivism, to which I have been invited. In particular, both Allan and Jim have helped to clarify a large number of issues about conceptual change on which my views were muddy. These meetings have been exemplary models of how to work through philosophical disagreements to achieve a better understanding of where we agree and, where we still disagree, of the substantial issues at stake in our disagreement.

Lennox on Concepts and Conceptual Change

Lennox's account of the stability of open-ended concepts, based on Rand's account of concepts in *ITOE*,[1] offers an important antidote to some radical versions of holistic theories of the meaning of theoretical concepts. It is important to distinguish, as Lennox does, between the sorts of conceptual change that he lists at the beginning of his essay[2] and change in the core concepts of a science. But it is also important to develop some sort of an account of how those core concepts can and do change. In addition to the sorts of conceptual change that Lennox recognizes in his essay, I shall argue that basic concepts in science (and, for that matter, in ordinary life) can be altered even while they are preserved. I shall restrict myself largely to scientific concepts, but at the end of this discussion I will try to show that the issues I raise are quite general and so must be faced in a general theory of concepts and conceptual change. But first, I want to emphasize the importance of Lennox's separation of the general topic of conceptual change from the analysis of the content of particular concepts and in the sets of entities (if any) that those concepts designate.

One of the problems faced by many philosophies of science that came into vogue during the last fifty years concerns their (implicit or explicit) analyses of the reference of theoretical concepts. Various approaches to this topic landed philosophers in so-called holist theories of meaning and reference, according to which the postulates, axioms, or relevant theoretical principles of the scientific theories of interest determined the meaning of the relevant theoretical terms (or concepts) and, in consequence, at least constrained their reference. This was the root of the controversies over incommensurability, as put forward, e.g., by Thomas Kuhn and Paul K. Feyerabend. We cannot go into theories of meaning here, but it is worth noting that several attempts to avoid this problem, for example, the causal theory of reference, still face the difficulty of meaning holism in dealing with such entities as atoms, electrons, or genes. The problem that remains in considering such entities is the indefiniteness of causal

---

1. I am neither widely nor deeply acquainted with Rand's philosophical works so, although I draw on parts of chapters 2, 5, and 6 and some other parts of *ITOE*, I rely mainly on Lennox's essay and some of the others in this volume for the views I examine and criticize.

2. In brief, these are: (1) devising new concepts to designate new sorts of entities, e.g., electrons or genes; (2) rejecting or replacing problematic concepts, e.g., "phlogiston" or "miasma"; (3) reclassifying entities by placing them in a different superordinate group, e.g., reclassifying cirripeds as a subclass of Crustacea rather than Mollusca; (4) accommodating

ascriptions such as "the gene is whatever it is that is responsible for the stable inheritance of Mendelian characters," or "the electron is whatever it is that caused these scintillations on the fluorescing screen in this experiment." Without further means of individuating the entities to which causal responsibility is ascribed, there is great uncertainty whether anything has genuinely been designated in such cases or, if designation has succeeded in particular cases, whether other instances of phenomena that are supposed to be caused by (e.g.) electrons or genes are genuinely effects of entities of the same sort as were involved in the phenomena previously identified. But the means of individuating theoretical entities involved in different phenomena typically depend on theoretical principles as well as experimental tools; the dependence on theory in this connection brings us back to the problems associated with meaning holism. (This point is, perhaps, clearer in the case of the concept of the gene than it is in the case of the concept of the electron, but there is not space here to elaborate on this issue.)

Lennox is entirely correct when he claims that we can often pin down what a concept designates adequately with inadequate or mistaken definitions. The initial locus for such claims is, of course, daily life, in which the success of communication depends on success in using concepts in such a way that, in different circumstances, we are able to agree about the correct use of those concepts to designate perceptually salient events, things, or processes. This can be done in spite of not having adequate definitions or of disagreeing about the proper formulation of definitions of the relevant concepts. For present purposes, the issue at the center of interest is how well this works when we go on to scientific concepts, particularly the concepts of "postulational" theories, that is, concepts like "electron" and "gene" that (if they refer to entities at all) refer to entities that are not perceptible.

Lennox is surely right that the relations among concepts, including theoretical concepts, can change in various ways without necessarily changing what is designated by those concepts and without changing what is designated in ways that damage communication and understanding. He is entirely correct that the fact that kind concepts designate open-

---

findings that identify specific groups of genes, e.g., regulatory genes and extranuclear genes, by adding specific subsidiary concepts, e.g., "regulatory gene" and "extranuclear gene"; and (5) developing additional or improved superordinate concepts, e.g., "eukaryote" or "vertebrate" for biological taxa.

ended classes of entities (things, events, processes, whatever) does not un-
dermine this point. Thus, Lennox's five sorts of conceptual change all can
take place without necessarily causing or requiring a fundamental change
in the content or definition of a concept or the class of entities designated
by that concept.

 Changes of classification are, of course, not innocent in these respects. Even if the designata of the focal concept of interest are not
changed, reclassification does alter the designata of other concepts. Consider Lennox's example of the concept "Cirripedia." Even if he is fundamentally right (which I think he is) that the reclassification of cirripeds as
crustaceans rather than mollusks did not, as such, require a fundamental
change in the referents of the concept *Cirriped*, it required *some* switch-
ing of definitions and alterations in the accepted designata for "Mollusca"
and "Crustacea"—after all, one of these lost and the other gained the
cirripeds. And, in fact, it also required some adjustment in the application of the concept "Cirripedia" (at least at the edges), for part of what
Darwin did was to bring in (and rule out) some marginal instances, supporting his judgments with strong evidence. To illustrate the importance
of the marginal cases, consider Darwin's evidence that some supposed
parasites found on or inside the females of several species turned out to
be the adult males, more or less reduced to sperm sacs with an attach-
ment organ by which they held fast to the shell or ovary of the female.[3]
Such dwarf males (Darwin called them "complemental males") do not
look like other cirripeds and had not previous been recognized to be cirripeds. Darwin showed that they were genuinely cirripeds by use of both
embryological and reproductive criteria.[4] This work depended heavily on
pioneering use of recent advances in microscopy.[5] These studies ended up
serving many other purposes for Darwin; one of them was to support the
view that embryological evidence ought to be given greater weight in the
classification (and later in tracing the evolutionary history) of organisms.

 3. Such instances are described in Darwin 1851a, 281–85 and plate 5. For the placement
of the research on cirripeds within Darwin's early work, see Love 2002 as well as other references that he provides.
 4. For further note, because it is relevant to the argument below, the embryological
and anatomical criteria (which, to this point, had been largely applied to adults) about which
organisms should be counted as cirripeds diverged; part of what went into the revision of
the classification was a reweighting of criteria that altered which organisms were counted as
cirripeds.
 5. On the importance of microscopy in these studies and on the ways in which Darwin
used microscopes, see Jardine 2009.

Thus, the particular classification of the dwarf males of barnacles, though it may be counted as a relatively routine (although surprising) correction and extension of stable knowledge, also had considerable weight in ongoing arguments for the revision of the criteria for classification and in the rethinking of the status of species as changing rather than static entities. This at least leaves open the extent and importance of the changes in the class of entities referred to in the change of classification involved in this case—for it speaks to a series of aberrant cases and that heightened the problems of drawing a border around the fossil members of the living and fossil cirripeds and led to the incorporation of hitherto unexpected organisms with the cirripeds.

This points me in the direction of the main point of these comments. Other things being equal, the revision of the placement of members in lower levels within the higher categories of a series of categories—e.g., the placement of species or genera within what systematists call "higher categories"—can be handled without great difficulties regarding the referents of the concept(s) at the base of the hierarchy; but the revision in the designata of concepts at more basal levels is problematic because it tends to force revisions at all the higher levels. With this caveat, all five types of conceptual change that Lennox addresses *can* take place without overly major disruption in the relationships among concepts and, for that reason, his classification is of genuine importance for our thinking about conceptual change. But the caveat is important, as should be clear already, and perhaps most important with respect to the first category—devising new concepts to designate new sorts of entities. Thus, in the long run, I believe that students of conceptual change will have to pay attention to concepts at the base level of scientific theories in order to resolve disagreements about conceptual change in science. This requires us to refocus attention from Lennox's central topic—the ways in which relations among concepts can change—a change that is unfair to Lennox since I delivered these comments to him just at the publication deadline. Still, let me introduce that topic, for it is where I think the argument must go.

Proper Formation of Concepts Is Not Sufficient to Determine What They Designate

One of the problems with Lennox's treatment of conceptual change concerns a role that he accords (following Rand) to the proper formation of concepts. Both Rand and Lennox treat the identity or meaning of "properly formed" concepts at the base of our conceptual structures (see the opening of Lennox's essay) as being fixed by the class of entities to which they refer.[6] This is, in part, because on their account those concepts are used in a way that fixes reference to open-ended sets of entities that hold a set of attributes in common. Although our knowledge of those entities and attributes may be adjusted in various ways, the meaning or identity of the concept is unchanged as long as the same open-ended class is referred to by the concept. This theory of concepts does not, of course, start with scientific concepts at its base, but with concepts that can be acquired by human perceivers in the course of perception and learning a (first) language.

On Lennox's and Rand's account, a properly formed concept in science may, occasionally, rest on false presuppositions that, when uncovered, lead to the replacement of that concept. (I do not believe that Rand allows "properly formed first level" perceptual [or perception-based] concepts to be replaced in this way.) Lennox holds, and I think that Rand held, that although scientific concepts must sometimes be replaced in light of new knowledge, first-order scientific concepts are seldom, if ever, retained if their identity or meaning is altered in a fundamental way. Rather, where the evidence so warrants, properly formed first-order scientific concepts are abandoned because they do not (as had earlier been thought) designate a coherent (open-ended) set of referents. It is striking that Lennox does not write anything about how a properly formed first-order scientific concept can be retained through a fundamental change in the open-ended set of entities that it is supposed to designate. He does, of course, allow reclassification of scientific concepts and the creation of *new* concepts that add or subtract constraints (or "measurements") and thus yield subordinate or superordinate concepts to the one from which one began. Furthermore, for Lennox as for Rand, as the relevant background knowledge changes, the definitions associated with concepts can change. However, at least for first-order concepts, such definitional changes occur because (and are acceptable only when) we have learned how better to understand which attributes characterize the already-designated (open-ended) class of things that had been picked out less efficiently and exactly; the inferior or less useful definition simply did not perform this task as

6. "All concepts are reducible to their base in perceptual entities [designated by first-level concepts], which are the base (the givens) of man's cognitive development" (*ITOE* 15). I use the terms "identity of a concept" and "meaning of a concept" with this sense, insofar as I understand it.

well as the improved definitions. One of the most important ways of organizing and advancing knowledge consists in identifying key attributes, especially those that most economically and exactly characterize the entities designated by a concept.

Lennox's implicit account of the proper formation of concepts is based primarily on "internal" analysis of the (putative) concept and its relation to other concepts. By this I mean that proper formation of a concept mainly depends on its freedom from internal contradictions and its being compatible with, and meshing coherently with, the other concepts in the mind(s) of the individual(s) who form the concept. However, if a concept is properly formed, it is connected to its referents and it will retain that class of referents across contexts (except, perhaps, for occasional corrections of errors in specific cases).[7] For concepts of natural and scientific kinds, the class or set of referents is open ended, but it is determined by those referents holding specific attributes in common, of which one or more can be used as an indicator of the entities referred to. These attributes may be used to give a provisional, revisable definition of the entities in question—e.g., that humans are two-legged animals that talk, similar to mother and father. In the instance of the concept "man" (as Rand terms it), Rand (and Lennox?) settle for "rational animal" as an essential definition, but they insist that this does not carry the metaphysical freight that is usually placed on the notion of essential definitions. Such definitions are revisable in the light of further knowledge—and just as the infant or young child comes to expand and alter the attributes used to identify humans (perhaps all the way to "rational animal"), so societies expand and alter the definitions associated with concepts. *These definitions provide the best available, most economical attribute(s) for picking out the correct open-ended class of entities.* The test of a good definition is *whether it preserves reference to the same* (intended) *open-ended class of entities* and is more economical and instructive about those entities than alternative proposed definitions. Thus, on this account, the only way to handle a fundamental alteration of the class referred to is to change the identity of the concept.

A stereotypical example of replacement of a scientific concept con-

---

7. I find this claim problematic. Whether a unique, stable class of referents has been picked out depends on externalities that cannot be determined by the concept's being well formed. There simply is no way to protect against the possibility that attempts to apply the concept in new circumstances will break down because the "natural" boundaries in the world do not coincide with those of the well-formed concepts and orderly conceptual scheme.

cerns the concept of phlogiston. The fundamental reason that this concept was abandoned is that it conflated two different phenomena (both handled in open-ended ways in the development of subsequent sciences). One of these concerned, roughly, the quantity of heat of a body (which, when the concept of phlogiston was abandoned came to be associated first with the quantity of caloric it contained, then with randomly directed kinetic energy of its component molecules), and the other concerned the degree of acidity (which ultimately came to be associated with the propensity of the chemical compounds composing that body to donate electrons to other compounds in a variety of conditions). It was a surprise to advocates of the concept of phlogiston that the attributes relevant to these phenomena picked out quite distinct sorts of entities. In a case like this, on the account Lennox offers, it seems that there is no choice but to abandon the concept that had mistaken presuppositions built into it.

First-Order Scientific Concepts May Be Systematically Altered

In contrast to Lennox I hold that first-order scientific concepts can sometimes be retained with major systematic revisions of the class of entities to which they refer. Such revisions often depend on the interactions among distinct disciplines that employ different tools to investigate the same scientific object, yielding initially discordant results that are, eventually, reconciled by modifications of the concept (Burian 1995). I will illustrate this process by use of a cartoon history of the concept (or concepts?) of the atom from Dalton's theory of the atom until, roughly, the middle of the twentieth century. Although the historical presentation is very rough, the moral that I draw will, I believe, withstand more careful scrutiny.

The fundamental point is that the concept of a chemical atom came under severe pressure for internal reasons within chemistry and was corrected in light of physical investigations of atoms, with strenuous efforts to show that chemists and physicists were designating exactly the same things in spite of their disagreements about atoms. Chemists and physicists employed numerous (conceptual, experimental, and mathematical) devices to show that their different investigative tools were "triangulating" on the same objects (specifically atoms of hydrogen, helium, lithium, carbon, nitrogen, oxygen, neon, and so on—as well as molecules of compounds of these and other elements) and so posed problems that required reconciliation of their discordant models, theories, and findings. The changes in the concept of the atom can be used to suggest (as I will show shortly) that a characteristic and important way of improving scientific knowledge results from calibrating the findings obtained by different instruments and from within different disciplines. For present purposes, the most important consequence of the revisions in the concept of the atom (as fundamental as any concept in chemistry since at least the nineteenth century) means that it was changed in ways that should count as altering the kinds of entities it designated. If this is correct, it puts great pressure on Lennox's and Rand's claim that properly formed (fundamental) concepts retain their meaning and identity in the face of increased knowledge.

So here is a selective sketch history of the atom to enforce the claims I just made, based on features chosen to highlight certain changes in the concept of the atom. Shortly after Antoine Lavoisier's account of chemical elements had taken hold (Lavoisier 1789), John Dalton proposed an empirically based theory of chemical atoms that provided measures of their relative masses. The main evidence for those masses was based on the law of multiple proportions (Dalton 1808). To illustrate that law, Dalton demonstrated that one oxide of tin combined one molecule of tin with one of oxygen, while the other oxide of tin combined one molecule of tin with two molecules of oxygen. Drawing on earlier work by Joseph-Louis Proust, who had proposed a law of constant composition and exemplified it in many instances, including two distinct oxides of tin, Dalton interpreted Proust's results for tin (one oxide had 88.1 percent tin and 11.9 percent oxygen; the other 78.7 percent tin and 21.3 percent oxygen). Dalton recalculated this result as follows: 100g of tin would combine with 13.5g of oxygen to form the first oxide and with 27g of tin to form the second oxide (van Melsen 1952). Dalton's law of definite proportions thus suggested specific combinations of atoms in certain molecules. To calculate relative atomic weights, Dalton used the simplest possible formulas for each element in the lowest proportion in the simplest molecules combining those elements. Thus, his formula for water was HO and his calculations were based on a 1:1 ratio of water atoms to oxygen atoms in the water molecule (Dalton 1808). On this, Dalton's position was subsequently corrected by Amadeo Avogadro, who first proposed in 1811 the law that the masses of equal volumes of (ideal, chemically pure) gases at a fixed temperature and pressure contain the same number of molecules, with the consequence that the masses of those volumes are proportional to their respective molecular weights.[8] This allowed him to recognize that the correct formula for water is H_2O, not HO, as Dalton thought.[9] What remained fixed in the definition of chemical atoms from around this time for nearly a century was that each atom of a given element had a distinctive attribute, namely its (atomic) mass. This clearly was an attribute of chemical atoms that belonged in the essential definition of (chemical) atoms until sometime after the beginning of the twentieth century.

In 1815 an anonymous publication by William Prout suggested that the hydrogen atom is the basal unit for all atoms, thus implying that atoms are structured and might not be indivisible, and that atomic masses would all be multiples of the mass of one hydrogen atom. Again, this suggestion was largely neglected at first and then remained contentious until almost a century had passed. While the question was held open because several elements had well-established atomic weights that could not be understood as multiples of the weight of hydrogen, the question of the reality and indivisibility of atoms remained in dispute. Several philosophers have taken Prout's hypothesis and the disputes over its correctness seriously (see, for example, Lakatos 1970, Laudan 1977), noting the serious difficulties it faced from anomalous cases, most notoriously that of chlorine, whose atomic weight was firmly established by various chemical means to be close to 35.5. The resolution of problems of this sort occurred only after significant revision of ideas about the chemical atom, revisions that were

8. I do not know the history well enough to know how early Avogadro's claim that the formula of water should be H_2O was generally accepted. Avogadro's first suggestion of this law was published in 1811, but his articulation and support of the claim was developed in a series of memoirs that spanned the period 1811–27. It was not widely accepted at first and was not considered to be definitively established in organic chemistry until the 1860s, and not until the 1870s in inorganic chemistry. Indeed, it was not until Jean Perrin suggested naming the Avogadro constant after Avogadro and provided many of the experimental and theoretical results for the culminating resolution of most of the contested questions relevant to the acceptance of Avogadro's number and the underlying molecular realities associated with it (Perrin 1909) that there was full acceptance of Avogadro's law and its implications. It was only then that it was established that the mass (in grams) of a mole of a molecularly pure substance is an exact reflection of the molecular mass of the molecules of which that substance is composed. The units and values involved were not standardized until Perrin's research confirmed the generality of the result.

9. Two liters of hydrogen at an appropriate temperature and pressure, combined with one liter of oxygen at that temperature, yield one liter of water vapor. Therefore, there are twice as many atoms of hydrogen as of oxygen in the water molecule. The mass of the liter of water vapor confirms this result: the formula for water is H_2O. Thus, the mass of a liter of a chemically pure gas such as oxygen does not necessarily serve as a measure of the mass of an atom of oxygen; the molecular structure of the gas must first be determined.

largely achieved by physicists with physical (rather than chemical) techniques. Rutherford finally ended skepticism on this point with his discovery of the atomic nucleus (Rutherford 1911) and the subsequent proofs that the hydrogen nucleus is present in other atomic nuclei and can be released, e.g., under bombardment by alpha particles (Rutherford 1919). By that time, Rutherford had already suggested that there might also be neutral particles (combining an electron and a proton) inside atomic nuclei to account for the measured masses of atoms.

A major step was the discovery of isotopes. Frederick Soddy (along with many others) played a key role in this discovery; he laid out the key claims in a series of papers in 1913. His Nobel lecture presents an engaging account of the sharp departures that were required from the standard chemical views about the atom. Part of what was at stake (though there was much more) was the recognition that chemically indistinguishable atoms of the same substance had strikingly different properties: some of them are highly stable, others extremely unstable. The unstable ones were changed by the emission of an α or β particle, at which point they were transmuted and acquired the identity of another chemical element (Soddy 1923).[10] J. J. Thomson quickly confirmed Soddy's claims by demonstrating the existence of (at least) two isotopes of neon (Thomson 1913). That line of work finally provided a basis for a partial resolution of the principal differences between atomic masses and atomic number. But it was not until James Chadwick's demonstration of the existence of the neutron in 1932 (within the framework of developments in quantum physics) that a satisfactory physical basis for resolving questions about the differences between nuclei of atoms of distinct isotopes of a single element were fully established.[11] By then, however, it had long been clear that anomalous chemical masses (like that of chlorine) result from averaging of the weights of different naturally present isotopes, whose chemical behavior was largely determined by their outer "rings" of electrons, isotopes whose main physical differences were determined by their nuclei.

10. As Soddy 1923 explains, it took about a decade and considerable conceptual adjustment to recognize that the "transmuted" atoms did not just behave like the atoms of other (already known) elements, but had been transmuted into atoms of those elements.

11. Even that is not the full story, of course. Relativistic and quantum considerations about the binding energy that holds atomic nuclei together provide a further understanding of the additional subtle departure of the masses of atomic nuclei from the masses that would result by adding together the masses of free protons and neutrons to obtain the mass of the nucleus. But we do not need to pursue these matters further to make the key points about changes in the concept of the atom.

The key point here is that the discovery of isotopes with different sta-
bilities means that chemical atoms of the same element are not chemically
homogeneous.[12] This means that the identity of the entities picked out by
the well-established attributes was not fully fixed by those attributes—
that we later had to choose which way to "fix" the reference to a single
isotope, to stable isotopes, or to all the isotopes of physical atoms with the
proper atomic number for the element in question.[13] Thus, I argue that the
entities designated by the chemical atoms of particular elements had to be
altered, not just by the recognition that atoms are divisible (which could
be dismissed as a simple error in our original conception of the entities
thus identified), but because the atoms in a given element in a chemically
pure sample are often inhomogeneous (e.g., have different masses) and
can behave in drastically different ways since some will, while others will
not, produce chemical impurities in a chemically pure sample that has not
had any relevant interaction with other bodies! This recognition surely
ought to be counted as requiring a change in the identity and meaning (in
Rand's and Lennox's sense) of the concept of the (chemical) atom.

The revised concept of the atom clearly derives from the original
(Daltonian or Lavoisierian) chemical concept of the atom, a concept that
(like that of the electron or the gene) that had open-ended reference *ab
initio*. But the "reference potential" of the new concept has now been altered from that of the original concept.[14] However, the fact that it referred
originally to physically distinct entities, some stable and some unstable,
casts doubt on the stability of reference of the original term in the face of

12. There are additional chemical differences between isotopes as is nicely shown in
Weisberg and Needham 2010. This article also reviews some of the issues discussed above and
supplies some useful additional references.

13. This choice is not as clear-cut as it may seem. Some isotopes have extremely short
half-lives, less than 10^{-3} seconds, and so have never been collected in sufficient quantities to
have their chemical properties tested. Their existence is not "merely" theoretical in the sense
that they have been detected by the radioactivity released by their decay and by other means,
but their existence has not been confirmed by standard chemical tests of the sort that are used
to ascertain properties like color, molecular weight, and the like.

14. As far as I know, the term "reference potential" was introduced into the literature by
Philip Kitcher (1978, 1982, 1984); I first used the term in Burian 1985. My use is slightly different than Kitcher's, for his use was strictly extensional and mine is not, but for present purposes the differences do not matter. The reference potential of a term or concept reflects the
devices that achieve "closure" pertaining even to open-ended concepts in virtue of which one
can judge whether new instances "fall under" or are designated by the concept or not. Thus,
"human," "square," and "justice" are open-ended concepts that an infant must learn—and

new knowledge—and the fact that resolution of such problems as that of the atomic weight of chlorine can be achieved by recognizing that there are (at least) two distinct entities referred to by the phrase "an atom of chlorine" makes it clear which way the choices have gone.

Lennox and I are, I am confident, in fairly close agreement about the historical tale that I told above, although I fear we will not yet be in agreement with the moral that I am trying to draw from it about the ways in which first-order scientific concepts can change. The issues between us do not turn on the details about the timing of discoveries or about the nature of the work that went into those discoveries. Rather, they turn on issues about the nature of concepts. One contrast that may help to illuminate the issues between us is the contrast between "phenomenal" and "postulational" concepts and their connection to perception. To help articulate that contrast, a briefer and more elementary sketch of another complicated case may be of help.

On one understanding of this distinction between phenomenal and postulational theories (which has been understood in several other ways), it clarifies two distinct readings of the first articulation of the concept of the gene.[15] That articulation is due to Wilhelm Johannsen, who coined it as a replacement for "pangene," "Anlage," "determiner," and other words committed to specific theories about the intrinsic structure, nature, or material of the causes of inherited traits: "We will simply speak of 'the gene' and 'the genes' instead of . . . [using these other terms]. The word 'gene' is completely free from any hypothesis. It expresses only the evident fact that, in any case, many characteristics of the organism are specified

---

learn to apply to instances in different circumstances. I maintain that there may be differences in the reference potential of these concepts (or the terms employed that reflect or represent the concepts) in different societies, within different circles within a society, and within an individual's life as he or she learns more about items that, initially, were thought to fall under the concept. Differences in reference potential can be reflected in definitions and qualifiers that are deployed—compare, for instance, the difference between the terms "distributive justice" and "retributive justice," terms that capture distinct but related concepts however well or poorly we can define them. But it also is brought about by the social creation of new circumstances that create new situations not previously entertained (compare the existence of cyborgs and the development of biotechnologies as altering the reference potential of "human," or the creation of manufacturing economies that alter the possible relationships within families, between families and employers, and thus the reference potential of "justice").

15. It also distinguishes the energeticist (allied with phenomenal) and materialist (postulational) interpretations of atomic theory in the late nineteenth century.

in the gametes by means of special conditions, foundations, and determiners which are present in unique, separate, and thereby independent ways—in short, precisely what we wish to call genes" (Johannsen 1909; translation here from Elof Carlson 1966, 20–22). According to the reading in which Johannsen is proposing a phenomenal concept, although there might be some sort of unknown entity involved, all we know about genes is that there is some unknown cause or constellation of causes for specific traits being inherited in Mendelian patterns. We have no knowledge of the intrinsic characteristics of such putative causes; that is, Johannsen denies that we know any (first-order) properties or attributes of genes (except the second-order property that they are present in germ cells).[16] True, there must be such attributes, but what we know is only that genes are the relevant causes of the inheritance of Mendelian differences in sexual organisms (and in the asexual offspring of plants) and that they are already present in germ cells that yield the organism in sexual crosses exhibiting Mendelian inheritance—and this is not sufficient for us to have any direct knowledge of their attributes. Thus, we do not have the sorts of assurance that we do in the case of concepts like those of "tree," "rectangle," "human," or "fire," concepts of entities in the presence of which we have actually succeeded in securing reference to a (homogeneous) class of entities that share a common attribute or attributes.

This contrasts with the "postulational" interpretation of scientific concepts such as "atom," "electron," and "gene."[17] Although we have at best first approximations of knowledge of those entities, that knowledge depends on theories employing the corresponding concepts. To be sure, in all such cases there are "phenomenal" and experimental regularities that are employed in constructing the concepts. These mean that, in good cases we will have picked out a homogeneous class of entities about which we have some significant knowledge. But it will often be the case that we have lumped together a series of different things and that we must adjust

16. That is not sufficient to guarantee that they have a precise location. Johannsen was already aware that William Bateson thought that genes might be something like stable harmonic resonances, a model that might allow them to dictate aspects of the form of an organism and to explain the inheritance of discrete characters like additional petals (in flowers) or vertebrae in animals (and other meristic parts of organisms that were added in whole units rather than by gradual accretion of material and the like). For some more details, see Burian 2000 and the references it contains.

17. "Postulational" because these concepts cannot be arrived at by straightforward extrapolation from first-order perceptual concepts. In this sense, the concept of gravity is no less a postulational concept than "atom" or "gene."

the theories and the concepts if we are to achieve homogeneous reference based on common attributes. The test is not whether we have formed the concepts properly, but whether the world behaves in accord with the expectations they generate as we learn and experience more.

Conclusions

For both Rand and Lennox as I understand their views, systematic changes in accepted attributes that alter the class of entities designated by a first-order concept are legitimate only as long as "the same" (open-ended) class of referents is retained. Since that class is open-ended, it is a significant epistemological challenge to determine whether a change in definition is legitimate. They insist that the challenge is fundamentally epistemological; the test of legitimacy is whether the key instances and the kinds of similarity (or identifying attributes) employed to identify new instances falling under the concept are sufficient to pick out the same open-ended class of referents as was picked out before. When this condition is met, a change in definition preserves the identity and meaning of the concept because it preserves the identity of the referents across the change of definition. (Remember that the meaning and identity of a concept are determined by the open-ended class of referents that the concept in question designates.) When it is not met, either we replace the concept or we face major difficulties about reevaluating first-order concepts. To this point, I have presented a prima facie case that first-order concepts of the sciences, such as the concepts of a (chemical) atom, an electron, or a gene, present just such difficulties. To close, I want to suggest that the same is de facto true of ordinary concepts as well.

Consider the concept of a rectangle. If we have not already done so, we learn how to define that concept when we are taught to define "rectangle" in elementary school. But the concept "rectangle" becomes problematic if one treats it as (necessarily?) according with Euclidean geometry since (as we now know, but the ancients did not) the axioms of Euclidean geometry do not apply exactly to many phenomenal rectangles—witness how surveyors' "rectangles" go wrong if they are laid out over a large enough portion of the surface of the earth. Or consider the concept "human." We have already reached the point of recognizing that new knowledge presents us with at least some difficulty about how to think about this concept. Should we count the brain-dead body of a human being as no longer a human being, or is the still-living body (in the full sense) a human being? What of fertilized eggs in a deep freezer that have not yet formed a blastula, let alone a gastrula? In the nineteenth century, fertilized eggs generally did not count as embryos—and in earlier centuries embryos did not count as human beings in Western cultures. Or to invoke what is still science fiction, but no longer undreamable—should we count human-ape hybrids as human if any are ever produced and if it turns out that they are not capable of (recognizable) rational thought? (May we never live to see the day when we face such a dilemma!)

The point here is one of principle. "Open-ended" really means that there is genuine openness of a sort that is compatible with divergent pathways, the end points of which are, well, different according to different initial criteria that seem to agree so far as they have been tested. That concepts are well formed does not guarantee that the world will behave in such a way as to conform to the limits and expectations we build into (or intend to build into) our concepts. We may find ourselves in a position analogous to that of anatomists and embryologists disagreeing about what to count as a cirriped, or chemists and physicists disagreeing about what to count as an atom, even when we are dealing with familiar concepts about the everyday world. It is not just the well-formedness of concepts that counts in these matters; another crucial factor is whether the world behaves in close enough accord with our expectations that we can still successfully apply the concepts with which we started.

One can be optimistic that we are doing pretty well on such fronts, at least when we stick fairly close to familiar experience (and I think there are good reasons to be optimistic that most of our first-order perceptual concepts are well grounded in this regard), but to be genuine fallibilists about such matters (which I, for one, think we should be and which, it appears, Lennox thinks we should be), we cannot presume that any of our concepts are guaranteed to hold fast in the face of advancing knowledge. That is the most fundamental reason for my resistance to what I take to be Lennox's conservatism, following Rand, about change in the identity and meaning of concepts in his excellent contribution to this volume.

Conceptual Development versus Conceptual Change
Response to Burian

JAMES G. LENNOX

In my essay in part 1 I characterized five categories of change in the conceptual structure of a science and stressed the importance of distinguishing them from the philosophically problematic notion of change in the meaning or identity of a concept. Richard Burian speaks approvingly of that distinction in his comment. Nevertheless, his comments suggest that he thinks at least some changes of the first sort entail changes of the second. In this response I challenge that suggestion, which in my view leads to the sort of skepticism about scientific progress that both of us think is untenable. To that end, I will say a bit more about what I have in mind by "conceptual development" and how I see it as importantly different from what philosophers of science have referred to as "conceptual change."

Burian characterizes his own position by contrasting it with the one that I defend: "In contrast to Lennox I hold that first-order scientific concepts can sometimes be retained with major systematic revisions of the class of entities to which they refer. Such revisions often depend on the interactions among distinct disciplines that employ different tools to investigate the same scientific object, yielding initially discordant results that are, eventually, reconciled by modifications of the concept."

The first sentence in this passage suggests a number of questions, among which are the following:

1. What are first-order scientific concepts?

2. What does it mean to say they are "retained" through revisions?

3. What constitutes a "major systematic revision of the class of entities to which they [first-order concepts] refer"?

I agree with the claim in the second sentence, that such revisions often arise due to interactions between different sciences employing different tools, and I find Burian's essays on the history and philosophy of biology enlightening on just this point. He adds, however, that the results that arise from the use of these different methods are sometimes initially discordant, and he states that harmony arises, when it does, through a "modification of the concept." What is at stake, of course, is what it means that a concept is "retained" (as the first sentence in the above quote says) and yet is "modified" in light of discordant findings (as the second sentence claims).

So let us consider the three questions occasioned by the first sentence above.

First, what are "first-order" concepts? Throughout his comments, Burian uses a number of different terms to designate a class of concepts that he wants to single out for special consideration, but I am uncertain about whether all of them refer to the same class. Thus, he refers to "core concepts," "base concepts," and (as above) "first-order" scientific concepts. He also distinguishes concepts in terms of their relative "basal" or "higher" level within a science. Finally, near the close of his comments in a discussion about the concept of the "gene," he introduces a distinction between "postulational" and "phenomenal" concepts, a distinction I believe he intends to pick out two different ways of thinking about the introduction of new concepts in science, when the referents of those concepts are not available to direct observation. That is, this is not a distinction between two categories of *concept*, but a distinction between two ways of *conceptualizing*.

It is because I believe that the process of introducing concepts that refer to such "hidden" or "theoretical" entities raise a number of special problems not raised by other abstract scientific concepts that I focused in my essay on a case of radical reclassification where the abstract, classificatory concepts ultimately refer directly to observable organisms. However, without going into details, the fact that Darwin's work on Cirripedia was the basis for a historical study (Jardine 2009, referred to by Burian) of his use of the microscope serves to make an important point: there may be more continuity between the formation of concepts such as "atom" and "electron" and concepts of newly discovered but more directly observable entities than is typically supposed.[1]

Now it sometimes sounds as if by a "base" or "first-order" concept Burian means a concept that is the least abstract in a scientific domain and, to use an Aristotelian expression, "nearest to perception." But on other occasions he seems to have in mind something like the "most fundamental" or "central" concept for a particular science or scientific theory, concepts such as "atom" in chemistry, "electron" in physics, or "gene" in biology. I will take Burian's decision to illustrate his view by sketching a history of the development of the concept of "atom" in chemistry to indicate that it is this latter sort of concept he has in mind, without being at all certain.

Second, what does Burian mean by his claim that concepts are "retained" through a "major systematic revision of the class of entities" to which the concepts refer? Since my essay also argues that, in cases where new knowledge does not lead us to eliminate a concept, the concept is retained, about that we do not disagree. So the disagreement, if such there is, must be about what is implied by such retention, and what sorts of modifications are permissible while claiming that the same concept has been retained. And that takes us to the third question, regarding concept retention through "major, systematic revisions" in reference.

The history of atomic chemistry is not an area in which I have any expertise (which is why I selected biological examples), but I am in agreement with Burian that our principal disagreements center on the philosophical lessons to be drawn from the history rather than the history itself (though the historical details may be important in resolving those disagreements). I will take his recounting of the story as accurate and assume it is intended to exemplify his claim about concept retention through systematic revision in reference. I will argue that there are problems with his way of handling such cases that can be avoided on the view I defended, properly understood. In order to do so, it will be useful to review a few key ideas that differentiate my Rand-inspired approach to conceptual development from Burian's.

1. On which see the suggestive comments toward the close of the section on the "Nature, Basis, and Formation of Concepts" in Gotthelf's essay in part 1.

First, we need to be clear on how I understand Rand's claim that concepts are open-end classifications. Burian often adopts that language in his comments, and as I noted in my essay, he has for many years himself been using the phrase "open reference" in a way that captures at least part of what Rand has in mind by concepts being "open-end." As far as I can tell, however, by this term Burian intends to capture only the very limited idea that a certain concept, say "atom," refers to all atoms—this is reflected in his language of "open-ended sets of entities" and "open-ended class of entities." The concept has an open extension, in other words. For Rand, as I understand her, the open-end nature of concepts is intimately connected to her views about the cognitive role of concepts. As I stress in my essay, and as is explained in more detail in those of Gotthelf and Salmieri, Rand is building on a theory of concepts that is normative in two respects: to be valid, concepts must be formed in conformity with appropriate methods; and concepts fulfill crucial cognitive needs that put constraints on whether, and when, a concept should be formed, eliminated, subdivided, and so on. These norms have implications for how one should respond to new information about a concept's referents. As I said in the essay, it "is a critical part of her view that such growth in knowledge *depends on* the concept retaining its identity through constant integrative updating." This entails a commitment to a *policy* of such "updating." To use the language adopted by Salmieri in his contribution to part 1, concepts, as forms of awareness, should be viewed not as static objects but as an "institutionalized policy of considering things in a certain manner." This involves a process of attempting to integrate new information with what is already known and reconsidering the relationship of the referents of a concept with those of other concepts as the context of our knowledge widens. Concepts are, as I put it at one point, loci of integration and reintegration. To take an example I alluded to in my essay: suppose you form the concept "mammal" on the basis of a readily observable network of similarities among land-dwelling, air-breathing, viviparous creatures with legs, and then discover that many water-dwelling animals that superficially appear to be more similar to fish are air-breathing and viviparous—and further study keeps turning up more similarities with mammals. At this point an interesting choice emerges, which can be illustrated historically. Aristotle, while knowing about many important similarities between cetacean physiology and the land-dwelling vivipara, does not form our concept "mammal"—his nearest equivalent category is (in Latin parlance) "viviparous quadruped." He decides to treat Cetacea as a distinct kind at the level of "fish" and "viviparous quadruped." When the evolutionary relationship of cetaceans to land mammals is discovered, placing them with the category "mammal" provides the most economical way of integrating that new understanding with what was already known. They are, along many important axes of similarity, mammalian, and a new causal understanding of these similarities is provided. This surprising extension of the concept to a large class of things not imagined to belong in the same order does not, from Rand's perspective, change the identity of the concept "mammal." It continues to refer to the same network of similarities, but there are a large number of unexpected aquatic members now included in its reference.

This is a "major systematic revision of the class of entities" to which the concept "mammal" refers. If it is Burian's claim that the view of conceptual development I am defending does not have the resources to deal with such changes, I hope that the above remarks will allay his fears.

The second aspect of Rand's view about the open-end nature of concepts that I stress is that a concept includes reference to the *yet-to-be-discovered characteristics* of the entities it subsumes. Returning to the previous example: we need to integrate new information about evolutionary relatedness, along with all the modifications of mammalian structures for an aquatic way of life found in cetaceans, into our concept "mammal," and to eliminate assumptions (if such there were) about mammals being essentially land dwellers. To say that a concept is "open-end" in nature is to say that the formation of a concept includes a commitment to integrating everything that will later be learned about its referents. And if we later learn things that indicate we were initially misled in *forming* the concept, we will need to eliminate or replace it.

This way of thinking about the open-end character of concepts is a natural implication of thinking of concepts as a form of being aware of the world that must be volitionally implemented and maintained. It also implies that concept-formation is a fallible process, and the history of science bears witness to its fallibility. Especially in science, where researchers are typically pushing on the limits of what information is currently accessible about the natural world, new information may require those researchers to reconsider previously formed concepts in a variety of ways. It was in the interests of spelling out some of that variety that I opened my essay by characterizing five ways future research might lead to such reconsideration—none of which, I argued, demanded that the concepts involved change their meaning.[2] I now turn to Burian's concerns on that front.

The insight in Rand's view that it is important to hold on to is that concepts are critical to the process of integrating new information with what is already known—they are the tools for that work. New concepts are formed in part to facilitate that process, and already formed concepts are important tools for dealing with new knowledge.

On the Objectivist view of concepts there are at least three kinds of change that may take place as a response to learning new information about the referents of a concept.

1. New knowledge can lead to various kinds of change in the *definition* of the concept.[3] The example of reclassification discussed in the third section of my essay showed how new information about the developmental life history of the cirripeds required that the phylum in which that order belonged be reconsidered. On Rand's view of concepts, that change depends on a complex process of reconsidering how these animals are related to and differentiated from other, similar animals—and, as I noted, reconsidering which features were most important in that reconsideration. Similarly, the new information about the complex internal structure of the atom discussed in Burian's comment raises fundamental questions about which features of that structure are causally fundamental, and thus essential. As I see it, such a reconsideration can, and as far as I understand the history in this case did, lead to a change in *definition*—but I do not see that the concept "atom" changed as a consequence.[4]

2. Rand typically discusses this issue in terms of the designation or denotation of concepts, rather than their meaning, but the fundamental point can be expressed in that language. On the view defended in my essay in part 1, the meaning of a concept includes both yet-to-be-discovered information about its referents *and* a standing policy to integrate new information about those referents by the same method that was used in forming the concept—and that new information may lead to a reconsideration of which attributes are most fundamental or how the existents subsumed are to be differentiated from others.

3. In the philosophical literature on this topic changes in definition are often assumed to entail changes in meaning, but on Rand's view that is a fundamental mistake. For a recent example, see Brigandt 2010.

4. It has occurred to me, however, that once it was determined that the "atom" had distinguishable constituents, and especially after the discovery that certain elements had isotopes with different atomic weights, it would be a reasonable question to ask whether a word, selected because of its etymological tie to the Greek for "indivisible," is the best *word* to denote the objects in question.

2. New information may, however, simply be "more of the same," that is, new information that is easily assimilated with what is already known. Though I have not made a careful study of this, it does not appear that what we have learned about Cirripedia (now termed an infra-class of the subphylum Crustacea) *since* they were reclassified has led to any significant changes in how the class is defined.

3. Finally, there is the sort of conceptual development raised by an example discussed in Burian's brief sketch of the development of atomic theory—the discovery, well after the concept of the atom was established in chemistry, that certain atoms came in more and less stable forms, eventually leading to the idea of certain elements having distinct isotopes.[5] This is the sort of case where Burian's work on the "triangulation" by the methods of different sciences on an object of investigation is so valuable. But in my view this does not indicate that the *concept* of the atom changed. What it indicates is that we learned a great deal about atoms between 1913 and 1940, which led, among other things, to a subdivision of the concepts for specific elements. What makes various isotopes forms of the same element, it came to be understood, after techniques for exploring atomic nuclei were developed, was a shared number of protons, specified in the atomic number for the element, and reflected in having very similar, but not identical, atomic weights; isotopes of an element are differentiated by have differing numbers of neutrons. For example, carbon has six protons, but may have either six, seven, or eight neutrons, giving rise to isotopes carbon-12, -13, or -14 with mass numbers 12, 13, and 14, respectively.

The development of this understanding, Burian claims, suggests that in the early stages of theoretical advance, "the identity of the entities picked out by the well-established attributes was not fully fixed" and that we later had to make a choice about whether the element name would be associated with a single isotope, the stable subset, or all isotopes. Burian claims that this case "ought to be counted as requiring a change in the identity and meaning (in Rand's and Lennox's sense) of the concept of the (chemical) atom."

But on the view defended in my essay, the stable identity of a *concept* only requires that at the time the concept is formed (on the basis of ini-

5. As far as I have been able to track it, this began with recognition of radioactive decay in a small number of elements, and was later generalized to all elements.

tially available evidence) it includes norm-governed policies for integrating new information about those entities in the future. Nor is the fact that new information about the relationship between an element's behavior, mass, and neutron number led to the need to make choices about how to conceptualize this new knowledge problematic. Chapter 7 of *ITOE*, "The Cognitive Role of Concepts," has advice, based on the importance of what Rand terms "unit economy" for human cognition, about such situations, but the implementation of that advice will depend on the extent to which the new information acquired is significant enough to require the formation of a new concept (such as "isotope"), a change in the definition of the concept (based, e.g., on information about atomic structure), or the concept's replacement or retirement.

As the history is sketched in Burian's comment, it seems that a complex interplay between new information about the mass and stability of various elements and new information about atomic structure led to the discovery of distinct elemental isotopes. The gradual recognition of the pervasiveness of such differences among samples of elements otherwise alike led to the formation of the concept "isotope" to denote *any* of these forms of the same element—and Burian rightly notes that a choice had to be made at that point about how to deal with this new complexity. Through this process, researchers came to know vastly more about atomic structure, but, to borrow Rand's metaphor, the more that they came to know went into the same file. Of course, that new knowledge had to be integrated with what was previously known, but that very process was facilitated by there being a stable locus for that integration.

These historical developments reflect, of course, a different sort of conceptual development than that discussed in my original essay. Every chemical definition I have seen of "isotope" refers to isotopes as "forms" or "variants" of an element (so, as noted above, there are three forms of carbon). This suggests that new chemical knowledge about atomic nuclei led to the need for a *subdivision* of concepts denoting chemical elements to reflect and systematize this new knowledge. But note that the system of concepts already in place for the atomically defined elements was critically important for this advance.

Let me close with a brief thought, requiring further exploration, about how concepts for what Theodore Arabatzis has called "hidden entities" are introduced into a science (Arabatzis 2011).[6] Burian in his com-

6. Arabatzis has self-consciously chosen this language to get away from the misleading distinction between "theoretical" and "observational" entities, a move I applaud.

ment distinguishes "postulational" from "phenomenal" concepts. But if I understand him correctly, these are not different *concepts*, but different normative stances one can take toward concept-formation when concepts for "hidden entities" ("gene," "electron") are being introduced and defined. It is of the very nature of such cases that relatively little is known initially about the referents beyond the fact that there is a set of correlated observations for which there are good reasons to think there is a common cause or source. There is, in other words, good reason to think that such a unifying cause exists before much is known about the nature of that cause.[7]

Early in his comment, Burian notes that when a concept for entities of this kind is introduced, there is typically "indefiniteness of causal ascriptions." One example of such indefinite ascription he gives is: "the gene is whatever it is that is responsible for the stable inheritance of Mendelian characters." I suppose this is a case of what he later refers to as the introduction of a "phenomenal" concept, a policy he sees being followed by Johannsen in his introduction of the term "gene" in 1909. And I suppose he refers to this way of introducing a concept as "phenomenal" because it prescinds from postulating a specific "hidden cause." He attributes to me the claim that in such cases the "designation" can be pinned down by "inadequate or mistaken definitions." This is not how I would put it, however. I would say that the "pinning down" is accomplished by means of a *contextually correct* definition, which may well be replaced or modified in the ways specified in my essay as our knowledge of the objects of investigation—that is, the context—widens and deepens. In any case, at this point in his comment he questions whether scientific concepts, particularly the core concepts of what he terms "postulational" theories, that is, concepts like "electron" and "gene," can be so pinned down. I not only believe they can, but I believe in specific historic circumstances it is the right policy. So let me now turn to Burian's later, specific introduction of this issue near the end of his comment to make my own, still evolving, views on this topic as clear as I can.

In that later discussion, Burian cites Wilhelm Johannsen's introduction of the concept "gene," and I believe it is intended to exemplify what he calls a "phenomenal" policy of concept introduction. The thought, I take it, is that Johannsen is not merely recommending that everyone in-

7. Aristotle discusses just such a stage of knowledge in *Posterior Analytics* II, the second in what David Charles refers to as Aristotle's three-stage view of inquiry (see Charles 2000, 23–56).

vestigating inheritance adopt the same term for the unit of inheritance to avoid confusion; he is, rather, introducing a concept based solely on agreed-to experimental results and recommending that it *replace* others that are tied to still speculative theoretical commitments, for example, about the material structure, location, or causal powers of those units. Johannsen may be recommending the latter *in order to* form a concept on which everyone, regardless of their more speculative commitments, can agree.

Burian introduces this distinction to help clarify differences between our positions, but as far as I can tell he never articulates how he thinks it does so. Because, in his conclusion, he characterizes my (and Rand's) position as "conservative," I suspect he thinks I will always recommend what he refers to as the phenomenalist strategy. I would prefer not to use that language, tied as it is to radical empiricism. I would prefer to frame my approach in terms of the kind, and the strength, of the observational/ experimental (i.e., inductive) evidence that gives rise to the need to form a concept. The issue is difficult to discuss without taking into account historical context, and thus without an example in view. Sticking with the history of genetics, I will briefly discuss its source document.

Earlier than Johannsen, Gregor Mendel, in his classic paper reporting his investigation of hybrid series in pea plants (Mendel 1866), exemplifies the norms that are well suited to such "hidden entity" cases. The paper is clearly divided into two distinct sections. In the first, he reports the observational results of an elaborate and beautifully designed series of experiments, reporting first the raw data, from which he abstracts arithmetic ratios and then further abstracts an algebraic formula for the series. All of this refers to the observable features of the plants—the colors of the seeds and flowers, the height of the stock, the shapes of the pods and seeds, and so on. But then Mendel turns to the question of what can be confidently inferred from these results about the internal makeup of the reproductive cells that would explain these results. He neither refrains from exploring the causal question nor speculates beyond what he has good evidence for. The language he uses is noncommittal—there are "factors" in the pollen and germinal cells that interact upon fertilization, but do not "blend." Though one clearly dominates over the other (e.g., the factor for yellow seed dominates over that for green, so that when you cross plants with these factors the first generation are all yellow), the patterns of inheritance over the next generations show that they remain independent. These "hidden" factors in the reproductive cells, he is confident from observational evidence, causally interact with each other in various ways and are causally responsible for the observable attributes of the plants; and he designs a distinct series of experiments to test his hypothesis about them.

Mendel, then, does not prescind from discussing these "hidden entities," nor does he go beyond what his experimental evidence supports. But note: that evidence supports confident assertions about the *causal powers* of these hidden factors, without providing support for their material structure, precise location within the cells, size, mode of causal action, and so on. Without wanting to impose the "phenomenal/postulational" labels on him, it strikes me that Mendel's approach is an exemplary way of introducing concepts of (currently) hidden entities without speculating beyond what is sanctioned by available knowledge. He has created a folder (later relabeled "gene" by Johannsen) within which to file an ever-expanding body of information.[8]

In this response I have provided more detail regarding Rand's thoughts on the open-end character of concepts and her understanding of conceptual development. I have done so by addressing, at least in a preliminary way, concerns that Burian has about what he refers to as the "core concepts" of a science in the interests of moving our ongoing dialogue on this topic forward another step or two.

---

8. A case I have been working on for the past year or so with this question in mind exemplifies the same approach, Robert Koch's research into the microbial agents of infectious diseases (see Koch 1880, 1881). An interesting aspect of both cases is the way in which the unanswered questions about the "hidden entities" drive innovations in observational technology and experimental design.

Perceptual Awareness

In Defense of the Theory of Appearing
Comments on Ghate and Salmieri

PIERRE LE MORVAN

A s a fellow direct realist, and as a proponent of the Theory of Appearing (TA) in particular, I am naturally sympathetic to the account of perception that Onkar Ghate and Gregory Salmieri attribute to Rand in their essays in part 1 of this volume. My primary aim in this response, however, is to defend the TA against Ghate's central criticism of William P. Alston's version of it.[1] In relation to this defense, I shall also critically discuss the infallibilist account of perception that Salmieri attributes to Rand and argue for a fallibilism consonant with the TA.[2] First, I delineate important similarities between the TA and what we may call Rand-

---

1. Ghate discusses Alston's version of the TA, and I shall be defending his version in this response. See Alston 1990, 1998a, 1999, 2002, 2005b. Note, however, that Alston was not the first or only defender of the TA. Other defenses of the TA have been given by Prichard 1909, Coffey 1917, Hicks 1938, Barnes 1945, Langsam 1997, and Le Morvan 2000, 2004. Views akin to it, reinvented later and apparently independently of it, include positions known as "disjunctivism" (see, e.g., Martin, unpublished manuscript; and Brewer 2011a); and "the relational view" (see, e.g., Campbell 2002). Moreover, as Coffey 1917 points out, the scholastic perceptionists anticipated the TA.

2. Unfortunately, space constraints will preclude me from commenting on other aspects of Salmieri's and Ghate's very interesting essays. For instance, I shall not comment on the account of concept-formation and justification that Salmieri attributes to Rand, although I

inspired presentationalism (RP) that Ghate finds in Rand's writings. I then critically discuss the infallibilist account of perception that Salmieri attributes to Rand and argue for a fallibilism consonant with the TA. Finally, I defend the TA against Ghate's central criticism and conclude with some synoptic remarks.[3]

Similarities between the TA and RP

From Ghate's discussion of presentationalism in the first two sections, we may note three crucial and interrelated points of agreement or contact between the TA and RP concerning the nature of perceptual awareness.

First, such awareness consists in a basic and irreducible presentation of mind-independent external objects to percipients. While propositional attitudes are representational in nature, perceptual awareness by contrast is essentially presentational.

Second, this presentation is ineluctably relational where the relata in question are external mind-independent objects on the one hand and percipients on the other, and where perceived objects are literally constituents of perceptual episodes.

Third, perceptual awareness is an awareness of objects or entities having various characteristics, and this perceptual awareness is a form of cognition distinct from conceptual cognition. While concepts may help direct our attention to objects and are essential to our forming beliefs about them, perceptual awareness provides the nonconceptual awareness that gives us something to conceptualize and to form beliefs about in the first place.

The TA and RP are thus both versions of direct realism: they are *realist* because they take perceived objects to be physical objects that exist independently of our perceptual awareness of them, and are *direct* realist because they deny that perceiving physical objects requires a logically prior awareness of some *tertium quid* (an idea, sense-datum, or what have you) putatively mediating between the perceiver and the perceived object. Both the TA and RP reject reifying appearances as objects of awareness.

---

must say that I find psychologically implausible the kind of volitionalism it involves. I shall also not have space to comment on Ghate's interesting discussion of hallucinations, conceptualization, and the Given.

3. In the ensuing discussion, I shall assume that Ghate and Salmieri are correct in their exposition of Rand's views of the nature of perception.

In light of these crucial similarities, one might wonder whether there is any real difference between the TA and RP. One might even wonder whether the latter is just a variant of the former. In light of such questions, let us consider the infallibilist conception of perception that Salmieri attributes to Rand.

Is Perception Infallible?

Consider Salmieri's instructive example of the myopic man looking at a tree without his glasses. While he sees the same tree he would see if he was wearing them, he sees it blurrily, and this blurriness is part of the way or form by which he sees the tree. As Salmieri notes in his section on "Epistemology and the Nature of Awareness," "An especially naïve realist would take the blurriness to be a feature of the very tree in front of which the man is standing." Such a naïve realist is, of course, mistaken, for he *mis*takes a way he perceives an object for a feature of the perceived object. But perceptual antirealists are also mistaken in supposing that to avoid this naïve realist error, one must posit some *tertium quid* between the tree and the myopic man, an object of awareness that actually has the feature of blurriness that the tree fails to have.

I wholeheartedly agree with Salmieri (and by extension Rand) that the correct way to avoid both these errors is to distinguish between perceived objects and the ways or forms by which we perceive them. To use the terminology of the TA, there is a distinction between perceived objects and how they phenomenally appear or are given or are presented to us.[4]

In light of Salmieri's blurriness example, one might think that perception is not infallible on Rand's view. According to Salmieri, however,

> Rand regarded perception as infallible in the sense of not being able to err. The many errors that are possible in identifying what one perceives are all posterior to the perception itself, on her view. An illusion, for example, is a case in which one object looks just like another object would in a more familiar circumstance, such that the first object is liable to be mistaken for the second. When such mistakes are made, however, the fault lies not in the perception, but in the judgments made about the perceived object.

4. Alston 1999 carefully distinguishes between phenomenal appearing and comparative, doxastic, and epistemic appearing. Phenomenal appearing is a matter of objects presenting distinctive qualitative features to us. When I talk of appearing, I mean it only in the phenomenal sense.

Salmieri also tells us: "Perception always occurs in a form. The form may be unfamiliar because of unusual conditions (as is the case in many illusions) or because of damage to the sense organs. Such perceptions might be less detailed, less useful, or more apt to be misinterpreted, than others, but they remain awarenesses of objects in the subject's environment, and there is no standard in accordance with which its *veridicality* can be impugned." Salmieri tells us as well that "perception's infallibility . . . consists in its inability to miscognize—to present the world as being other than as it is. In this way, perception is necessarily veridical." By contrast, he notes that "other cognitive states, however, including those at the perceptual level, can be nonveridical, in that they can represent the world as being other than it is. This is possible because perception's more basic presentation of the world forms a standard against which these other cognitions can be impugned."

Though Salmieri does not discuss the TA, his characterization of the Rand-inspired infallibilist position on perception helps to bring out a salient divergence between the two views. Let me therefore address why I find quite implausible the kind of infallibilism Salmieri attributes to Rand.

Salmieri sometimes sounds as if he is contending that there is no standard by which the veridicality of particular perceptions (or perceptual episodes) can be impugned. Take the myopic man. Without his glasses, the tree looks blurry to him. Suppose that, given his myopia and the viewing conditions, the tree cannot but look blurry to him. Does this mean that the veridicality of his seeing the tree under these conditions cannot be impugned? No. He can put on his glasses and look at the tree again, or ask others with 20/20 vision about how the tree looks; in such ways he can come to realize that although the tree looked blurry to him without his glasses, there is good reason to think that the tree itself is really not blurry. Appealing to one's later perceptions or to the perceptions of others can provide a standard by which one can impugn the veridicality of particular perceptions and discover that they were not presenting the world as it is. Contrary to Salmieri's (and by extension Rand's) contention, particular perceptions *can mis*cognize and present the world in ways other than it is; accordingly, particular perceptions are *not* necessarily infallible. We sometimes misrepresent the world in our judgments and beliefs *because* particular perceptions have presented it in ways other than it is.

Now suppose that the Rand-inspired perceptual infallibility is not that all particular perceptions are infallible, but rather that perception as a faculty or ability taken as a whole is infallible. For instance, when we appeal to other perceptions to correct particular perceptions, are we not ultimately appealing to the tribunal of perception itself? And do not our representational states concerning the world ultimately rest on our perceptions of it? This form of perceptual infallibilism strikes me as more defensible than supposing that (all) particular perceptions are infallible.

Perceptual *fallibilism* even at this level, however, strikes me as more sensible. Here is why. To be a realist about perception is to hold that what we perceive are physical objects, and that their existence (and that of at least some of their features) does not depend on our being perceptually aware or conscious of them, nor do all of their features exist only in relation to us. Contrast this with a perceptual antirealist, such as an idealist who thinks that the objects of awareness are existentially dependent on someone's perceiving or being conscious of them. While we realists can agree that such idealism ought to be rejected, notice how well infallibilism squares with such an account: *if* what we perceive depends on our perceiving or being conscious of it, it makes some sense to suppose that our perception is infallible for there can be no gap between the existence of the immediate object of awareness and the awareness of it.[5]

Insofar as we are realists, however, we take the objects that we perceive to have an existence independent of our perceiving or being conscious of them (and accordingly that not all their features exist only in relation to us). Moreover, we are not gods and are not endowed with god-like powers. Accordingly, the epistemic modesty of perceptual fallibilism strikes me as more befitting of a realist position. Perceptual fallibilism does not entail holding that perception never presents the world as it is or that it is not generally reliable (see Alston 1996). Rather, it holds that it is possible (at least sometimes) that features that objects are perceptually presented to us as having might not be features they actually have and/or that perceived objects might not be presented with all the features they actually have. While our judgments about the world ultimately rest on our perceptions of it, these perceptions provide us with prima facie and not infallible grounds for them. Such is the epistemic modesty of the per-

5. Recall here, for instance, Bishop George Berkeley's insistence on the infallibility of perception given the putative immediacy of the perception of mind-dependent sensory ideas (*Principles* §§85–90, esp. 90 [in Dancy 1998]).

ceptual fallibilism one finds with the TA, a view that is not only realist but *realistic,* given our human epistemic condition as finite beings.[6]

Ghate's Criticism of the TA

I earlier delineated some crucial similarities between the TA and RP, and I sympathize with Ghate's direct realism and his defense of the Given. In this section, however, I shall focus on his central criticism that, contrary to what the TA maintains, we should "reject the idea that perceptual awareness can 'match' or 'fail to match' the objects of awareness." Before doing so, however, I want to note a preliminary point concerning what he says about the language of appearance.

In an oblique criticism of the TA, Ghate complains that "the terminology of 'appearances' is misleading when used to describe perceptual awareness" on two counts: appearances are often reified into objects of awareness, but even when they are not, "'appearance' is normally used in a context where one seeks to distinguish something from fact: the person sitting over there in the bleachers appears to be Tom but is, in fact, Harry." On the first count, it is worth remembering that the TA is explicitly committed to *rejecting* the reification of appearance and treats it as a relation. On the second, Ghate fails to note that "appearance" is normally used not just in the sense to which he alludes, but also as a generic term encompassing phenomenal looking, sounding, tasting, and the like.[7]

With this preliminary point aside, let us now consider Ghate's key criticism of the TA. Recall that Ghate objects that, contrary to what the TA maintains, "we should reject the idea that perceptual awareness can 'match' or 'fail to match' the objects of awareness."[8] Ghate offers three main interconnected lines of reasoning for this conclusion, each of which fails.

First, while assuming that there are (only) two perspectives on the matter, he claims the following: "From one perspective, there can be no 'match' because sensory qualities are not characteristics of an object but of a relation; they are (aspects of) the object-*as-it-is-being-perceived-by-*

---

6. Ironically, while I take it that Rand strenuously opposed perceptual antirealism, the conception of perception that Salmieri attributes to her amounts to a kind of epistemic immodesty that one finds with appearance reifying infallibilists in supposing that human perception is infallible.

7. See the *OED*'s definitions of "appearance," especially entries 8–14.

8. Recall that perceptual awareness on the TA consists in one or more external objects appearing in certain ways to percipients.

the-subject. From another perspective, they always match because they are (aspects of) the *object*-as-it-is-being-perceived-by-the-subject." A major problem with this line of reasoning is that the TA in no way denies, and in fact it maintains, that sensory qualities "are (aspects of) the *object*-as-it-is-being-perceived-by-the-subject.*" By saying there is no guaranteed match between how an object appears and how it really is, Alston means that just because an object appears (e.g., looks, tastes, sounds, feels, or smells) *F* (e.g., blurry, circular, green, sour, etc.) to someone *S,* it does not automatically follow that the object really is *F,* although its appearing so to *S* gives *S* a prima facie ground for believing that it is. Just because a tree looks blurry to me under certain perceptual conditions, it does not follow that it really is blurry. Even if the tree really has (or even must have) the relational property of looking blurry to me under certain perceptual conditions, it does not follow that it is blurry independently of those conditions. The tree's nature does not depend on my consciousness of it even though its aspect of looking blurry partially depends on my consciousness of the tree. It is in this sense that how an object appears can fail to match how it really is, for it has an existence independent of my (or any finite being's) consciousness of it. Does Ghate really want to deny the possibility of failure of matching *in this sense?* If RP is committed to such a denial, this seems to me good reason to prefer the much more realistic realism of the TA.

A second line of reasoning he adduces also fails. Ghate insists that perception is awareness of an object no matter what "the specific forms of a perceiver's perceptual awareness of those objects, and however those forms vary from episode of perception to episode of perception as the perceiver's means of perception or his conditions of perception change." Recall that the TA and RP are in agreement on this matter. Ghate then points out that "there is no standpoint from which one could declare that, say, visual awareness of the cylindrical pen presents the pen 'as it really is,' but tactile awareness of the cylindrical pen fails to presents the pen 'as it really is'—or vice versa. And when one rejects naïve realism, when one recognizes that perceptual *awareness* itself has a nature, there is no need to privilege one form of awareness over another, as presenting the way the object 'really is.' Every form of perceptual *awareness* of some objects is a form of perceptual awareness of those *objects.*"

Ghate then declares that "Alston thinks that a non-naïve version of presentationalism can reject this conclusion, but it is not clear why he thinks this." However unintentionally, Ghate's charge here traduces

Alston's version of the TA. In fact, the passage from Alston that he cites makes no such claims: "TA, as I understand it, is not saddled with the thesis that objects only appear perceptually as what they actually are. It is not that 'naïve' a direct realism. . . . It is a familiar fact of life that perceived objects are not always what they perceptually appear to be. . . . The directness and givenness [of perceptual awareness] has to do with the absence of any mediation in the awareness, not with any guaranteed match between how X appears and what it is" (Alston 1999, 183).

As I have indicated before, Alston's point here is that it is possible for perceived objects to not appear as they really are. But this does not entail privileging one form of awareness (e.g., visual awareness) over another (e.g., tactile awareness), or denying that awareness itself has a nature, or that every "form of perceptual *awareness* of some objects is a form of perceptual awareness of those *objects*." While I trust he has done so unintentionally, Ghate has mischaracterized Alston's version of the TA.

This brings us to his third main line of reasoning. After quoting the passage above, Ghate notes correctly that, according to Alston, the converse of "'a perceiver is perceptually aware in a certain way of external objects' is 'those external objects appear in a certain way to the perceiver.'" Ghate then insists *on a point that Alston or any other defender of the TA has not denied*, namely, "A particular appearance, a particular presentation, of the external objects to the perceiver has itself a specific nature, an identity." He asks, "What would it mean for a presentation of external objects to 'fail to match' what those objects are?" and avers that presentation and objects presented are not comparable in this way. Ghate proceeds to examine a number of ways that he speculates one might try to make sense of this, and finds them all unsatisfactory. Curiously, however, he fails to directly address the way that the defenders of the TA such as Alston *have* made sense of this, namely, that an object may appear (e.g., look, taste, sound, feel, or smell) *F* (e.g., blurry, circular, green, sour, etc.) to someone without actually being *F*. What could be more obvious? To use a previous example, a tree can look blurry under certain perceptual conditions without actually being blurry in its existence independent of our perceptual awareness of it.

What seems to escape Ghate in his inability to make sense of the above noted failure to match is that the TA distinguishes between (1) the way(s) a perceived object is in perceptual relation to someone, and (2) how it is independently of its perceptual relation to someone. The first is concerned with the perceived object as it appears to someone, and the second with the perceived object independently of how it appears to someone. Yes, both concern the perceived object. Yes, a perceived object is an actual relatum in the appearing relation. Note, however, that when they talk about the perceived object *as it actually or really is,* defenders of the TA, such as Alston, mean how it is independently of its appearing to someone. What the TA allows for is the possibility that (at least sometimes) the features perceived objects are perceptually presented or given to someone as having might not be features they have *independently of their being so presented or given,* and/or perceived objects might not be presented or given to someone with all the features they have *independently of their being so presented or given.*[9]

The TA's allowance for this possibility does not require denying that "the presentation is a relational phenomenon," or taking external objects themselves to be "relational phenomena," thereby abandoning presentationalism in favor of some version of representationalism," or supposing that "external objects and their characteristics should be presented in only one way to the perceiver," or ruling out "that we can be perceptually aware of the cylindrical pen through vision and through touch."

It is unfortunate that Ghate is unable to make sense of a possibility that on the TA is very much a live one.[10] His (and by extension Salmieri's and Rand's) inability to make sense of this possibility stems I suspect from a fundamentally erroneous supposition about the nature of perceptual error that he ironically shares with representationalists, namely, the idea that perceptual error can occur *only if* perceptual awareness is representational in nature.[11] Of course, *if* one accepts this idea, one may very well suppose that, if perceptual awareness is not representational but presentational in nature, it is infallible. The TA, however, advances a *presentationalist* challenge to this supposition, for it shows how one can account for perceptual error presentationally. How? In terms of *phenomenal fidelity,* which is a function of the extent to which perceptual awareness

9. For instance (assuming color realism), just because a red object may look (say) gray to a deuteranope, it does not follow that the perceived object really is gray independently of its appearing gray to this person. Even if the object cannot but look gray to that person, it does not follow that the object really is gray.

10. And insofar as RP cannot make sense of this possibility, this strikes me as a good reason to prefer the TA.

11. This mistake is related to another that I suspect he shares with the appearance-reifying defenders of the Given, namely, that perceptual awareness of the Given must be infallible. The TA by contrast is committed to a fallibilist construal of the Given. See Alston 2002 on this matter.

presents perceived objects as they are. Perceptual veridicality and non-veridicality can, in turn, be understood in terms of phenomenal fidelity and the lack thereof: perceptual awareness is veridical to the extent that it presents perceived objects as they are (e.g., square objects appear square, red objects appear red) and falsidical to the extent that it does not (e.g., square objects appear other than square, red objects appear other than red).[12] This account of perceptual error is, of course, related to a core principle of the TA: that just because something appears (is given or presented as) *F* to *S,* it does not automatically follow that it is *F,* although its appearing so gives *S* a prima facie ground to believe that it is *F.*[13] The TA is not a form of naïve realism that supposes that perceived objects are always presented as they are; in *this* sense of realism, however, RP *is* naïve.

Before closing, let me add that Ghate has interesting and insightful things to say about illusions, hallucinations, conceptualization, and the Given that I do not have space to discuss. I shall limit myself to two brief points concerning what he says about illusions.

First, concerning the straight stick partially immersed in water, Ghate curiously fails to note that it *looks bent* when he claims that "you, the perceiver, are aware of the stick *and* its straight shape." Yes, you are aware of the stick in these conditions. Yes, the stick is straight. But (contra Ghate and RP) you are not perceptually aware in these conditions of its being straight because it does not look straight.[14] Note, moreover, that your prior experience of straight sticks being immersed in water can lead you to judge that it is straight *despite* its looking bent in these conditions. Therefore, it seems to me implausible that the illusion is a function of one's judging and conceptualizing the straight stick as bent (based on perceptual similarity with previously perceived bent sticks on dry ground), because the stick can (and typically does) look bent even to someone who judges and conceptualizes the stick as being straight.

Second, Ghate's more general contention that the sense of illusion arises from the perceiver's conceptualization of what he is seeing also strikes me as psychologically implausible. Consider, as another example,

---

12. How we find this out is a matter of epistemology, but the epistemology of perception ought not to be confused with its ontology. Note that perceptual veridicality and falsidicality come in degrees, and the same perceptual awareness can be veridical in some respects (e.g., shape) but falsidical in others (e.g., color).

13. Prichard 1909 made this point long ago in criticizing Kant's epistemology from the TA's presentationalist standpoint.

14. As for bent sticks partially submerged in water, their shape also looks distorted.

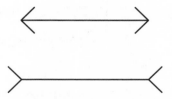

FIGURE 3. The Müller-Lyer illusion.

the oft-discussed Müller-Lyer illusion where two lines of equal length are such that one looks longer than the other.

Suppose I judge the lines to be equal in length (and conceptualize them accordingly) because I have carefully measured them. Even so, despite my conceptualizing and judging them as equal in length, they can still look different in length. Therefore, to maintain as Ghate does that the sense of illusion arises from "a perceiver's powers to classify and judge" strikes me as inadequate to account for illusion.

Conclusion

In this discussion, I have defended the TA against the central criticism that Ghate has leveled against Alston's version of it. I have also critically discussed the infallibilist account of perception that Salmieri attributes to Rand, and argued for a fallibilism consonant with the TA. While the TA and RP have numerous affinities as closely related forms of direct realism, in light of the considerations I have adduced above, I conclude that there is good reason to prefer the TA.

Forms of Awareness and "Three-Factor" Theories

GREGORY SALMIERI

I n my contribution to part 1 of this volume, I discussed Rand's view of awareness as an activity the identity of which is not exhausted by its objects, and I emphasized her distinction between the *form* of an act of awareness and its *object,* which I illustrated with a brief discussion of its application to sense-perception. I indicated there how the distinction can be used to counter some standard objections to direct-realist views of perception like Rand's, and Onkar Ghate treated this topic in much greater detail (and in somewhat different terminology) in his contribution to part 1.[1]

In the last decade especially, there has been a lot of interest in direct realism, and some views have emerged that are similar to Rand's in that their analysis of perception includes, in addition to the subject and the object, a "third factor" that plays a role similar to Rand's idea of form. Among the proponents of such a position are Bill Brewer and John Campbell, the latter of whom is of particular interest because he takes his third factor to be a feature not just of perception, but of consciousness as such.

1. For more in-depth treatments of perception based on Rand's, see Kelley 1986 and Ghate 1998.

Considering Brewer and Campbell's positions, and what I take to be an inadequacy they share, will help to bring out what is distinctive and significant about the idea of forms of awareness.

In order to set a context for this contrast, I will begin by cataloging some significant points on which Rand, Ghate, Campbell, Brewer, and I are in agreement. We view perception as the foundation of thought and knowledge and endorse a direct realist, relational, and nonconceptual account of perception. It is worth pausing over the several shared points of agreement here. The first is *realism* (as opposed to idealism)—the position that in perception we are aware of mind-independent things rather than only of intramental items. The second point of agreement is that, in many cases at least, we are aware specifically of *entities,* as opposed to merely being aware of qualities, dispositions, etc. (as we might, perhaps, speculate that some of the lower animals are). Finally, this perceptual awareness of entities is *direct* in that it is not grounded in some more basic awareness of nonentities (either of mind-dependent objects of any sort, or of qualities, dispositions, etc.).

Direct realism is to be distinguished from a position that used to be called representationalism, is now sometimes called indirect realism, but that I will call "traditional representationalism." According to this view, we are aware directly of internal mental items which resemble or otherwise represent objects out in the world, and we are aware derivatively of these external objects either simply because of the relationship in which they stand to the representations or by means of some sort of inference that there must be something that stands in this relationship.

Our shared position is also to be distinguished from views that hold that, though we are aware directly of some mind-independent things, the objects of our awareness do not include entities but only qualities or dispositions—things like sounds or expanses of color. On this view, our awareness of the entities that have the qualities or dispositions works in just the same way as it does in the case of traditional representationalism, except that the intermediate object, by knowing which we are derivatively aware of the entities, is extramental rather than mental.

Finally, the shared position on perception can be contrasted with what Brewer calls "the content view"—a position that is sometimes now referred to as "representationalism" and which I will call "newfangled representationalism." Whereas both our consensus position and traditional representationalism agree in thinking of perception primarily as a relation between the subject and an object (whether mind-dependent or mind-independent), newfangled representationalism sees it as a relation to a judgeable content—something like a proposition which *represents* the world as being a certain way (with this ability to represent then being cashed out usually in functional and/or information-theoretic terms).

This last view is like traditional representationalism in that it takes perception to consist in having some state, which one could have whether or not the object one would normally be said to perceive exists, and in that this state can correspond or fail to correspond with the world. Campbell and Brewer have argued convincingly that the various forms of the newfangled representationalism view lead to something very much like the "veil of perception" by which traditional representationalism separates subjects from the outside world. On both views, we are related to external objects only by having certain mental contents that could be just as they are even if the external objects were quite different.[2]

Representationalism of one form or another has typically been seen as the only viable alternative to idealism because it has been thought that direct realism cannot account for such phenomena as the relativity of perception—i.e., the fact that the same object can appear differently to perceivers in different circumstances or conditions.[3] Brewer and Campbell account for this phenomenon by introducing a "third factor" in addition to the conscious subject and the external object of his perception.

The third factor is that which differs when the same subject perceives the same object differently. For example, the same coin might look circular to a subject when viewed from one angle and elliptical when viewed from another; an oar may look straight when viewed in a single medium, but bent when partially submerged in water; the same pail of water may feel cold to a subject when his hand is warm and warm to him when his hand is cold; and Venus may look one way when viewed in the morning and another when viewed in the evening (thus making it possible, as in Gottlob Frege's famous example, for someone to have two names for the planet without realizing that they refer to the same entity). Brewer (2011a, 96) explains: "Perceptual experience is a matter of a person's conscious acquaintance with various mind-independent physical objects *from a given spatiotemporal point of view, in a particular sense modality, and in*

2. See Campbell 2002, 124–32, 145–56; and Brewer 2011a, chap. 4.

3. Illusions, which direct realism is often thought to be unable to account for, are specialized cases of the relativity of perception. The other phenomenon for which direct realism is often thought to be unable to account is hallucination, on which see Ghate's essay in part 1 of the present volume.

certain specific circumstances of perception (such as lighting conditions in the case of vision). These factors effectively conjoin to constitute a third relatum of the relation of conscious acquaintance that holds between perceivers and the mind-independent physical direct objects of their perceptual experience." Campbell (2009, 657), speaking of consciousness more broadly, writes: "We should think of consciousness of the object not as a two-place relation between a person and an object, but as a three-place relation between a person, a standpoint and an object. You always experience an object from a standpoint. And you can experience one and the same object from different standpoints."

Once the presence of a third factor is recognized, explaining the relativity of perception becomes simple, as Brewer (2011a, 96) observes:

> the experiential variations noted [between the way a coin looks from different angles and in different circumstances], and any others along similar lines, may all perfectly adequately be accounted for by variations in this third relatum. For example, head-on v. wide-angle experiences, and those of the head side v. the tail side involve different spatial points of view. Experiences of the newly minted v. tarnished and battered coin involve different temporal points of view. Seeing v. feeling it clearly involve different sense modalities; and bright light v. dim light viewings involve different circumstances of perception. Still these are all cases of conscious acquaintance with the very same mind-independent physical coin—with variations in the third term of the perceptual relation.

What I would like to consider is how we should understand this third factor. Any realist (as opposed to idealist) needs to appeal to *some* factor other than subject and object to account for the relativity of perception. Since the phenomenon to be explained is how there can be differences in the perception despite the subject and object being the same, clearly something other than these two must be appealed to. Notice that the representationalist's representations are themselves a third factor that is supposed to account for these differences.

The difference between these representations and the third factors appealed to by Brewer and Campbell is that the representations are supposed to somehow stand between the subject and the object, making the former's awareness of the latter indirect. This is clearest in traditional representationalism, according to which the subject stands to the representation in the very same relation that a naïve person would have thought the subject stood to the (external) object: the subject is aware of the representation, and this awareness counts derivatively as an awareness of the object because of some relation between the representation and the object. In either event, the representation takes the place that the naïve person would have attributed to the external object. Something similar occurs in the case of newfangled representationalism. Here, too, the *content* of one's perception is something that is only contingently related to the world—to the objects that we would ordinarily say that we see.

Brewer's and Campbell's third factors are not supposed to mediate between the subject and object. They are third factors not just in the sense of being something else involved in an episode of perception besides the subject and the object, but in that they are supposed to play *a different sort of role* than either of these two. The representationalist's third factor is not a third factor in this sense. Perception remains for them essentially a two-place affair, with their third item usurping the place of the object. (It is this usurpation that leads to the veil of perception.)

If there is a third factor (or sort of factor) in the sense upheld by Brewer and Campbell, how should we understand it and its relation to the other two? Brewer says little about how the several factors he cites in addition to subject and object cohere into a third factor, and it is not clear that he needs to for his immediate purposes. Campbell has more to say on the subject. His third factor, recall, is *standpoint*, and he arrives at it by broadening the ordinary visual notion of a standpoint to enable it to do the work done by the Fregean notion of "sense"—that is, to explain how statements of the identity of two co-referential terms can be informative.

To "articulate the notion of standpoint" he advocates considering the sense modalities severally and noting for each what factors other than the subject and object are responsible for the differences in the view one can have of an object. (This will be a literal view in the case of vision, and an analog of a literal view in the case of the other modalities.)

> For example, suppose the modality is vision. Then we need, further, position, but also the relative orientations of the viewer and object, how close the viewer is to the object, whether there is anything obstructing the light between them, and so on. In the case of hearing, a rather different set of factors would be relevant: not just which object was in question, but what sounds it was making, and the obstruction of light would not be to the point, though the obstruction of sound would be. We do not usually spell out all these conditions, though we are perfectly capable of articulating them when they are important in particular cases. (Campbell 2009, 658)

The goal of this procedure is to "show how we can characterize a way of experiencing an object without appealing to either the idea that 'ways' are characterized by associated representations [as is held by the newfangled representationalists] or the idea that 'ways' are characterized by the idiosyncrasies of the mental paint involved [as is held by the traditional representationalists]. Rather than either the idea of an intervening level of mental representation or the idea of an intervening level of mental paint, we can simply appeal to the notion of experience as a three-place relation between an object, an experiencer and a standpoint" (Campbell 2009, 658). The third factor is, then, the *way* in which the object is perceived by the subject. Or, to use a phrase of Frege's, it is the *mode of presentation*. Frege, of course, used this phrase to describe "senses," and it is worth observing two things in this connection.

First, whatever Frege intended senses to be (and I think he oscillated between different conceptions of it), the tradition that followed from him treated the senses as *intermediates* between subjects and the things to which we would naïvely take them to be referring. For the better part of a century, senses were almost universally understood to be descriptions (or description-like items) that the subject is acquainted with more directly than with the referents (if, indeed, in any given case, there are any referents at all).

Gareth Evans (1982) called attention to those aspects of Frege's writing on sense that tell against this way of reading it, and he suggested that we can make use of the notion to understand how we can be directly acquainted with extramental objects (rather than only with "mental paint," as Campbell calls the mental objects posited by traditional representationalists). But Evans himself, in his execution of this idea, fell into newfangled representationalism—a view that, no less than the traditional reading of Frege, distances us from mind-independent objects.

This thumbnail history suggests that, whatever insight may be contained in Frege's idea of a mode of presentation, there is something difficult about developing it in a way that does not collapse the mode in which something is presented into a thing that is itself presented (and which then somehow presents something further).

The second thing I would like to observe about "modes of presentation" is that they are modes in which an object can present itself to a subject, rather than modes in which the subject can be acquainted with the object. It is the object or its availability to the subject that admits of variation, and any variations in the subject's awareness of the object is to be explained by these variations, which are external to the awareness itself. This point was important to Frege, who was reacting against a psychologism in logic that was connected with nineteenth-century German idealism.

By contrast, Rand viewed awareness as an *activity* that can be performed on an object in different *ways*. It can be analogized to the activity of physically grasping something. In order for me to grasp something, there must be some object that I grasp, and I must grasp it with some grip or other. The variations in grip are differences in how I handle the object rather than variations in how the object is available for handling.[4] Likewise, the differences between various forms in which I can perceive an object are differences in the activity I perform in perceiving it, rather than differences in its mode of presentation. Rand's forms are ways in which a subject is aware of an object, whereas a Fregean mode is independent of any subject (or type of subject) and his faculties.

What about Campbell and Brewer's third factors? Both Brewer and Campbell include the sense-modality in their third factors. However, it is striking that neither includes in his description of the third factor anything about the subject's internal conditions or internal operations, but only factors such as where the subject is located relative to the object, and any other physical conditions external to the subject that are relevant to perceiving in the relevant sense-modality (e.g., the lighting, whether there are obstructions, etc.).

Campbell's choice of the term "standpoint" is significant in this connection: a literal standpoint is a *place* from which an object can be viewed, and specifying it does not require specifying anything about the faculties of the person occupying it. Creatures with very different types of eyes— for example, a nautilus, a housefly, and a human being—can, in turns, occupy the same literal standpoint. Campbell does not say anything in explaining his extended notion of standpoint that would prevent such different creatures from sharing one. Nor is there anything in Brewer's description of his third factor that would present such radically different creatures from sharing one—unless, that is, we think of their vision as a different sense-modality from our own.

Perhaps it is plausible to say that the vision of a nautilus or a housefly is a different sense modality than our own, but what about the vision

---

4. Of course, facts about the objects do place constraints on the sorts of grips by which we can grasp them, and in order to keep my grip on a changing object (e.g., a melting snowball), I may need to alter my grasp.

of animals that are more similar to us—hawks and dogs, for example? Surely they share the modality of vision with us, yet equally surely objects look different to them than to us, even when we occupy the same standpoint. A hawk's vision is keener than ours, and dogs see less keenly than we do and with more limited color perception, but they have a wider field of vision. Someone might, perhaps, take these sorts of differences to mean that their sense modality is different from ours, but we could say this with as much justice for differences in vision among human beings, or in the same man's vision as it changes across the course of his life.

If one is willing to parse sense-modalities this finely, then the idea of a modality approaches Rand's of a form of perception. But this is not what is ordinarily meant by "sense-modality," nor is it what I think Campbell or Brewer means by it. Their third factors, then, do not include anything about the subject's internal conditions or activities. They include only the specification of a sense-modality, "a spatiotemporal point of view" and the "circumstances of perception," where this last term is understood to mean *external* circumstances—things such as the lighting conditions or the level of ambient noise.

The context in which they formulated their positions sheds light on why Brewer and Campbell do not incorporate the state and activities of the subject into the third factor of perpetual awareness. Both are concerned to fend off newfangled representationalism and so emphasize the idea of being *acquainted with objects*. In developing the idea of acquaintance, both take their inspiration from philosophers who think of states of acquaintance as having no characteristics other than those contributed by their objects.

Brewer (2011a, xi–xii, 3–4, 95) uses the British empiricists to fix his conception of a direct object and argues that we have the kind of acquaintance with extramental objects that they thought we only have with "ideas" (or, in Hume's case, ideas and impressions). Notice, though, that while the empiricists recognize many sorts of variation among ideas, they recognize no variation in the *manner* in which one is aware of an idea. Locke, for example, catalogs many dimensions along which ideas can vary—simplicity versus complexity, clarity versus obscurity, distinctness versus confusion, reality versus fantasticality, adequacy versus inadequacy, truth versus falsehood—but there is no corresponding list of different ways in which the same idea can be in the mind. There is, for him, no such thing as possessing an idea clearly or obscurely; only possessing a clear or an obscure idea. Any characteristics that one might ascribe to the *awareness* of an idea, Locke instead ascribes to the idea itself; leaving the awareness bereft of identity of its own. We can find this same view of awareness in G. E. Moore, who *"denies that experiences have intrinsic features. Instead, they owe everything they are to their relation to objects."*[5] Campbell draws heavily on Moore's view of awareness as a "generic relation between the thinker and the object."

Of course, there is hardly anyone who speaks of acquaintance or direct awareness without seeing this relation as being bereft of identity, so it is not surprising that the figures that Brewer and Campbell reference in motivating the idea view consciousness in this way. Moreover, their "third factors" are supposed to rectify the error these earlier thinkers made when they denied that states of awareness have any characteristics other than those contributed by their objects, and Campbell in particular is quite explicit that this error made it impossible for Moore and others to account for phenomena like the relativity of perception without denying that we are acquainted with the ordinary extramental objects that we normally take ourselves to perceive: "This is a problem for Moore's radical transparency. If your experience of the object is fully characterized simply by saying that we have a generic relation of consciousness holding between you and that thing, then we do not seem to have the resources to explain how there could be different kinds of conscious experience of the thing" (Campbell 2009, 654). To solve this problem Campbell thinks of consciousness "not as a two-place relation between a person and an object, but as a three-place relation between a person, a standpoint and an object" (657). However, it remains a *generic* relation, all of the features of which are supplied by its relata.

It is instructive here to return to my earlier analogy between being aware of something and physically grasping it. The analog of Moore's position would be that a grasp is a generic relation between the grasper and

---

5. James Van Cleve (2005), quoted by Campbell (2009, 653). This view of acquaintance as a *generic* relation is common, especially in the first half of the twentieth century. Another example can be found in H. H. Price, who writes that sensing "differs from other acts of acquaintance only in its object, not in its nature, and it has no species" (Price 1950, 18). His reasoning is as follows: "Are there several different sorts of acquaintance, e.g., sensing, self-consciousness, and contemplation of mental images? I cannot see that there are. The difference seems to be wholly on the side of the data. If so, *a fortiori* there are not different kinds of sensing. Visual sensing will simply be the acquaintance with color-patches, auditory sensing the acquaintance with sounds, and so on; the acquaintance being the same in each case" (Price 1950, 5).

the object grasped, to which object the grasp owes all its features. But, Campbell would observe, this view gives us no way to differentiate between grasping something with a precision grip and grasping it with a power grip, so he would instead think of a grasp as a generic three-place relation between a subject, an object, and a grip. How does this position relate to the one I advocated earlier, according to which grasps and, by analogy, states of awareness have characteristics of their own?

Campbell treats the characteristics that I attribute to the state of awareness as parts of the third factor. This is analogous to Locke's (de facto) strategy of exporting the clarity or obscurity of one's awareness to the objects. However, since the third factor is not the object, exporting (what I think of as) the state's features to it does not eliminate the possibility of a subject's being aware of the same object in different ways. Moreover, since the third factor is essentially the sum of all of the things that I would treat as characteristics of the state, we might think of Campbell's position and the one I have been advocating as notational variants. Indeed, if you wanted to represent my view in a formal system like the predicate calculus you would have to do so, just as Campbell suggests, by treating awareness as a three-place relation, and, for many purposes, I would have no objection to doing so. However, I see no reason to treat awareness in this way that does not apply equally well to grasping or walking or any other action that can be performed on (or with respect to) an object. And unless there is some such reason, awareness is no more a generic, three-place relation than any other action is: all can be represented this way (though not without being somewhat misleading ontologically).

My sense is that Campbell is anxious to treat awareness in particular as a generic relation because he thinks that any identity possessed by the state of consciousness itself would constitute a barrier between us and external objects. We can see this worry in his analogizing the brain's role in visual perception to that of a medium that remains transparent only by a process of "constant adjustment and recalibration" that is "always sensitive to the finest details of the scene being viewed." On this view, the brain is not "constructing a conscious inner representation whose intrinsic character is independent of the environment"; rather, "there is a kind of complex adjustment that the brain has to undergo, in each context, in order that you can be visually related to the things around you; so that you can see them, in other words." However, Campbell adds that "the adjustment and recalibration may not always yield full transparency," and he gives as an example of this "looking at the world through a jaundiced eye," which he analogizes to looking at it through yellowish (rather than "purely transparent") glass (Campbell 2002, 119).[6]

Granted, this is a metaphor, and Campbell says earlier that any metaphor is bound to have its limitations, but it is striking that the metaphor he gives for the workings of the brain and nervous system in producing perception is one in which they are working to *get out of the way*. An observer, viewing an object through a fallibly transparent medium, would have a better and more reliable view of the object if the medium were removed; for it adds nothing other than the threat of opacity. Similarly, the analogy implies, we would better perceive the world if we were not encumbered by our brains and nervous system. The view Campbell is trying to fend off is that the brain's activity in perception creates an internal object. Notice, though, that both views depict the subject ultimately as being aware of the object *no how*. Either the brain's activity constructs an internal object with which we are acquainted *without doing anything*, or else the brain's activity consists in keeping itself transparent so that we can be acquainted with the object again *without doing anything*. But once we recognize being aware of objects as something we *do*, rather than viewing it as a "generic relation" in which we stand, the fact that there are physiological processes involved in awareness ceases to be troubling, and instead of facing an alternative between our nervous systems either working to construct a veil of perception or working to get out of our way, we can understand our nervous systems as doing the work of acquainting us with the world.

Campbell's comment on the jaundiced eye is similarly interesting. It implies that there is some *right way* for things to look—the way they would look if the mechanisms were functioning properly and were fully transparent. We find the same idea in Brewer, who makes the following suggestion about "supposed general yellowing of the jaundiced person's perception": "Their experience, at least according to the standard philo-

6. Compare Fumerton 2006, 9: "One could suppose that in veridical perception the relevant changes in the brain simply open the shades to reveal what is there before the perceiver. But the metaphor is in the end devastating to the direct realist who wants to identify the phenomenal reality, the character of the reality that is given to one in experience, with features of external reality. The opening of a window shade does not causally determine the scene revealed. What one sees through a window depends on what is there outside the window. Change the environment and you see something different. But I take it that the changes that take place in the brain, however produced, causally determine the phenomenological scenery, so to speak."

sophical description of the case, consists in visual acquaintance with the objects before them partially obscured by a general hallucinatory super-imposition introspectively indistinguishable from the presence of a wash of yellow light" (Brewer 2011a, 116). Both Brewer and Campbell think that the world really looks as it does without the yellow tint, which they see as obscuring the world from view. I disagree.

One of my friends reports having noticeably different tints in his two eyes, so that when he switches back and forth between eyes, the effect is like that of rocking the tint knob on a television back and forth. For this to be the case, must one of his eyes be damaged (less than fully transparent)? Suppose (as for all I know is the case) that my friend is equally able to discriminate gradations of color with each eye. On what grounds, then, would we say that one eye saw correctly, while the other saw through an obscuring tint? Perhaps on the grounds that one of the two eyes sees the world as most people see it? For all we know, such variations in tint may be ubiquitous, with the result that there is no normal tintless view by con-trast to which certain eyes may be identified as afflicted with an obscur-ing tint (just as there is no "normal" way of speaking by contrast to which everyone else can be identified as speaking with an accent). Or, switch-ing to another sense modality, given that the same water feels hotter or colder depending on the temperature of one's hands, must it be that there is some condition of our hands that would allow us to feel the way the water *really* feels, with all of the other conditions partially obscuring the true feel of the water from us?

Switching examples again, how are we to understand color-blind or myopic people on this transparency model? Is their medium not trans-parent enough to let the colors or fine details of shape through? Clearly their way of perceiving is worse than that of normally sighted people in various respects, but are they not seeing the objects as they really are? Surely we should say, with Brewer, that such people perceive objects "in a degraded visual modality" (2011a, 116). But the modality is degraded only by the standard of what is normal *for a human being*. Some animals surpass us in distance vision or in their ability to distinguish colors. Pre-sumably their visual experiences differ from ours in something like the way the experience of a normally sighted person differs from that of a myopic or color-blind person. If we regard the degradation of the myopic or color-blind person's vision as doing anything analogous to *obscuring* his view of the world, then we have to regard the nature of human sense organs as doing the same for all human perception.

Since any sense faculty will be limited in its acuity, regarding these limits as obscuring the world from us amounts to taking as one's standard of awareness the sort of omniscience that Moore, Bertrand Russell, and others thought that we had of sense-data.[7] But it is impossible to live up to this (supernatural) standard, and so it will push us toward the conclusion that our acquaintance with external objects is always partially obscured or else superimposed with a hallucinatory material. Any view that includes this (supernatural) standard of direct awareness will, if developed consistently, lead us to regard ourselves as trapped behind a veil of perception (even if some versions will permit us to regard the veil as less than fully opaque).

By contrast, if we acknowledge that to be aware of something is to be aware of it *in some form*, then differences in acuity or in tint or in how things feel to us when we are in different conditions will not lead us to conclude that we are perceiving the world through an obscuring medium. And, if we think of this form as standing to the act of awareness as a grip stands to the act of grasping, we will not fall into the error of treating the form as the object anymore than we mistake a grip for the object grasped. How we are aware of the objects around us depends on all sorts of facts about us and our faculties and conditions. The same person experiences the same object differently when he is in different conditions, other people may experience it more differently still, and other animals surely experience it quite differently. But these differences in *how* we are aware of an object are not differences in *what* we are aware of, because what we are aware of is the object, rather than the form in which we are aware of it—just as what we physically grasp is an object rather than the grip we have on it.

If we accept this view, differences between the ways in which people perceive the same objects—or between human perception and that of various animals—need not puzzle or trouble us. These differences will be analogous to the differences in physical grips that result from subtle differences among normal human hands, or from the more dramatic dif-

7. Russell, for example, describes his acquaintance with a sense-datum as follows: "so far as concerns knowledge of the colour itself, as opposed to knowledge of truths about it, I know the colour perfectly and completely when I see it, and no further knowledge of it itself is even theoretically possible. Thus the sense-data which make up the appearance of my table are things with which I have acquaintance, things immediately known to me just as they are" (Russell 1912, 73–74).

ferences between healthy and deformed hands, or between human hands and the claws or talons of various animals.

Indeed, we can accommodate much more radical differences in forms of perception than this. This is well illustrated by a science fiction example that has long circulated in Objectivist circles. Imagine a Martian who experienced colors or the temperature of his environment in the way in which we experience musical tones.[8] When his eye was trained on a green object, for example, he might have the experience we have when hearing middle C on a piano, and when a red object came into view, he might have an experience like that of hearing the A just below it. Perhaps, when multiple colors were in view he would have an experience like that of hearing a chord. The Martian would be aware of the same attributes that we are aware of in ordinary color perception, but he would be aware of them in a very different form (just as vision and touch enable us to be aware of shape in very different forms, and echolocation enables bats to be aware of it in yet a third form).[9]

If we do not distinguish between form and object in this way, the fact that we can perceive attributes like shape both visually and tactilely will be mysterious. Moreover, within any given sense modality, the differences of acuity among people and between people and other animals, will require us to postulate obscuring media, hallucinatory tints, and the like. This is the view of perception suggested by Campbell's example of the medium that struggles to remain transparent, but it is not clear to me whether Campbell accepts it. The use of the metaphor does not commit him to it, and there are passages, such as the following, in which he seems to reject it: "On the Relational View of perception, we have to think

8. Various examples of Martians experiencing the objects of one of our sense modalities in the way we experience the objects of another have been in circulation since at least the 1960s. The version of the example I give here is based on Gotthelf 2000, 56.

9. The example concerning vision and touch is from Binswanger 1989. Of course, such a Martian's awareness of a color would include an awareness of the form in which he experiences it, just as our awareness of the same color includes an awareness of the very different form in which we experience it. A special act of introspection is required on the part of the perceiver (whether earthling or Martian) to isolate the form from the object and to conceptualize them separately. Indeed, our terms for sensory qualities are typically ambiguous: it is unclear whether they refer to qualities in the objects themselves or to features of the way in which we are aware of them. (And they have been used in both ways in Objectivist circles.) This makes examples like that of the Martian difficult to formulate. For the purposes of this example, I am using color terms to name qualities of the objects, but I am not taking a position on the nature of these qualities.

of the cognitive processing as 'revealing' the world to the subject; that is, as making it possible for the subject to experience external objects. . . . On the Relational View of experience, we have to think of experience of objects as depending jointly on the cognitive processing and the environment. Experience, on this view, cannot be understood simply as a matter of cognitive contents becoming subjectively available" (Campbell 2002, 118).

But if our own cognitive processing makes experience of external objects possible, so that the experience depends in part on it, then we would expect facts about these processes—facts about how they are being performed in a given instance, about the condition of the faculties that perform them, and so on—to have an influence on the *way* in which we experience the objects. This influence would be of the same broad sort as that had by the vantage point from which we view the objects and the lighting conditions in which we do. And just as there is no single *correct* vantage point from which to view an object—one by reference to which we can consider the view from every other vantage point to be somehow incorrect or faulty—we should not think that there is some one correct way for our perceptual faculties to operate, such that, for example, when one person's vision has a different tint than another's, one of them must be viewing the world through an obscuring medium.

Thus, we arrive at Rand's position that awareness is an activity that has a nature, such that awareness will always be in some form or other, and the form will be determined by internal features of the perceiver as well as by such external factors as his spatial relation to the object and the lighting conditions. I think this is an implication of Campbell's position, but it is one that he and Brewer seem reluctant to embrace. I worry that this is due to some remnant of what Rand describes as "the unchallenged premise that any knowledge acquired by a process of consciousness is necessarily subjective and cannot correspond to the facts of reality, since it is 'processed knowledge'"—the idea that "identity [is] the disqualifying element of consciousness"—"the notion that only an ineffable consciousness can acquire a valid knowledge of reality, that 'true' knowledge has to be causeless, i.e., acquired without any means of cognition" (*ITOE* 80). Because their views of perception do contain something analogous to Rand's idea of form, a comparison with them highlights what I think is Rand's distinctive insight into the nature of awareness. I will give her the last word: "All knowledge *is* processed knowledge—whether on the sensory, perceptual or conceptual level. An 'unprocessed' knowledge would be a knowledge acquired without means of cognition. Consciousness (as I said in the first sentence of this work) is not a passive state, but an active process. And more: the satisfaction of every need of a living organism requires an act of *processing* by that organism, be it the need of air, of food or of knowledge" (*ITOE* 81).

Direct Perception and Salmieri's "Forms of Awareness"

BILL BREWER

I believe that what Salmieri calls "three-factor views" contain a deep and important insight about the nature of our perceptual relation with the mind-independent physical world around us. He correctly contrasts such views with representationalism, both old and new. I argue that his own understanding of the insight ultimately collapses into the bad old representationalism that we both reject. His view is effectively a version of indirect realism. I explain how the insight should instead be developed in such a way as to maintain the crucial contrast with representationalism, and to preserve the vindication that three-factor views offer of a genuine direct empirical realism.[1]

What I regard as the basic insight of the three-factor view goes back to the early modern empiricists' conception of perception as a matter of a person's *acquaintance* with a *direct object* of experience. In their hands this is conjoined with an equivalence between the way things *look,* in vision, say, and the nature of the direct object in question: something looks *F* in an experience if and only if its direct object is *F*. Consideration of illusion and hallucination then *force* the characterization of the direct ob-

---

1. For extended development and defense of these ideas see Brewer 2011a.

jects of experience as mind-dependent things distinct from any mind-independent objects we may nevertheless indirectly perceive. Three-factor views retain the relational structure of this view but deny the equivalence thesis that entails the mind-dependence of direct objects, insisting instead that perception is a relation between a perceiver and a direct object of experience *in a particular sense modality, from a given spatiotemporal point of view, and in certain specific circumstances.* These last features of modality, point of view and circumstances, determinate in any actual perceptual situation, constitute the third relatum of the perceptual relation in question. (I will follow John Campbell in calling this a *standpoint* in what follows [Campbell 2009].) This explains the way in which a mind-independent physical direct object of perception, *o*, may look *F*, say, although it is not actually *F*, in virtue of its perceptually relevant similarities from the standpoint in question with paradigm *F*'s, without any need for the introduction of mind-dependent intermediate relata.

A good question that Salmieri raises is how to develop the three-factor approach in such a way as to avoid collapse into the newfangled representationalism that replaced indirect realism with the idea of perception as a specific *way* of being conscious, where such ways are effectively indexed by *representations* of how the mind-independent world might be around the perceiver. Very crudely, perceptual experience is a matter of being conscious *that-p-ly* for some relevant content *p*.

The threat of collapse may be exacerbated by Salmieri's appropriation on behalf of the three-factor theorist of talk of perception as a *way* of being aware of *o*. Formally this is straightforward. Suppose that we do indeed think of perception as a three-place relation, A, of acquaintance between a subject, S, object, o, and standpoint, Σ, and suppose that c is a specific visual standpoint, then we can define a way of being conscious A_c as follows: $A_c(S, o) \Leftrightarrow A(S, o, c)$, and think of this as S being conscious of o c-ly. So far as it goes there is nothing wrong with this. But we must remember that it is on a par with the a-ly way that S may be conscious from a standpoint Σ, where $A_a(S, \Sigma) \Leftrightarrow A(S, a, \Sigma)$, for example, as a simple restriction on the fundamental three-place relation. Our only possible understanding of which *way* of being conscious is being conscious c-ly is derived from our understanding of $A(S, o, \Sigma)$, instantiated by c at Σ. By contrast, the whole point of new representationalism is to understand a perceptual condition in terms of a more basic understanding of the notion of the representational content p that indexes the way of being conscious in question.

Furthermore, the purely formal c-ly restriction on A(S, o, Σ), A_c, is absolutely not *contentlike* in nature. Characterization of this particular way of being conscious has nothing to do with truth-conditions or any determinate degree of predicational generality. It is simply a matter of a subject being visually acquainted with the particular thing in question from a specific point of view and in specific perceptual circumstances. Specifying the point of view and circumstances, the standpoint, in question simply involves a specification of certain determinate features of the particular perceptual situation, some determination of which is essential to any case of perceptual-relational acquaintance with that, or any other, thing.

In any case, my central concern in this area is that Salmieri's own development of the three-factor view is really just a version of *old-fashioned* representationalism—indirect realism—at best paying lip service to the genuine empirical realism that the three-factor approach strives to vindicate.

We can approach this worry from an explicit difference that he registers between Campbell's approach and his own inspired by Rand: the former asserts whereas the latter denies that there is a *right way* for a red, round object to look independently of the idiosyncrasies of the perceiver's nervous system. According to the three-factor view, what it is like for the perceiver in vision, say—that is, the way things look to her—just is the way *things* look: the looks that the things she sees have from the standpoint in question. If an object is red and round and her standpoint is head-on in good lighting, then, provided that her visual system is functioning normally, the way things look will be constituted by the shape and color of that very thing. In this way, as the extended quotation from Campbell that Salmieri gives makes clear, our nervous system works to present us with the natures of the very things that are out there in the world around us. Malfunction may result in less than perfect success in all sorts of ways. But this is a quite different matter from correctly accessing the elliptical look that that same red, round object has from an angle, say, although cases may be constructed in which the subject cannot tell these two conditions apart. Similarly with respect to color. Supposing that any further difficulties involved in establishing *conclusively* which of two subjects in fact has the color of the thing right are of any deep theoretical significance strikes me as giving in to a kind of idealism or verificationism that is at odds with the realism supposedly agreed from the start.

Salmieri's Martian example seems to me to give the game away completely. According to the three-factor view as I understand it, there is a mind-independent world out there of colored and shaped objects. Given our point of view and circumstances in perceiving them, their objective nature constitutes the subjective nature of our experience of them. The redness and roundness of the object itself constitute the way it looks head-on in good lighting conditions, given a well-functioning perceptual system apt to reveal the nature of that thing. If all and only red things sound to me at the pitch of tuning fork A and all and only green things at middle C, and if I were blind, I would *not* thereby perceive the colors of those things, albeit in a different way. I would not have the foggiest idea which properties those color properties are. Those objects would be causally responsible for the way things sound to me, and the sounds I hear would be systematically correlated with their color properties; but this is perception *of color* only on the old-fashioned indirect realist model, on which the sensations that we are directly aware of in perception are a medium of indication, "blank signs," in Michael Ayers's (1991) phrase, individuated prior to and independently of any question of what their external correlates may be.

The contrast between visual and tactual shape perception is entirely different from that between genuine and purportedly auditory color perception as just described. The former is a matter of different standpoints on the very same objective shape. For that very shape property, individuated prior to and independently of any question of how it may appear in perception, plays a fundamental and essential role in the subjective characterization of the nature of the experience itself in both modalities, and is therefore transparent to the subject of such experience. In vision, this transparency is evidently sensitive to lighting, viewpoint, and obstruction; in touch, the enabling and disabling conditions are evidently different; and this explains the contrasting character of the two experiences of the same shape. Shape perception in both modalities is a presentation of that very shape, though, *not* a matter of being subject to some sensation or other which as a matter of brute fact systematically correlates with the shapes of things out there, whatever these may be.

Genuine transparency of this kind, as Campbell describes, is precisely what the three-factor empirical realist needs from perception, and I would say provides. Rand's *form* as elaborated by Salmieri offers instead the idea of a subjective medium, indicating by mere biological covaria-

BILL BREWER

tion what may be out there in a way that leaves the nature of the mind-independent world itself entirely hidden. So far as I can see this is precisely the old-fashioned representationalism that we all supposedly reject.

It is a criterion for getting this right that ways things appear are to be individuated in terms of the natures of the mind-independent things themselves that we perceive; and therefore that there *is* a right way for things of a given nature *to* appear. In denying this, Salmieri's position is not a development of the three-factor view as I understand it, and certainly not one that the empirical realist should go along with.

Salmieri seems to suggest that unless we think of perceptual experience as he does, as a medium that is characterized quite independently of the natures of physical objects and that provides a *form* for our apprehension of those things, with different subjects potentially apprehending the very same features of those same objects in radically disparate such ways, then we are left with a notion of perceptual consciousness that has no identity of its own. This is not right. The three-factor view offers a conception of perceptual consciousness precisely as the transparent presentation of the natures of those very physical objects themselves from a given perceptual standpoint in the world. Its nature—the nature of perceptual consciousness—is to be characterized directly in terms of those objects—the familiar colored and shaped things in the world around us—as a particular subject's acquaintance with them from a given standpoint.

Keeping Up Appearances
Reflections on the Debate over Perceptual Infallibilism
BENJAMIN BAYER

everal contributors to this volume (Onkar Ghate, Pierre Le Morvan, Gregory Salmieri, and Bill Brewer) share an interest in defending direct realism (sometimes also called presentationalism) about the senses. They agree that perceptual awareness is the awareness of objects or even facts in the world, not of mental intermediaries such as sense-data or some other kind of "representational" content. But they differ over the commitments of accepting the existence of this direct form of awareness. A central point of contention is over whether treating perception as direct commits the realist to *infallibilism* about the senses, the view that there is an important sense in which the senses cannot be wrong. In this volume, Ghate and Salmieri each affirm a version of this view which they attribute to Rand, seeing it as essential to the case for anti-skeptical realism. Le Morvan and Brewer, by contrast, critique the case for infallibilism, seeing it as lending comfort to skepticism or idealism. Central to the dispute is the felt need to reconcile with direct realism various truisms about illusions and other cases of the relativity of perception that suggest the possibility of a gap between sensory appearances and facts.

I am in general agreement with Salmieri and Ghate on the merits of Rand's theory, and so I want to help showcase the resources available in their essays to address the objections from Le Morvan and Brewer. I will begin by arguing that direct realists can acknowledge fairly mundane truisms about "appearances" without maintaining that there is any important sense in which the senses are fallible. I will also address the concern that infallibilist direct realism collapses into some version of representationalism or worse.

Le Morvan

Le Morvan's case for perceptual fallibilism rests on the premise that "just because an object appears (e.g., looks, tastes, sounds, feels, or smells) F (e.g., blurry, circular, green, sour, etc.) to someone S, it does not automatically follow that the object really is F." Because an object can look F without being F, he concludes that perception can fail to "match" its objects. Even if the perceptual awareness per se does not come in a propositional form that is either true or false, that it might fail to "match" in this way is sufficient to establish fallibilism.

I want to maintain that we can accept ordinary claims about objects that look F but are not F without accepting fallibilism. It does not follow from these truisms that the senses are sometimes mistaken. Indeed, Ghate's chapter describes a sense of "appears F" or "looks F," which makes unambiguously clear why there is no such consequence. Ghate's proposed description of the bent stick illusion suggests the following analysis of the language of "looks F" or "appears F":[1]

(1) An object appears F in a context a if and only if a subject's perceptual awareness of an object in context a is similar to his perceptual awareness of an F object in context b.

We can formulate the claim whose possible truth is supposed to imply fallibilism according to Le Morvan as follows:

(2) An object appears F in context a, and that object is not F in context a.

If we apply Ghate's analysis of "appears F" and substitute it into (2), making necessary adjustments for grammar, we get:

---

1. At one point Le Morvan expresses curiosity about why Ghate's initial description of the bent stick illusion does not use the language of "appearance." But Ghate does use the language of "looks."

(3) A subject's perceptual awareness of an object in context *a* is similar to the subject's perceptual awareness of an *F* object in context *b*, and the object is not *F* in context *a*.

Once we analyze "appears *F*" this way, the perceptual state is not being compared to the fact in a way that generates any "mismatch." The analysis does not describe the perceiver's awareness as expressing any content that is logically inconsistent with facts about the object of awareness. It does not express any content *that the object in context* a *is* F, which is the content it would need to express to contradict the fact *that the object in context* a *is not* F. There would be a contradiction only if we equivocate and suppose that the presence of "*F*" in "appears *F*" means that the perceptual state expresses a content effectively identical to that of a *belief* that the object in context *a* is F. (As we will discuss later, it is possible that the illusion may *prompt* one to form this belief, but it is important that a belief that contradicts the fact has a very different kind of content than perceptual awareness, a point that both Le Morvan and William P. Alston concede.)

In point of fact, if it is meaningful to talk about such a thing as perceptual *content*, then "content" refers to the nature of a state of awareness, a nature that is, by the admission of all parties to this dispute, a product of facts about the nature of the object and of the perceiver. To speak of the similarity between one's awareness in one context and one's awareness in another is to make a point about what Ghate and Salmieri (following Rand) call the *form* of awareness. Shortly I will say more about whether it is possible for *any* description of perceptual form to be inconsistent with the objects of perception.

So if we can describe perceptual awareness in a way that makes sense of the possibility of illusion, without portraying any contradiction between perceptual content and fact, there is no reason to suppose that the perceptual awareness *fails to match* the way things actually are, at least not in a sense of "failure" that counts as relevantly epistemic. (I will consider some other possible senses of "failing to match" shortly, but I doubt these cases of "mismatch" are epistemically interesting.) This means that we can affirm Le Morvan's possibility (2) without being committed to perceptual fallibilism.

Le Morvan might object to the infallibilist's attempt to rescue the language of "appearance" by appealing to Alston's claim that "the appearing (looking) relation [is] *irreducible* to theoretically more fundamental factors. X's looking a certain way to S is a bottom line concept" (Alston 1999, 183). He might take this point to imply that "appears *F*" should not be defined in terms of anything else, let alone similarities among states of awareness. Both Le Morvan and Alston may be correct to treat perceptual awareness itself as a "basic and irreducible presentation of mind-independent external objects to percipients." Sensory qualities, by virtue of being aspects of perceptual awareness, may be metaphysically irreducible.

But, I will suggest, the metaphysical irreducibility of sensory qualities would not imply the *epistemic* irreducibility of a *concept* of "sensory quality" (or "appearance"). To know about the existence of such a thing as the quality of one's sensory awareness is a sophisticated conceptual act, the complexity of which is reflected in the definition of a concept like "appear." Le Morvan and Alston would concede that perception affords us direct awareness of objects in the world; it does not involve a hidden introspective component, the awareness of some internal mental state, as the representationalist maintains. To know of the qualities of one's state of awareness is not a simple act of turning one's awareness on itself. Introspection of sensory qualities is made possible only by a process of interrelation among various states of extrospective awareness (a process Ghate reminds us about in his essay). One perceives a chair, for example, and moves around it, noticing that something changes even as the chair does not: this kind of observation helps bring into relief that *there is* a quality of one's state of awareness of the chair which is changing. Eventually one notices not only that there are differences in one's state of awareness with respect to the same object, but that there can be similarities between different states of awareness of different objects—as our awareness of a straight stick in water is similar to our awareness of a bent stick out of water. By quasi-experiments like this, one learns to abstract the contributions of the nature of the perceiver from the contributions of the nature of the object of perception. Only through this process of isolating differences and similarities do we become aware of sensory qualities, sometimes described as "appearances." A definition of "appears *F*" should reflect the fact that our knowledge of the concept is dependent on our knowledge of these relationships.

Understanding the point above about our formation of the concept of "appearance" helps to make sense of why Ghate would think there is a hidden representationalist element in the theory of appearing as presented by Le Morvan and Alston. When they claim that perception and reality can "mismatch," they assume that "appears F" is an epistemically irreducible concept (insofar as they do not consider any definition of the concept, including one that would explain away the mismatch). But to think it is irreducible in this way, they would need to think that one could form the concept of "appears F" merely by distinguishing primitive instances of appearing-F from, say, instances of appearing-not-F, *as if these appearances presented themselves directly to the mind for our comparison—just as the representationalist suggests.* If, however, we take our commitment to direct realism seriously and accept that we begin by grasping objects in the world, and only later notice that something about our awareness changes when the same object is perceived in different contexts, we will be led to define "appears F" in the relational way I have suggested. And this definition, of course, saves the language of appearances for the perceptual infallibilist.

This perspective on the formation of concepts of sensory qualities is complementary to Ghate's more explicit reasons for rejecting the possibility of a mismatch between sensory qualities and the objects of perception, reasons Le Morvan does not really address. Ghate emphasizes—and Le Morvan agrees—that perceptual awareness is a relational phenomenon, and that the nature of this relation is determined by both the nature of the object of perception and by the nature of the perceiver. As aspects of this relation, sensory qualities are not properties of the external object alone, but characteristics of "the object-as-it-is-being-perceived-by-the-subject." For this reason, Ghate claims, no description of our sensory qualities (as we might give using the language of "appearing F") can contradict a description of properties of objects in the world (even if it uses the language of "F").

It is simply a *category mistake* to expect some acts of perception to match and other acts of perception to mismatch objects in the world. For there to be a match or mismatch in qualities or the concepts of those qualities, these qualities or concepts must be *commensurable.* Insofar as perceptual awareness is seen as a relational phenomenon, however, sensory qualities are aspects of that relation, and *concepts* of sensory qualities are concepts of aspects of that relation. They are not aspects or concepts of characteristics of objects. There is a strong case, then, that the fallibilist tries to compare incommensurable things. Even if words for sensory qualities incorporate *language* that can also be used to describe characteristics of the world, these words are used in different senses, and on pain of equivocation there can be no contradiction or mismatch between a description of the aspect of a relationship between a perceiver and objects, and a description of aspects of those objects alone.

The category mistake involved in the attempt to compare sensory qualities with properties in the world becomes clearer when we consider Le Morvan's discussion of Salmieri's example of a myopic man looking at a tree:

> Without his glasses, the tree looks blurry to him. Suppose that, given his myopia and the viewing conditions, the tree cannot but look blurry to him. Does this mean that the veridicality of his seeing the tree under these conditions cannot be impugned? No. He can put on his glasses and look at the tree again, or ask others with 20/20 vision about how the tree looks; in such ways he can come to realize that although the tree looked blurry to him without his glasses, there is good reason to think that the tree itself is really not blurry. Appealing to one's later perceptions or to the perceptions of others can provide a standard by which one can impugn the veridicality of particular perceptions and discover that they were not presenting the world as it is.

To claim that one's blurry vision of a tree impugns the veridicality of one's perceptual experience implies a comparison between the bluriness of one's vision with non-blurry objects. But this is a comparison between metaphysical apples and oranges. We never speak of such things as "blurry" material objects. Perhaps we speak of fuzzy objects, like cotton balls or clouds. But if we see a cotton ball or cloud clearly and distinctly, do we say that our senses mismatch reality? It makes no more sense to say this than to say that seeing a non-fuzzy tree in a blurry way is also a mismatch. Fuzzy objects are nothing like blurry perception. The point is not even that they *look different*. They're not the kinds of things whose looks we can compare. One is a thing, the other is a way things look.

To clarify this further: supposing that there could be a contradiction or mismatch between sensory qualities and characteristics of the world is like supposing that there could be a contradiction or mismatch between an object's weight and its mass. Just like the nature of the perceptual relation is determined by the nature of the object and the nature of the perceiver, a thing's weight is a function of its mass and the nature of other massive bodies in its vicinity. Just like our language for qualities is sometimes etymologically derived from our language for characteristics ("looks bent" derives from "is bent"), our language for weight is sometimes derived from our language for mass (it is not uncommon for nonscientists to measure weight in "kilograms," even though kilograms are a unit of mass, not of weight, which is measured in newtons). Even if we use the loose language of "kilograms" for weight, it would be a category mistake to say that a weightless astronaut's weight "mismatches" his mass. Only the similarity of equivocal language creates the illusion of a mismatch: he weighs 0 on a scale using "kilograms," but we know that his mass of 150 kilograms has not changed. We can avoid the illusion of a mismatch altogether if we measure his weight in newtons and his mass in kilograms, just like we can avoid the illusion of a mismatch between a state of perceptual awareness and an object in the world, if we eliminate the misleading language of "appearing F" and simply describe the state of awareness as similar to another state of awareness of an object that is F in a different context.[2]

There may be other reasons for thinking that cases in which an object appears F but is not F (even as I have defined "appears F") are evidence of a "mismatch" between perceptual awareness and reality of a sort that does not involve *contradiction* between two "contents." For example, one might claim that even if nothing about the content of a perceptual quality that we can describe using the language of "appears F" contradicts the fact that the object is not F, one might characterize the mismatch in terms of what *judgment* this appearance leads one to form, and the fact to which this judgment fails to correspond if it is false. Insofar as Ghate is happy to account for cases of illusion using a distinction between perception and judgment, I do not see any reason he would object to speaking of this kind of mismatch. If one makes the judgment that a stick in water is bent, and this turns out to be a false judgment, then one could say very loosely that one's senses cause a "mismatch" between the mind and reality, but only insofar as they lead one to form a false judgment. But the real mismatch is between the judgment and the fact in that one can make sense of a notion of matching or mismatching by reference to a correspondence theory of truth. Speaking of a mismatch between the sensory appearance and the fact is merely sloppy shorthand that is parasitical upon this better

2. One might challenge the eliminability of the language of "appears F" by rejecting the definition of "appears F" that I have proposed on the grounds that there is something else about the nature of perceptual awareness that gives us reason to associate it with Fness. One might propose, for instance, that perceptual awareness has conceptual content, which would make it possible that perceptual awareness qua perception could have the content *that something is* F. But Le Morvan appears to agree with Ghate that this is an unacceptable concession. I will not explore this option further, especially since many philosophers have challenged the idea that perception has conceptual content, and I will not repeat their analysis here.

understood mismatch. And, since we know that these judgments are correctable, if one learns to recognize the illusion and avoids any disposition to make the judgment, there is not even a sloppy sense in which the senses would "deceive" us because of some kind of mismatch.[3]

It is worth making a brief comment on *why* beliefs can be mistaken about their objects while perception cannot. The difference depends on a difference in their respective types of content. Thanks to formal logic, we understand clearly what it is for one belief to contradict another belief. What is it for a belief to "contradict" facts in reality? One might argue that if it is a category mistake to look for a match or mismatch between facts about sensory qualities and facts about the objects of perception, then surely it is also a category mistake to make a similar comparison between beliefs and their objects. In one respect this is true. The *qualities* of beliefs cannot be compared to the qualities of the world. There are, for example, no *foolish* objects in the world which foolish beliefs either match or mismatch. (There are foolish people, but they are foolish only by reference to their beliefs.) But there are important differences between perception and belief that account for the possibility of error in the case of the latter but not the former. Salmieri explores the difference between perception and belief by exploring the more general difference between perception and the various forms of cognition that (he argues) are based on it. I will not describe his position further here, but merely indicate that it is available to explain why comparing beliefs to facts in reality is no longer a category mistake: the special facts Salmieri cites about beliefs qua nonbasic forms of cognition are offered as an explanation for the possibility of error.

Some direct realists have thought that describing states of perceptual awareness in terms of appearing *F* is essential to making sense of how the senses could have the cognitive content needed to stand in a relationship of justification to beliefs. If the direct realist does not read this cognitive content off descriptions of appearances, how can he make a case for a foundationalism about justification, as Rand, Ghate, and Salmieri want to? Elsewhere in this volume, Salmieri and Gotthelf argue that Rand's theory of concepts is in a unique position to provide a justificatory bridge between infallible perception and the remaining structure of our knowledge. In another essay, I have argued that direct realism about perception uniquely informs just such a theory of abstraction (Bayer 2011). I argue in particular that we need a direct realist theory that regards perceptual

3. Charles Travis, in his aptly titled "The Silence of the Senses" (2004, 64–65, 67–68), makes a similar point, invoking Austin (1962, 11) and even Descartes.

awareness as neither true nor false to avoid various regress problems. Epistemologists who assume that foundational justification is internalistic will argue that if a perceptual state is the sort of thing that could match or mismatch facts, then to use it as a source of justification for our beliefs we must suppose that we are justified in believing that the perceptual state actually matches, and this generates a regress or meta-regress.[4] The internalist foundationalist can avoid the regress only by supposing that perceptual states confer justification but do not require it, because they are not the sorts of things that face an alternative of matching or mismatching the facts. An additional advantage of perceptual infallibilism, then, is the role it plays for the internalist in defending against these regress problems.[5]

I mention this last point not only to cite an advantage of perceptual infallibilism, but also to reinforce one of Ghate's criticisms of Alston. Le Morvan claims that Ghate misrepresents Alston by claiming that Alston denies that awareness has a nature and that perceptual awareness is a form of awareness of objects. He disputes Ghate's interpretation by citing a passage in which Alston claims explicitly that, in his theory, the directness of perceptual awareness stems from the absence of any intermediate representational object, not from a guaranteed match. But I do not think that Ghate is unaware of Alston's claim: I think what he is saying is that by countenancing the possibility of a mismatch, Alston's theory *implies* that perceptual awareness has no nature and that it is not always an awareness of objects (whether or not he would admit this implication). Consider Ghate's point that perceptual awareness gives us a nonpropositional form of awareness of the matter of what a proposition would designate as subject and as predicate. On this view, objects *are* the integrated unity of their characteristics, characteristics that are only separated by the act of conceptualization and brought together again in the act of judgment. If perception mismatches the facts, if there is a mismatch between a sensory quality of appearing F and an object that is not F, the claim is that our awareness of the object as an object matches, but not our awareness of it as an object that is F. But since objects just *are* the unity of their characteristics, our perception cannot succeed in matching its object without "matching" the characteristics of the object. If, therefore, our awareness

4. This is precisely the point advanced by BonJour (2004), the target of my (2011) critique.

5. Elsewhere I have argued (Bayer, forthcoming) that direct realism about perception gives us good reasons to be internalists rather than externalists. I mention this because Le Morvan and Alston, in particular, may not care to classify themselves as internalists.

of a thing that looks F does count as a mismatch in characteristics, we are not perceiving the object after all. Such an account of awareness would degenerate into a representationalist theory: to reunify objects and characteristics, we would have to posit the existence of internal mental objects, on the grounds that our awareness of external objects is somehow degenerate in virtue of its being mediated.

Brewer

Brewer, in his comments on Salmieri, also contends that "there is a *right way* for a red, round object to look independently of the idiosyncrasies of the perceiver's nervous system"—implying that there is a *wrong* way for it to look.

After giving an example of "normal" perception of a red, round object (the subject's "standpoint is head on in good lighting . . . [and] . . . her visual system is functioning normally"), he claims that "malfunction may result in less than perfect success in all sorts of ways." Presumably one example of imperfect perception of color would be to perceive a red, round object that looks mauve in poor lighting conditions. Salmieri would claim that this is not imperfect perception, but merely an unusual form of perception (a form that is similar to perceiving a mauve object in normal lighting conditions). But we do not need to rehearse this debate here. What is new in Brewer's discussion is his treatment of a more radical case of alleged perception in an unusual form. If infallibilism can maintain that even this is a case of perception, albeit in an unusual form, it will be even more plausible that the ordinary cases of perception in an unusual form are not cases of imperfect or erroneous perception.

For Brewer, some alleged ways of perceiving colored objects are so radically different from the usual ways that they do not count as ways of perceiving colored objects at all. Brewer evaluates the example of a Martian perceiver, radically different from ourselves, as follows: "If all and only red things sound to me at the pitch of tuning fork A and all and only green things at middle C, and if I were blind, I would *not* thereby perceive the colors of those things, albeit in a different way. I would not have the foggiest idea which properties those color properties are." Salmieri, by contrast, is willing to entertain the possibility of two perceivers who perceive the same objects, and the same characteristics of those objects, but in radically different forms. Here Salmieri is drawing on Rand's distinction between the form and the object of awareness, which is in turn informed by Rand's view that the nature of our perceptual activity is not a barrier to but an enabler of our awareness of objects in the world. Different organisms may exploit very different processes to apprehend the same properties of objects in the world, but these are still different ways of *apprehending* these properties.

Brewer objects that Salmieri's and Rand's position implies a "collapse" back into a form of traditional representationalism. We could count the experience of the Martian as genuine perception of color, he argues, only if we say that perceiving color is nothing but the causal connection and correlation between color properties and "the way things sound." But according to Brewer, this presupposes that the "sensations that we are directly aware of in perception are a medium of indication," a presupposition of traditional representationalism.

If we understand the Martian example in one way, I think Brewer is correct to think that the infallibilist's use of the example would involve a representationalist assumption. If we suppose that the Martian's auditory experience of color involves an experience that is *identical* to our experience of middle C, then it might be supposed that our auditory experience has a metaphysically separable component, "the sound of middle C." This *does* sound like representationalism, insofar as it suggests that the nature of a sensory quality is *not* the product of the relationship between the object and the perceiver. A genuine direct realist cannot regard the nature of perceptual awareness (described in terms of "looks" or "sounds") as metaphysically separable in this way: the nature of perceptual awareness, we are all agreed, is dependent on facts about both the object and the perceiver.

But I do not think that one needs to interpret the Martian example in the way that suggests this kind of metaphysical separability of the nature of perceptual awareness. Perhaps there is a way we can make sense of what it is like to be a Martian; if we cannot, we cannot compare his experience to ours. But then all that Salmieri needs to say is that the Martian's way of experiencing color properties is *radically different* from ours, in just the same way that we normally say that the bat's way of experiencing shape is radically different from ours—even if we do not know what it is like to be a bat. Salmieri could simply propose that the Martian's auditory perception of color is no different than the bat's perception of shape through auditory means (which is quite real).

In any case, Brewer's evaluation of another broadly similar case is interestingly different from his evaluation of the Martian example. I refer to his analysis of our visual and tactile perception of shape properties.

The difference in his evaluation is interesting, because everyone acknowledges that we can perceive shape by both sight and touch, even though visual and tactile sensory qualities are very different from each other. The differences are so dramatic that they give rise to the classic problem first posed by William Molyneux to John Locke: would a man born blind who learned to distinguish shape by touch be able to identify shape visually upon the restoration of his sight?[6] Brewer wants to accommodate the possibility of both visual and tactile perception of shape without accommodating the possibility of both visual and auditory perception of color. Salmieri, by contrast, wants to suggest that the way our tactile perception of shape differs from our visual perception of shape is hardly less radical than the way a Martian's auditory perception of color differs from our visual perception of color. If we want to resolve the dispute between Salmieri and Brewer, then, we must see if Brewer can state a principled reason for allowing for one possibility but not the other.

Brewer allows for the possibility of visual and tactile perception of shape for the following reason: "[The possibility of visual and tactile shape perception] is a matter of different standpoints on the very same objective shape. For that very shape property, individuated prior to and independently of any question of how it may appear in perception, plays a fundamental and essential role in the subjective characterization of the nature of the experience itself in both modalities, and is therefore transparent to the subject of such experience." Presumably Brewer would say that the *Martian's* experience, unlike our awareness of color, is not characterizable in a "fundamental and essential" way by reference to color properties individuated prior to their appearance in perception. What does Brewer mean by saying that in ordinary color perception, our experience *is* characterizable by color properties, and why does he think that, in the example of the Martian, it is not? And why does he think that color cannot be perceived via different modalities but that shape can be?

To answer the second question first, part of his reason seems to depend on his estimate of the actual difference between visual and tactile awareness of shape, which at times he appears to regard as fairly trivial. He says that vision and touch have (merely) different "enabling and disabling conditions": visual apprehension of shape works through unobstructed reception of light rays; touch does not. But surely this oversimplifies the

---

6. Locke, *Essay* 2.9.8 (Nidditch 1979). See also Degenaar and Lokhorst's summary (2010) of the philosophical and empirical debate surrounding the problem.

difference. It is not that seeing is simply a way of "touching" light rays and discovering shape in the same way as touch. There are radical differences between the way the nerve endings on the retina process light signals and the way they process physical displacement on the skin. There is *certainly* a significant qualitative difference in these sensory modalities. Note just one major difference: whereas there is the possibility of perceiving shapes from different visual perspectives, there is no obvious equivalent of perspective in the tactile perception of shape. Of course, one side of an object will feel different than other sides, but we can grasp a whole object in three dimensions in a way that we cannot see things in three dimensions. There are truly deep differences in these sensory modalities.

Brewer makes crucial use of the idea that some mind-independent properties can be used to "characterize" the nature of perceptual experience. When he claims that the nature of the Martian's experience is not characterizable by color properties, my first reaction is to think that it is another way of claiming that qualities of auditory perception do not *match* mind-independent color properties. If so, my critique of Le Morvan above would seem to apply to Brewer as well. As I have argued above, to speak of the possibility of a match or a mismatch would involve various category mistakes. Before I allege this, however, I need to examine what Brewer actually means by this "characterization" of experience by mind-independent properties.

In a recent essay, Brewer (2011b) clarifies what it means for a property individuated independently of its appearance in perception to play a role in the characterization of the nature of experience. He compares his view on this matter to a standard view he rejects, the empiricist's traditional understanding of color as a secondary quality. According to this standard view, we can characterize "looking red" independently of any worldly property; the worldly property of "redness," if it is anything, is whatever property has the disposition to cause the appearance of looking red in perception. So, as Brewer puts it, the standard view maintains that appearances are individuated independently of mind-independent properties, and that reference to them explains which worldly properties count as color properties. Brewer, by contrast, insists that both shape *and* color are individuated independently of appearances, and aid in explaining the nature of the appearances, not the other way around. In this way, Brewer explicitly models his understanding of all mind-independent properties on the traditional empiricist understanding of primary qualities. He argues that the following kinds of explanations are characteristic of the way in which mind-independent properties explain the nature of the appearances, that is, the nature of our perceptual experience:

> The coin looks circular to Janet because it is circular and she is viewing it from head on.
>
> The coin looks elliptical to John because it is circular and he is viewing it from an angle.
>
> The jumper looks red outdoors because it is red and lighting conditions are normal outdoors.
>
> It looks mauve in the store because it is red and the lighting conditions are artificially dingy [in] the store. (Brewer 2011b, 70)

I think these kinds of explanations are what Brewer would describe as *characterizations* of our experience by reference to mind-independent properties. Indeed, it is in accepting such explanations that Brewer thinks we regard these properties as mind-independent.

Why, then, does Brewer say that reference to mind-independent color properties does not help explain the nature of *the Martian's* experience in the way that color properties do explain the nature of *our* experience in the last two examples above? Here it is useful to propose a way in which mind-independent color properties might be alleged to do just that, and describe Brewer's likely response. One could propose, for example, that color properties are the mind-independent underlying reflectance properties of objects described by physics. The advocate of this rather crude proposal could still claim that it is precisely these properties which *do* cause the Martian to see as he sees, and reference to these properties would therefore explain the nature of his awareness.

But Brewer contends that such underlying physical properties are "absolutely not" the properties presented in the perceptual experience of color. They are not, because on his view the fundamental physical properties are simply not presented in perception. "Perceptual presentation provides us with at least a rough and provisional conception of what the objects are with which we are presented; and we have no conception whatsoever of what the most fundamental scientific-physical primitives are simply on the basis of perception" (2011b, 75–76). It matters to Brewer that we have no conception of what these properties are, because if we have no idea what the underlying physical property of redness is, we could not make use of redness in explanations like this: "The jumper looks red outdoors because it is red and lighting conditions are normal outdoors"

(2011b, 70). We could not make use of such a property because the following would not be *knowable* to the commonsense knower who nonetheless
knows that color is a mind-independent property: The jumper looks red
outdoors because it [has such and such underlying physical property] and
lighting conditions are normal outdoors.

Of course, I agree with Brewer that nothing in our perceptual awareness gives us any *conception* of what the fundamental constituents of matter are. If we assume that the task of perceptual awareness is to give us
a *conception* of what things are, it will come as no surprise if we are led
to conclude that the Martian does not perceive. But we should see if we
evaluate the Martian problem in the same way if we suppose instead that
perception has nonconceptual and nonpropositional content, which is the
usual assumption of the infallibilists anyway.[7] For if we suppose this, we
need not deny that what we see when we see the color of an object is its reflectance properties (or whatever underlying properties color consists of).
A nonconceptual perceiver may not be able to *isolate* these underlying
properties qua underlying properties, but he may be able to isolate them
as against other properties (such as shape). To be sure, we see an object's
properties *in a form* that does not reveal facts about these properties. But
on the view of perception that I have been pursuing, to suppose that the
perceptual form must somehow match or reveal every fact about some
property is to confuse the form and object of perception. The fact that we
can see properties the natures of which are not revealed to us in their entirety is not surprising if we think of the statement "color is a reflectance
property" (for example) as a *de re* identity, rather than a *de dicto* one.[8]

Brewer will maintain, of course, that any account of perception depending on the mere covariance between color properties and auditory
modes of perception would be an account of the merely "brute" causal

7. Even longtime advocates of the idea that perception has conceptual, propositional
content, like McDowell (2009a), have come to qualify their view and to maintain that perceptual content is not propositional and is conceptual only in the sense that it is *conceptualizable.*

8. That our form of awareness of a property does not reveal every fact about it should not
be surprising, given that, as Salmieri suggests, the distinction between the form and object
of perception has important affinities to Frege's sense/reference distinction. A Fregean would
say we do not believe *de dicto* that Hesperus is Phosphorus (because "Hesperus" and "Phosphorus" have different senses), even if we believe *of* Hesperus (*de re*) that it is Phosphorus (because "Hesperus" and "Phosphorus" refer to the same thing). Likewise, the perceiver may not
see color *as* a reflectance property (in a conceptual sense of "seeing as"), but the perceiver who
sees color is still seeing a reflectance property. Scientific conceptualization of color and visual
perception of color are different forms of awareness of the same property, and we might have
one without the other.

connection between these properties and the "medium" which supposedly covaries with them. I have already indicated that a direct realist
should regard it as a mistake to think of the "medium" as a metaphysically separable entity. Salmieri does not speak of a "medium" *of which*
the perceiver is directly aware. What Brewer calls the "medium," Salmieri
calls, following Rand, the *form* or *means* of awareness, that *by* which or
that by means of which one is aware, and this is not the same as the *object,*
that *of* which one is aware. On this view, the fact that a causal process is
necessary for awareness of an object does not imply that it is the causal
process of which we are directly aware. By the same token, involving a
causal process in the means of awareness does not transform this view
into indirect realism, whereby the object of awareness becomes *whatever*
causal factors antecede one's experience. The form/object distinction still
contends that what one is aware of is an *object,* and some identity conditions for objects are part of the proposal. The object of awareness, whether
an entity or a property of it, is not just any causal antecedent, but the
object *consciously distinguished* by the perceiver that determines (along
with many other antecedent conditions and the nature of one's perceptual
apparatus) the nature of one's awareness.

Of course, bringing in the form/object distinction at this point does
not imply that we can explain color appearances by reference to mind-
independent color properties if we know nothing of them. I accept that
the commonsense knower cannot explain why the jumper looks red outside by reference to reflectance properties he knows nothing about. This
does not mean that the commonsense knower is not able to understand
at all why the jumper looks red outside; I am simply conceding that it's
not an understanding in terms of reflectance properties.[9] But the fact
that our commonsense explanations do not make reference to properties
grasped through science should not dissuade us from identifying properties grasped by common sense with those grasped by science.[10]

9. He can still say it looks red because it is red (his *understanding* of "looks red" derives
from what it is to be red). See my proposal below about how the characterizability of "looks
red" by reference to "being red" is best understood as an explanation in the sense of describing a causal connection. If we characterize "looks red" by reference to "being red," this may
be because we *form our concept* of "looking red" only after having formed the concept of "being red," and what we do when we say "it looks red because it is red" is citing a paradigm case
of what it means to look red.

10. It might be that "explanation" also admits of a *de re* and *de dicto* sense. We might not
explain anything about color appearances by reference to reflectance properties *de dicto,* but
by reference to colors, even though colors *are* reflectance properties (if they are).

Brewer thinks that it is in offering *substantive* explanations for why things appear as they do by reference to mind-independent properties that we grasp them as mind-independent (2011b, 73). Since he thinks we cannot give substantive explanations by reference to such things as reflectance properties, he argues, as a direct realist, that we lose the mind-independence of color if we regard it as a physical property such as this. To bolster my case against ruling out the possibility that colors are physical properties of some kind, I want to claim that it is a mistake to see our ability to offer substantive explanations as constitutive of our grasp of the mind-independence of the properties involved in these explanations: if we need to be able to give substantive explanations to grasp the mind-independence of properties, there will be few mind-independent properties we can grasp.

Even an explanation as seemingly straightforward as "The coin looks elliptical to John because it is circular and he is viewing it from an angle" involves specialized scientific knowledge. Brewer offers it as a common-sense explanation available to John or anyone else. But prior to the systematization of geometrical optics, it would have been at best only implicit for much of humanity if not mysterious (as witness, the lack of perspective in most painting before the Renaissance). Facts about the geometry of projection are, of course, easier to discover than quantum physics or even other less fundamental physical properties, and this probably explains why it has been thought that there is a distinction between primary and secondary qualities. Philosophers in the early modern period understood geometry and could think of properties like shape in terms of it; they did not understand the quantum physics behind reflectance properties. But there is little excuse for formulating a fundamental metaphysical distinction on the basis of humanity's present state of knowledge. Brewer, of course, does not endorse anything like Locke's primary/secondary quality distinction. But I think that a version of it survives in his contention that shape is a mind-independent physical property (courtesy of geometry) while color is a mind-independent but nonphysical property. We should not say that one is a physical property while the other is not only because the one is easily understood as a physical property, while the other is not.

Further to my point, it is interesting that Brewer's example of an explanation for a "false" color appearance—one parallel to his explanation of the elliptical look of the coin—is "It looks mauve in the store because it is red and the lighting conditions are artificially dingy in the store." Without specialized scientific knowledge like that provided by geometry in the case of the explanation of the elliptical look of the coin, this explanation is not actually much of a "robust" explanation. *Why* does something look mauve under these dingy lighting conditions? Why does it not retain its color? If it still seems like saying that the light is dingy explains why the red object is mauve (and remember that mauve is a kind of purple), what about cases where the "false" appearance varies even more from the origin? Are there commonsense explanations available for why distant green hills look blue, why the orange sun at sunrise appears pink, why blue paper under yellow light looks black, why transparent water looks blue, and so on?

So, to the extent that Brewer thinks that a mind-independent property characterizes the nature of perceptual experience only if it is presented to the perceiver in a way that provides information from which one could in effect know everything there is to know about this property, I think he is still assuming something like the "matching" view in Le Morvan I have already critiqued for attempting to compare incommensurable facts about the form and object of perception. When Brewer says that the Martian does not perceive color because nothing about mind-independent color properties characterizes his experiences, he is assuming that to perceive color one must have color experiences that "match" color properties, in the sense of providing the knower with all of the information about those color properties. To account for how we can perceive color without having to know information about underlying physics, Brewer says that color is a mind-independent but nonphysical property that we apprehend "transparently." Infallibilist direct realism based on the form/object distinction does not countenance the idea of "transparent" perception: all perception is of an object by a definite means in a definite form, and this includes perception of properties we do not know everything about.

Furthermore, there is a looming threat of skepticism if a property like color is a nonphysical property revealed transparently only to those with the *right* sensory apparatus (unlike Martians). A Martian who can know nothing of this property through perception also cannot infer it from anything: if it is a nonphysical property, it is not causally connected to any physical facts that he otherwise does know. This would not be such a concern for us if it were not for the fact that there are so many other modes of awareness which *we* do not possess, say those possessed by bats and bees and countless other real or conceivable species. For every conceivable mode of awareness, there would be more nonphysical properties revealed transparently only to creatures with these modes, and not to us. A universe of unknowable properties opens before us. The problem does not merely suggest a barrier to acquiring certain kinds of knowledge: it actively challenges knowledge we think we have. We think that scientists who study reflectance properties are teaching us something about *colors*. We also think that the universe has a certain causal unity, that it is not a series of atomic fact-properties which are knowable as the "shell" of objects only to properly constructed organisms. And if we accept that to know a property we must know everything about it transparently, we may find that we do not even know anything about shape or other physical properties. (Euclidean geometry may not reveal everything there is to know about shape in relativistic reference frames, for example.)

I agree with Brewer that appearances are not characterizable without reference to mind-independent properties, but I do not think that the characterizability in question is an explanatory relation. More likely it is a relationship of priority in the order of concept-formation: in the manner suggested above, I think we only come to grasp the concept of "looking red" by reference to the concept "red." The same process of concept-formation is likely involved in understanding why some properties are mind-independent. Indeed, I think that the same kinds of quasi-experiments by which we abstract our knowledge of the form of perception from our knowledge of the object are involved in grasping the mind-independence of an object's properties: when we are impressed by the fact that something about us changes when we move around a table and see something about our awareness of it change, the fact that something about the table stays the same (its shape) is brought into relief. Similar quasi-experiments could be performed with color: even if something about an object changes as our distance from it or the lighting conditions under which we see it change, there is still something about it that stays the same (its color). The fact that there is some regularity in how the appearances of various shapes and colors change (J. J. Gibson's "invariant properties") reflects this fact. If this account of how we grasp the mind-independence of properties is correct, then it is no longer a liability of regarding colors as physical properties that this identity does not help us offer commonsense explanations of the appearances. We do not need an account of explanation to make sense of how we grasp the mind-independence of properties.

In the end, I cannot see how allowing for the possibility of visual and tactile perception of shape, but not for the possibility of visual and auditory perception of color is anything other than question-begging. We can perceive shape in radically different forms: via touch as well as via sight. There is no reason to think there could not be radically different forms of perceiving color, not unless we think color is a property revealed only "transparently." To insist that some property can be perceived transparently is to assume that perception of it cannot be characterized without knowing everything about it, without "matching" form to object. And whether or not perception must "match" its object is precisely the question at issue. Salmieri and Ghate argue that the very expectation of the possibility of a "match" or "mismatch" between properties in the world and sensory qualities is a kind of category mistake, engendered by the attempt to compare incommensurable properties and/or concepts. As far as I can see, Le Morvan and Brewer have not addressed these objections. Until and unless they offer a rival account that answers the category mistake objection, I cannot see how this debate can proceed fruitfully.

Conclusion

I want to close by pointing to an especially interesting part of Salmieri's essay that I think has the effect of highlighting why it is important that direct realists be infallibilists, as Rand would recommend. Salmieri notes that if we must accept the idea that standard examples (like the myopic perceiver) count as cases of mistaken or degraded perception, we can do so only by reference to human standards of "normal" perception. But why privilege human perception, when we know of animals that surpass us in the same sensory modalities? If our visual perception is mistaken when it runs together light with and without ultraviolet (unlike bees), or if our auditory perception is mistaken when it gives us only a very "blurry" awareness of location (compared to a bat, or even to the blind), then since we can always imagine another being that discriminates even more properties than the bee or the bat, Salmieri has a point when he says that describing the limits of perception as errors implies "taking as one's standard of awareness the sort of omniscience that Moore, Bertrand Russell, and others thought that we had of sense-data." As we have seen previously in consideration of Brewer's demand that genuine awareness reveal the properties of an object "transparently," this demand implies a form of skepticism for all to whom such transparent awareness is not available.

It is significant, then, that in advocating perceptual fallibilism, Le Morvan makes the following remark: "Insofar as we are realists, however, we take the objects that we perceive to have an existence independent of our perceiving or being conscious of them (and accordingly that not all their features exist only in relation to us). Moreover, we are not gods and are not endowed with godlike powers. Accordingly, the epistemic modesty of perceptual fallibilism strikes me as more befitting of a realist position." Though Le Morvan maintains that he and Alston do not deny that perceptual awareness has a definite nature, I take it that Salmieri would regard the above as a confession to the contrary. The explicit suggestion here is that we are not gods, and therefore our senses can (and must, on certain occasions) be in error. Salmieri and Ghate have given us reason to think that if we count the senses' limited ability to discriminate (like myopia) as a source of error, we may have to consider the possibility that perception is always in error (since we can always imagine a being that discriminates more characteristics). But this means, in effect, that we are limited, not omniscient; therefore, we are in error. But the limits of a creature are its *nature*. To say that our limits necessitate error is to say that the *nature* of consciousness necessitates error. But this *is* a yearning for magical access to the world that works by no means in particular. Perceptual infallibilism, by contrast, acknowledges and embraces the limits, the *nature* of our consciousness.

UNIFORM ABBREVIATIONS OF WORKS BY AYN RAND

(with indication of the editions cited from)

Rand's philosophical output took many different forms (e.g., monographs, essay collections, journal entries, lecture courses subsequently transcribed—not to mention the novels, which contain specific philosophical content and are themselves philosophical novels) and some items appear in several different editions with differing pagination. Because there is not yet a standard edition of her works, we decided to adopt for the series this list of uniform abbreviations and a standard set of (easily accessible) editions to which to refer for page numbers in citations.

*Centennial trade editions (with facsimile original covers), New York: Plume, 2005
**Centennial mass-market editions, New York: Signet, 2005

Anthem Anthem (*1953)

Anthem '38 Anthem (London: Cassells, 1938)

AOF The Art of Fiction: A Guide for Writers and Readers,
ed. T. Boeckmann (New York: Plume, 2000)

AON The Art of Nonfiction: A Guide for Writers and Readers,
ed. R. Mayhew (New York: Plume, 2001)

ARL The Ayn Rand Letter, 1971–1976 (New Milford, CT: Second
Renaissance Books, 1990)

Atlas Atlas Shrugged (*1957)

Column The Ayn Rand Column: Written for the Los Angeles Times,
with additional essays, 2nd ed. (New Milford, CT: Second
Renaissance Books, 1990)

CUI Capitalism: The Unknown Ideal (**1966)

EAR   *The Early Ayn Rand: A Selection from Her Unpublished Fiction*, ed. L. Peikoff (**1984)

Fountainhead   *The Fountainhead* (*1943); "Introduction" Introduction to the twenty-fifth anniversary edition of *The Fountainhead* (New York: Bobbs-Merrill Co., 1968)

FTNI   *For the New Intellectual: The Philosophy of Ayn Rand* (**1961)

Interviews   *Objectively Speaking: Ayn Rand Interviewed*, ed. M. Podritske and P. Schwartz (Lanham: Lexington Books, 2009)

ITOE   *Introduction to Objectivist Epistemology*, expanded 2nd ed. (New York: Meridian, 1990)

Journals   *Journals of Ayn Rand*, ed. D. Harriman (New York: Dutton, 1997)

Letters   *Letters of Ayn Rand*, ed. M. S. Berliner (New York: Dutton, 1995)

Lexicon   *The Ayn Rand Lexicon: Objectivism from A to Z*, ed. H. Binswanger, The Ayn Rand Library, vol. IV (New York: Plume, 1986)

Marginalia   *Ayn Rand's Marginalia: Her Critical Comments on the Writings of Over Twenty Authors*, ed. R. Mayhew (New Milford, CT: Second Renaissance Books, 1995)

Plays   *Three Plays: Night of January 16th; Ideal; Think Twice* (**2005)

PWNI   *Philosophy: Who Needs It* (**1982)

Q&A   *Ayn Rand Answers: The Best of Her Q & A*, ed. R. Mayhew (London: New American Library, 2005)

RM   *The Romantic Manifesto: A Philosophy of Literature* (**1969)

ROTP   *Return of the Primitive: The Anti-Industrial Revolution*, ed. P. Schwartz (New York: Plume, 1999)

TO   *The Objectivist 1966–71* (New Milford, CT: Second Renaissance Books, 1990)

TON   *The Objectivist Newsletter 1962–65* (New Milford, CT: Second Renaissance Books, 1990)

VOR   *The Voice of Reason: Essays in Objectivist Thought*, ed. Leonard Peikoff, The Ayn Rand Library, vol. 5 (New York: Plume, 1990)

VOS   *The Virtue of Selfishness: A New Concept of Egoism* (**1964)

WTL   *We the Living* (New York: Random House, 1959)

WTL '36   *We the Living* (New York: Macmillan, 1936)

REFERENCES

Adrian, Edgar Douglas. 1932. *The mechanism of nervous action.* London: Humphrey Milford Oxford University Press.

Alberts, Bruce, et al. 2002. *Molecular biology of the cell.* 4th ed. New York: Garland Science.

Alston, William P. 1990. Externalist theories of perception. *Philosophy and Phenomenological Research, Supplement* 50:73–97.

———. 1996. *The reliability of sensory perception.* Ithaca: Cornell University Press.

———. 1998a. Perception and conception. In *Pragmatism, reason, and norms,* ed. Kenneth R. Westphal, 59–88. New York: Fordham University Press.

———. 1998b. Sellars and the "myth of the given." APA Eastern Division meetings. (Available online at www.ditext.com/alston/alston2.html; see Alston 2002.)

———. 1999. Back to the theory of appearing. *Philosophical Perspectives* 13:181–203.

———. 2002. Sellars and the "myth of the given." *Philosophy and Phenomenological Research* 65:69–86.

———. 2005a. *Beyond "justification": Dimensions of epistemic evaluation.* New York: Cornell University Press.

———. 2005b. Perception and representation. *Philosophy and Phenomenological Research* 70:253–89.

Anglin, Jeremy M. 1977. *Word, object, and conceptual development.* New York: Norton.

Arabatzis, Theodore. 2011. Hidden entities and experimental practice: Renewing the dialogue between history and philosophy of science. In *Integrating history and philosophy of science: Problems and prospects,* ed. S. Mauskopf and T. M. Schmaltz, 125–39. Berlin: Springer Verlag.

Austin, John Langshaw. 1962. *Sense and sensibilia.* 2nd rev. ed. Ed. G. J. War-nock, Oxford: Oxford University Press.

Ayers, Michael. 1991. *Locke.* Vol. 1. London: Routledge.

Barnes, Winston F. H. 1945. The myth of sense-data. *Proceedings of the Aristotelian Society* 45:89–118.

Barrett, P. H., and R. B. Freeman, eds. 1988. *The Works of Charles Darwin.* 29 vols. New York: New York University Press.

Bayer, Benjamin. 2011. A role for abstractionism in a direct realist foundationalism. *Synthese* 180.3: 357–89.

———. Forthcoming. Internalism empowered: How to bolster a theory of justification with a direct realist theory of awareness. *Acta Analytica. Online First,* 2 February 2012, http://www.springerlink.com/content/qp62435124544157.

Binswanger, Harry. 1998. *The metaphysics of consciousness.* Gaylordsville, CT: Second Renaissance. Audio recording.

———. 1989. *Consciousness as identification.* Irvine: Second Renaissance Books. Audio recording.

Bloch, Corinne L. 2010. Towards a unified approach to concepts. Paper presented at the 22nd Biennial Meeting of the Philosophy of Science Association (Montreal, November 4–6, 2010).

———. 2011. Scientific kinds without essences. In *Properties, powers and structures: Issues in the metaphysics of realism,* ed. Brian Ellis, Alexander Bird, and Howard Sankey, 233–55. London: Routledge.

Bonevac, Daniel. 2002. Sellars vs. the given. *Philosophy and Phenomenological Research* 64.1: 1–30.

BonJour, Laurence. 1978. Can empirical knowledge have a foundation? *American Philosophical Quarterly* 15:1–14.

———. 1985. *The structure of empirical knowledge.* Cambridge, MA: Harvard University Press.

———. 2004. In search of direct realism. *Philosophy and Phenomenological Research* 69.2: 349–67.

Boyd, Richard. 1991. Realism, anti-foundationalism and the enthusiasm for natural kinds. *Philosophical Studies* 61:127–48.

Brewer, Bill. 2006. Perception and content. *European Journal of Philosophy* 14:165–81.

———. 2011a. *Perception and its objects.* Oxford: Oxford University Press.

———. 2011b. Realism and explanation in perception. In *Perception, causation, and objectivity,* ed. Johannes Roessler, Hemdat Lerman, and Naomi Eilan, 68–81. Oxford: Oxford University Press.

Brigandt, Ingo. 2003. Species pluralism does not imply species eliminativism. *Philosophy of Science* 70.5: 1305–16.

———. 2010. The epistemic goal of a concept: Accounting for the rationality of semantic change and variation. *Synthese* 177.1: 19–40.

Brock, Thomas D., ed. 1999. *Milestones in microbiology: 1546–1940.* Washington, DC: ASM Press.

Brown, R., et al. 1999. Eliminating emotions? Review symposium on *What emotions really are: The problem of psychological categories* by Paul E. Griffiths. *Metascience* 8.1: 5–62.

Burian, Richard Martin. 1985. On conceptual change in biology: The case of the gene. In *Evolution at a crossroads: The new biology and the new philosophy of science,* ed. David J. Depew and Bruce H. Weber, 21–42. Cambridge, MA: MIT Press.

———. 1995. Comments on Hans-Jörg Rheinberger's "From experimental systems to cultures of experimentation." In *Concepts, theories, and rationality in the biological sciences: The second Pittsburgh-Konstanz colloquium in the philosophy of science,* ed. Gereon Wolters and James G. Lennox, 123–36. Konstanz and Pittsburgh: Universitätsverlag Konstanz and University of Pittsburgh Press.

———. 2000. On the internal dynamics of Mendelian genetics. *Comptes rendus de l'Académie des Sciences, Paris. Série III, Sciences de la Vie / Life Sciences* 323.12: 1127–37.

———. 2005. *The epistemology of development, evolution, and genetics: Selected essays.* Cambridge: Cambridge University Press.

Campbell, John J. 2002. *Reference and consciousness.* Oxford: Oxford University Press.

———. 2009. Consciousness and reference. In *Oxford Handbook of Philosophy of Mind,* ed. Brian McLaughlin, Ansgar Beckermann, and Sven Walter, 648–62. Oxford: Oxford University Press.

Carey, Susan. 2000. Knowledge acquisition: Enrichment or conceptual change? In *Concepts: Core readings,* ed. E. Margolis and S. Laurence, 459–87. Cambridge, MA: MIT Press.

Carlson, Elof Axel. 1966. *The gene: A critical history.* Philadelphia: W. B. Saunders.

Charles, David. 2000. *Aristotle on meaning and essence.* Oxford: Oxford University Press.

Charles, David, ed. 2010a. Definition and explanation in the *Posterior Analytics* and *Metaphysics.* In Charles 2010b, 286–328.

———. 2010b. *Definition in Greek philosophy.* Oxford: Oxford University Press.

Chisholm, Roderick. 1957. *Perceiving: A philosophical study.* Ithaca: Cornell University Press.

Coffey, Peter. 1917. *Epistemology or the theory of knowledge: An introduction to general metaphysics,* 2 vols. London: Longman Green.

Corvini, Pat. 2007. *Two, three, four and all that.* Irvine: Second Renaissance. Audio recording.

———. 2008. *Two, three, four and all that: The sequel.* Irvine: Second Renaissance. Audio recording.

Dahl, Per F. 1997. *Flash of the cathode rays: A history of J. J. Thomson's electron.* Bristol: Institute of Physics Publishing.

Dalton, John. 1808. *A new system of chemical philosophy.* Manchester: Printed by S. Russell for R. Bickerstaff.

Dancy, Jonathan. 1998. *George Berkeley: A treatise concerning the principles of human knowledge.* Oxford: Oxford University Press.

———. 2005. Epistemology, problems of. In *The Oxford companion to philosophy,* 2nd ed., ed. Ted Honderich, 263–65. Oxford: Oxford University Press.

Darwin, Charles R. 1851–1854. *A monograph on the sub-class cirripedia, with figures of all the species:* vol. 1, *The lepadidae; or, pedunculated cirripedes.* London: The Ray Society, 1851a; repr. Barrett and Freeman 1988, vol 11; vol. 2, *The balanidæ, (or sessile cirripedes); the verrucidæ, etc.* London: The Ray Society, 1854a; repr. Barrett and Freeman 1988, vols. 12–13.

———. 1851b. *A monograph on the fossil lepadidae, or, pedunculated cirripedes of Great Britain.* London: The Palaeontographical Society; repr. Barrett and Freeman, 1988, vol. 14.

———. 1854b. *A monograph on the fossil balandidae and verrucidae of Great Britain.* London: The Palaeontographical Society; repr. Barrett and Freeman, 1988, vol. 14.

Davidson, Donald. 1983. A coherence theory of truth and knowledge. In *Kant oder Hegel,* ed. Dieter Henrich, 423–38. Stuttgart: Klett-Cotta. Repr. in *Subjective, intersubjective, objective,* 137–53. Oxford: Oxford University Press, 2001.

Degenaar, Marjolein, and Gert-Jan Lokhorst. 2010. Molyneux's problem. In *Stanford encyclopedia of philosophy* (Fall), ed. Edward N. Zalta. http://plato.stanford.edu/archives/fall2010/entries/molyneux-problem.

Devitt, Michael. 1996. *Coming to our senses: A naturalistic program for semantic localism.* Cambridge: Cambridge University Press.

Doris, John M. 2000. Review of Paul E. Griffiths, *What emotions really are: The problem of psychological categories. Ethics* 110.3: 617–19.

Duhem, Pierre. 1906. *La théorie physique: Son objet—sa structure.* Paris: Chevalier & Rivière. English translation of 1914 2nd ed. by Philip P. Wiener as *The aim and structure of physical theory.* Princeton: Princeton University Press, 1954; repr. 1991.

Dupré, John. 1993. *The disorder of things: Metaphysical foundations of the disunity of science.* Cambridge, MA: Harvard University Press.

———. 2004. Review of Joseph LaPorte, *Natural kinds and conceptual change.* In *Notre Dame Philosophical Reviews,* 2004.06.01. http://ndpr.nd.edu/review.cfm?id=1439.

Efron, Robert. 1969. What is perception? *Boston Studies in the Philosophy of Science* 4:137–73.

Evans, Gareth. 1982. *The varieties of reference.* Oxford: Oxford University Press.

Feest, Uljana. 2005. Operationism in psychology: What the debate is about, what the debate should be about. *Journal of the History of the Behavioral Sciences* 41.2: 131–49.

Feyerabend, Paul K. 1962. Explanation, reduction and empiricism. In *Scientific explanation, space and time,* ed. H. Feigl and G. Maxwell, 28–97. Minneapolis: University of Minnesota Press.

Fodor, Jerry A. 1998. *Concepts: Where cognitive science went wrong.* Oxford: Clarendon Press.

Fodor, Jerry A., et al. 1999. Against definitions. In *Concepts: Core readings,* ed. Eric Margolis and Stephen Laurence, 491–512. Cambridge, MA: MIT Press.

Fumerton, Richard. 2006. Direct realism, introspection, and cognitive science. *Philosophy and Phenomenological Research* 73.3: 680–95.

Geach, Peter. 1957. *Mental acts: Their contents and their objects.* London: Routledge and Kegan Paul.

Ghate, Onkar. 1998. The argument from conflicting appearances. PhD dissertation. University of Calgary.

Gilbert, Scott F. 1997. *Developmental biology.* 5th ed. Sunderland, MA: Sinuauer Press.

Gotthelf, Allan. 2000. *On Ayn Rand.* Belmont, CA: Wadsworth.

———. 2012a. Aristotle as scientist: A proper verdict (with emphasis on his biological works). In Gotthelf 2012b, 371–98.

———. 2012b. *Teleology, first principles, and scientific method in Aristotle's biology.* Oxford: Oxford University Press.

———. 2012c. Understanding Aristotle's teleology. In Gotthelf 2012b, 67–89.

———. Forthcoming. Ayn Rand as Aristotelian: Concepts and essences. In *Ayn Rand and Aristotle: Philosophical and historical studies,* ed. Allan Gotthelf and James G. Lennox. Ayn Rand Philosophical Studies No. 3. Pittsburgh: University of Pittsburgh Press.

Gotthelf, Allan, and Gregory Salmieri, eds. 2014. *Ayn Rand: A companion to her works and thought.* Oxford: Wiley-Blackwell.

Grecco, John, and John Turri. 2011. Virtue epistemology. In *The Stanford encyclopedia of philosophy* (Spring), ed. Edward N. Zalta. http://plato.stanford.edu/archives/spr2011/entries/epistemology-virtue.

Griffiths, Paul E. 1997. *What emotions really are: The problem of psychological categories.* Chicago: University of Chicago Press.

———. 1999. Squaring the circle: Natural kinds with historical essences. In *Species: New interdisciplinary essays,* ed. R. A. Wilson, 209–28. Cambridge, MA: MIT Press.

———. 2004. Emotions as natural kinds and normative kinds. *Philosophy of Science* 71:901–11. Supplement of the proceedings of the 2002 Biennial Meeting of the Philosophy of Science Association. Part II: Symposia Papers.

Hacking, Ian M. 1991a. The making and moulding of child abuse. *Critical Inquiry* 17:253–88.

———. 1991b. On Boyd. *Philosophical Studies* 61:149–55.

———. 1991c. A tradition of natural kinds. *Philosophical Studies* 61:109–26.

———. 1992. World-making by kind-making: Child abuse for example. In *How classification works: Nelson Goodman among the social sciences,* ed. M. Douglas and D. L. Hull, 180–238. Edinburgh: Edinburgh University Press.

———. 1995. *Rewriting the soul: Multiple personality and the sciences of memory.* Princeton: Princeton University Press.

Hanson, Norwood Russell. 1958. *Patterns of discovery.* Cambridge: Cambridge University Press.

Harré, Rom, and Edward Madden. 1975. *Causal powers: A theory of natural necessity.* Oxford: Basil Blackwell.

Harriman, David. 2010. *The logical leap: Induction in physics.* New York: New American Library.

Hendry, Robin Findlay. 2006. The elements of chemistry from Lavoisier to IUPAC. *Philosophy of Science* 73:864–75.

———. 2010. The elements and conceptual change. In *The semantics and metaphysics of natural kinds*, ed. H. Beebee and N. Sabbarton, 137-58. London: Routledge.

Heshka, Stanley, and David B. Allison. 2001. Is obesity a disease? *International Journal of Obesity* 25:1401–4.

Hessen, Beatrice. 1970. The Montessori method. *TO* 9.5–7: 844–48, 856–62, 870–74.

Hicks, G. Dawes. 1938. *Critical realism.* London: Macmillan.

Hinde, Robert A. 1985. Was 'the expression of emotions' a misleading phrase? *Animal Behaviour* 33:985–92.

Hodge, Jonathan. 1985. Darwin as life-long generation theorist. In *The Darwinian heritage,* ed. D. Kohn, 207–43. Princeton: Princeton University Press.

James, William. 1890. *The principles of psychology.* New York: Henry Holt.

Jardine, Boris. 2009. Between the beagle and the barnacle: Darwin's microscopy, 1837–1854. *Studies in History and Philosophy of Science* 40:382–95.

Johannsen, Wilhelm. 1909. *Elemente der exakten erblichkeitslehre.* Jena: G. Fischer.

Kelley, David. 1984. A theory of abstraction. *Cognition and Brain Theory* 7:329–57.

———. 1986. *The evidence of the senses: A realist theory of perception.* Baton Rouge: Louisiana State University Press.

Kelley, David, and Janet Krueger. 1984. The psychology of abstraction. *Journal for the Theory of Social Behaviour* 14:43–67.

Kitcher, Philip S. 1978. Theories, theorists and theoretical change. *Philosophical Review* 87:519–47.

———. 1982. Genes. *British Journal for the Philosophy of Science* 33:337–59.

———. 1984. 1953 and all that: A tale of two sciences. *Philosophical Review* 93: 335–73.

Koch, Robert. 1880. Investigations into the etiology of traumatic infectious diseases. In Brock 1999, 96–100.

———. 1881. Methods for the study of pathogenic organisms. In Brock 1999, 101–8.

Kuhn, Thomas H. 1962. *The structure of scientific revolutions.* Chicago: University of Chicago Press.

———. 1996. *The structure of scientific revolutions.* 3rd ed. Chicago: University of Chicago Press.

Lafortuna, Claudio et al. 2006. The combined effect of adiposity, fat distribution and age on cardiovascular risk factors and motor disability in a cohort of obese women (aged 18–83). *Journal of Endocrinal Investigation* 10:905–12.

Lakatos, Imre. 1970. Falsification and the methodology of scientific research programmes. In *Criticism and the growth of knowledge,* ed. I. Lakatos and A. Musgrave, 91–136. Cambridge: Cambridge University Press.

Langsam, Harold. 1997. The theory of appearing defended. *Philosophical Studies* 87:33–59.

Laudan, Larry. 1977. *Progress and its problems: Towards a theory of scientific growth.* Berkeley: University of California Press.

———. 1990. *Science and relativism: Some key controversies in philosophy of science.* Chicago: University of Chicago Press.

Lavoisier, Antoine Laurent. 1789. *Traité élémentaire de chimie présenté dans un ordre nouveau et d'après les découvertes modernes.* Paris: Cuchet.

Lawrence, Andrew D., and Andrew J. Calder. 2004. Homologizing human emotions. In *Emotions, evolution and rationality,* ed. D. Evans and P. Cruise, 15–50. Oxford: Oxford University Press.

Le Morvan, Pierre. 2000. *A defense of the theory of appearing.* PhD diss., Syracuse University.

———. 2004. Arguments against direct realism and how to counter them. *American Philosophical Quarterly* 41:21–34.

Lennox, James G. 1987. Kinds, forms of kinds, and the more and the less in Aristotle's biology. In *Philosophical issues in Aristotle's biology,* ed. A. Gotthelf and J. G. Lennox, 339–59. Cambridge: Cambridge University Press. Repr. in Lennox 2001a, 160–81.

———. 2001a. *Aristotle's philosophy of biology.* Cambridge: Cambridge University Press.

———. 2001b. *Aristotle: On the parts of animals I–IV*. Oxford: Clarendon Press.

Leslie, Alan M., and Stephanie Keeble. 1987. Do six-month-old infants perceive causality? *Cognition* 25:265–88.

Levin, Benjamin. 1990. *Genes IV*. Oxford: Oxford University Press.

Love, Alan C. 2002. Darwin and cirripedia prior to 1846: Exploring the origins of the barnacle research. *Journal of the History of Biology* 35:251–89.

Machery, Eduoard. 2009. *Doing without concepts*. Oxford: Oxford University Press.

———. 2010. Précis of *Doing without concepts*. *Behavioral and Brain Sciences* 33:195–244.

Margolis, Eric, and Stephen Laurence, eds. 2000. *Concepts: Core readings*. Cambridge, MA: MIT Press.

Martin, Michael. G. F. Unpublished manuscript. *Uncovering appearances*.

McDowell, John. 1994. *Mind and world*. Cambridge, MA: Harvard University Press.

———. 1998. Having the world in view: Sellars, Kant, and intentionality. *Journal of Philosophy* 95.1–3: 431–91. Repr. in McDowell 2009b, 3–65.

———. 2009a. Avoiding the myth of the given. In McDowell 2009b, 256–74. Cambridge: Harvard University Press.

———. 2009b. *Having the world in view: Essays on Kant, Hegel, and Sellars*. Cambridge, MA: Harvard University Press.

McGinn, Colin. 1984. The concept of knowledge. *Midwest studies in philosophy* 9:529–54. Repr. in McGinn 1999, 7–35.

McGinn, Colin 1999. *Knowledge and reality: Selected essays*. Oxford: Oxford University Press.

Mendel, Gregor. 1866. Experiments in plant hybridization. In Stern and Sherwood 1966, 1–48.

Michotte, A. 1963. *The perception of causality*. New York: Basic Books.

Moore, George Edward. 1903. The refutation of idealism. *Mind* 12:433–53.

Moser, Paul. 1999. Epistemology. In *The Cambridge dictionary of philosophy*, 2nd ed., ed. Robert Audi, 273–78. Cambridge: Cambridge University Press.

———. 2002. Introduction. In *The Oxford handbook of epistemology*, ed. Paul Moser, 3–24. Oxford: Oxford University Press.

Moss, Lenny. 2001. Deconstructing the gene and reconstructing molecular developmental systems. In *Cycles of contingency: Developmental systems and evolution*, ed. S. Oyama, P. E. Griffiths, and R. D. Gray, 85–97. Cambridge, MA: MIT Press.

———. 2002. *What genes can't do*. Cambridge, MA: MIT Press.

Napier, J. R. 1956. The prehensile movements of the human hand. *Journal of Bone and Joint Surgery (British Volume)* 38-B.4: 902–13.

Nidditch, Peter H. 1979. *John Locke: An essay concerning human understanding*. Oxford: Clarendon Press.

Oatley, Keith, and Jennifer M. Jenkins. 1996. *Understanding emotions*. Oxford: Blackwell.

Pasnau, Robert. 1997. *Theories of cognition in the later Middle Ages*. Cambridge: Cambridge University Press.

Peikoff, Leonard. 1981. Maybe you're wrong. *Objectivist Forum* 2.2: 8–12.

———. 1987. *Objectivism: The state of the art*. Oceanside, CA: Second Renaissance Books. Audio recording.

———. 1991. *Objectivism: The philosophy of Ayn Rand*. New York: Dutton.

———. 1993. *Understanding objectivism*. Gaylordsville, CT: Second Renaissance Books. Audio recording.

———. 1994. *The art of thinking*. Gaylordsville, CT: Second Renaissance Books. Audio recording.

———. 1996. *Unity in epistemology and ethics*. Gaylordsville, CT: Second Renaissance Books. Audio recording.

———. 1998. *Objectivism through induction*. Gaylordsville, CT: Second Renaissance Books. Audio recording.

———. 2005. *Induction in physics and philosophy*. Irvine: The Ayn Rand Bookstore. Audio recording.

Perrin, Jean. 1909. Mouvement brownien et réalité moléculaire. *Annales de Chimie et de Physique*, 8th ser., 18:1–114.

Pojman, Louis, ed. 2002. *The theory of knowledge: Classic and contemporary readings*. 3rd ed. Belmont: Wadsworth.

Price, Henry Habberle. 1950. *Perception*. London: Methuen.

Prichard, Harold Arthur. 1909. *Kant's theory of knowledge*. Oxford: Clarendon Press.

Prinz, Jessie. 2001. *Furnishing the mind*. Cambridge, MA: MIT Press.

Pryor, James. 2000. The skeptic and the dogmatist. *Nous* 34:517–49.

———. 2001. Highlights of recent epistemology. *British Journal for the Philosophy of Science* 52:95–124.

———. 2005. There is immediate justification. In *Contemporary debates in epistemology*, ed. Matthias Steup and Ernest Sosa, 181–202. Malden, MA: Blackwell.

Putnam, H. 1977. Meaning and reference. In *Naming, necessity and natural kinds*, ed. S. Schwartz, 119–32. Ithaca: Cornell University Press.

Quine, Willard Van Orman. 1951. Two dogmas of empiricism. *Philosophical Review* 60:20–43.

Quinn, Paul C. and Eimas, Peter D. 1996. Perceptual cues that permit categorical differentiation of animal species by infants. *Journal of Experimental Child Psychology* 63:189–211.

Quinn, Paul C., Peter D. Eimas, and Stacey L. Rosenkrantz. 1993. Evidence for representations of perceptually similar natural categories by 3-month-old and 4-month-old infants. *Perception* 22:463–75.

Rakison, David H., and Lisa M. Oakes, eds. 2003. *Early category and concept development: Making sense of the blooming buzzing confusion*. New York: Oxford University Press.

Rakison, David H., and Yevdoklya Yermolayeva. 2010. Infant categorization. *Wiley Interdisciplinary Reviews: Cognitive Science* 1.6 894–905.

Rey, Georges. 1983. Concepts and stereotypes. Repr. in *Concepts: Core readings*, ed. Eric Margolis and Stephen Laurence, 279–99. Cambridge, MA: MIT Press, 2000).

Rheinberger, Hans-Jörg. 1997. *Towards a history of epistemic things: Synthesizing proteins in the test tube*. Stanford, CA: Stanford University Press.

———. 2000. Gene concepts: Fragments from the perspective of molecular biology. In *The concept of the gene in development and evolution*, ed. P. J. Beurton, R. Falk, and H.-J. Rheinberger. Cambridge: Cambridge University Press.

Rosch, E. 1978. Principles of categorization. In *Cognition and categorization*, ed. E. Rosch and B. Lloyd, 27–48. Hillsdale, NJ: Lawrence Erlbaum Associates.

Russell, Bertrand. 1912. *The problems of philosophy*. London: Williams & Norgate.

Rutherford, Ernest. 1911. The scattering of α and ß particles by matter and the structure of the atom. *Philosophical Magazine* 21:669–88.

———. 1919. Collisions of alpha particles with light atoms. IV. An anomalous effect in nitrogen. *Philosophical Magazine* 37:581–87.

Salmieri, Gregory. 2006. *Objectivist epistemology in outline*. Irvine: The Ayn Rand Bookstore. Audio recording.

———. 2008. *Aristotle and the problem of concepts*. PhD diss., University of Pittsburgh.

———. 2013. The Objectivist epistemology. In Gotthelf and Salmieri 2014.

———. Unpublished. Aristotle's conception of universality.

Salmieri, Gregory, and Gotthelf, Allan. 2005. Ayn Rand. In *Dictionary of Modern American Philosophers*, ed. John J. Shook, 1996. London: Thoemmes Press. Repr. with revisions as "Ayn Rand and Objectivism: An overview," http://www.aynrandsociety.org/#Overview.

Scerri, Eric R. 2006.*The periodic table: Its story and significance*. New York: Oxford University Press.

Scholl, B., and P. Tremoulet. 2000. Perceptual causality and animacy. *Trends in Cognitive Science* 4.8: 299–305.

Schulz, Laura, Tamar Kushmir, and Alison Gopnik. 2007. Learning from doing: Intervention and causal inference. In *Causal learning: Psychology, philosophy and computation*, ed. Alison Gopnik and Laura Schulz, 67–85. New York: Oxford University Press.

Selby-Bigge, Louis Amherst, and Peter H. Nidditch. 1978. *David Hume: A treatise of human nature*. Oxford: Clarendon Press.

Sellars, Wilfrid. 1963. Empiricism and the philosophy of mind. In *Science, perception and reality,* chap. 5. London: Routledge and Kegan Paul.

———. 1967. *Science and metaphysics: Variations on Kantian themes.* London: Routledge and Kegan Paul.

Shapere, Dudley. 1966. Meaning and scientific change. In *Mind and cosmos: Essays in contemporary science and philosophy,* ed. Robert G. Colodny, 41–85. Pittsburgh: University of Pittsburgh Press.

Sloan, Philip. 1985. Darwin's invertebrate program, 1826–36: Preconditions for transformism. In *The Darwinian heritage,* ed. D. Kohn, 71–120. Princeton: Princeton University Press.

Sloutsky, V. 2003. The role of similarity in the development of categorization. *Trends in Cognitive Sciences* 7.6: 246–51.

Smith, Linda B., Susan S. Jones, and Barbara Landau. 1996. Naming in young children: A dumb attentional mechanism? *Cognition* 60:143–71.

Soddy, Frederick. 1923. The origins of the conceptions of isotopes. Nobel lecture, 12 December 1922 [prize for 1921, awarded in 1922]). In *Les Prix Nobel en 1921–1922,* ed. Carl Gustaf Santesson, 1–29. Stockholm: The Nobel Foundation. Repr. 1966 in *Nobel Lectures, Chemistry 1901–1921,* 371–99. Amsterdam: Elsevier.

Sommers, Fred. 1982. *The logic of natural language.* Oxford: Clarendon Press.

Steinle, Friedrich. 2006. Concept formation and the limits of justification: 'Discovering' the two electricities. In *Revisiting discovery and justification: Historical and philosophical perspectives on the context distinction,* ed. Jutta Schickore and Friedrich Steinle, 183–95. Berlin: Springer Verlag.

Stern, Curt, and Eva R. Sherwood, eds. 1966. *The origins of genetics: A Mendel source book.* San Francisco: W. H. Freeman.

Stevens, June. 2003. Ethnic-specific cutpoints for obesity vs. country-specific guidelines for action. *International Journal of Obesity* 27:287–88.

Thomson, Joseph John. 1913. Rays of positive electricity. *Proceedings of the Royal Society* A 89:1–20.

Toulmin, Stephen. 1961. *Foresight and understanding.* Bloomington: Indiana University Press.

———. 1972. *Human understanding.* Vol. 1, *The collective use and evolution of concepts.* Princeton: Princeton University Press.

Travis, Charles. 2004. The silence of the senses. *Mind* 113:57–94.

Van Cleve, James. 2005. Troubles for radical transparency. http://www-bcf.usc.edu/~vancleve/papers/Transparency%20draft%202.doc. Forthcoming in *Supervenience in Mind: A Festschrift for Jaegwon Kim,* ed. Terence Horgan, David Sosa, and Marcelo Sabatés. Cambridge, MA: MIT Press.

Van Melsen, Andrew G. 1952. *From atomos to atom: The history of the concept atom.* Mineola, NY: Dover.

Waters, C. Kenneth. 1994. Genes made molecular. *Philosophy of Science* 61:163–85.

———. 2000. Molecules made biological. *Revue Internationale de Philosophie* 4 (214):539–64.

Wear, Andrew ed. 1990. *William Harvey: The circulation of the blood and other writings.* London: Everyman Library.

Weisberg, Michael, and Paul Needham. 2010. Matter, structure, and change: Aspects of the philosophy of chemistry. *Philosophy Compass* 5:927–37.

Whewell, William. 1860. *On the philosophy of discovery.* Repr., New York: Burt Franklin, 1971.

Williams, Michael. 1999. *Groundless belief.* 2nd ed. Princeton: Princeton University Press.

Wright, Darryl. 1999. *Reason and freedom* Gaylordsville: Second Renaissance Books. Audio recording.

Benjamin Bayer is visiting assistant professor of philosophy at Loyola University New Orleans. He is the author of two articles in *Synthese* and *Acta Analytica* that apply insights from the direct realist account of perception to the defense of foundationalist and internalist theories of justification, respectively. His current work focuses on building a case for evidentialism from the perspective of doxastic voluntarism.

Jim Bogen is emeritus professor of philosophy at Pitzer College and an adjunct professor of history and philosophy of science at the University of Pittsburgh. His publications include papers on Aristotle, causality, and the role of data in evaluating scientific claims. He is presently working on the development of a neuroscientific counterexample to some common ideas about mental-physical reduction, a paper on what regularities of different kinds have to do with causal connectivity and the individuation of mechanisms, and a book-length project with J. E. McGuire on the metaphysical basis of Aristotle's modalities.

Bill Brewer is Susan Stebbing Professor of Philosophy at King's College, London. He previously taught at Warwick, Oxford, Cambridge, Brown, and the University of California, Berkeley. He works in philosophy of mind, metaphysics, and epistemology, and his books include *Perception and Reason* (1999) and *Perception and Its Objects* (2011), on the metaphysics and epistemology of our relation with the mind-independent physical world in perception. He has also published numerous articles in journals and collections. Having written two books on perception, his next major project concerns the nature of its persisting mind-independent physical objects themselves, and their parts.

Richard M. Burian is emeritus professor of philosophy and science studies at Virginia Polytechnic Institute. As a historian/philosopher of biology, he focuses on conceptual change in science, the theory of the gene, and the impact of molecularization on biology. His recent writings include *The Epistemology of Development, Evolution, and Genetics: Selected Essays* (2005); "Selection Does Not Operate Primarily on Genes" (2009); "From Genetic to Genomic Regulation: Iterativity in microRNA Research" (with M. A. O'Malley and K. C. Elliott, 2010); and "On the Need for Integrative Phylogenomics and Some Steps toward Its Creation" (with E. Bapteste, 2010).

Onkar Ghate is a senior fellow and vice president at the Ayn Rand Institute in Irvine, California. He specializes in Ayn Rand's philosophy of Objectivism and is the institute's senior instructor and editor. He wrote his PhD dissertation on the philosophy of perception, and has published and lectured extensively on many aspects of Rand's philosophy and fiction, including the application of the philosophy to cultural and political issues. His current research focuses on religion, morality, and the separation of church and state.

Allan Gotthelf is Anthem Foundation Distinguished Fellow for Research and Teaching in Philosophy at Rutgers University and professor emeritus of philosophy at The College of New Jersey. From 2003 to 2012 he was visiting professor of history and philosophy of science at the University of Pittsburgh, where he held the university's Fellowship for the Study of Objectivism. He was one of the founding members of the Ayn Rand Society and chairs its steering committee. He is the author of *On Ayn Rand* (2000) and coeditor of the forthcoming *Ayn Rand: A Companion to Her Works and Thought*. He has also published extensively on Aristotle, including *Teleology, First Principles, and Scientific Method in Aristotle's Biology* (2012).

Paul E. Griffiths is university professorial research fellow in philosophy at the University of Sydney and professor of philosophy of science, ESRC Centre for Genomics in Society, at the University of Exeter. He is author of *What Emotions Really Are: The Problem of Psychological Categories*

(1997) and coauthor (with Kim Sterelny) of *Sex and Death: An Introduction to the Philosophy of Biology* (1999). He has published many articles in the philosophy of biology and the philosophy of psychology, especially on the nature of the gene and on evolutionary developmental biology. He is currently working on an introduction to the philosophy of genetics, co-authored with Karola Stotz.

Pierre Le Morvan is associate professor of philosophy at The College of New Jersey (TCNJ). He specializes in epistemology, philosophy of perception, and philosophy of religion. He has published in such journals as *American Philosophical Quarterly, Australasian Journal of Philosophy, British Journal for the History of Philosophy, Metaphilosophy,* and others. He is currently working on articles on the nature of ignorance, healthy and unhealthy skepticism, and the nature of knowledge, as well as a book defending the Theory of Appearing, a direct realist account of the nature of perceptual awareness.

James G. Lennox is professor of history and philosophy of science at the University of Pittsburgh. He was one of the founding members of the Ayn Rand Society and serves regularly on its steering committee. He is the author of *Aristotle's Philosophy of Biology* (2001) and *Aristotle on the Parts of Animals I–IV* (2001) and coeditor of *Philosophical Issues in Aristotle's Biology* (1987), and *Concepts, Theories, and Rationality in the Biological Sciences* (1995). Currently he is working on a book on Aristotle's norms of inquiry and collaborating on a translation and commentary of Aristotle's *Meteorology* IV.

Gregory Salmieri is visiting scholar and Fellow in Objectivity and Values in the department of philosophy at Boston University, having taught for four years at the University of North Carolina, Chapel Hill, as a visiting assistant professor. He has published on issues in Aristotle's epistemology and ethics and on Rand's philosophy and novels and is coeditor of the forthcoming *Ayn Rand: A Companion to Her Works and Thought.* Currently he is working on a monograph on Aristotle's view of conceptual knowledge and editing a multiauthor volume on Aristotle's epistemology.

abstraction, x, 4–5, 4n3, 52–53, 74n51, 93, 105, 148; as a mental process, 19–23, 28; as a mental product/synonym for "concept", 22–23; definition of the process of, 12n31, 20, 21n29; involved in which stage of concept-formation, 20–24. *See also* concept-formation; concepts; measurement-omission

abstractionism, 4–5, 19, 28. *See also* abstraction

abstractions from abstractions, 24, 78, 116; narrowings or subdivisions as, 24, 24n33, 59, 157–58; widenings as, 24, 24n33, 59; cross-classifications, 59. *See also* concept-formation, hierarchical order of; first-level concepts

actions, 56–57; awareness of in forming entity concepts, 57, 66–67; concepts of, 20, 117n10. *See also* causality; characteristics; entities

acquaintance, 233, 234n5, 238n7, 242. *See also* consciousness; perception, as a direct form of awareness

Adrian, E.D., 169–71, 179–80

adverbial theory of perception, 47n10

agnosia, visual object, 7n8. *See also* perception; hallucination

Alberts, B., et al., 171

Alston, W., x, xii, 87nn2–3, 88–92, 91n7, 97, 97n16, 104n21, 107–8, 108nn25–26, 215, 215n1, 217n4, 219, 221–23, 223n11, 225, 249–51, 255, 255n5, 267. *See also* appearing, theory of

analytic-synthetic distinction, 16, 32–33, 32n47, 34n52, 71, 155–56. *See also* concepts, meaning of; concepts, open-end reference of; definitions, as distinct from the meaning of the concept

Anglin, J., 58n22

analogy, 81

anti-conceptual mentality, 72n46. *See also* concrete-bound mentality

appearance (perceptual), 89, 96, 98–99, 101–2, 101n18, 216–17, 217n4, 220–21, 223n11, 242–44, 247–50, 248n1, 253–54, 259–61; conceptualization of and judgment about, 107–8; definable vs. undefinable, 249–51. *See also* form vs. object of awareness; sensory qualities

appearing, theory of, x, xii, 89–90, 97, 97n16, 215–17, 215n1, 218, 220–25, 223n10, 224n13, 251. *See also* Alston, W.; direct realism/ presentationalism (about perception)

a priori and a posteriori knowledge, 155–56

Aquinas, T., 46, 46n7

Aquapendente, F., 130n27

Arabatzis, T., 208, 208n6

arbitrary assertion, 69n37, 83. *See also* belief; evidence; judgment

Aristotle: 14n17, 15n20, 31n46, 35, 35n54, 38, 65n31, 73, 74n51, 93, 118–19, 122n18, 172n5, 204; *History of Animals*, 14n18, 38n59, 130n27; *Parts of Animals*, 15n20, 38n59; *Topics*, 31n46; *Posterior Analytics*, 31n46. *See also* measurement-omission; realism (about universals)

artifacts, concepts of, 153–54. *See also* abstractions from abstractions

atom (concept of), 186, 192–97, 203, 206–9, 206n4. *See also* conceptual development

attributes, awareness of in formation of concepts of entities, 21n32, 24n35, 56–57; concepts of, 15, 21n29, 21n31, 24–25, 56–57, 56n19, 117n10. *See also* characteristics; "Conceptual Common Denominator" (CCD); entities, concepts of

Austin, J., 8n8, 49, 254n3

Avogadro, A., 193–94, 194n8

awareness. *See* acquaintance; consciousness; knowledge

axiomatic concepts, 30n44, 61n25, 73n49, 76

axiomatic knowledge, 75n53, 80n57

Ayers, M., 245

Barnes, W., 215n1

Bateson, W., 198n16

Bayer, B., xii–iii, 5n5, 48n14, 54, 58n22, 75n52, 88n4, 94n14, 255nn4–5

Berkeley, G., 230n20, 219n5. *See also* idealism; nominalism (about universals)

belief, 42–43, 254, defined, 64. *See also* fallibility, of beliefs/judgments; judgment; knowledge

Binswanger, H., 5n7, 16, 46n6, 239n9

Bloch, C., 180

Bogen, J., xi–ii, 34n50, 173–76, 173n1, 174n2, 176n4, 179–81

Bonevac, D., 108n26

BonJour, L., 108, 255n4

borderline case problem, 17n20, 37–39, 39n61. *See also* nominalism (about universals); similarity

Boyd, R., 9n11, 118n12

Brewer, B., xii, 8n8, 9n8, 88n4, 94n14, 215n1,

226, 228–30, 228n2, 232–34, 236–37, 240, 242n1, 247–48, 256–66

Brigandt, I., 141, 152, 206n3

Brock, T., 211n8

Brown, R., 146

Burian, R., xi, 5n4, 117n8, 121, 121n16, 192, 196n14, 198n16, 201–11

Campbell, J., xii, 88n4, 94n14, 215n1, 226, 228–36, 228n2, 239–40, 243–45

Carey, S., 115n5

Carlson, E., 197–98

causal theory of perception, 86. *See also* representationalism/indirect realism (about perception); perception

causal theory of reference, 186–87. *See also* natural kinds; realism (about universals)

causality, 68; and concept-formation, 211; concept of, 65n31; perception of, 47, 48n22, 66. *See also* actions; axiomatic concepts; fundamentality; induction

Chadwick, J., 195

characteristics, 66; concepts of, 58, 58n22, 68n34, 73n47; defined, 58n21; included in meaning of entity concepts, 117–19, 155–56, 205; perception of, 58, 91–93, 95. *See* actions; attributes; concepts, open-end reference of; "Conceptual Common Denominator" (CCD); distinguishing characteristics; entities; relations

Charles, D., 31n46, 35n54, 122n18

Chisholm, R., 47n10

choice. *See* volition

Coffey, P., 20n31, 215n1

coherentism (about epistemic justification), 74–75. *See also* foundationalism; "Myth of the Given"; perception, as the foundation of knowledge

colors, concepts of, 12, 14, 29, 262n9, 265; perception of, 245, 257–65, 261n8

color blindness, 237. *See also* colors; relativity of perception; sensory qualities

commensurable characteristics. *See* characteristics; "Conceptual Common Denominator" (CCD); similarity

concept-formation, 10–22, 35, 52–53; as volitional, 22, 53, 70, 77, 215n2; hierarchical order of, 8–9, 13n17, 14n18, 24–28, 27n39,

30n45, 58n22, 71; knowledge required for, 11–17, 55–57, 70, 72, 74–75, 78; norms of, 5, 10, 24–25, 35n55, 35–36, 70–73, 153–54, 204; whether it guarantees successful reference, 186–87, 189–91, 191n7, 196, 198–200. *See also* abstraction; abstractions from abstractions; concepts; first-level concepts; measurement-omission

concepts, application of, 57, 61, 63, 65–66, 68–69, 71, 74, 78; and induction, 9, 9nn10–11, 140–41; and scientific progress, x, 4n4, 8–10, 19, 112, 115, 119–22, 126, 129–30, 153–54, 201; as analogous to file folders, 9, 61–62, 120, 126, 131, 151–52, 155–56, 163–64, 166–67, 169, 172, 208, 211; as central to epistemology, ix–x, 5, 8, 10, 41–43; as forms of awareness, 3, 32, 53–56, 61, 69n37; as "mental entities," 20, 55; as integrations, 8, 17, 19–20, 20n28, 22–23, 32, 52, 55, 61–62, 61n25, 118, 122–23, 156, 206; as policies, 54–55, 61–62, 69n37, 117–18, 122, 204–5, 207–8; as valid or invalid, 22, 55, 70n38, 71, 141–42, 205–6; based both on mind-independent and cognitive facts, 83, 148–49; function of, 8, 10–11, 34, 36, 56–57; defined, 17, 17n21, 20, 20n28, 52; meaning of, 32–34, 32n47, 113–15, 115nn4–5, 117–22, 125, 199, 206; open-end reference of, 9, 9n12, 16–17, 23, 32n47, 116–22, 117n8, 125–26, 132, 190, 200, 204–5, 211; perceptual basis of, 9–10, 12, 48, 52, 55, 104; possession conditions of, 3, 61, 117; psychological vs. philosophical accounts of, 11, 12n17; role in identification, 51–53; role of in epistemic justification, 3–4, 42, 74–75, 254–55; unitary character of, 3, 17, 53–55; universality of, 3, 22, 105–7. *See also* abstraction; concept-formation; conceptual development; conceptual level of awareness; definitions; measurement-omission; perception; similarity; universals, problem of "conceptual change." *See* conceptual development

conceptual development, 27n39, 32–33, 33n48, 112–15, 115n5, 147, 185; in conceptual narrowing or subdivision, 113–14, 186–87n2, 190, 207–8; in conceptual widening, 114, 186–87n2, 190; in forming

concepts to identify newly discovered facts, 113, 186n2, 189; in reclassification in light of deeper knowledge of units, xi, 114–15, 120n13, 122, 126–33, 128n23, 131n28, 186n2, 188–90, 188n4, 206; in rejection or replacement of concepts, 33n48, 114, 121n15, 131n28, 186n2, 190–92, 209–10; vs. idea of "conceptual change," 126, 201, 203; whether involving change in meaning, xi, 113–15, 114n4, 115n2, 119–22, 124, 127, 129–33, 186–93, 196, 198–207. *See also* abstractions from abstractions; concepts, and scientific progress; conceptual level of consciousness; definitions, as revisable in new contexts of knowledge

conceptual level of consciousness, 6, 52. *See also* concepts; conceptualization; form vs. object of awareness, conceptual; judgment; propositions; reason

"Conceptual Common Denominator" (CCD), 53, 115–16, 131, 178; role of in differentiating units of first-level concepts, 14, 35; role of in differentiating units of higher-level concepts, 13n17, 25; role of in process of abstraction and the resulting integration, 16, 20, 23–24, 35, 35n56, 54, 56; role of in formulation of definitions, 30, 56, 118–19; role of in judgment, 65, 71; role of in perception of similarity, 12–13. *See* characteristics; measurement-omission; similarity

conceptualization, x, 52, 72, 74, 77–78, 80–81, 83. *See also* concept-formation; concepts, role in identification; method; validation

concrete-bound mentality, 80. *See also* anti-conceptual mentality

consciousness, 45–46; as an active process, x, 6, 44–45, 232, 236, 240–41; axiomatic concept of, 61n25, 89n6; cognitive and non-cognitive states of, 44, 50; concepts of states of, 9, 21n29, 25–26, 26n37, 29; different forms of, 43, 45–46; essential functions of, as differentiation and integration, 30, 52; faculty of vs. state of, 43–44, 44n4; reducible vs. irreducible to physical processes, 45, 45n5; whether it can be objectless, 43–44, 47–48;

whether its form is without identity, 47,
47n10, 88, 96, 222, 233–36, 234n4, 236n6,
239–40, 246, 249, 266. *See also* awareness;
existence, primacy of over consciousness;
form vs. object of awareness
conditional statements, 64–65
context, concepts as dependent on, 30n45;
knowledge as dependent on, 25n35. *See
also* concept-formation, hierarchical
order of; definitions, as revisable in new
contexts of knowledge; hierarchy
counterfactuals, 65n31
cross-classification (form of conceptualization), 149, 157–58. *See also* abstractions
from abstractions; taxonomies
Corvini, P., 29n42
Cuvier, G., 127

Dahl, P., 28, 28n40
Dalton, J., 192–94, 196–97
Dancy, J., 41
Darwin, C., 127–29, 128nn23–25, 188, 188n3
Davidson, D., 74, 108
deduction, 68–70, 68n35. *See also* induction;
inference
definitions, xi, 5; as revisable in new
contexts of knowledge, xi, 25n35, 33–34,
33n49, 57n20, 73–74, 73n47, 112–13, 118–19,
122–26, 130–31, 140, 142, 148–49, 154–55,
190–91, 207n2, 206, 209; as distinct
from the meaning of the concept, 32–33,
119, 121–22 , 155–57, 206n3; as factual
or empirical, 34, 140–41, 148–49; as
integrators of knowledge, 30–31, 83, 176,
180–81; as aiding in unit-reduction, 30–31,
164–65, 174; cognitive purpose of (stating
the essential characteristic), 10, 30–33,
36, 77–78, 118, 122–23, 156–57, 164–65, 174,
190–91; defined, 30; determined by cognitive vs. by pragmatic factors, 142–45,
152–53, 157–58, 167–69, 172; differentia of,
30, 73, 73n47, 118, 122; genus of, 30, 36n57,
73, 73n47, 116, 118, 122; "operational,"
166–69, 172, 174, 179n9; ostensive,
30n44, 73n49, 79n56, 84, 156; role of in
concept-formation, 10, 20, 20n28, 29–30,
73, 164; role of in preserving hierarchy
of concepts, 30, 73, 73n47, 77, 79n56; role

of in scientific knowledge, 25n35, 33n49;
rules/norms of, 10, 30, 33–34, 73, 74n51,
166; stipulative vs. objective, 140; valid (or
objective) or invalid, 113, 156–57, 176n4;
vs. specification of a concept's differentia,
178–79; whether necessary for cognition/
communication, 164–65, 168–69, 187;
whether requiring a fundamental distinguishing characteristic, 170–77, 179–80.
See also analytic-synthetic distinction;
concepts; conceptual development;
distinguishing characteristics; essences/
essential characteristics
Degenaar, M., Lokhorst, G., 258n6
Descartes, R., 86, 254n3
Devitt, M., 122
descriptions, 63, 63n28, 177, 231. *See also*
phrases
determinates and determinables, 14, 14n18
difference. *See* differentiation; similarity
differentiation, as essential to consciousness
generally, 6, 43n2, 44–45, 52, 122; in
concept-formation, 20, 35, 55, 114–16; in
definitions; 30; in perception, 44, 62,
91. *See also* abstraction; integration;
similarity
differentia. *See* definitions, differentia of;
distinguishing characteristics
direct realism/presentationalism (about
perception), 87–89, 87n3, 88n4, 91, 93–94,
96–100, 103–4, 106, 109–11, 215–16, 220–21,
223, 224n14, 225–29, 228n3, 247, 251,
254–55, 255n5, 257, 264, 266; defined, 90,
216, 219. *See also* naïve realism (about perception); perception, as a direct form of
awareness; representationalism/indirect
realism (about perception); three-factor
theories of perception
discrimination. *See* differentiation
disjunction (form of judgment), 64–65
disjunctivism (about perception),
103n29, 215n1. *See also* direct realism/
presentationalism (about perception);
hallucination; perception
distinguishing characteristics, 59, 166;
as omitted in conceptual widening,
116; causal role of, 56; fundamental or
non-fundamental, 174; role of in concept

application, 78; role of in concept-formation, 15, 17, 29–30; identification of in definitions, 30–31, 33–34, 35n55, 36, 118, 126, 164. *See also* "Conceptual Common Denominator" (CCD); definitions; differentiation; essences/essential characteristics

Dorris, J., 146

dreams, 50–51, 104. *See also* hallucination; perceptual level of awareness

Duhem, P., 121n16

Dupré, J., 142, 145

education, Montessori, 80n58; progressive, 81n59

Efron, R., 7n8, 26n36

electron (concept of), 186–87, 186n2, 198, 209. *See also* theoretical concepts

elements (concepts of), 150–51. *See also* atom, concept of

Ellis, B., 141–42

emotion, 50; concepts of, 145. *See also* perceptual level of consciousness

empiricism, 233, 242, 259–60

entities, concepts of, 15–16, 21n32, 24–25, 24n40, 55; defined, 48n13. *See also* attributes, concepts of; concepts

epistemic norms, 74n50, 75–76. *See also* concept-formation, norms of

epistemology, ix, 5n4, 41–43, 41n1, 78, 84; defined, 42

error, 44; concept of, 64. *See also* fallibility; knowledge

essences/essential characteristics, 165; stated by definitions, 5, 10, 31–33, 36, 118, 121–23, 156–57; defined, 33, 125, 156, 174–75; discovery of as mandating new concepts, 37–38, 125; metaphysical vs. epistemological, x, 10–11, 31n46, 34–35, 34n53, 35n55, 119, 122, 122n18, 125, 131, 150, 174, 179, 191. *See also* concepts; definitions; distinguishing characteristics; nominalism (about universals); realism (about universals)

ethics/metaethics, basis of in Objectivist theory of concepts, 25–26, 25n35, 26n37, 73n48

Evans, G., 231–32

evidence, 7, 69n37. *See also* perception; justification.

existence, as a self-evident axiom, 44, 44n3, 50; axiomatic concept of, 61n25; primacy of in relation to consciousness, 6, 10, 43–44, 44n3, 75n53. *See also* consciousness; metaphysics

explanation, 141. *See also* fundamentality

extension. *See* intension and extension (of concepts)

externalism (about epistemic justification), 43n2, 75; defined, 76

facts, 64, 93–94

fallibilism (about perception). *See* perception, fallible vs. infallible

fallibility, 42, 44, 219–20; of beliefs/judgment, 106–8, 253–54; of concepts, 48, 52, 77; of non-conceptual expectations, 50–51. *See also* concepts; perception, fallible vs. infallible

Feest, U., 167

Feyerabend, P., 115, 186

file folders, concepts as analogous to. *See* concepts, as analogous to file folders

first-level concepts, 80–81, 203; application of, 57, 65, 68–69, 78; cognitive function of, 57–58; defined, 58–59, 58n23; formation of, 24–25, 37, 55–57, 66, 78, 153–54, 190; role in first-level generalization, 65, 68; role of in foundation of knowledge, 71, 75. *See also* abstractions from abstractions; concept-formation, hierarchical order of

"floating abstractions" (invalid concept), 71. *See also* concept-formation, norms of; concepts, valid or invalid

form vs. object of awareness, xii, 46–48, 105n22, 226, 232, 238–40; as analogous to grips, 45–46, 232, 232n4, 234–35, 238; conceptual, 32; conflation of, 46–47, 51, 95, 96–98, 217, 238, 261; introspective discrimination between, 239n9, 261, 265; perceptual, 8n8, 46, 49–50, 94–96, 94n13, 97–98, 100–104, 107, 217, 221–22, 226, 232–33, 245–46, 249, 256–57, 261–62, 261n8, 264–66. *See also* concepts; consciousness; perception, content of determined by objects and perceiver; sensory qualities

Fodor, J., 3n1, 34n52

foundationalism (about epistemic justification), 70, 74–75, 254–55. *See also* coherentism; perception, as the foundation of knowledge; hierarchy of knowledge

Frege, G., 3n1, 32n47, 46n7, 68n35, 228, 230–32, 261n8. *See also* sense (Fregean mode of presentation)

"frozen abstraction" (invalid concept), 72, 72n45. *See also* concepts, valid or invalid

Fumerton, R., 236n6

fundamental characteristics, 180n10; and causality, 31n46, 34–35, 34n51, 48, 56, 151, 178; discoveries about as occasioning conceptual reclassification, 73n47, 125–26, 128, 132, 150–51; role of in concept-formation/definition, 15n19, 31, 33, 70, 73, 119, 142, 165–66, 174–75, 179. *See also* conceptual development; definitions; distinguishing characteristics; essences/essential characteristics; similarity, as cognitively economical/fundamental or not

Geach, P., 3n1, 4, 4n3, 19, 22, 24, 28

generalization, 63; defined, 66; first-level (from direct perception), 65, 67–68; higher-level, 69. *See also* induction

genes (concept of), 143–45, 158, 185–87, 186n2, 197–98, 209, 211. *See also* theoretical concepts

genus. *See* "Conceptual Common Denominator" (CCD); definitions

geometry, 199

Ghate, O., x–xii, 5n6, 7n8, 11n13, 34nn52–53, 35n55, 39n61, 49n15, 51, 174n1, 215–16, 215n2, 216n3, 220–24, 226, 226n1, 228n3, 247–51, 248n1, 253–55, 266–67

Gilbert, S, 123

given, myth of the. *See* "Myth of the Given"; Sellars, W.

Glymour, C., 164n1

Gotthelf, A., ix–xi, 8nn8–9, 15n18, 25n35, 30n43, 30n46, 39n61, 46n6, 57n20, 70n39, 73–75, 106n23, 116n6, 117n9, 118n11,

125n20, 142, 148, 153, 163–65, 185, 203n1, 204, 239n8, 254

grammar, concepts of, 29. *See also* consciousness, concepts of

Grant, R., 128n23

Grecco, J. and Turri, J., 61n25

Griffiths, P., xi, 11n13, 34n52, 35n55, 39n61, 118n12, 120, 126n21, 128n11, 142–43, 145, 148, 150, 152–53, 156–58

Hacking, I., 9n11, 139, 145–46, 158

hallucination, 51, 99n17, 103–4, 103n26, 104n21, 224, 228n3, 243. *See also* illusion (perceptual); imagination; perceptual level of awareness

Hanson, R., 113

Harré R., and Madden, E., 48n14, 65n31

Harriman, D., 48n14, 59n23, 66n32, 69n36, 70n38, 74n50

Harvey, W., 130n27

Hendry, R., 33n49

Heshka, S., and Allison, D., 176n6

Hessen, B., 80n58

Hicks, G.D., 215n1

hierarchy of knowledge, 8, 24–25, 25n35, 27; epistemic norms associated with, 25, 71; vs. scientific taxonomy, 60, 61n24. *See also* concept-formation, hierarchical order of; context; taxonomy (scientific)

higher-level concepts. *See* abstractions from abstractions

Hinde, R., 140

Hobbes, T., 13. *See also* nominalism (about universals)

Hodge, J., 128n23

holism (about conceptual meaning), 121, 121n17, 186; defined, 186

Hume, D., 13n17, 17n20, 18–19, 18nn24–25, 65n31, 93, 233. *See also* nominalism (about universals)

human being (concept of), 199

humors (invalid concept of in disease theory), 130. *See also* concepts, valid or invalid

idealism, 86n1, 219, 219n5, 227–29, 231–32, 244, 247

identification, 45, 52–53, 62. *See also* concepts, role in identification

identity, axiomatic concept of, 61n25; law of, 75n53, 83. *See also* noncontradiction, law of; logic

identity of consciousness. *See* consciousness, whether its form is without identity

illusion (perceptual), 49, 97n16, 99–103, 224, 228n3, 242–43, 247, 249, 253. *See also* hallucination; perception, fallible vs. infallible; relativity of perception

imagination, 50, 64n30, 104. *See also* hallucination; perceptual level of awareness; supposition

incommensurability of concepts, 132, 186. *See also* conceptual development; holism (about conceptual meaning)

indirect realism (about perception). *See* representationalism/indirect realism

induction, 9, 9nn10–11, 65–68, 139, 141; and causality, 48, 66; problem of, 66, 70, 70n38. *See also* causality; concepts, and induction; deduction; inference; generalization

inference, 69–70, 79. *See also* deduction; induction; judgment

integration, as essential to consciousness/ knowledge generally, 5–6, 30, 44, 52, 83, 122; and identification, 62; in concept-formation, 30n45, 35, 55, 115–16; in definitions, 30–31; perceptual, 45; norm of, 72, 75. *See also* concepts, as integrations; consciousness, functions of; differentiation; perception, as integrating sensations

intension and extension (of concepts), 155–56. *See* definitions, as distinct from meaning of the concept

intentionality, of perception, 91n7. *See also* perception, content of

internalism (about epistemic justification), 75–76, 81–82, 255, 255n5; defined, 75

interoception, 104. *See also* hallucination; perception

introspection, 29, 44, 104–5, 239n9, 250–51, 265. *See also* consciousness, concepts of

isolation. *See* differentiation

James, W., 66on12

Jardine, B., 188n5, 203

Johannsen, W., 197–98, 198n16, 209, 211

judgment, x, 64n29, 69; as a form of awareness, 63, 69; as concept application, 4, 57, 62–65, 69, 74, 93, 106–8; content of, 63–64; defined, 63–64; first-level or perceptual, 7, 51–52, 65, 67–68, 75, 78, 81; higher-level, 68–69; simple and complex forms of, 64–65; subject and predicate of a, 63, 69. *See also* belief; fallibility, of judgments; perception, as distinct from judgment or propositional thought; propositions

justification (epistemic), x, 5n6, 41–43, 70, 74–77, 108–11; and objectivity, 5; non-propositional, 8n8. *See also* concepts, role of in epistemic justification; epistemic norms; externalism (about epistemic justification); foundationalism (about epistemic justification); internalism (about epistemic justification); knowledge; objectivity

Kant, I., 3, 4n2, 16, 47, 47n11, 71, 81n59, 224n13

Kelley, D., 7n8, 8n8, 12n16, 89n6, 91nn8–9, 93n12, 226n1

Kelley, D., and Krueger, J., 12n15

Kitcher, P., 196n14

knowledge, as requiring activity, 82; concept of, 26, 43, 43n2, 64, 76; conceptual, 43, 48, 53; inferential, 69–70; definition or analysis of, x, 76; perceptual, 50–51, 69, 110–11, 254; propositional and non-propositional, x, 43, 43n2, 46, 65, 69, 74; relation to belief, 43n2; validation of, 76–77, 79–80. *See also* consciousness; epistemic norms; epistemology; justification; propositions

Koch, R., 211n8

Kuhn, T., 113, 186

Lafortuna, C., 168

Lakatos, I., 194

Lamarck, J-B., 127

Langsam, H., 215n1

language. *See* words

Laudan, L., 121, 194

Lavoisier, A., 193, 196

Lawrence, A., and Calder, A., 143

Le Morvan, P., xii, 88n4, 215n1, 247–52, 248n1, 255, 255n5, 259, 264, 266

Lennox, J., x–xii, 5n18, 16n19, 25n35, 27n39, 33nn48–49, 34n53, 38n59, 57n20, 73, 142, 148, 153, 173, 180n10, 181n11, 185n, 186–92, 186n1, 199–200, 207

Leslie, A. and Keeble, S., 48n14

Levin, B., 113

Locke, J., 4–5, 4n3, 17n20, 19–20, 32n47, 36–37, 39n61, 47n8, 233–35, 258, 258n6, 263. See also nominalism (about universals); realism (about universals); representationalism/indirect realism (about perception)

logic, 74n51

logical positivism, 16

looks. See appearances.

Love, A., 128n23, 188n3

Machery, E., 163

Margolis, E. and Laurence, S., 120n14

Martin, M., 215n1

mathematics, concepts of, 29, 29n42; relation of to concept-formation, 19, 19n26. See also consciousness, concepts of; measurement; measurement-omission; method, concepts of

McDowell, J., 4, 4n2, 74, 261n7

McGinn, C., 43n2

meaning. See concepts, meaning of

measurement, 26, 54, 178–79; defined, 54; implicit, 13, 55. See also mathematics; measurement-omission; similarity

measurement-omission, x, 54n17, 83, 178; as facilitating integration and abstraction, 19n27, 20n28, 23–23, 54; as facilitating open-end reference to attributes of concepts' units, 15n21, 16, 17n20, 55–56; as facilitating open-end reference to concepts' units, 15–16, 19, 19n26, 54; in formation of abstractions from abstractions, 24–25, 24n33, 116, 190–91; in formation of concepts of characteristics, 58n22, 178; in formation of first-level concepts, 67. See also abstraction; concept-formation; concepts, open-end

reference of; "Conceptual Common Denominator" (CCD); measurement; similarity; universals, problem of

memory, 500, 104. See also perceptual level of awareness

Mendel, G., 198, 210–11

metaphysics, ix, 6

method, concepts of, 26–27, 26n37; epistemic need for, 42–43, 52, 79–80, 80n57, 80n58, 82–83, 84n62. See also consciousness, concepts of; fallibility; justification (epistemic); objectivity; validation

Michotte, A., 48n14

Mill, J.S., 140

modality, sensory. See sensory modality

Molyneaux, W., 258, 258n6. See also sensory modality

Montessori method (in education), 80n58

Moore, G.E., 47n9, 234, 238, 266

morality. See ethics/metaethics; normative concepts

motion. See action

Moser, P., 41n1

Moss, L., 144

Müller-Lyer illusion, 225

"Myth of the Given," 4–5, 74, 88, 108–10, 108n26. See also coherentism; foundationalism (about epistemic justification); perception, as the foundation of knowledge; Sellars, W.

naïve realism (about perception), 47, 87–88, 94, 99, 217, 224; vs. presentationalism or direct realism, 88–89, 94, 96–97, 99–100, 99n17, 221–22. See also direct realism/presentationalism (about perception); form vs. object of awareness, perceptual

Napier, J., 45

narrowing, conceptual. See abstractions from abstractions

natural kinds, xi, 9n11, 11n13, 34n53, 139–42, 145–50, 164, 166, 173n1, 191, 191n7, 198–99; defined, 141–42, 150, 153–56. See also concepts; definitions; nominalism (about universals); realism (about universals)

nominalism (about universals), 11, defined, 11n14, 13n17; vs. the Objectivist theory of concepts 17n20, 18, 36–38, 125, 153–56. *See* Berkeley, G; concepts; essence; universals, problem of; Hobbes, T.; Hume, D.; Locke, J.; realism (about universals)

noncontradiction, law of, 75n53. *See also* deduction; identity, law of; logic

normative concepts, 146

Oatley. K. and Jenkins, J., 140

object-dependence of consciousness. *See* primacy of existence

Objectivism, ix

Objectivist theory of concepts. *See* concepts

objectivity (epistemic), as a norm of cognitive processes, 5, 10, 14n18, 39, 39nn62–63, 40n64, 60, 82–83, 84n62, 111, 157; as the status of cognitive products that adhere to norms, 35n55, 38–40, 112, 142. *See also* justification (epistemic); method; validation

Ockham's razor, 38n60

omniscience, 42, 121, 219, 238, 267. *See also* fallibility

open-end reference of concepts. *See* concepts, open-end reference of

Owen, R., 128n25

"package deals" (invalid concept), 71, 71n40. *See also* concepts, valid or invalid

Pasnau, R., 46n7

Peikoff, L., x, 5n7, 7n8, 8, 9n11, 25n35, 33n49, 34n52, 39nn61–62, 44n3, 46n6, 48n13, 51, 58n23, 66, 66n32, 67, 69n37, 70n38, 71, 71nn41–42, 72n44, 74, 74n50, 80n57, 83, 88n5, 89n6, 91n10, 94n13, 96n15, 97, 106n23, 120n14, 123n19, 131n28, 155

perception, as an active process, 44; as a basic form of knowledge, 6–7, 43, 50–51, 74, 110–11, 254; as a direct form of awareness, x, 48, 52, 87, 91–92, 109, 222, 227, 247, 250; as awareness of particular entities/characteristics, 8n8, 85–88, 91–94, 91n8, 97–99, 104, 216, 227, 255–56, 266–67; as distinct from concepts, x, 4, 6–7, 50, 92–93, 92n11, 93n12, 216, 253n2, 261, 261n7; as distinct from judgment or propositional thought, x, 7, 8n8, 49–52, 93–94, 98, 101, 109–10, 217, 224, 248–49, 253, 255; as

distinct from sensation, 6–8, 48n12, 93; as integrating sensations, 8, 30, 52; as non-volitional, 51–52; as the foundation of knowledge, 4–5, 50, 52, 55, 74–75, 108–11, 219, 227; content of, 105n29, 249; content of determined by objects and perceiver, 90–91, 91n7, 94–96, 100, 216, 223, 227, 251–53; content of not representational, 86–90, 96, 99n17, 216, 227–28; defined, 48n12; fallible vs. infallible, 7, 42–43, 49–52, 75, 80n57, 87–88, 96–98, 106, 215–25, 220n6, 223n9, 223n11, 228, 237, 240, 244–67; objects of as mind-independent, 219, 221–23, 227–29, 243, 245–46, 263–65; reducible vs. irreducible to physical causes, 88–89, 94; specificity of, 7n8, 26, 49; theory of informs theory of concepts, 6. *See also* appearance (perceptual); concepts; consciousness; direct realism/presentationalism (about perception); form vs. object of awareness; naïve realism (about perception); perceptual level of consciousness; relativity of perception; representationalism/indirect realism (about perception); sensation; sensory modality; sensory qualities

perceptual level of consciousness, 19, 50–51, 104, 218. *See also* dreaming; emotion; imagination; introspection; memory

perceptual relativity. *See* relativity of perception

Perrin, J., 194n8

phenomenal vs. postulational concepts, 197–99, 197n15, 202, 209. *See also* concepts; theoretical concepts

phenomenalism, 86n1

phlogiston (invalid concept of), 33n48, 114, 186n2, 192. *See also* concepts, as valid or invalid; conceptual development, in rejection or replacement of concepts

phrases, 63, 63n27. *See also* descriptions; judgment

Plato, 11, 14, 35n54. *See also* realism (about universals); universals, problem of

Pojman, L., 41n1

presentationalism (about perception). *See also* direct realism/presentationalism (about perception)

Price, H.H., 234n4

Prichard, H., 224n13

primacy of existence. *See* existence, primacy of in relation to consciousness

primary/secondary quality distinction, 259, 263. *See also* appearance (perceptual); sensory qualities

Prinz, J., 120n14

Proust, J., 193

Prout, W., 194

propositions, 27–28, 49, 62–65, 69, 69n37, 76; defined, 63. *See also* beliefs; judgment; knowledge, propositional and non-propositional; perception, as distinct from judgment or propositional thought; propositional attitudes

propositional attitudes, 64, 64n30. *See also* propositions

Pryor, J., 8n8, 89, 108–9, 108n25, 108n34, 110

psychologism (about logic), 232

Putnam, H., 122n18

qualia (sensory). *See* sensory qualities

Quine, W.V.O., 121n16

Quinn, P., et al., 12n15

Rakison, D.H., and Oakes, L., 12n15

Rakison, D.H., and Yermolayeva, Y., 12n15

Rand, A.: *AOF*, 22; *AON*, 22; *ARL*, 71n40; *Atlas*, 25n35, 43–44, 44n4, 49, 51, 53, 69n37, 71, 82; *CUI*, 71n40; *FTNI*, 19, 22, 25n35, 47, 88n5, 89n6; *ITOE*, ix, 3n1, 5–6, 5n6, 9n10, 9n13, 12–13, 15–17, 17nn21–23, 19n26, 20–25 20nn28–29, 21nn30–32, 24n33, 25n35, 26n36, 27, 27n39, 28n40, 29–31, 29n42, 30n44, 32n47, 34–39, 34n50, 34nn52–53, 36n57, 41–42, 44, 47–48, 52–54, 57n20, 58n22, 60, 61n25, 70, 71n41, 72, 75n53, 77–78; 78n55, 79n56, 80, 83, 84n62, 88n5, 89n6, 91, 93, 94n13, 96n15, 104, 106n23, 112–22, 117n7, 117n10, 124–25, 127, 130, 148–50, 152–57, 163–65, 166n2, 173n1, 175n3, 177, 180n10, 186, 186n1, 190n6, 208, 240–41; *Journals*, 22; *PWNI*, 69, 71n41, 81n59; *RM*, 158; *VOR*, 69n37, 80n58, 81n59; *VOS*, 25n35, 72n45, 73n48, 73n48, 158

Rand's "razor" (norm of concept-formation), 38, 70–71. *See also* concept-

formation, norms of; similarity, as cognitively economical or not; unit-economy, principle of

realism (about universals), 10–11, vs. the Objectivist theory of concepts, 11, 14, 16, 22–23, 34, 38, 125, 174n1, 178. *See also* concepts; natural kinds; universals, problem of

reason, 73n48, 52–53; defined, 52. *See also* concepts; logic

reduction. *See* concept-formation, hierarchical order of; hierarchy of knowledge

reference potential, 196–97, 196n14. *See also* concepts, open-end reference of

referential stability (of concepts), 127–30, 132, 196–97. *See also* conceptual development, whether it involves change in meaning; units, expanding knowledge of vs. change in the meaning of a concept

referents (of a concept). *See* concepts, meaning of; units (of a concept)

regress, epistemic (problem of), 254–55. *See also* foundationalism (about epistemic justification); justification (epistemic)

relations, concepts of, 29, 117n10

relativity of perception, 97n16, 99–103, 228–29, 247. *See also* form vs. object of awareness distinction; illusion (perceptual); perception; three-factor theories of perception

representationalism/indirect realism (about perception), 86–90, 99n17, 105n22, 217, 223–24, 223n10, 227–20, 231, 242–46, 248, 250–51, 255–57, 262; defined, 227; vs. direct realism, 87–88, 97–98, 104, 105n22, 216, 233. *See also* direct realism (about perception); perception, content of not representational

Rey, G., 120n14

Rheinberger, H., 141

Rosch, E., 58n22

Russell, B., 3n1, 47n8, 238, 238n7, 266

Rutherford, E., 195

Salmieri, G., x, xii, 5n5, 7n8, 8n9, 9n11, 11n14, 13n17, 14n18, 15n21, 25n35, 30n45, 34n51, 37n58, 39n63, 40n64, 46n6, 48n14, 57n20, 58n22, 59n23, 74n50, 88n4, 94n14, 116n6,

117n9, 118n11, 174n1, 177n7, 181n11, 204, 215–18, 215n2, 220n6, 223, 242–45, 247, 249, 252, 254, 256, 258, 261n8, 262, 266–67

Salmieri, G., and Gotthelf, A., 9n10, 25n35, 39n61, 174n1

Scerri, E., 33n49

scholastic perceptionism, 215n1

Scholl, B., and Tremoulet, P., 48n14

Schulz, L., Kushmir, T., and Gopnik, A., 113n1

science, philosophy of, 5n4, 27n39, 113–14. *See also* concepts, and scientific progress

Sellars, W., 4, 4n2, 8n8, 108, 108n26. *See also* "Myth of the Given"

self-evidence, 72n46. *See also* axiomatic concepts; axiomatic knowledge

sensation, 6, 6n7, 8, 86; concepts of, 30n44; defined, 48n12. *See also* colors, concepts of; consciousness, concepts of; perception, as integration of sensations; sense data theory; sensory qualities

sense (Fregean mode of presentation), 230–32; vs. form of awareness, 232, 261n8. *See also* Frege, G.

sense data theory, 89, 238, 238n7. *See also* representationalism/indirect realism (about perception), sensation

sensory modality, 228–30, 232–33; differences in with respect to awareness of same property, 95, 239, 245, 257–59, 265–66. *See also* Molyneaux, B.; perception; sensory qualities

sensory qualities, 95–96, 96n15, 221, 232, 235; as incommensurable with properties in the world, 251–53, 253n2; concept of, 239n9, 251–52, 262n9, 265; introspective awareness of, 250. *See also* appearance (perceptual); form vs. object of awareness, perceptual; perception; sensation

sentences, 77

shape, awareness of in formation of first-level concepts, 56–57, 66–67; concepts of, 199–200, perception of, 245, 257–59. *See also*, attributes; characteristics; "Conceptual Common Denominator" (CCD); first-level concepts

Shapere, D., 115n4

similarity, 140, 149, 54; arbitrary or factual,

11–13; as cognitively economical/fundamental or not, 36, 54, 70–71, 114, 150–51, 205; as grasped through awareness of comparative difference, 11–13, 13nn16–17, 20, 53; perceptual and abstract, 12, 12n15, 13n17, 24–25, 59–60; role of in concept application, 57; role of in concept-formation, 7, 9–10, 15, 19n27, 35, 55, 55n18, 57, 78, 105, 115–16, 122n18; role of in perceptual illusion, 101–3. *See also* concepts; nominalism (about universals); perception; realism (about universals)

skepticism, 44, 247, 264

Sloan, P., 128n23

Sloutsky, V., 58n22

Smith, L., et al., 12n15

Socrates, 34n54

Soddy, F., 195, 195n10

Sommers, F., 68n35

species (biological concept of), 140–43, 151, 157, 186n2; reclassification of, 114, 127–33, 188–89, 188n4. *See also* conceptual development; taxonomies, scientific

states of affairs, 93–94

Stern, C., and Sherwood, E., 210

"stolen concepts," 71. *See also* concept-formation, norms of; concept-formation, hierarchical order of; concepts, valid or invalid;

supposition, 64n30. *See also* conditional statements; propositional attitudes; imagination

Steinle, F., 5n4

Stevens, J., 166, 168

Stotz, K., 143

taxonomies (scientific), 139–40, 151–52, 157–58. *See also* conceptual development; definitions; hierarchy of knowledge

teleological concepts, 26, 180. *See also* ethics/metaethics

theoretical concepts, 8–9, 25, 27–28, 28n41, 186–87, 199, 202–3, 209. *See also* abstractions from abstraction; concepts, and scientific progress; phenomenal vs. postulational concepts

theory-ladenness of perception. *See* perception, as distinct from concepts thinking/thought, 53. *See also* concepts; judgment

Thompson, J.V., 127

Thomson, J.J., 28, 195

three-factor theories of perception, xii, 226, 228–35, 242–46; vs. representationalism, 230, 242–44. *See also* direct realism/presentationalism (about perception); form vs. object of awareness; perception; sense (Fregean mode of presentation)

Toulmin, S., 113

transparency of consciousness. *See* consciousness, whether its form is without identity

Travis, C., 7n8, 49, 88n4, 254n3

truth, correspondence theory of, 69n37

universals, problem of, 3, 13n17, 19n27, 22; Objectivist solution to, 11–12, 14, 35, 35n56. *See also* concepts, universality of; measurement-omission; nominalism (about universals); realism (about universals)

unit-economy, cognitive function of concepts is to provide, 58, 118, 150–51, 180–81; definitions needed to achieve, 118–19, 123; principle of as norm of concept-formation, 36–38, 59, 153, 207–8. *See also* concept-formation, norms of; concepts, function of; similarity, as cognitively economical or not

unit-perspective, 54–56, 65–66, 149, 156, 174–75. *See also* concepts, based on mind-independent and cognitive facts; concepts, as integrations; similarity; units

units (of concepts), 24n33, 25–26, 29–30, 54; as the meaning of concepts; 32–33, 121–22, 125; defined, 53–54, 149; expanding knowledge of vs. change in the meaning of a concept, 32, 57n20, 121–23, 127–29; of higher-level concepts, 116. *See also*

concepts, meaning of; conceptual development, whether it involves change in meaning; similarity

unit-reduction. *See* unit-economy.

unobservables (concepts of). *See* phenomenal vs. postulational concepts; theoretical concepts

validation (of knowledge), x, 42–44, 52, 76–77, 79–81. *See also* concepts, as normative; concepts, valid or invalid; justification (epistemic); objectivity

van Cleve, J., 234n4

van Melsen, A., 193

veil of perception, 228, 230, 236, 238. *See also* representationalism/indirect realism (about perception); skepticism

veridical perception. *See* perception, fallible vs. infallible

verificationism, 244

virtue epistemology, 61n25

volition, as basis of need for epistemology, 42–43, 50–53, 62; role of in concept-formation/conceptualization, 22, 53, 70, 215n2. *See also* concept-formation, as volitional; fallibility

Waters, C.K., 143

Wear, A., 131n27

Weisberg, M., 33n49

Weisberg, M., and Needham, P., 196n12

Whewell, W., 140

widening, conceptual. *See* abstractions from abstractions

Williams, M., 108

Wittgenstein, L., 4, 13n17, 71n43

Wright, D., 69n37

words, 11, 63n27; as denoting concepts, 52; role of in conceptual integration, 17–18, 20, 30, 54, 118. *See also* concepts; nominalism (about universals); unit-economy